REASON, FAITH AND HISTORY

Spanning the breadth of philosophical, historical and theological interests articulated in the work of Paul Helm, including chapters on Calvinism, philosophical theology, philosophy of mind, Christian Doctrine and epistemology, *Reason, Faith and History* offers an accessible text for students of contemporary philosophy of religion as well as those interested in philosophical theology more broadly.

Reason, Faith and History offers a unique collection of essays on key topics in the philosophy of religion. Published in honour of Paul Helm, a major force in contemporary English-speaking philosophy of religion, this book presents newly commissioned chapters by distinguished philosophers and theologians from North America, Israel, the UK and Continental Europe.

Contributors include: Robertson, Trueman, Hughes, Swinburne, Torrance, Clark, Robinson, Pink, Gellman, Cross, Byrne, Hossack, and Crisp.

Paul Helm

Reason, Faith and History
Philosophical Essays for Paul Helm

Edited by

M.W.F. STONE
Katholieke Universiteit Leuven, Belgium

ASHGATE

Published by
Ashgate Publishing Limited
Gower House
Croft Road
Aldershot
Hampshire GU11 3HR
England

Ashgate Publishing Company
Suite 420
101 Cherry Street
Burlington, VT 05401-4405
USA

www.ashgate.com

British Library Cataloguing in Publication Data
Reason, faith and history: philosophical essays for Paul Helm
  1. Religion – Philosophy
  I. Stone, Martin II. Helm, Paul
  210

Library of Congress Cataloging-in-Publication Data

Reason, faith, and history: philosophical essays for Paul Helm / edited by Martin Stone.
    p. cm.
  Includes bibliographical references and index.
  ISBN 978-0-7546-0926-1 (hardcover : alk. paper) 1. Religion–Philosophy. I. Helm, Paul.
II. Stone, M. W. F. (Martin William Francis), 1965–
  BL51.R328 2007
  210–dc22

2007029633

ISBN 978-0-7546-0926-1

Mixed Sources
Product group from well-managed forests and other controlled sources
www.fsc.org Cert no. SGS-COC-2482
© 1996 Forest Stewardship Council

Printed and bound in Great Britain by
TJ International Ltd, Padstow, Cornwall.

They therefore as to right belonged,
So were created, nor can justly accuse
Their maker, or their making, or their Fate,
As if predestination over-rul'd
Their Will, dispos'd by absolute Decree
Or high foreknowledge; they themselves decreed
Their own revolt, not I: if I foreknew,
Foreknowledge had no influence on their fault,
Which had no less prov'd certain unforeknown.
Milton, *Paradise Lost*, iii, 111–119

Contents

Notes on Contributors

Peter Byrne is Professor of Ethics and Philosophy of Religion, Department of Theology and Religious Studies, King's College London. He is the author of many books including *Natural Religion and the Nature of Religion* (1989); *The Philosophical and Theological Foundations of Ethics* (1992); *The Moral Intepretation of Religion* (1998); and *God and Realism* (2003). He is the editor of the journal *Religious Studies*; and of the Ashgate series *Studies in the History of Philosophical Theology*.

Stephen R.L. Clark is Professor of Philosophy at the University of Liverpool. He is the author of many well-known books including: *The Moral Status of Animals* (1977); *From Athens to Jerusalem: The Love of Wisdom and the Love of God* (1984); *God, Religion, and Morality*; and *Biology and Christian Ethics* (2000).

Oliver D. Crisp is Reader in Theology at the University of Bristol. A former research student of Paul Helm, he is the author of *Divinity and Humanity: The Incarnation Reconsidered* (2007); *Jonathan Edwards and the Metaphysics of Sin* (2005) and *An American Augustinian: Sin and Salvation in the Dogmatic Theology of William G.T. Shedd* (2007). With Paul Helm he has edited *Jonathan Edwards: Philosophical Theologian* (2003), and with Michael C. Rea he has co-edited and contributed to *Analytic Theology: New Essays in the Philosophy of Theology* (forthcoming in 2009).

Richard Cross is John A. O'Brien Professor of Philosophy at the University of Notre Dame, Indiana. He is the author of many important articles in philosophical theology and medieval philosophy, and the monographs *The Physics of Duns Scotus* (1998); *Duns Scotus* (1999); *The Metaphysics of the Incarnation: Thomas Aquinas to Duns Scotus* (2002); and *Duns Scotus on God* (2005).

Jerome I. Gellman is Professor of Philosophy at Ben-Gurion University of the Negev, Beer-Sheva, Israel. He is the author of many articles in the philosophy of religion, and of the books *The Fear, the Trembling, and the Fire: Kierkegaard and Hasidic Masters on the Binding of Issac* (1994); *Experience of God and the Rationality of Theistic Belief* (1997); and *Mystical Experience of God: A Philosophical Inquiry* (2001).

Keith Hossack is Reader in Philosophy at Birkbeck College, University of London. He has published widely in the areas of philosophical logic, philosophy of language and philosophy of mathematics, and is the author of the groundbreaking study *The Metaphysics of Knowledge* (2007).

Christopher Hughes is Reader in Philosophy at King's College London. He is the author of many influential articles in metaphysics, and philosophical theology, and has published widely in the area of medieval philosophy. He is the author of *On a Complex Theory of a Simple God* (1989); *Kripke: Names, Necessity, and Identity* (2004); and *Aquinas* (2007).

Thomas Pink is Reader in Philosophy at King's College London. He has published in ethics, philosophy of action, and the history of philosophy. He is the author of *The Psychology of Freedom* (1996); *Free Will: A Very Short Introduction* (2004); and joint editor with M.W.F. Stone of *The Will and Human Action: from Antiquity to the Present Day* (2004). A major two-volume study: *The Ethics of Action*, and a critical edition of *The Questions Concerning Liberty, Necessity and Chance* by Thomas Hobbes and John Bramhal, are forthcoming from Oxford University Press.

David G. Robertson is Assistant Professor of Philosophy at Felician College, New Jersey, USA. He is the author of several articles in ancient philosophy and its relationship to patristics, and has translated many excerpts from the Church Fathers for *The Sourcebook in the Philosophy of the Ancient Commentators 200-600 AD*, 3 vols., edited by Richard Sorabji. His forthcoming book, *Word and Meaning in Ancient Alexandria*, will be published by Ashgate.

Howard Robinson is Professor of Philosophy at the Central European University, Budapest, Hungary, and Honorary Research Fellow in the Department of Philosophy at the University of Liverpool. He mainly specializes in metaphysics, including the philosophy of religion, and the philosophy of mind, and has interests in the history of philosophy. His principal publications are: *Matter and Sense: a Critique of Contemporary Materialism* (1982); *Objections to Physicalism* (1993); *Perception* (1994); and an edition of Berkeley's *Principles and Three Dialogues* (1996).

M.W.F. Stone is Professor of Renaissance and Early Modern Philosophy at the Institute of Philosophy, Katholieke Universiteit Leuven in Belgium, and Visiting Professor of Philosophy at King's College London. He is author of numerous articles on medieval philosophy and early modern scholasticism, and is the editor of several collections including, with Jill Kraye, of *Humanism and Early Modern Philosophy* (2001). His forthcoming two volume study of the casuistical tradition, *The Subtle Arts of Casuistry*, will shortly be published by Oxford University Press.

Richard Swinburne FBA is Emeritus Professor of Philosophy at the University of Oxford, having been Nolloth Professor of the Philosophy of the Christian Religion. One of the leading authorities in English-speaking philosophy of religion, he is the author of many influential books including his triology, *The Coherence of Theism* (1977, revised edition 1993); *The Existence of God* (1979, new edition 2005); *Faith and Reason* (1981, new edition 2005); and a tetralogy on the philosophy of the Christian religion: *Responsibility and Atonement* (1989); *Revelation: From Metaphor to Analogy* (1992); *The Christian God* (1994); and *Providence and the Problem of*

Evil (1998). His more recent books include *Epistemic Justification* (2001); and *The Resurrection of God Incarnate* (2003).

Alan J. Torrance is Professor of Systematic Theology at St. Mary's College of the University of St. Andrews, Scotland. He is the author of many articles in systematic theology, and has published the monographs *Persons in Communion: An Essay on Trinitarian Description and Human Participation* (1996); and with Hilary Regan and Antony Wood *Christ and Context: The Confrontation between Gospel and Culture* (1993).

Carl R. Trueman is Professor of Church History and Historical Theology at Westminster Theological Seminary, Philadelphia, USA, specializing in Reformation history. He is the author of *Luther's Legacy: Salvation & English Reformers 1525-56* (1994); with R.S. Clark, *Protestant Scholasticism: Essays in Reassessment* (1999); and with Paul Helm, *The Trustworthiness of God: Perspectives on the Nature of Scripture* (2002).

Acknowledgements

Like so many academic publications in these unremitting times, this venture was commissioned with enthusiasm, begun in earnest, sustained with diminishing alacrity, and completed many, many, moons after its agreed date of submission. The editor can only apologize to the contributors, publisher, and the recipient of this festschrift, for the woeful delay in bringing this volume to final fruition. He alone is responsible. Still, with its publication he can now console himself with the ancient and liberating thought of '*abit onus*'. The editor would also like to thank Sarah Lloyd, and her colleagues at Ashgate, for their exemplary patience, repeated encouragement, and justifiable scolding. Several years ago when the idea for a volume honouring the work of Paul Helm was first mooted, the editor received some useful advice from Daniel Hill, Peter Byrne, and the late Colin Gunton. Along the way, he has been cheered, as well as shamed, by the graciousness and good humour of Paul Helm, who has had to wait much longer than he thought for this celebratory volume. It is to be hoped that Paul will come to recognize this tome as a fitting tribute to his splendid work as a philosopher.

M.W.F. Stone, *Feast of St. Stanislaus*,
Bishop and Martyr, Leuven, 11 April 2007

Introduction

M.W.F. Stone

> The philosophy of religion is not a particular type of philosophy, as the wines of the Loire are a particular type of wine, and the fact that some aspect or other of a religion is being addressed does not give us license to depart from usual standards of philosophical strictness and rigour.
>
> Paul Helm[1]

As it is recognized and practised in the analytic tradition of English-speaking philosophy, the philosophy of religion presents several intellectual challenges to anyone foolhardy enough to submit themselves to its exacting discipline. First and foremost, one must realize that to broach and scrutinize the central arguments of the philosophy of religion is to engage with philosophy itself. For the subject matter of the field, as it ranges over issues in philosophical theology, the justification of religious belief, quandaries concerning religion and morality, the topic of God and other minds, or questions emanating from ancient and more recent formulations of the so-called 'problem of evil', is always conditioned by developments in the core areas of philosophy; especially, philosophical logic, metaphysics, ethics, epistemology, and the philosophy of mind. Thus, the philosophy of religion is not a *sui generis* subject beholden to an internal framework of coherence and its own standards of verisimilitude. Progress or otherwise in the discipline, will be predicated upon the emulation and endorsement of normative standards of clarity, rigour and sagacity, as these pertain to analytic philosophy as a whole.

A second, and much more specific, challenge concerns the requirement that those prepared to engage with the philosophy of religion must cultivate an appreciation of those finer points of theology (whether Jewish, Christian, or Islamic) that prompt genuine philosophical puzzlement, and which require further elaboration of their dogmatic scope and point. Under this heading, the student of the philosophy of religion must be cognizant of the basic details of theological argument, in just the same manner as a philosopher of physics or mathematics, will marshall his technical understanding of those disciplines in order to provide a conceptual clarification, or else a reasoned justification, of some mathematical theorem or physical theory. The practice of philosophy of religion thereby requires a sympathetic and informed understanding of Western theology and its rich and complex history, whereby ideas and concepts gleaned from the distant past are brought into critical engagement with techniques and methods of philosophical analysis distilled from the present.

The revival of the intellectual fortunes and institutional profile of the philosophy of religion over the last thirty years or so, can be attributed (at least in part) to the fact that so many of its leading figures have risen to the challenges specified above. Whatever else might be said of their work, it should be beyond dispute that

---

1   *Faith With Reason*, Oxford: Clarendon Press, 2000, p. 1.

the seminal writings of philosophers such as Alvin Plantinga, Richard Swinburne, William Alston, Robert Adams, Marilyn McCord Adams, and Norman Kretzmann, have not only ameliorated the general intellectual level of the discipline, but have helped to restore something of the philosophical integrity of the field which had been lost during those long and gloomy years in which self-styled 'philosophers of religion' were overtly fixated with non-cognitive accounts of religion, or else sold their souls to one or more suggestive intepretations of the religious legacy of Ludwig Wittgenstein. Up to the present day, 'analytic philosophy of religion', as it is now known, continues to blossom in many philosophy departments in North America, Great Britain, and parts of continental Europe. Centrally connected with on-going developments in English-speaking philosophy, as can be illustrated in the work of leading exponents such as Peter van Inwagen, Eleonore Stump and Brian Leftow, it shows little sign of conceptual ill-health or lack of creativity as it negoitates the profound challenges of a new millenium.

Aside from those luminaries of the subject listed above, there is another philosopher, Paul Helm, whose commitment to the best practices of analytic philosophy and whose formidable knowledge of many important areas of the history of Christian theology, have enabled him to make a genuine contribution to the philosophy of religion over the last thirty-five years. His industry and achievements are honoured in this book of essays by friends, admirers, former colleagues, and students. Educated at Worcester College Oxford, Helm has enjoyed a distinguished academic career, in which he was for several years a Lecturer and then Reader in Philosophy at the University of Liverpool, before taking up from 1993 to 2000 the prestigious chair of the History and Philosophy of Religion at King's College London.[2] Subsequent to taking early retirement from King's in 2000, Helm moved to Regent's College, Vancouver, where he became J.I. Packer Professor of Philosophical Theology, a post he held until 2005. He continues as a Teaching Fellow at the College. Helm remains an active presence in contemporay philosophy and theology, not least by virtue of his attendance at many conferences, and by dint of a continual flow of publications on an assortment of academic and topical issues. Ever willing to indulge his taste for innovation, he has even established his own web blog, 'Helm's Deep',[3] in which

---

2   In English universities of the post-war period, named chairs in the philosophy of religion were few and far between. Other than the Nolloth Professorship of the Philosophy of the Christian Religion at Oxford University, most recently held by Richard Swinburne, and now by Brian Leftow, the chair of the History and Philosophy of Religion (originally a chair of the University of London before its translation to King's College, whose incumbents before Helm included H.D Lewis, Stewart Sutherland, and Keith Ward), was the only other recognized senior post to which philosophers of religion could aspire. The Norris Hulse chair of the Divinity Faculty of Cambridge University, has more often than not been the preserve of systematic theologians with little or no interest in English-speaking philosophy of religion, the only real exception to this rule being the tenure of Donald MacKinnon. It is a cause of great regret that on Helm's departure from King's, the College decided not to renew the post with the consequence that the chair is now suspended. That said, it should be emphasized that Helm's old department remains an internationally recognized centre for the study of philosophy of religion.

3   See http://paulhelmsdeep.blogspot.com/.

his current philosophical interests and theological predilections can be enjoyed and contested by all those at ease with the vagaries of cyberspace.

On the basis of the publication of several highly focused monographs that tackle some of the more recalcitrant issues of the subject, Helm has become one of the most respected philosophers of religion of his generation. In numerous works that straddle the domain of epistemology and other cognate disciplines, he has analysed the nature and meaning of faith and its more general relationship to other forms of belief, and to the exercise of the will. In the course of these enquiries he has advanced an original account of the relationship between faith, reason and volition, one which is opposed to many influential arguments in post-foundationalist religious epistemology, especially those postulated by philosophers smitten by the contrivances of so-called 'Reformed Epistemology'. From the publication of his first major book *The Varieties of Belief* (1973),[4] and continuing with *Belief Policies* (1994),[5] and on to *Faith and Understanding* (1997),[6] and *Faith with Reason* (2000),[7] Helm has ploughed his own furrow on the taxing subject of the justification of religious belief. Neither beholden to the siren voices of contemporary fashion, nor obstinate in his advocacy of the putative verities of the past, his work is always characterized by a sane and proportionate commitment to reason and argument. Whether read in chronological sequence or else consulted as self-standing contributions, Helm's books on religious epistemology repay serious study, and will be read for many years to come.

Helm's extensive corpus also includes works of great interest in the area of philosophical theology. His widely admired *Eternal God* (1988),[8] sought to defend the classical Christian view that God exists in timeless eternity, rebutting the charge of modern critics that it is incoherent. By arguing that the idea of divine timelessness is grounded in the notion of God as creator, Helm contended that this was sufficient to enable one to advance a plausible description of divine omniscience. The eternity of God is then considered in the context of a unified treatment of the main concepts of philosophical theology, and one of the main strengths of Helm's account, was to identify the important ramfications which a sketch of God's timeless existence might be said to have for issues related to divine and human freedom. Alongside acclaimed studies such as the famous article 'Eternity' by Eleonore Stump and Norman Kretzmann,[9] and the book by Brian Leftow, *Time and Eternity*,[10] Helm's

---

4   Paul Helm, *Varieties of Belief* (Muirhead Library of Philosophy), London: Allen and Unwin, 1973.

5   Paul Helm, *Belief Policies* (Cambridge Studies in Philosophy), Cambridge: Cambridge University Press, 1994.

6   Paul Helm, *Faith and Understanding* (Reason and Religion Series), Edinburgh: Edinburgh University Press, 1997.

7   Paul Helm, *Faith With Reason*, Oxford: Clarendon Press, 2000.

8   Paul Helm, *The Eternal God: A Study of God Without Time*, Oxford: Clarendon Press, 1988; Second edition paperback, Oxford: Clarendon Press, 1997.

9   Eleonore Stump and Norman Kretzmann, 'Eternity', *Journal of Philosophy*, 78, 1981: 429-458.

10   Brian Leftow, *Time and Eternity* (Cornell Studies in the Philosophy of Religion), Ithaca, NY: Cornell University Press, 1991.

Eternal God is widely acknowledged to be one of the more influential conceptual assessents of this divine attribute in recent philosophical theology.

Helm's other notable contribution to this area of philosophical religion can be seen in his discussion treatment of the knotty problem of divine foreknowledge, and its impact on issues related to counterfactual conditionals, fatalism, human freedom, and providence. In a series of papers and discussion notes published in the 1970s,[11] Helm defended with great clarity and determination a position commensurate with his own Reformed Tradition. A later book, *The Providence of God* (1993),[12] sets out his mature account of God's prescience and its general implications for an account of divine providence.

Mention of the Reformed tradition brings us to the last area in which Helm has made a palpable contribution to contemporary theological learning. A sincere yet restrained advocate of Calvinian Christianity, a position which he deems to be nothing more than the unequivocal teaching of biblical revelation, Augustine, and selected medieval scholastics, Helm has found cause to write about his great hero John Calvin, either with a view to expounding the Reformer's ideas in such a way as to make them philosophically tractable and plausible, or else to defend his own view of the development of the Reformed Tradition against what he deems to be unscholarly and suggestive reinterpretations of historical Calvinism, especially those forms that found expression in the British Isles in the sixteenth and seventeenth centuries.

The second of these traits is in evidence in his most polemical opsuculum, *Calvin and the Calvinists* (1982),[13] a small tract written at the expense of R.T. Kendall's *Calvin and English Calvinism to 1649* (1981).[14] It is the burden of Kendall's study to show that there exists a profound rupture between Calvin and his later followers such as the English Puritans, with the consequence that Puritan theology had departed significantly from the spirit and the letter of Calvin's own dogmatic teaching. At the time at which Kendall's study appeared, it had become commonplace among a prominent cohort of Protestant theologians (here one thinks of T.F. Torrance and his many enthusiasts and imitators), as well as among some historians of the Reformation, to oppose the historical teaching of Calvin to the mediated ideas of the 'Calvinists'. Rejecting this position as simply false, Helm sought to argue that, within the period covered by Kendall's monograph, Calvin and the English Puritans were speaking in one and the same theological voice. He prosecuted his case on the basis of a detailed exposition of the doctrines of the Atonement and of 'Saving

---

11   See especially: 'Divine Foreknowledge and Facts', *Canadian Journal of Philosophy*, 4, 1974: 305-315; 'On Theological Fatalism Again', *Philosophical Quarterly*, 24, 1974: 360-362; 'Fatalism Once More', ibid, 25, 1975: 289-296; 'Timelessness and Foreknowledge', *Mind*, 84, 1975: 516-527; and 'Foreknowledge and Possibility', *Canadian Journal of Philosophy*, 6, 1976: 731-734. For an excellent discussion of some of the ideas on divine foreknowledge and omniscience defended by Paul Helm, see the essay by Christopher Hughes 'No Way Out', in this collection.

12   Paul Helm, *The Providence of God* (Contours of Christian Theology Series), Leicester: Inter-Varsity Press, 1993.

13   Paul Helm, *Calvin and the Calvinists*, Edinburgh: Banner of Truth Trust, 1982.

14   R.T. Kendall, *Calvin and English Calvinism to 1649*, Oxford: Clarendon Press, 1981.

Faith', showing that there was no real warrant for anything like the conclusion that Kendall had proposed.

Helm's other great gift to the scrutiny and analysis of the doctrines and legacy of the Reformed Tradition is the ambitious and pioneering, *John Calvin's Ideas* (2005),[15] a book entirely without precedent,[16] and the product of its author's long and studious engagement with Calvin's ideas and historical context. While never denying that Calvin was first and foremost a theologian, and by stating that he was not a 'philosopher' in our accepted understanding of that term, Helm proceeds to explain Calvin's own familarity with a range of philosophical ideas, and the ways in which he was prepared to put such ideas to work in the elucidation of his theological positions. Given the length and sophistication of this tome, its conclusions and proposals have yet to be fully absorbed by scholars of Reformation thought. Still, without exaggeration, one can envisage that the general dissemination of Helm's analysis will lead to a thorough reappraisal of Calvin's theological method, his relationship to late medieval thought, and to later Reformed scholasticism. When viewed alongside the recent completion of Richard A. Muller's important *Post Reformation Reformed Dogmatics*,[17] Helm's volume, like those of Muller, provides a new and radical means whereby our existing understanding of the intellectual context and development of Reformed theology can be liberated from antecedent theological assumptions, especially those associated with T.F. Torrance and the ahistorical neo-Barthian school, and viewed in a different and much more appealing light.

An interesting by-product of greater topicality which *John Calvin's Ideas* bequeaths to its readers, however, is Helm's own powerful critique of some of the staple ideas of contemporary 'Reformed Epistemology', a position associated with the writings of Alvin Plantinga and others.[18] At many places, Helm is eager to show his reader that at crucial points Calvin's own ideas are not those of Plantinga, and that in certain instances the strictures of self-styled Reformed epistemology and those of Calvin, particularly on matters concerning warrant and the rational justification of belief in God and on natural theology, are not always in full accord.[19] While several scholars have recently taken Plantinga to task for his interpretation of Calvin,[20] the singular merit of Helm's own exposition is to call into question some of the more confident historical assertions that Plantinga makes on behalf of Calvin and the

---

15   Paul Helm, *John Calvin's Ideas*, Oxford: Oxford University Press, 2004; paperback edition 2006.

16   The only other comparable study would be Charles Partee, *Calvin and Classical Philosophy* (Studies in the History of Christian Thought, 14), Leiden: Brill, 1977, which restricts itself to a study of Calvin's use and appropriation of the ideas of ancient philosophy.

17   Richard A. Muller, *Post Reformation Reformed Dogmatics: The Rise and Development of Reformed Orthodoxy, ca. 1520 to ca. 1725*, 4 vols., Grand Rapids: Baker Academic, 2006.

18   See Alvin Plantinga, 'Reason and Belief in God', in Alvin Plantinga and Nicholas Wolterstorff, eds., *Faith and Rationality*, Notre Dame: University of Notre Dame Press, 1983, pp. 16-93; and *Warranted Christian Belief*, New York: Oxford University Press, 2000.

19   See Helm, *John Calvin's Ideas*, pp. 210, 241-242, 265-268, 269-270.

20   See especially the articles by Michael Sudduth, 'Calvin, Plantinga, and the Natural Knowledge of God: A Response to Beversluis', *Faith and Philosophy*, 15, 1998: 92-103; and the 'Prospects for 'Mediate' Natural Theology in John Calvin', *Religious Studies*, 31, 1995: 53-68.

Reformed Tradition. The detail as well as the sobriety of Helm's exegesis invites any scholar and philosopher to approach Calvin's writings with greater tact and nuance, the effect of which will surely help to introduce a greater critical distance between some aspects of the teaching of John Calvin and the research programme of Reformed epistemology.

Further to his achievements in the philosophy of religion and in the history of Reformed theology, Helm has also edited several significant collections of essays. For many years his 'Oxford Readings' paperback, *Divine Commands and Morality* (1981),[21] was an undergraduate's first port of call as they got to grips with this distinctive and, at times, perplexing approach to ethics. His years at King's College saw him produce two major collections, the first being an anthology of texts for Oxford University Press entitled *Faith and Reason* (1999);[22] and the second being the proceedings of a conference he organized on Jewish and Christian approaches to God, subsequently published as *Referring to God: Jewish and Christian Philosophical and Theological Perspectives* (2000).[23] When in Vancouver he produced with his friend, and contributor to this volume, Carl Trueman, a volume of essays dealing with *The Trustworthiness of God: Perspectives on the Nature of Scripture* (2002);[24] and also co-edited with his former research student, Oliver Crisp, *Jonathan Edwards: Philosophical Theologian* (2003),[25] a volume which has been roundly praised as one of the more significant assessments of Edwards's career to appear in the last twenty years. Once again in these highly successful books, one can see so many of the traits that have won Helm the esteem of his peers: a thorough knowledge of the history and complexity of the Christian tradition; philosophical acuity and imagination; and perspicuous and thought-provoking commentary.

The essays that follow this inadequate appreciation need little by way of introduction. All the contributors gladly accepted the editor's invitation to write in honour of Paul Helm, and some choose to address themes directly related to ideas and issues that are represented in his published corpus, while others decided that the most felicitous way to pay tribute to their friend or former colleague was to offer a piece of their current research. This is why the volume is loosely organized around the themes of *reason*, or those pertaining to philosophical analysis; *faith*, or those issues which direct our attention to the content of specific theological beliefs; and *history*, or those areas of the Christian tradition which continue to intrigue and delight our speculative instincts and which call forth for further clarification and debate.

---

21   Paul Helm ed., *Divine Commands and Morality* (Oxford Readings in Philosophy), Oxford: Oxford University Press, 1981.

22   Paul Helm, ed., *Faith and Reason* (Oxford Readers), Oxford: Oxford University Press, 1999.

23   Paul Helm ed., *Referring to God: Jewish and Christian Philosophical and Theological Perspectives* (Curzon Jewish Philosophy Series), Richmond: Curzon, 2000.

24   Paul Helm and Carl Trueman eds, *The Trustworthiness of God: Perspectives on the Nature of Scripture*, Grand Rapids: Eerdmans, 2002.

25   Oliver Crisp and Paul Helm eds, *Jonathan Edwards: Philosophical Theologian*, Aldershot: Ashgate, 2003.

The volume begins with an article by David Robertson, who considers questions concerning the philosophy of language that can be found in the theological heritage of patristic writers such as Basil of Caesarea, and by Carl Trueman who offers a reinterpretation of the significance of a neglected early modern divine, Stephen Charnock. From there, Christopher Hughes invites us to consider his own novel proposals concerning the solution of Alvin Plantinga and others (Paul Helm included) to traditional perplexities concerning divine omniscience, while Richard Swinburne urges Paul Helm to take natural theology more seriously than he has been diposed to do hitherto. Alan Torrance provides us with a series of reflections on theological epistemology, and Howard Robinson tackles the rarefied subject of God's existence and His essence. Stephen Clark provides a repose for the reader in the quiet and agreeable thoughts of G.K. Chesterton, a pause which is followed by Thomas Pink, whose subtle excursus into several salient themes in the history of moral psychology and theological anthropology, affords the reader great insight into several issues touched on by the work of Helm. Jerome Gellman provides the volume with a further set of reflections on the epistemic quandaries that court any analysis of mystical experiece, and Richard Cross offers a polished exposition of a perennial difficulty in Western Christology. The last three essays of the volume contain a critical study on Helm's account of the authorship of sin by Peter Byrne, a highly innovative philosophical analysis of concepts by Keith Hossack, and an adroit discussion by Oliver Crisp of the thorny issue of multiple incarnations.

The fact that these essays embrace such a wide variety of themes and issues is perhaps the best and most appropriate tribute to Paul Helm. In these sad and trying times of excessive specialization, and the profileration of increasingly myopic and quite ghastly academic approaches to both philosophy and theology, it is important that we celebrate the achievements of a civilized and cultivated colleague who writes on a great number of topics in philosophy, philosophy of religion, theology, and Reformation studies, with learning, wit and authority. Helm's work is always attuned to the need to bring important areas of philosophy of religion into a genuine dialogue with the study of the history of our magisterial Christian tradition. He does this in order that one can recapture and reassess ways of thinking about the philosophical issues that attend the justification of religious belief, or else the description of God's nature, which have been forgotten or arbitrarily rejected. The philosophical imagination is broadened and ameliorated by the introduction of new and interesting things to think about. Paul Helm's industry and creativity as a philosopher of religion can be measured against those novel insights he has introduced to the areas of religious epistemology, philosophical theology, and the history of the Reformed Tradition. For this, and for so much more, we remain in his debt.

Significant Publications of Paul Helm

Books

Editor, *Jonathan Edwards' Treatise on Grace and Other Posthumously Published Writings* (Cambridge, James Clarke, 1971).

The Varieties of Belief (Muirhead Library of Philosophy) (London and New York, George Allen and Unwin, Humanities Press, 1973).

Calvin and the Calvinists (London, Banner of Truth Trust, 1982; Korean Edition, Seoul, Word of Life Press, 1988).

Editor, *Divine Commands and Morality* (Oxford, Oxford University Press, 1981; Spanish Edition, Mexico, Fondo De Cultura Economica, 1986).

Editor, *The Divine Revelation* (London, Marshall, Morgan and Scott 1983; Reprinted Vancouver, BC. Regent Publishing, 2004).

Editor, *Objective Knowledge: A Christian Perspective* (Leicester: Inter Varsity Press, 1987).

Eternal God (Oxford: Clarendon Press, 1988; Paperback Edition 1997).

The Providence of God (Leicester: Inter Varsity Press, 1993).

Belief Policies (Cambridge, Cambridge University Press, 1994; Digital Reprint 2007).

Faith and Understanding (Edinburgh, Edinburgh University Press, 1997).

Editor, *Faith and Reason* (Oxford, Oxford University Press, 1999).

Editor, *Referring to God* (Richmond, Curzon Press, 2000).

Faith with Reason (Oxford, Clarendon Press, 2000).

Editor (with Carl R. Trueman) *The Trustworthiness of God* (Grand Rapids, Eerdmans, 2002).

Editor (with Oliver D. Crisp) *Jonathan Edwards, Philosophical Theologian* (Aldershot, Ashgate, 2003).

John Calvin's Ideas (Oxford, Oxford University Press, 2004; Paperback Edition 2006).

Calvin: A Guide for the Perplexed (London, T & T Clark, 2008).

Calvin in the Centre (Oxford, Oxford University Press, 2008).

Articles, including Contributions to Volumes

Philosophy of Religion

'Revealed Propositions and Timeless Truths' *Religious Studies* 8 (1972): 127-136.

'God and Free Will' *Sophia* 13 (1974): 16-18.

'Divine Foreknowledge and Facts', *Canadian Journal of Philosophy* 4 (1974): 305-315

'Omnipotence and Change', *Philosophy* 5 (1976): 454-461.

'A Theory of Disembodied Survival and Re-embodied Existence', *Religious Studies* 14 (1978): 15-26.

'God and Whatever Comes to Pass', *Religious Studies* 14 (1978): 315-323.

'On Grace and Causation', *Scottish Journal of Theology* 32 (1979): 101-112.

'God and Spacelessness', *Philosophy* 55 (1980): 211-221. (Reprinted in *Essays in the Philosophy of Religion*, eds Steven M. Cahn and David Shatz (New York, Oxford University Press, 1982), pp. 99-112).

'God and the Approval of Sin', *Religious Studies* 20 (1984): 215-222.

'Time and Place for God', *Sophia* 24 (1985): 53-55.

'Omniscience and Eternity' *Proceedings of the Aristotelian Society*, Supplementary Volume 63 (1989): 75-87.

'The Impossibility of Divine Passibility', in *The Power and Weakness of God*, ed. Nigel M. de S. Cameron (Edinburgh, Rutherford House, 1990), pp. 119-140.

'The Perfect and the Particular', Inaugural Lecture, King's College, September, 1994.

'Eternal Creation', *Tyndale Bulletin* 45 (1994): 321-338.

'One Truth, One Way' (London, Evangelical Library, 1996).

'Eternal Creation: The Doctrine of the Two Standpoints', in *The Doctrine of Creation* (ed. Colin Gunton) (Edinburgh, T & T Clark, 1997), pp. 29-46.

'Perfect Goodness' in *A Companion to the Philosophy of Religion*, ed. Philip Quinn and Charles Taliaferro (Oxford, Blackwell, 1997), pp. 243-259.

'Time and Trinity', in *Questions of Time and Tense*, ed. Robin Le Poidevin (Oxford, Clarendon Press, 1997), pp. 251-265.

'Eternality', in *Philosophy of Religion: A Guide to the Subject*, ed. Brian Davies (London, Cassell, 1998), pp. 75-79.

'Maimonides and Calvin on Divine Accommodation', in *God and Reference*, ed. Paul Helm, (Richmond, Curzon Press, 1999), pp. 149-170.

'Image of the Spirit and Image of God', in *Creator, Redeemer, Consummator, a Festschrift for Meredith Kline*, eds Howard Griffith and John R. Muether (Jackson, Miss.: Reformed Academic Press, 2000), pp. 203-213.

'Wittgensteinian Religion and "Reformed"' Epistemology' in *Wittgenstein and Philosophy of Religion*, eds Robert L. Arrington and Mark Addis (London and New York, Routledge, 2001), pp. 101-118.

'The Augustinian Calvinist View', in *Four Views of Divine Foreknowledge*, eds James K. Beilby and Paul R. Eddy (Downers Grove, Inter Varsity Press, 2001), pp. 161-206.

'Divine Timeless Eternity', in *God and Time: Four Views*, ed. Gregory Ganssle (Downers Grove, Inter Varsity Press, 2001), pp. 28-60.

'Can God Love the World?', in *Nothing Greater, Nothing Better*, ed. Kevin J. Vanhoozer (Edinburgh/Grand Rapids MA, Rutherford House/Eerdmans, 2001), pp. 168-186.

'The Indispensability of Belief to Religion', *Religious Studies*, 37 (2001): 75-86.

'The Problem of Dialogue', in *God and Time: Essays on the Divine Nature*, eds Gregory E. Ganssle and David M. Woodruff (New York: Oxford University Press, 2002), pp. 207-220.

'Augustine's Griefs', *Faith and Philosophy*, 20 (2003): 448-459. (Reprinted in *Augustine's Confessions: Critical Essays*, ed. William E. Mann (Lanham, Rowman and Littlefield, 2006), pp. 147-160.)

'All Things Considered: Providence and Divine Purpose', in *Comparative Theology: Essays for Keith Ward*, ed. T.W. Bartel (London, S.P.C.K., 2003), pp. 100-109.

'Synchronic Contingency in Reformed Scholasticism: A Note of Caution', *Nederlands Theologisch Tijdschrift* 57 (2003): 207-222.

'Reid and "Reformed" Epistemology' in *Thomas Reid: Context, Influence and Significance*, ed. Joseph Houston (Edinburgh, Dunedin Academic Press, 2004), pp. 103-122.

'Of God's Eternal Decree' in *Reformed Theology in Contemporary Perspective*, ed. Lynn Quigley (Edinburgh, Rutherford House, 2006), pp. 143-161.

'B.B. Warfield on Divine Passion', *Westminster Theological Journal*, 69 (2007): 95-104.

'Karl Barth and the Visibility of God', in *Engaging with Barth*, eds David Gibson and Daniel Strange (Leicester, Apollos, 2008), pp. 273-299.

'The Classical Calvinist Perspective', in *Perspectives on the Doctrine of God*, ed. Bruce A. Ware (Nashville, Tenn., Broadman and Holman, 2008), pp. 5-52.

John Locke

'John Locke and Jonathan Edwards: A Reconsideration', *Journal of the History of Philosophy* 7 (1969): 51-61.

'John Locke on Faith and Knowledge', *Philosophical Quarterly* 23 (1973): 52-66.

'Locke's Theory of Personal Identity', *Philosophy* 54 (1979): 173-185.

'A Forensic Dilemma: John Locke and Jonathan Edwards on Personal Identity', in *Jonathan Edwards, Philosophical Theologian*, eds Paul Helm and Oliver D. Crisp (Aldershot; Ashgate 2003), pp. 45-60.

Calvin and Calvinism

'Calvin, English Calvinism and the Logic of Doctrinal Development', *Scottish Journal of Theology*, 34 (1981): 179-186. (Reprinted in *Articles on Calvin and Calvinism*, ed. Richard C. Gamble, *vol. 14. Calvinism in France, Netherlands, Scotland, and England* (Hamden, Conn. Garland Publishing Inc., 1993).)

'Thomas Reid, Common Sense and Calvinism', in *Rationality in the Calvinian Tradition*, eds H. Hart, J. Van De-Hoeven and N. Wolterstorff (Lanham, Maryland, University Press of America, 1983), pp. 71-89.

'Calvin and the Covenant: Unity and Continuity', *The Evangelical Quarterly*, 55 (1983): 65-81. (Reprinted in *Articles on Calvin and Calvinism*, ed. Richard C. Gamble, *vol. 8. An Elaboration of the Theology of Calvin* (Hamden, Conn. Garland Publishing Inc., 1993).)

'Calvin and Natural Law', *Scottish Bulletin of Evangelical Theology*, 2 (1984): 5-22. (Reprinted in *Articles on Calvin and Calvinism*, ed. Richard C. Gamble, *vol. 7. The Organizational Structure of Calvin's Theology* (Hamden, Conn. Garland Publishing Inc., 1993).)

'Calvin (and Zwingli) on the Providence of God', *Calvin Theological Journal*, 29 (1994): 388-405.

'John Calvin, the *Sensus Divinitatis* and the noetic effects of sin', *The International Journal for the Philosophy of Religion*, 43 (1998): 87-107.

'Calvin, the "Two Issues", and the Structure of the *Institutes*', *Calvin Theological Journal*, 42 (2007): 341-348.

Other Articles in Philosophy

'Defeasibility and Open Texture', *Analysis* 28 (1968): 173-175.
'Pretending and Intending', *Analysis* 31 (1971): 127-132.
'Are "Cambridge" Changes Non-events?', *Analysis* 35(1975): 140-144.
'Detecting Change', *Ratio* 19 (1977): 34-38.
'On Pan-critical Irrationalism', *Analysis* 47 (1987): 24-28.

Chapter 1

Mind, Language, and the Trinity in Basil of Caesarea

David G. Robertson

It has often been said that the fourth-century debates that followed the landmark Council of Nicaea in 325 were conducted in such a way that Greek philosophy had been finally and decisively purged from orthodox trinitarian thought. In honor of the unity of philosophical and theological concerns exemplified in Paul Helm, I will try to bring to light a remarkable case of the power of philosophical ideas within Christian theology in even the most eminent of Greek theologians, even when discussing the Trinity. I hope to show that philosophical ideas about mind and language inherited from the Stoics inform the theological use of the distinction between inner speech (*logos endiathetos*) and language expressed (*logos prophorikos*) in the work of a cornerstone of trinitarian orthodoxy, Basil of Caesarea.[1]

I

Although the Stoics were not the first philosophers to draw a distinction between inner and outer speech, they developed the notion as received from Plato (*Soph.* 263E3-9; 264A1-2; *Phil.* 38E; *Theaet.* 189E6-190A; 206D1ff.) and Aristotle (*An. Post.* 76b24; *Cat.* 4b34), and gave it their stamp.[2] Following Plato and Aristotle, the wide dissemination of the Stoic *logos*-distinction in Hellenistic and Later Greek philosophy must also be taken into account. Of the many uses of the distinction, the Hellenistic debates on speech and human rationality are particularly relevant to the theological uses of the distinction I will discuss. So I will introduce the Hellenistic debates with the Stoics.

The Stoics do not seem to have concentrated on thought and its precise relation to language, as is now such a focus of interest in philosophy, cognitive science, and

---

1   For recent notices of the importance of the analogical arguments in Basil based on the distinction, there is Philip Rousseau, *Basil of Caesarea* (Berkeley and Los Angeles: University of California Press, 1994): 114-116 and Volker Henning Drecoll, *Die Entwicklung der Trinitätslehre des Basilius von Cäsarea* (Göttingen: Vandenhoeck and Ruprecht, 1996): 92-93 and 166.

2   On the question of Stoic origins, there is a classic discussion by Max Pohlenz, 'Die Begründung der abendländischen Sprachlehre durch die Stoa', *Nachrichten von der Gesellschaft der Wissenschaften zu Göttingen*, Phil. Hist. Kl., N. F., Bd. 3, N. 6 (Göttingen: Vandenhoeck & Ruprecht, 1939): 151-198 at 196-197. On Plato there is a summary of the evidence from the dialogues in Wolfram Ax, *Laut, Stimme und Sprache* (Göttingen: Vandenhoeck & Ruprecht, 1986): 105.

related fields. At least we can see that the Stoics have a notion of inner speech or 'linguistic thought'. The distinction is key to marking off human beings from other animate creatures, in such a way that there is a close relation between language and the rationality of human thought. The Stoics seem to take up this distinction in the first part of their dialectic, the part dealing with signifiers rather than what is signified (Diogenes Laertius 7.55ff.; 7.62).

The Skeptic philosopher Sextus Empiricus reports the Stoics on the relevance of the distinction between inner and outer *logos*:

> A human being differs from other animals not by using speech which is uttered (for crows, parrots and jays pronounce articulated words), but rather inner speech.[3]

This idea is loosely in accord with the views of the Stoic philosopher Diogenes of Babylon on human rationality reported elsewhere (Diogenes Laertius 7.55-56), so perhaps Sextus is drawing from Diogenes.[4] We also find from the doxagraphy of Diogenes Laertius (7.55-56) that for Diogenes of Babylon, the human voice as distinguished from animal sounds is articulate and sent forth from the mind; animal voices are merely bits of air struck by impulse. Thus in its semantic capacity, human vocal sound becomes speech. Speech is defined as signifying vocal sound sent out from the mind.

For the Stoics, the key characteristic of human rationality is the capacity for language.[5] Standard Stoic theory defines thoughts in terms of 'rational impressions', which are internally ordered and articulated in sentences, but also have a certain correspondence to non-corporeal things which are said or can be said.[6] In fact, the 'impressions' of rational creatures are spoken of as 'thoughts' or 'cognitive processes',[7] and it is clear that the Stoic notion of thought which follows a 'presentation' or

---

3   Sext. Emp., *Math.* 8.275 (Mutschmann and Mau) = SVF 135 and 223. All translations from Greek are my own unless noted otherwise.

4   For Diogenes, the difference between mere utterance and speech is also associated with the Stoic theory of the 'sayable' (Diogenes Laertius 7.57 = LS 33A, reporting Diogenes of Babylon): 'Speaking differs from utterance, for sounds are uttered, while things, which are actually just sayables, are said.'

5   Catherine Atherton, *The Stoics on Ambiguity* (Cambridge: Cambridge University Press, 1993): 42ff. provides an excellent account of the link between language and rationality, including the 'sayable' and its significance in connection with the distinction of *logos*. Also there is Max Mühl, 'Der *logos endiathetos* und *prophorikos* von der älteren Stoa bis zur Synode von Sirmium 351', *Archiv für Begriffsgeschichte* 7 (1962): 7-56 at 8-18.

6   The Stoics define (Sext. Emp., *Math.* 8.70 (Mutschmann) = LS 33C and Diogenes Laertius 7.63 = LS 33F) the 'sayable' as 'that which subsists in accordance with a rational impression', and define the rational impression as 'that in which the content of the impression is presented by means of language'. Sextus (*Math.* 8.12 = LS 33B) reports that the Stoics say that the true and the false are dealt with 'in what is signified', and sets forth a three-level Stoic semantic theory of thing signified, sign, and object. There is further discussion in Michael Frede, 'The Stoic notion of a *lekton*', *Language*, ed. Stephen Everson (Cambridge: Cambridge University Press, 1994): 109-128.

7   Diogenes Laertius, 7.51 = LS 39A6.

'appearance' is directly associated with language. 'The presentation precedes, and then thought, which possesses the capacity for speech, expresses with language that which is experienced by the agency of the presentation.'[8]

Accordingly, the Stoics have a sense in which they regard mental speech as unspoken, an internal phenomenon. The linguistic character of thought is important.[9] In an argument attributed by Galen to Chrysippus for locating the ruling part of the soul in the heart, what goes on in the mind is spoken of as inner discourse.

> He [*i. e.* Chrysippus] seems to me to be making use in this argument of his work on vocal sound. I prove this on the basis of what he says in addition: 'Then from the mind', he says, 'must come speaking and speaking in oneself or producing vocal sound and thinking and producing vocal sound in oneself and sending outwards.' For he takes something agreed as his first premiss, namely that speaking and speaking in oneself belong to the same part [of the soul], then he takes as his second premiss that speech is a work of the heart, and from these two premisses he deduces the conclusion, that speech in oneself takes place in the heart.[10]

This bit from Chrysippus contains obscurities, but there seems to be a notion that speakers articulate language within the mind which is then reflected in the utterance spoken to other (hearers, that is) speakers. The relation between inner and outer speech is not causal like the relation of speaker's mind and speaker's utterance but rather is a relation of having the same character.[11]

Later Peripatetics were happy to appropriate the Stoic terminology. For our purposes, let us take up the influential Stoicizing Peripatetic philosopher Porphyry, who wrote an entire (extant) treatise on animals. Porphyry says in *On Abstinence from Animal Food* that the definition which he gives of *logos prophorikos* is not the sole property of any philosopher or philosophical school, but is very widely recognized and contains a notion inherent in the concept of *logos*. The *logos* which is speech articulated by means of the tongue is 'signifying of the inner and psychic affections'.[12] Presumably, Porphyry thinks that the notion is found in Plato and Aristotle as well as the Stoics, representing philosophical consensus.[13]

---

8   Diogenes Laertius, 7.49 = LS 33D.

9   Julia Annas, *Hellenistic Philosophy of Mind* (Berkeley and Los Angeles: University of California Press, 1992): 63ff. goes into the importance of articulable content in Stoic philosophy of mind.

10   Galen, *Plac. Hippocr. Plat.* 3.7.42-43 (De Lacy, 220.16-18) = FDS 451. See Atherton, *The Stoics on Ambiguity*, 95-97 for further discussion of this text.

11   Chrysippus is said by Galen to be drawing upon his philosophy on vocal sound, where presumably Chrysippus presents his treatment of the distinction between inner and outer speech. For it is reported (Diogenes Laertius 7.55) that among the Stoics, there is general agreement that in dialectical theory one must begin from a treatment of vocal sound.

12   Porphyry, *Abst.* 3.3 (Nauck, 188.17-20).

13   David Sedley has pointed out that at least in the bit about signifying internal affections Porphyry says something that is distinctively Aristotelian (*Int.* 16a5-6) and not close to anything reported of the Stoics. Besides the texts adduced here from the Stoics, Sextus, and Porphyry, Pohlenz, 'Die Begründung', 191ff.; 197-198 includes references to Plotinus, Galen, and the Rhetoricians on the *logos*-distinction.

II

Next we will see how the Stoic distinction between inner and outer speech is used in the Hellenistic rationality debates. The legacy of these philosophical arguments will then be traced in some of Basil's work.

Much of what is known today of the Hellenistic debates is preserved from the Skeptics. To start with, there is a valuable report of the third-century AD Pyrrhonist philosopher Sextus Empiricus (*Hyp.* 1.65ff.), who attacks the Stoics within the framework of internal and expressed speech. Sextus is here presenting his ten modes of skepticism. The first mode has to do with sense-perception; it is an argument which points to the physical variations among animals on account of which different animals do not receive the same impressions from the same objects. On these grounds Sextus argues (*Hyp.* 1.59) that human beings can only know how things appear to us, and must suspend judgement as to what they are like in their nature. Accordingly, human beings cannot determine whether the impressions of animals are to be preferred to those of humans. Sextus provides strong evidence for the Stoic use of the *logos*-distinction in this debate, for the Stoics are said (*Hyp.* 1.62-65) to argue for a fundamental divide between irrational animals and rational humans. (He often refers to 'dogmatists' but in this passage picks out the Stoics by name, while his attack is clearly preoccupied with Stoic ideas.)

> So then, let us move on to reason. There is reason which is internal and there is reason which is expressed in language. So let us first look at the former kind. According to the dogmatists who think in a way particularly opposed to us, those from the Stoa, inner reason is anchored in these things, in the choice of what is appropriate (with a view to the fulfillment of our rational nature) and avoidance of what is alien to it, in the knowledge of the skills which contribute to this end, in the grasp of the virtues in accordance with our nature and the virtues which concern the passions.[14]

Significantly, Sextus of all the animals chooses the dog as his example for discussion in the passage immediately preceding (*Hyp.* 1.64). To support his position, namely that the perceptions of animals are no less trustworthy than those of humans, Sextus argues that animals possess rationality to the same degree as humans. Thus he takes up 'internal reasoning' first (*Hyp.* 1.66ff.),[15] in order to show that his representative animal, the dog, is 'perfectly equipped' in every respect that humans are perfectly equipped: The dog chooses what is 'well-suited' to himself and avoids what is harmful, the dog has a 'technical skill', namely hunting with which to obtain what is suitable, and the dog possesses virtue.

Sextus's dog is also a dialectician. This is illustrated (*Hyp.* 1.69) by means of the famous 'dog syllogism' of the great Stoic philosopher Chrysippus. Chrysippus is said to be 'particularly hostile' to irrational animals, yet for some reason accords the

---

14   Sext. Emp., *Hyp.* 1.65 (Mutschmann and Mau).

15   At *Hyp.* 1.73 Sextus moves on to speaking about *logos prophorikos*. Obviously, Sextus has a problem with this side of the matter. He takes recourse not in dogs but in animals which utter human sounds such as jays (cf. birds and expressed speech at *Hyp.* 1.77) and advances the possibility that humans just cannot understand the utterances of animals.

dog a share in dialectic. For the dog makes use of the fifth undemonstrable argument with several disjuncts when, tracking an animal, he or she arrives at a crossroads, and having sniffed at the two alternative roads, pursues the third without sniffing.[16] With regard to the Stoic view of animal reasoning in this case, Sextus tells us that 'the old [philosopher] says that he reasons this out virtually.' So to this counter-example, the Stoics would reply that no syllogism is carried out by the dog in the 'full' sense that is exemplified in human reasoning. As Sorabji argues, for Chrysippus the dog performs this in a way that is analogous yet inferior to the way in which human reason operates, for animals only possess a distorted image of complete rationality.[17] However, the behaviour of the dog at the crossroads can be expressed *by us* as an argument, and the same conclusion reached.

Sextus also addresses the question of rational humans and irrational animals in another passage in the course of his arguments that there is no sign.

> The dogmatists...who hold a position which is the opposite, say that man does not differ from the irrational animals by virtue of reason which is expressed (for in fact both ravens and parrots and jays pronounce articulate vocal sounds), but rather by virtue of reason which is internal; nor by virtue of the simple impression alone (for animals too receive impressions), but by virtue of the impression which involves inference and combination. On account of which the human being, when he conceives a notion of consequence, also in that very thought registers the cognition of a sign by virtue of the consequence; and the sign itself is of such a sort, 'if this, then this'. So then the existence of the sign hinges upon the nature and construction of the human being.[18]

Here the distinguishing mark of human rationality according to the Stoics is inference from signs.[19] On top of this, the Stoics would presumably add that the

---

16 There are several reports of the Stoic 'dog syllogism', conveniently listed by Karlheinz Hülser, *Die Fragmente zur Dialektik der Stoiker* (Stuttgart-Bad Cannstatt: Frommann-Holzboog, 1988): 4.1154-1159. The argument can be represented as follows:

A or B or C.

Not A and not B.

Therefore, C.

Michael Frede, *Die stoische Logik* (Göttingen: Vandenhoeck & Ruprecht, 1974): 153-157 discusses further the original Stoic argument which passed into later writers.

17 Richard Sorabji, *Animal Minds and Human Morals* (London: Duckworth, 1993): 89. 'Why then do animals not infer? The Stoics' best answer might be that they define reason (*logos*) as a collection of concepts, so reasoning (*logizesthai*) should involve the application of concepts, and they deny that animals have any.'

18 Sext. Emp., *Math.* 8.275-276 (Mutschmann and Mau) = FDS 529; 1031 = SVF 2.223 (part) = LS 53T. The translation and discussion here owes much to the suggestions of Richard Sorabji in personal correspondence. I also acknowledge the work of Myles Burnyeat, 'The Origins of Non-Deductive Inference', *Science and Speculation. Studies in Hellenistic Theory and Practice*, eds. Jonathan Barnes, Jacques Brunschwig, Myles Burnyeat, and Malcolm Schofield (Cambridge: Cambridge University Press, 1982): 193-238 at 206-207.

19 Burnyeat, 'Origins', 209ff. goes into some problems involved in the standard Stoic account of what a sign is (*Math.* 8.245): 'A sign is a proposition which forms the antecedent in a sound conditional, being revelatory of the consequent.' Burnyeat points out rightly that *Math.* 8.275-276 should not be understood to imply that signs amount to conditional propositions.

difference also lies in the meaningful quality of human utterances,[20] a position that Porphyry labours to overcome in his treatise on animals.[21]

Porphyry in his treatise *On Abstinence* likewise builds his arguments for the rationality of animals along the lines of the distinction, echoing some of the same points covered by Sextus.[22] Porphyry provides valuable testimony on Stoic theory in the course of his concise summaries of the opinions of 'the ancients' on reason and language. Before anyone else, he turns to the Stoics.

> Seeing that reason is two-fold according to the Stoics, being internal in one respect, and expressed in another, and again being correct in one aspect, and incorrect in another, it is appropriate to distinguish which of the two [kinds] they deny to the animals.... Since then reason is two-fold, being present in speech, while being present in the (mental) disposition, let us take our starting point from the former, which is ordered according to the voice. So if reason expressed is vocal sound [uttered] through the tongue, semantic of the affections which are inward and of the soul – for this definition is the commonest and is not at all the property of a philosophical sect, but only is based on the notion of reason.[23]

Porphyry then goes on to defend animal speech according to this definition, insofar as animals have their own language, which they possess not by convention like humans but in conformity to the guidance of nature and the gods.[24] It so happens that humans cannot understand animal speech,[25] the same line as found in Sextus (*Hyp.* 1.73ff.).[26]

There is controversy over what is allowed by the Stoics to animals in this passage. For further discussion of the issues, see Burnyeat, 'Origins', 209ff.; Sorabji, *Animal Minds and Human Morals*, 27.

20 With regard to 'impressions' and the inner-outer speech distinction, I take it that the Stoic position would spot the difference in the more sophisticated structuring of thoughts or 'rational impressions'. As we might claim in a different context today, exclusively in the case of *homo sapiens* is a developed theory of meaning or a theory of inference for a natural language appropriate.

21 Porphyry, *Abst.* 3.4 (Nauck, 191.3-13) brings up the same three birds as Sextus (ravens, parrots, and jays), and in general argues along very similar lines for meaning-loaded utterances of animals.

22 Pohlenz, 'Die Begründung', 192 notes the agreement both in content and in presentation between Sextus and Porphyry, and on this basis posits a common source. But then, oddly enough, he tries to use this observation as leverage in order to compromise Porphyry's clear and sound testimony to the Stoic origin of the doctrine.

23 Porphyry, *Abst.* 3.2 (Nauck, 187.20-188.20). In the translation, the square brackets supply what serves to fill out the Greek.

24 Atherton, *The Stoics on Ambiguity*, 147 n. 11 forwards some interesting criticisms of Porphyry's argument.

25 Porphyry, *Abst.* 3.6 (Nauck, 194.3-9). Soon after (*Abst.* 3.7), he turns to a discusson of inner reason, but seems less interested in it than Sextus, who argues heavily from this standpoint.

26 Writing on the basis of the same tradition, the Platonist philosopher Plutarch's entertaining treatise *On the Cleverness of Animals* plays variations on some of the same philosophical themes although without bringing in the thought and speech distinction. Plutarch presents arguments in this anti-Stoic treatise in favour of considering animals as

By this point, we can see the relevance of the Stoic distinction to the rationality debates. We are now in a position to take up a Greek Christian viewpoint on mind and language. In *Hex.* 9 and *Hom.* 3[27] of Basil the main strands of the philosophical tradition as sketched above are reworked into a Christian exposition of particularly impressive features of the created order, which show the wisdom of the creator. Basil discusses the untaught, innate nature of all creatures, which bear the mark of their maker's wisdom.

As with the Stoics, there are important distinctions to be made between humans and animals – Basil points to reason (*logos*) as the factor which marks the difference. 'In the case of irrational animals, the familial bonds between offspring and parents are untaught and unreflecting, by virtue of the fact that the God who formed them has made due allowance for the lack of reason with the excellence of the faculties of perception.'[28] A slightly different view is presented shortly before this text from his homilies on creation, where Basil says that the difference between animals and humans has its basis in bodily posture, insofar as it *reflects* the soul.[29] Basil is confident that animals possess souls, but he thinks that they are still without reason in spite of all that sense-perception does.[30] However, Basil looks less Stoic and more Platonic (*Hom.* 3.7 Rudberg) when he asserts that the human soul is immaterial, being divided into two parts, a rational and an irrational part.

The relationship of animal perception and rationality is elaborated a bit more in the following passage from *Hex.* 9, where Basil uses several animals as his examples, including the important case of the dialectical dog as inherited from the Stoics and reflected in the anti-Stoic polemics of Porphyry and Plutarch. He discusses the loyalty of dogs to their masters, but most impressive of all is the logical ability of the dog.

> The dog does not partake of reason, but nevertheless possesses a faculty of perception which accomplishes the work of reason. Seeing that the things which the wise men of this world have discovered with difficulty, working them out with much diligent study, I mean the construction of syllogisms, in these things nature instructs the dog. For the dog, while pursuing the track of a wild beast, when he finds that the track splits into several different directions, approaches each path which bears off, by his actions all but emits the

---

rational and indeed as dialecticians, *Soll. Anim.* 961C-969C (Helmbold). Plutarch's treatise is of relevance to Basil not only by virtue of its content, but also on account of its character as some type of school exercise – Basil may have read this popular treatise. William Helmbold takes up the question of the school-traditions behind Plutarch in his introduction to *Plutarch's Moralia* 12, eds. and trans. Harold Cherniss and William C. Helmbold, Loeb Classical Library (Cambridge, MA and London: Harvard University Press, 1957). Plutarch helps us to see how the Hellenistic debates were passed down through indirect channels in the Imperial period.

27   Jean Bernardi, *La Prédication des Pères Cappadociens* (Marseille: Presses Universitaires de France, 1968): 67-68 dates *Hom.* 3 to the period of Basil's priesthood, a few years before the dating of *Hom.* 16 generally agreed upon in the literature (371-372 AD). Moreover, Bernardi sees important points of similarity between *Hom.* 3 and *Hom.* 12 on the beginning of *Proverbs*, which he dates (56) as a quite early homiletical work (about 364 AD).

28   Basil, *Hex.* 9.4 (de Mendieta and Rudberg, 153.4-6).

29   Basil, *Hex.* 9.2 (de Mendieta and Rudberg, 148.23-149.6). Cf. Plato, *Tim.* 90A-B; Aristotle, *Part. Anim.* 2.10, 656a10-13; 4.10, 686a27-28.

30   Basil, *Hex.* 9.3 (de Mendieta and Rudberg, 149.11-149.13).

syllogistic utterance: Either this path, he says, the wild beast has taken, or this path, or in this direction; but neither this path nor this path, so the remaining option is that the beast has gone off in this final direction; and so by the denial of the false alternatives he finds the true one. What more do those men achieve who apply themselves to impressive diagrams and draw figures in the dust, by denying two of the three disjuncts and in the remaining disjunct deducing the true one?[31]

The most important point here, besides the unmistakable traces of Stoic influence, is that the notion of inner and outer reason would be deeply established in the background of his distinction between the work of nature and reason. For, as sketched above, the Stoics seem to work *logos endiathetos* and *logos prophorikos* into their discussions of rationality.

Basil remarks that in the case of the dog, perception which amounts to the work of nature does the work of human reasoning. Plutarch's account of Stoic canine syllogistic is similar but a bit finer-grained in that only the minor premiss is supplied by perception, while reason supplies the major premiss and the conclusion. On the other hand, Basil's dog 'all but utters the syllogistic speech', agreeing with Sextus' inclusion of 'virtually' in his testimony of Stoic animal reasoning. That is, Basil thinks that the dog accomplishes, under the guidance of nature, what could be arrived at by means of an argument by a human being.[32]

Actually, this idea is already present in an earlier homily (*Hom.* 3) where it is said that what is needed with a view to what is good and suitable for irrational creatures is secured by the guidance or control of divinely instituted nature, while the same ends are served in the case of humans by means of reason. Here we find some further reflections on the nature of human rationality.

> So God, who is our educator, has issued this great injunction [i.e. to attend to oneself], to the end that whatever is to their benefit from nature, might be added to us from the saving assistance of reason, and that whatever sets irrational animals aright without their paying attention, is gained by us through the work of attention and the continual application of reasoning.[33]

---

31   Basil, *Hex.* 9.4 (de Mendieta and Rudberg, 153.21-154.3) = FDS 1157, cf. Aelian, *Nat. Anim.* 6.59 (Hercher, 166.10-28).

32   Taking the idea about nature and perception a bit farther, Basil, *Hex.* 9.3 (de Mendieta and Rudberg, 150.20-151.10) accords a degree of rational understanding to animals with respect to the prognosis of things that are consequent upon other things: 'And the foreknowledge of changes in the air, does it not reveal some sort of rational understanding?' Basil adduces the examples of sheep, oxen, and bears, and then remarks on this testimony to the providential governance of the cosmos in terms familiar to Stoicism as well as the 'perception of the future' which irrational animals exercise.

33   Basil, *Hom.* 3.2 (Rudberg, 25.12-16). This homily is not easy to date with much degree of confidence. Seeing that *Hex.* is agreed to be one of his latest works, Paul J. Fedwick, 'A Chronology of the Life and Works of Basil of Caesarea', *Basil of Caesarea: Christian, Humanist, Ascetic*, ed. idem (Toronto: Pontifical Institute of Mediaeval Studies, 1981): 3-19 at 9 n. 32 remarks of *Hom.* 3 that although it is probably earlier, it is still a fitting complement to the unfinished *Hex.* 1-9.

And it seems that such a notion of human rationality in this text is forecast in the introductory section of the homily (*Hom.* 3.1), which remarks on the relation of the mind (the hidden) to speech (the revealed).

> God, our creator, has given the use of reason to us, in order that we might reveal the deliberations of our hearts to one another, and each person might impart something to his or her companion by virtue of what is common to human nature, as if speaking forth the deliberations from some inner chambers, from the hidden regions of the heart.... But since the soul, hidden under the veil of the flesh, produces thoughts, it requires verbs and names with a view to making public the things stored in its depths. So then whenever our thinking takes to itself semantic vocal sound, as if being conveyed with speech as a kind of ferry, crossing through the air, it arrives from the speaker to the hearer.[34]

Here human reason forms vocal utterances for the sake of expressing what is in the mind. Thought takes on language (which is termed *logos*) with a view to attaining a vehicle of expression. We might say that here is a notion of a 'language of thought' which, if strictly faithful to the Stoic legacy, has structural correspondences to natural languages. However, Basil is rather uninformative here on mind and the content of mental states: Basil only says that thoughts from deep within the speaker emerge and hitch a ride on utterances. The utterance is encoded in natural language by the speaker and then on the other end is decoded by the hearer, suggestive of contemporary 'communicative' theories of language and the mind. Indeed this idea must have been a commonplace in Late Antiquity, for Augustine says something quite similar in his homilies on the gospel of John (*Hom. in Joh.* 37.4.14-24). In Augustine's hands, it is supposed to explain the transfer of information from one person to another, to show how teaching is possible. Basil thinks that individuals express their thoughts by means of the divinely-instituted benefits of linguistic interchange: human nature is equipped with the capacity for rational thought and its expression through speech. These thoughts are in turn apprehended successfully by hearers on the basis of certain key characteristics that all people have. Inner speech does not seem to be conceived as a silent monologue or debate – I take it that the soul is simply occupied with private thoughts.

To sum up the argument of this section, Basil thinks that animals perform actions under the guidance of nature in such a way that animal minds are entirely programmed in their responses to external stimuli. Animal perception can accomplish what reason does for us, at least for purposes of action. On the question of the distinguishing mark between animal and human rationality, Basil usually sticks to the view that inner, unspoken reason is constitutive of human rationality. These texts bear the marks of the Hellenistic debate on reason and animal rationality, which in turn involves the Stoic distinction. Now, we are ready to take up the discussions of inner and outer speech in a few selected Basilian homilies (*Hom.* 12, *Hom.* 16, *Homs. in Psalmos*).

---

34 Basil, *Hom.* 3.1 (Rudberg, 23.1-11). The concealed in thought as opposed to revealed in language theme is developed further, *Hom.* 3.1 (Rudberg, 24.17-25.7).

III

Max Mühl has already shown in an influential article that the philosophical background to *logos endiathetos* and *logos prophorikos* makes its mark on the theological tradition of the first few Christian centuries. Yet beyond his work, very little on this distinction has been written about the great Patristic writers of the later fourth century, nor as regards its more general career in Greek and Latin Patristics after Nicaea. I will argue that an important, if unexpected, use of the distinction appears in an important doctrinal homily of Basil (*Hom.* 16) on the opening sentence of John's gospel, 'in the beginning was the Word'.[35]

Two basic problems need to be considered. The first problem is why Basil takes up the distinction for theology, along with the surprising statement that the *logos* issues from the mind analogous to human speech, in a departure from his major theological predecessors and contemporaries: Eusebius, Athanasius, Meletius, and the leaders of the Homoiousian party that attended this issue.[36] Unfortunately, I cannot go too far into the complicated historical questions. Secondly, there is the obscurity of the relation of the philosophical tradition to the ideas of *Hom.* 16: I will argue that Basil is the first ancient thinker to definitely and clearly claim that thought is timeless and that human speech is produced from the mind without passion.[37]

---

35 Basil, *Hom.* 16.3 (PG 31, 475C-479A). This homily tends to be treated in scholarly literature together with *Hom.* 15, which bears the title 'On the Faith'. Fedwick, 'Chronology', 9-10 thinks that *Hom.* 16 can be dated to the same year (372 AD) as *Hom.* 15 and yet a little earlier than *Hom.* 15, which bears the likely dating to 7 September. This dating would place *Hom.* 16 securely before the composition of the major work on the Holy Spirit and around the beginning of Basil's separation from the views of Eustathius of Sebaste. (The personal watershed of the break with Eustathius is treated by Rousseau, *Basil of Caesarea*, 239.) Bernardi, *La Prédication*, 86-87, also dates *Hom.* 16 to the same period as Hom. 15. If the loose chronological consensus of these scholars is correct, then the boldness and spirit of this sermon may provide a useful indication of Basil's personal and theological outlook at this stage of his career. The increased prominence of the Marcellan issue, so important for the theological background to *Hom.* 16, also loosely supports the view of Fedwick and Bernardi. On the eventual rejection of Marcellus, see Rousseau, *Basil of Caesarea*, 246-247; Rousseau cites three homilies in connection with the emergence of Basil's homiletical responses to the Sabellian issue, namely *Hom.* 24, *Hom.* 27, and our *Hom.* 16.

36 Christopher Stead, 'The Concept of Mind and the Concept of God in the Christian Fathers', *The Philosophical Frontiers of Christian Theology*, eds. B. Hebblethwaite and S.R. Sutherland (Cambridge: Cambridge University Press, 1982): 39-54 at 39 claims that 'in the fourth century Eusebius and Athanasius seem to be noticeably reluctant to characterize God as Mind'. Unfortunately, it is far beyond the scope of this chapter to evaluate this interesting point. Stead does not say too much about the Cappadocian Fathers or indeed about Marcellus. He attributes a use of the distinction to Athenagoras, Theophilus, Irenaeus, and Tertullian.

37 I note in passing that traces of similar Stoic ideas regarding the *logos* distinction can be seen here and there in the Eastern Origenist tradition which Basil inherits, particularly in Origen himself, but also in Dionysius of Alexandria and Gregory of Nazianzus. One text from Gregory's poetry deserves special mention, *Carm.* 2.1.12, 267-269 (PG 37, 1185). Also cf. Gr. Naz., *Or.* 28.13 (Barbel); Gr. Nyss., *Eun.* 1.539-542 (Jaeger, 182.17-183.15).

Does our mind seek to know, who was in the beginning? 'The *Logos*', he says. What kind of *logos*? The language of men? Or rather, the speech of angels? In fact, the Apostle has indicated to us, that the angels speak in their own tongue, saying, 'if I should speak with the tongues of men and angels'. But also there are two meanings of '*logos*' which can be distinguished. For one sense of the term means the *logos* which is expressed by means of vocal sound, the speech which dissipates in the air after being uttered; and another sense of the term means the speech which is inward, located in our hearts, the speech which is involved in thought. And there is another, the expertise that is employed in the arts. Observe the senses of the term carefully, that the homonymy of the word does not mislead you.... But instead hear the *Logos* in a manner that is worthy of God. When he [i.e. John] speaks to you concerning the Only-Begotten, he calls him the *Logos*. So then just as he will call him a little later light, and life, and resurrection, and when you hear light, you are not carried down to that which is perceptible and visible to the eyes, and when you hear life, you do not think of this mundane existence, which even the irrational animals live; just so when you hear '*Logos*', beware lest ever you are carried down by dint of the weakness of the mind to earthly and lowly thoughts. Rather, search out the meaning of the term. On what account does John use the term of *logos*? In order that it might be made plain, that he issued from the mind. Why *logos*? Because he was generated without passion. Why *logos*? Because he is the image of the one who generated him, making known the one who generated as a whole in himself, being no partition from him, although he exists in his own perfection. So also our *logos* represents our thought as a whole. That which we conceive in the heart, we express in speech, and that which is spoken is the image of the thought in the heart. For from the outflow of the heart, *logos* is brought forth. And our heart is like a source, while speech when spoken forth is like a stream, which flows from this source. So great is the outflow, so much also is that which is referred back to the origin; and of what is hidden, so great also is that which appears in the open. He uses the term '*Logos*', in order that he might set the passionless generation of the Father before you, and speak theologically to you of the perfect reality of the Son, and through these things indicate to you the timeless union of the Son with the Father. In fact our speech is the offspring of the mind, begotten without passion, for it is not severed, nor is it divided, nor is it effluent; rather, the mind as a whole remains in its own nature, emitting speech which is whole and complete. And the *logos* which issues outwards contains in itself the meaning in its entirety of the mind which generates it. To the extent that is pious and reverent, appropriate from the term '*Logos*' with a view to the theology of the Only-Begotten; whatever you find which appears alien and unfitting, this you must reject, and step beyond it by every means. 'In the beginning was the *Logos*.' If he had said, 'in the beginning was the Son', the notion which involves passions would enter along with the term 'Son'. For since human generation takes place over time, and involves passion, for this reason he says '*Logos*', correcting in advance the unsuitable conceptions, to the end that he might keep your soul from harm.[38]

So here we see the analogy to human speech and the mind at work. When the semantic ambiguity is resolved into the distinct senses, Basil uses various forms of a verb (*propheromenos*, *propherein*) which is a cognate of the descriptive term in the philosophical tradition (*prophorikos*). On the other hand, the term for inner reason or speech (*endiathetos*) is of course identical to the term in the philosophical tradition.

---

38 Basil, *Hom.* 16.3 (PG 31, 476C-480A).

The theological use of the distinction amounts to illustrating the relation of the divine *logos* to the inner nature of God, by the notion of speech which is expressed, originating from the mind of an individual who uses speech for communication. We do not see here a notion of the theology of divine thought as *inner* speech, although there is talk about the divine mind. (Recall the passages discussed above in Basil where the idea that thought is constituted by language or has the character of 'inner speech' is absent.) The passage reworks the classic Greek theology of the image of God in a striking way; care is taken to point out the perfection of the image, and the characteristic of permanence, of existing in its own right, balanced by the union of image to what is imaged.

Now I will address the second of the two basic problems. The supposition that Basil is simply working with standard philosophical ideas about the relationship of speech to thought is somewhat wrong. Rather, I would argue that there is surprising originality to the ideas he works into his theological arguments. The most interesting philosophical points are (1) that speech is a kind of image of the speaker's mind and (2) the passionless, timeless production of speech.

With regard to point (1), Basil's idea of speech as the image or reflection of the mind of the speaker must be understood in light of its prominence in the philosophy of the Imperial period. Ptolemy, a contemporary of Galen and a leading mathematician and astronomer of the Imperial period, wrote an extant short treatise entitled *On the Criterion and the Rational Part of the Soul*. This work shows how certain features of the earlier debates between sceptics and dogmatists were passed down for general appropriation by philosophers and scientists, like Ptolemy himself. The treatise takes up various topics in the theory of language, including the traditional distinction between inner and outer speech.

> To the rational faculty, according to which the unique property of human beings is defined, belong thought and speech. Thought is inner *logos*, being a certain exposition and repetition and differentiation of what has been remembered, while speech [is] the vocal symbols through which thoughts are expressed to those who are nearby. And vocal sound is a certain image of the mind itself, voice [is an image] of mental activity, speech [is an image] of thought, and generally, expressed *logos* [is an image] of inner *logos*.[39]

Ptolemy's remarks on inner and outer speech in this passage emphasize speech as the image of the mind. So we discern in Ptolemy a theory of signs, echoing both Aristotle and the Stoics, reworked into a 'spoken image' doctrine of language.

In Basil, on the other hand, there is a development of the inherited 'spoken image' doctrine in the idea of the *logos* as the image which expresses thought completely and unerringly. A Fregean take along similar lines might be that each thought can be apprehended by everyone and that whatever is expressed in language is in some prior sense an object of thought.[40] But the notion of Basil is stronger in that *all* the contents of the mind are expressible in language and thus can be grasped by others. The idea seems to be that nothing is lost in translation into language. This

---

39   Ptolemy, *On the Criterion* 6.1-8 (Lammert).

40   Gottlob Frege, 'The Thought', *Collected Papers on Mathematics, Logic, and Philosophy*, ed. B. McGuinness (Oxford: Basil Blackwell, 1984): 351-372.

would presumably be the point of the insistence on the commensurateness of what is inner and what is outer. Otherwise, there might be problems in the theological epistemology: something would be 'held back' from the expression of what God has in God's mind.

As for point (2), the passionless and timeless issue of *logos*, we are dealing with a rather odd view of freedom from passion characterizing the issue of human language from the mind.[41] It is difficult to determine exactly what is meant by this claim, but I take him to mean not the absence of any involvement of emotions or desires in human speech, but rather the absence of any disruption in the connection of thought and utterance (the notion that people say what they have in their minds to say).

Strangely enough, Basil in this passage avoids Son-language where one would expect it, as we find nowhere else in his received corpus of works. He claims that John cleverly and purposely passes up the sentence 'in the beginning was the Son' in favour of the sentence 'in the beginning was the Word', with a view to eliminating harmful connotations of the term 'Son'; John sets himself to exclude all passion from the eternal generation of the Son, and moreover the begetting of the Son must be timeless. This is unusual insofar as talk of the generation of the Son, or at least the passionless generation of the Son, seems quite acceptable to him elsewhere – in fact it is a cornerstone of Basil's trinitarian thought, frequently upheld in his theological works. For example, the idea is clearly present in one of Basil's major treatises, the *Contra Eunomium*,[42] where is found an interesting passage discussing the timeless issuing of the Son from the Father, taking up the analogy to the human mind.[43] The idea of the Son as the perfect image or seal of the Father is present, as in *Hom.* 16, but missing is talk of speech in relation to thought.

Let us consider the bearing of the philosophical tradition on point (2). The point about time and the mind might be found in the Stoics, in something reported of Diogenes of Babylon. As discussed above, quite possibly it is Diogenes who employs the notion of *logos endiathetos* and *prophorikos* in his theory of vocal sound in arguments which are designed to show how human rationality operates beyond the

---

41 Although I cannot find the idea of the passionless generation of human word from human mind anywhere else in Basil, other homiletic passages speak of the *perfection* of human reason in terms that evoke the simplicity of God, in accordance with a strong notion of undeviating moral singleness, e.g. *Hom.* 12 (PG 31, 400C) on the prologue of *Proverbs*. Right theological thinking is conceived as a static and straightforward rational exercise. Also compare the discussion in *Hom. in Ps.* 14 (15) (PG 29, 253C-256B), on the words of the psalm, 'who speaketh truth in his heart, on whose tongue is found no deceit'. Here the idea of reason in the hiddenness of the heart is present along with the contrast between truth in the heart and straightness in speech. The theme of the simplicity of orthodox doctrine is explored in detail by Mario Girardi, "Semplità' e ortodossia nel dibattito antiariano di Basilio di Cesarea: la raffigurazione dell' eretico', *Vetera Christianorum* 15 (1978): 51-74.

42 Drecoll, *Die Entwicklung*, 165 argues that *Hom.* 16 represents a step beyond the *Contra Eunomium*, for in *Eun.* Basil had treated every word of *John* 1.1 up to but not including *logos*. Since *Hom.* 16 was probably delivered almost ten years after the composition of *Eun.* (cf. footnote 35), it appears that Basil chose homiletic occasions later in his career to treat the fundamental early Christian concept of *logos*.

43 Basil, *Eun.* 2.16, 33-45 (SC 305: 64).

pale of animal rationality. Now Galen preserves an argument of Diogenes for the location of the 'leading part of the soul' in the heart (not the head) which talks about significant vocal sound being sent out from the mind.[44] The report says that the utterance is semantically imprinted by thoughts in the mind, and thus formed or stamped issues outward in speech, being then extended in time. Hence the implication might be that thoughts (inner speech) are timeless insofar as they remain in the head. Not much, I admit, but worth a mention.

However, it appears that the philosophical tradition does not dwell at all on the possibility of *passionless* generation of speech from the mind, however conceived. (The frivolous student of Antiquity might point out that more philosophers than bishops were enmeshed in marital relations.) With respect to the Stoics, the standard view is that humanity, and human speech in particular, is fundamentally rational. For the Stoics, ordinary language naturally reflects the order of the rational cosmos and should be brought into perfect concord with it. On the other hand, Stoic orthodoxy conceives the passions or emotions as movements of the soul disobedient to reason, reflecting the Chrysippean psychology of a wholly rational soul without an irrational part.[45] But there is no sign of any Stoic worry about speech production *per se* involving a passion of any kind.

Aristotle, like the Stoics, presents a semantic theory with three levels (*Int.* 16a3-9 and 24b1-2), where on the level of the mind he talks about the 'affections' of the soul. In the *De Interpretatione* Aristotle says that things which are spoken are symbols of 'things that happen to the soul', while 'things that happen to the soul' are likenesses of objects. (Aristotle also says that the utterances, which are signs, are *primarily* signs of things that happen to the soul, and one might assume, only secondarily signs of objects.[46]) Clearly, Basil's view of language and thought borrows nothing from the Peripatetic tradition, and the Stoics don't appear to have much to say either.

In closing, I hope that my readers would agree to the depth of philosophical infiltration in late fourth-century orthodox trinitarian discourse and argument, which I have tried to bring to light in this contribution. But if we take the philosophy seriously, we soon run into puzzles – such as the unresolved question as to why Basil assumes so readily the passionless quality of speech. Perhaps by the fourth century this was commonly held; we might hope (vainly) that evidence from the Hellenistic rationality debates would shed some light on the question. Or perhaps the notion of begetting, once it was treated as distinct by Patristic writers from the philosophical notion of generation, took on philosophical assumptions of its own: It may be an entirely Christian idea. This view of language may have been a natural position to

---

44   Galen, *Plac. Hippocr. Plat.* 2.5.9-13 (de Lacy, 130.7-19) = FDS 450.

45   Thanks to Richard Sorabji for discussion of these ideas. Atherton, *The Stoics on Ambiguity*, 119-122 presents texts (particularly from Galen), translations, and further discussion of these points. In contrast to the Stoics, Basil believes that the soul is immaterial, *Hom.* 3.7 (Rudberg, 35.16ff.), and is divided into two parts, a rational part and an irrational part, *Hom.* 3.7 (Rudberg, 35.6-8).

46   The later Peripatetic tradition understands things that happen to the soul in this text to amount to thoughts (cf. *Int.* 16a9ff.)—see Jonathan Barnes, 'Meaning, Saying and Thinking', *Dialektiker und Stoiker*, hrsg. Klaus Döring und Theodor Ebert (Stuttgart: Franz Steiner Verlag, 1993): 47-61 at 50-53.

advocate, given Patristic theological preoccupation with the timeless and passionless generation of the Son from the Father. Further, I am told that the timelessness of thought is taken up and developed in Medieval Philosophy. But I must leave the afterlife of these ideas to others.[47]

47　I owe special thanks to M.W.F. Stone for his encouragement of this sort of work over several happy years. I must also acknowledge the copious debt to my dissertation supervisor Richard Sorabji, my examiners Bob Sharples and David Sedley, as well as to M.W.F. Stone, Paul Helm, and Sir Anthony Kenny for their helpful responses at the British Society for the History of Philosophy Conference, 'Athens and Jerusalem: Christianity and the History of Philosophy', University of Keele (Keele, 6-9 April 2000).

Chapter 2

Reason and Rhetoric: Stephen Charnock on the Existence of God

Carl R. Trueman

Charnock's Life

Stephen Charnock was born in 1628 in the parish of St Katherine Cree, London. As a young man, he attended Emmanuel College, Cambridge, an establishment well-known for its Puritan pedigree, where he studied under William Sancroft, who later became Archbishop of Canterbury, and where he appears to have been converted to the Puritan cause. From there, he went to a parish in Southwark, where he enjoyed a brief but fruitful ministry prior to being made a Fellow of New College, Oxford, by the Parliamentary Visitors in 1649. Then, in 1652, he was made Senior Proctor of the University, a position he held until 1656, at which point he left for Ireland, where he spent time as chaplain to Richard Cromwell, the Lord Protector's brother.

With the Restoration of Charles II in 1660, and the subsequent draconian legislation that made up the Clarendon Code, Charnock found himself ejected from the Established Church in 1662, under the terms of the Act of Uniformity.[1] His ministry continued, however, as he served the non-conformist cause in secret, and even managed to visit Reformed centres in Holland and France. In 1675, with the partial relaxation of legislation against non-conformists, Charnock accepted a call to become co-pastor of a church in Crosby Square, London, with the ejected presbyterian minister (and one-time delegate to the Westminster Assembly), Thomas Watson. Watson, as the author of, among other things, an influential commentary on the Westminster Shorter Catechism, was a man of some distinction, and the presence of two such powerful Puritan intellects in the one charge made Crosby Square a significant stronghold of non-conformity.

The congregation, organized upon broadly presbyterian lines, met in the hall of Crosby House, an ancient mansion on the east side of Bishopsgate Street. The hall was owned by one Sir John Langham, an Alderman of the city, who was himself a committed presbyterian and allowed the congregation to have use of the building. It was here that Charnock delivered the series of addresses that have come down to us as his *Discourses upon the Existence and Attributes of God*, a series which was cut short by the death of Charnock on 27 July 1680, at the age of fifty-two.[2]

---

1 The Clarendon Code is a term which describes four Acts of the Cavalier Parliament: the Corporation Act (1661); the Act of Uniformity (1662); the Conventicle Act (1664); and the Five Mile Act (1665).

2 The extant sermons are collected in Stephen Charnock, *Discourses upon the Existence and Attributes of God*, 2 vols (Grand Rapids: Baker, 1979).

The Context of the Treatise

Charnock's life spanned the most turbulent decades of the seventeenth century and yet it must not be forgotten that he reached his adulthood during the time when the Puritan cause within the Church of England was in the ascendant. The bitter persecutions of the 1630s would not have had a great immediate impact upon him as it was in the 1640s, the decade of the Civil Wars and the Westminster Assembly, that Charnock's own theological convictions matured within a context where they were increasingly to represent the dominant cultural and theological orthodoxy. This point is worth noting, as the contrast between his early membership of the intellectual and political establishment and his later status as a marginalized non-conformist provides at least part of the background to the *Discourses*.

We must not, of course, isolate Charnock's theological development from the broader contours of the intellectual culture of which he was a part. He was a graduate of Cambridge and a Fellow at Oxford, neither of which institution represented a monochrome intellectual culture during this period, enjoying the presence of Puritan and Laudian scholars throughout the 1640s and 1650s. Thus, in addition to the obvious continuities of library resources and basic curriculum structure during this time, it is evident that the 1640s, and even the 1650s, did not mark clean breaks with the intellectual traditions of the past in these institutions but, to a large extent, represented a continuation of the development of the medieval pattern under the impact of the English renaissance. Thus, for example, in the 1650s at Oxford, the Laudian Edward Pococke remained as professor of Oriental Languages during the Vice-Chancellorship of the Independent John Owen – a symbol of the importance of scholarship in the Commonwealth period and, perhaps, of the limitations of ambition which the Puritan project embodied. The Cambridge and Oxford which would have shaped the mind of the young Charnock – and into which he apparently fitted so well – were Renaissance institutions geared to the production of Renaissance men. Indeed, Charnock did not disappoint on this score, emerging, so we are told, with a broad intellectual training which evidenced itself, among other things, in a strong interest in medicine – a passion which he shared with other men of the age, including the famous Richard Baxter who seems to have enjoyed conducting his own medical experiments on his parishioners in Kidderminster.

If the intellectual cultural background of Charnock the man lies in the Renaissance milieu of Cambridge and Oxford, we must not forget that the social and political background of the *Discourses* lies very much in the struggles of the 1660s. It is indeed very difficult to overestimate the impact upon the Puritan consciousness of the collapse of the Puritan project which the Restoration of 1660 heralded and the Clarendon Code. For one hundred years before the Civil War there had been a more or less continual struggle within the Church of England to achieve a more thorough reformation of its doctrine and liturgy. While there had been no single, unified, organized movement which we might call 'Puritanism', there had been numerous attempts to organize opposition to the establishment and a number of high-profile individuals, such as Cartwright, Chaderton, Perkins and Ames, whose lives and writings had become focal-points for internal dissent. In the 1640s, however, with the actions of Parliament in establishing the Westminster Assembly and then engaging in military conflict with the King, a large number of Puritans had, for a short time at least, enjoyed a degree of unity of purpose. In the late 1640s and 1650s, this had become somewhat fractured, with the execution of the King being opposed in large part by the presbyterians, the failure of Parliament to impose the presbyterian settlement on England to which many English puritans felt that the Solemn League and Covenant with Scotland had committed them, and the rise to prominence under Cromwell of leading Independents such as John Owen and Philip Nye. Nevertheless, a strong belief in God's providence often combined with an acute eschatological sensitivity, meant that for many the events of the 1640s and even the 1650s heralded a significant movement of God and pointed forward to even greater things. The events of 1660 and beyond, therefore, precipitated something of a crisis in confidence in many puritan circles and raised acute theological questions in many minds.

Of course, we have no reason to believe that Charnock, as a presbyterian, was particularly enamoured of the Protectorate, although his enjoyment of high office under the Protector's brother might indicate a more sympathetic stance than we might have expected. Nevertheless, even if Charnock was not devastated by the restoration of Charles II in 1660, the advent of the Clarendon Code must have been a grievous blow to him, entailing as it did a dramatic loss of status and influence both for him and the kind of theological and political policies he represented. To be moved so rapidly from the corridors of power to the wilderness of anonymity must have had a significant effect upon his whole life, including his theology. Whatever his attitude to the Protectorate, he can scarcely have stood apart from the crisis in identity which the Great Ejection precipitated for the puritan cause. A group that had seen themselves as having the God-given responsibility and opportunity to reform the Church of England from the inside were now placed permanently on the outside, with neither the resources nor the opportunities for continuing the project. Loss of personal status, loss of theological influence, and loss of the traditional purpose for existence were all part of the Puritan's – now non-conformist's – lot in the 1660s and 1670s, and to these Charnock was no exception. His role was no longer that of establishment insider but of the outsider, looking on with frustration at political and theological developments within the Church of England, and pastoring congregations who, thanks to their outwardly marginalized status, needed to be reassured of the fundamental justice of their cause.

These then are the two basic elements to the background of Charnock's great discourses on God: the renaissance culture of Cambridge and Oxford and the impact of the struggles of the 1660s. It is against this background that the *Discourses* must be read.

The *Discourses*: Scope and Structure

The text of the *Discourses* which we have today represents the extent of the project at the time of Charnock's death in 1680. Thus, it is incomplete and does not contain the whole of what he intended to say in this area. As its stands, the work consists of fourteen individual discourses, originally given as lectures to his congregation in Crosby House. These are, in order: on the existence of God; on practical atheism; on

God's being a Spirit; on spiritual worship; on the eternity of God; on the immutability of God; on God's omnipresence; on God's knowledge; on the wisdom of God; on the power of God; on the holiness of God; on the goodness of God; on God's dominion; and on God's patience. Thus, the treatise as it stands does not move beyond the traditional locus of the doctrine of God.

Each discourse is presented as a commentary upon a selected verse of scripture, representing the homiletic context of the original sermon. The opening paragraphs are devoted each time to the standard contextualization and analysis which one would expect from a Puritan preacher addressing himself to a particular text. Nevertheless, while the chosen text provides a basic exegetical reference point for the ensuing discourse, Charnock's approach is far more discursive than a straightforward exposition of the relevant passage. Instead, the text operates more as a biblical statement of the theme of each of the discourses which are in practice far more comprehensive in their treatments than mere exposition and application would generally allow.

For the sake of brevity, my interest is in the first discourse, that dealing with the existence of God, as this, I believe gives the reader a good idea of Charnock's approach and agenda throughout the whole and also, because it contains examples of the so-called 'proofs for God's existence' allows us to address the important question of the relationship between Charnock's thought and medieval antecedents, a point which will help to draw this work into current debates about seventeenth-century Reformed thought.

The proofs for God's existence are, of course, a classic point to examine in order to determine the nature and scope of reason and rationality within a theologian's scheme. From Anselm to Barth, one can tell a lot about an individual's theology by looking at the status and the nature of the proofs. Within the specific context of the history of Reformed thought, they have come to play a pivotal role in analysing the relationship between Reformed Orthodoxy, the Reformation, the Middle Ages, and the Enlightenment. Is the apparent resurgence of the proofs in Protestant theology in the seventeenth century continuous with the thought of the Reformers, a retrogression to the theology of the Middle Ages, or a step towards Enlightenment rationalism? It is these questions which I wish to develop an approach towards today; and it will be my contention that such questions, although of an essentially theological kind, can only really be approached if we are willing to think beyond mere theological answers to look at the wider historical context within which they occur.

Discourse I: On the Existence of God

The Argument of the Discourse

Charnock's text for this discourse, as for the subsequent one on practical atheism, is Psalm 14:1, 'The fool hath said in his heart, There is no God. They are corrupt, they have done abominable works, there is none that doeth good'. Charnock divides the verse into two: the fool's intellectual and moral convictions, as evidenced in his declaration, and the fool's subsequent immoral actions, the practical atheism that flows from his cognitive atheism. While this latter issue is dealt with in much more detail in the second discourse, it is still an underlying concern in this first lecture.

The first distinction, the fool's intellectual atheism, Charnock divides into three subsections, that of absolute denial of God's existence, denial of his providential care, and denial of one or more of his perfections.[3] The division is important because it points immediately to the fact that atheism, and thus the arguments which are to be opposed to it, are not simply matters of abstract metaphysics, dealing only with the existence of God; rather they also deal with the essence or identity of God. In fact, while Charnock initially distinguishes denial of divine providence from denial of divine attributes, he soon elides the two so that the one explicitly involves the other:

> Those that deny the providence of God, do in effect deny the being of God; for they strip him of that wisdom, goodness, tenderness, mercy, justice, righteousness, which are the glory of the deity.[4]

In other words, atheism can be either the denial or doubting of God's bare existence (absolute and sceptical atheism respectively, as Charnock categorizes them), but also includes the denial or drastic revision of God's essence – the classic seventeenth-century meaning of the term. Charnock justifies this point exegetically from his understanding of the Hebrew text of Psalm 14:1 which uses the Hebrew form he transliterates as Eloahia, and Latinises as *potestas Dei*, 'power of God'.[5] The fool is not so much involved in denying the bare existence of God as in the denial of God's power and jurisdiction, a denial which inevitably has profound practical implications. In fact, what Charnock is really going to deal with in this treatise is not atheism as understood in the modern world, but *practical* atheism: the rejection of God's character as demonstrated in licentious living. This, of course, allows Charnock to broaden the application of the verse, and thus the 'foolishness' of its subject to include the usual suspects: Arminians and Socinians. Though not mentioned explicitly, there is no doubt that it is them he has in mind.

The close connection of atheism with the perceived positions of Arminians and Socinians on issues such as divine sovereignty and providence is not original with Charnock. John Owen (1616-1683) makes precisely this point in his attacks on Arminianism in the 1640s when he describes rejection of the immutability of God's decrees, a position which he imputes to the Arminians and which he sees as the eternal foundation of providence, as 'transcendent atheism'.[6] What one has, therefore, explicitly in Owen and implicitly in Charnock is the forging of a link, an association, between the idea of atheism and the rejection, not of God in the absolute sense but of a particular view of God. Given the historical context of Charnock's *Discourse*, it is not hard to imagine who the 'practical atheists' are whom he has in

---

3   'There is a threefold denial of God, 1. *Quoad existentiam*; this is absolute atheism. 2. *Quoad providentiam*, or his inspection into, or care of the things of the world, bounding him in the heavens. 3. *Quoad naturam*, in regard of one or other of the perfections due to his nature.' *Existence*, p. 24.

4   *Existence*, p. 24.

5   *Existence*, p. 24.

6   Owen, *Works* 10, p.14.

mind, especially when he makes dark references to the 'swarms' of atheists and their 'barefaced debauchery' who are more numerous now than at any time before:[7] those cavaliers and royalists who were prospering under the Restoration. He could not, of course, say so explicitly because of the difficult political situation, but his non-conformist congregation could not have failed to have understood that the perennial Puritan language of moral lament was primarily referring to all that was going on around them. The result is a rhetorical connection which the rest of Charnock's discourse serves merely to reinforce.

The arguments Charnock proposes against atheism in all its forms are grouped together under four general reasons: everyone has always acknowledged some kind of divine being;[8] the whole of nature indicates the existence of a divine being;[9] human nature witnesses to the existence of a divine being;[10] and miracles indicate the existence of a divine being.[11] The litany of proofs is entirely conventional and these provide the basic framework for Charnock's marshalling of more detailed arguments for the existence of God, and it is to these we now turn.

Under the first reason, Charnock subdivides the argument into three: the acknowledgement of a higher divine being has been, first of all, universal; secondly, it has been constant and uninterrupted; and, thirdly, it is natural and innate.[12] The striking thing about each of these arguments is the profoundly non-speculative nature of each, based rather upon empirical phenomena than upon metaphysics. Indeed, at the one point where the argument could have been developed in a speculative direction, that concerning the innate nature of theistic convictions, Charnock in fact roots his argument in the fact that any other explanation for the first two points – universality and constancy – is completely absurd and that the argument from human structure is the only plausible explanation. Thus, in an argument strangely analogous to those from mechanical causality, he rejects tradition as the source because every tradition requires a source and cannot regress into the past indefinitely; furthermore, traditions generally fail to generate the kind of certitude so typical of theistic beliefs. He then proceeds to reject some kind of governmental conspiracy theory, whereby the ancient equivalent of the New World Order, the Freemasons, or the Knights

---

7   *Existence*, p. 26.

8   'Reason 1: Tis a folly to deny or doubt of that which hath been the acknowledged sentiment of all nations, in all places and ages. There is no nation but hath owned some kind of religion, and, therefore, no nation but hath consented in the notion of a Supreme Creator and Governor.' *Existence*, p. 29.

9   'Reason 2: It is a folly to deny that which all creatures or all things in the world manifest. [To which he adds:] Let us view this in Scripture, since we acknowledge it, and after consider the arguments from natural reason.' *Existence*, p. 42.

10   'Reason 3: It is a folly to deny that which a man's own nature witnesseth to him. The whole frame of bodies and souls bears the impress of the infinite power and wisdom of the creator.' *Existence*, pp. 63-64.

11   'Reason 4: As it is a folly to deny that which all nations in the world have consented to, which the frame of the world evidenceth, which man in his body, soul, operations of conscience, witnesseth to; so it is folly to deny the being of God, which is witnessed unto by extraordinary occurrences in the world.' *Existence*, p. 74.

12   *Existence*, pp. 29-42.

Templar, met together and cooked up a scheme to dupe the helpless millions of the world into believing in God for some reason unspecified in the text. Apart from being completely crazy, Charnock notes that there is no corroborative evidence that such a conspiracy was ever concocted, and, even if such evidence were found, it could not account for the persistence of such beliefs. Finally, he rejects innate fear as the motive for the simple reason that one cannot fear something unless one first believes in its existence: thus, belief in God must precede the fear of him. The result: belief in some kind of god, all other options having been excluded, must be innate.[13]

The second category of argument, that of the universal manifestation of a divine being, is the context in which Charnock develops the metaphysical heart of the discourse. In this section, the reader is treated to an arsenal of arguments for God's existence which would have been familiar to anyone acquainted with the standard kind of theistic proofs so common in theology from the Middle Ages onwards. Charnock divides this particular argument into four sub-arguments: from production; from harmony; from preservation, and from teleology.[14] In the first, he proposes the standard theses concerning the impossibility of self-motivation from potency to act, the impossibility of an infinite causal or temporal regression, and the principle of sufficient reason all as bases for positing the existence of a single, infinitely perfect creator God. In addition to these, he also adds the Platonic argument, also used by Descartes though of a much earlier vintage, that the idea of perfection in the human mind requires a divine archetype as its ultimate cause.[15] The result overall is a standard and unexceptional litany of theistic proofs.

The second major strand of argumentation is that from the harmony of creation. Again, this section represents a marshalling of standard arguments: the balance of contrary qualities; the hierarchy of creaturely being, culminating in human as the highest creatures, and the constant stability of this hierarchy all point to a master architect who has created and structured the universe in such a balanced and perfect way.[16] All the arguments in this section are, of course, rooted in the assumption that order cannot ultimately be the cause of itself: order requires an orderer, and that orderer is God.[17]

The third strand of argumentation in this section concerns creaturely teleology: as even non-rational creatures act by instinct to achieve certain ends, this implies that they are driven to these ends by an ordering instinct – and such an ordering instinct presupposes a prior cause which provides such order. Again, this cause is identified as God.[18] Finally, the argument from preservation – that every creature depends ultimately upon some transcendent source of being for its continuation – rounds off this particular section.[19]

---

13 *Existence*, pp. 37-41.
14 *Existence*, pp. 43-63.
15 *Existence*, p. 52.
16 *Existence*, pp. 52-60.
17 *Existence*, p. 59.
18 *Existence*, pp. 60-62.
19 *Existence*, pp. 62-63.

The third major section, that dealing with arguments from the nature of humanity, focuses on three particular aspects: body, soul, and conscience.[20] In the first, the body, Charnock praises the physical virtues of heart, mouth, brain, ear, eye, tongue, teeth and lungs, demonstrating incidentally that he clearly had a keen interest in, and sound amateur knowledge of, the embryonic science of human anatomy.[21] While other theologians of the seventeenth century indulged in ichthyotheology, whereby God's existence was seen to be demanded by the anatomical peculiarities of various kinds of fish, Charnock sticks to the more mundane territory of human physiology. Then, in dealing with the soul, he uses the standard arguments regarding the knowledge of the soul's substance solely through its operations to establish its immateriality, and then to argue that its surpassing gifts point clearly to the transcendent God.[22] Next, Charnock points to the existence of conscience, with its innate moral law, and the inescapable fear generated by the transgression of that law, as demonstrating the existence of a transcendent moral law, and thus of a transcendent moral law-maker.[23] Finally, he argues that humanity's constant desire to transcend itself – the fact that it has desires which cannot ultimately be satisfied by creaturely comforts and achievements – indicates clearly that there is some higher purpose – and thus some higher being – to which humanity is answerable.[24]

The final major section, before Charnock moves in classic Puritan fashion to the 'uses of the doctrine', deals with the evidence for God's existence provided by extraordinary judgements, miracles, and the fulfilment of prophecies. Under the first heading, Charnock mentions only one – the death of Herod Agrippa, recorded in Acts 12:21-23 but also corroborated by Josephus in Book 19 of his *Antiquities*.[25] As for the second, miracles, Charnock mentions briefly that even the Jews 'to this day' acknowledge the miracles of Christ, and then adds that many pagan thinkers (he explicitly cites Dio and Seneca) have noted the miraculous preservation and prosperity of the Jews, despite all the attempts by others to crush them. Such miraculous preservation is ascribed by Charnock to their special status in God's purposes.[26] Finally, he points to the fulfilment of prophecy, again focusing on those which refer to figures and events which are not confined to sacred history, in this case the prophecy of Cyrus by Isaiah, and the impact of reading the Book of Daniel on Alexander the Great.[27] With this reference, the main section of the discourse, that dealing with the positive proofs, comes to an end.

---

20 *Existence*, pp. 63-74.
21 *Existence*, pp. 64-66.
22 *Existence*, pp. 67-69.
23 *Existence*, pp. 69-73.
24 *Existence*, pp. 73-74.
25 *Existence*, p. 75.
26 *Existence*, p. 76.
27 *Existence*, p. 77.

Assessing the *Discourse*

The question which immediately comes to mind upon reading the first discourse, particularly when one encounters the various metaphysical arguments for God's existence in the second group of proofs, is 'Is this not a return to the medieval theological tradition of theistic proofs?' The question is undoubtedly a valid one – especially in the context of current discussions regarding the relationship of medieval theology to Reformation and post-Reformation developments – but it is nonetheless impossible to answer in any helpful manner when posed in such a blunt form. Issues of continuity and discontinuity are more subtle than such a question allows and so, in an attempt to do justice to such subtleties and to produce a more nuanced answer, I propose to break my evaluation down into two separate pairs of issues: the nature of Charnock's sources and the content of his arguments; and the function and style of the discourse as a whole. In examining each of these points in turn, we may find that Charnock does not fit neatly into any of the boxes we might like to slot him into; but we will be able to position him far more accurately in the historical stream of Christian thought than if we simply attempted a straightforward 'yes or no' answer to the question initially proposed. I am increasingly convinced that dogmatic problems in historical theology often require answers that are, in part at least, non-dogmatic, and Charnock's discourse is an excellent example of how this is so.

The Sources and Content of the Arguments

Of all the arguments used by Charnock, those metaphysical points raised under the second general heading concerning the universal testimony of nature to the existence of God, stand in most obvious continuity with the medieval theological tradition. The arguments from causality, infinite regression etc are so common in the medieval tradition that it is, of course, impossible to point with certainty to any specific source for those which Charnock himself cites no source. The one medieval actually quoted in the main text in this section is Thomas Aquinas, the quotation being from *Summa Theologiae* 1.2.3.[28] Here, Charnock uses with approval Thomas's argument that goodness in the creaturely realm requires a perfect good as its source and cause, an argument which enjoyed general acceptance among Puritan theologians. In addition to the quotation from Thomas, however, there are quite a number of marginal references throughout this section pointing to other sources which Charnock was using or at least citing as support for his position. Thus, Charnock's exegesis of Romans 1:19-20, which he regards as the scriptural basis for the arguments under this section, is supported earlier on in the treatise by a bald marginal reference simply to 'Aquinas'[29] and then later by a more specific reference to Bañes's commentary

---

28 'Those things that are good must flow from something perfectly good: that which is chief in any kind is the cause of all that kind. Fire, which is most hot, is the cause of all things which are hot. There is some being, therefore, which is the cause of all that perfection which is in the creature; and this is God.' *Existence*, p. 43.

29 *Existence*, p. 27.

on Thomas's *secunda secundae*.[30] The necessity of even sceptics acknowledging a first cause is undergirded by a reference to Cocceius's *Summa*,[31] a work which is also cited in defence of a kind of anthropic principle,[32] the transcendence of the creature's purpose and of the creature's inability to fully understand even itself.[33] In addition to these sources, throughout the dissertation Charnock also makes explicit marginal references to works by Voetius, the French sceptic, Charron (*de la Sagesse*), Pierre Gassendi, Amyraut, Amyrant, Cicero, some little known English commentators, King and Pink, Charleton and Fotherby, and various others, some of whom are well-known to us, others have long since passed into well-deserved oblivion; all of whom, however, supply support of one kind or another for proving the existence of God. What is significant is that, with the exception of Aquinas, Charnock is not drawing consciously on the medievals, at least not in a manner which he considers to require explicit marginal references, but is locating himself within a much more recent tradition of theistic proofs of the kind that he finds in the work of scientists such as Gassendi, theologians such as Bañes, Voetius and Cocceius, and the emerging tradition of general studies of religion as an empirical phenomenon. His sources, therefore, even for the metaphysical arguments of his *Discourse* are better characterized in general as Renaissance and post-Reformation than as medieval.

This diversity of sources, of course, reflects the diversity of argumentation: universal consent, universal manifestation, the microcosmic nature of humanity, and the reality of providence and miracles, indicate a breadth of proofs which is much wider than that found in, say, either of Aquinas's *Summe*. At the very least, therefore, we have in Charnock's *Discourse* a very considerable expansion of the medieval tradition of proofs to include many other elements which serve to persuade people of God's existence and which are not medieval but distinctively Renaissance in both source and character. For example, when one looks at the detailed knowledge of anatomy in the section on the body as proof of a divine maker, there is clear evidence of substantial knowledge of contemporary medicine, with Charnock clearly aware of matters such as the structure of the inner ear and the nature of the flow of blood around the body. Indeed, in this context, Charnock even makes explicit reference to the structure of the heart and the important role of the arterial valve system.[34] Although no text books are cited, what we have is considerably more elaborate and sophisticated in its detail than the analogous discussion in Calvin's *Institutio*.[35] The argument as Charnock phrases it is, in its overall thrust, traditional, but in its content entirely up-to-date. As with his use of the medieval proofs, we have another example of the expansion and elaboration of an argument with details supplied by more recent discoveries and knowledge.

---

30 *Existence*, p. 42.
31 *Existence*, p. 51.
32 *Existence*, p. 56.
33 *Existence*, pp. 60-61.
34 *Existence*, p. 65.
35 *Institutio* 1.5.3.

Thus, when we look more closely at the arguments marshalled by Charnock to prove the existence of God, whether they be of the more metaphysical variety so common since the Middle Ages, or those based upon the wonder of empirical phenomena, a picture merges of a thinker whose thought stands in definite continuity with the Middle Ages but which cannot simply be reduced to redux of the medieval arguments. Much of what he has to say points quite clearly to the impact of Renaissance learning on his work, particularly in his elaboration of the proof based on the physical make-up of humanity, where his knowledge of human anatomy and physiology serves to expand and, if you will pardon the pun, flesh out the arguments found in earlier Renaissance Protestants such as John Calvin. Nevertheless, even in the metaphysical territory of causality, however, Charnock is far from dependent upon medieval sources for his arguments, choosing instead to cite more recent sources, and in particular the work of Pierre Gassendi, in order to reinforce what are in general very traditional arguments. Thus, in answering our first question, whether Charnock's treatise marks a return to medieval proofs, we must answer with both a yes and a no: yes, to the extent that his discourse embodies the traditional litany of proofs from causality, perfection etc., that were the stock-in-trade of medieval theologians; but no to the extent that he massively expanded the range of arguments under the impact of Renaissance thinking on his theology, and also undergirded his arguments, even of the most traditional kind, with reference not, in general, to medieval sources, but to Renaissance and post-Reformation works.

The Function and Style of the Discourse

If the content and sources of the arguments in the discourse present a complex picture which, while allowing for continuity, prevents a straightforward identification of Charnock's position with that of his medieval antecedents, it is yet possible that the function and style of the overall argument might yet prove to be a point of just such identity. Do Charnock's arguments function in the same way as, say, those of Thomas Aquinas within his great *Summae*? And are the proofs presented in a manner such that their argumentative force is substantially the same as that of earlier arguments? It is to these questions we now turn.

First, a cautionary note must be sounded. The context of Charnock's discourse, and thus of the arguments which it contains, is emphatically not that of the university classroom, the great medieval *summe*, or even of an elementary textbook of theology. What Charnock is doing in his famous work is *preaching* the doctrine of God to his congregation – and that a non-conformist and thus socially marginalized congregation. The context, while pedagogical in a sense, is thus predominantly homiletical. He is not attempting a systematic synthesis of doctrine. He is not presenting a series of disputed questions on the more controversial topics of divinity. He is not even presenting a thorough doctrinal exposition of one of the classic catechisms, a popular undertaking among English Puritan theologians, not least Charnock's co-pastor, Thomas Watson. No – Charnock is preaching to his people and this point is a decisive factor in understanding his discourses. We should therefore be sensitive to the issue of genre when considering the relationship between Charnock's display of proofs and those of others such as Thomas Aquinas, and must take into account the possible – if not highly probable – differences in intention that lie behind the two works.

This basic difference in genre between Charnock and, say, Aquinas or even Francis Turretin, is highlighted by the fact that the discourse on God's existence (as all the other discourses in the work) ends with a series of practical applications of the foregoing arguments. What we have here, as the Puritans would no doubt have said, is a piece of practical divinity cast in sermonic form, intended in the first instance for the immediate benefit of Charnock's listeners, his congregation of faithful believers in the Bishopsgate. Indeed, these practical applications are themselves illuminating. Divided into four main 'uses', they are as follows:

- Use 1: If atheism be folly, it is then pernicious to the world and to the atheist himself. Wisdom is the band of human societies, the glory of man. Folly is the disturber of families, cities, nations; the disgrace of human nature.[36]
- Use 2: How lamentable is it, that in our times this folly of atheism should be so rife.[37]
- Use 3: If it be the atheist's folly to deny or doubt of the being of God, it is our wisdom to be firmly settled in this truth, that God is.[38]
- Use 4: Is it a folly to deny or doubt of the being of God? It is a folly also not to worship God, when we acknowledge his existence; it is our wisdom then to worship him.[39]

These four applications in fact form two pairs, the first dealing with the social ramifications of the belief in or denial of God's existence while the second group deal with the significance of what Charnock has said for the believer.

To take the first pair, Charnock's position is the classic one which regards the existence of God as the objective foundation of social order and justice (a position embodied in some of the proofs themselves) and thus the denial of God's existence, either intellectually or, just as serious, practically as leading to the complete breakdown of society. This much is laid out in the first use, while the second is little more than an extension of this, lamenting the current desperate state of affairs in England. To this, Charnock appends a series of statements concerning atheists: it is impossible to prove that God does not exist (a subtly different point to arguing that one can prove that God exists); atheism sets one on a collision course with the whole of nature; many atheists live in fear that they are wrong (an interesting twist on the problem of assurance!); atheists are motivated by the desire to live licentious lives; atheism is a high-risk strategy (echoes of Pascal's wager here); atheists can never be sure they have looked at all the evidence and thus can never be certain that their opinion is correct.[40] The kind of arguments brought forward are very familiar though, in the specific context of Charnock's own time, with the collapse of the Puritan project and the Draconian measures embodied in the Clarendon Code, they no doubt

---

36 *Existence*, p. 77.
37 *Existence*, p. 79.
38 *Existence*, p. 84.
39 *Existence*, p. 87,
40 *Existence*, pp. 81-83.

took on a particular urgency and relevance. Charnock, the one-time member of the ruling establishment, now ejected from the corridors of power, looks on with dismay as the work of the godly brethren is undone by a pampered and corrupt regime which has no time for the true gospel. As a result, he fulminates against the atheistic decadence of the times, pointing his congregation to the intellectual incoherence, absurdity, malice, and – let us not forget – mortal danger of what is going on around them. What is particularly noteworthy at this point is that the power of this section lies not in any positive connection Charnock makes with the earlier proofs (any such connection is implicit at best) but in the awful and terrifying nature of the motives, risks and results of atheism for society and for the individual. Gone are the appeals to rarified metaphysics and to the intricate structure of the inner-ear; of far more importance now are the emotive descriptions of the catastrophic social and personal consequences of denying God.

From here, he proceeds to the second pair of arguments: his people should be sure that God is, and they should therefore worship him. What is interesting in this final part of the treatise is that Charnock makes no explicit connection between the various arguments he has proposed in the earlier section for God's existence and the efforts to which he now urges his congregation and his readers. Again, as with the first couplet, the power of his argument resides not in any connection with the formal proofs outlined earlier – they are mentioned here but only in passing as a basis for looking at the world as well as at scripture for confirmation of who God is[41] – but in the terrible consequences of believers doubting of God's existence: they will never worship him as they should; they will never be able to order their lives; they will never have any comfort or assurance; and they will never be able to have full confidence in the scriptures.[42] The ultimate appeal here, as in the first couplet, has been to the emotions of the audience, not to their intellects.

This, then, leads to my final major point concerning Charnock's discourse on the existence of God. It is not, in the final analysis, a presentation of the proofs to establish the foundation of a theological scheme or to determine which truths about God are available both from nature and from revelation, as is arguably the case in the medieval tradition epitomized by Aquinas. It is, I would argue, not part of this kind of project at all but rather an example of rhetorical argumentation which uses the classic proofs as elements within a larger framework with the purpose of *persuading* the audience of the validity of their position and of warning them away from alternative, atheistic (whether absolute, sceptical, or practical) convictions. Several elements of the discourse lead me to this conclusion, none of which is, perhaps, on its own conclusive yet which, when taken together, have a persuasive force.

First, there is the failure of Charnock to make any major positive connection between the metaphysics of the mediaeval proofs which he utilizes and the theology that follows. There are allusions throughout the whole set of discourses to metaphysical argumentation, but these are occasional and not built into the essential method or structure of what he is doing. Indeed, it is arguable that, when this *Discourse* is taken as a whole Charnock has a decided lack of interest in the metaphysics which underlie

---

41   *Existence*, pp. 85-86.
42   *Existence*, pp. 84-85.

the proofs – not that he does not believe in their metaphysical truth; it is just that it is not this that is important. The traditional scholastic proofs stand alongside others – consent of the nations (itself a classic rhetorical strategy and one frequently used in Puritan theology), structure of the human body, soul, and conscience, and the reality of the miraculous and of prophetic fulfilment. What one has is not a piece of work the ultimate purpose of which is to set out in systematic fashion all of the known proofs for God's existence and then to use this as a basis for theological construction but an attempt to present a barrage of arguments whose cumulative force will prove to be irresistibly persuasive to those in his congregation and beyond whose faith needs reinforcing. He is, after all, preaching to a marginalized congregation of believers who, presumably, did not need to be told how to construct a metaphysical basis for further theological construction. No – they needed rather to be reminded again and again that the sacrifices which they were making by placing themselves in opposition to the political and religious establishment were worthwhile. Persuading and reassuring them of God's existence and sovereignty was part and parcel of Charnock's task as pastor.

Second, there are Charnock's own stated purposes behind the discourse, none of which shows any remote interest in the production of proofs for any apologetic or systematic theological reason, and which parallel the comparative lack of metaphysical interest in the treatise as a whole. Of particular note in this context is the fact that Charnock nowhere employs the proofs for the kind of theological purpose evident in the first part of Calvin's *Institutio*, where the existence of general revelation is used as a basis for asserting the universal accountability of the human race. Charnock has no real concern in this discourse for arguing about the nature and status of the human race in such a narrow theological and soteriological manner. Instead, the focus at the end is rather on the terrible consequences of atheism and the awful responsibilities entailed by theism for society and for the individual. Indeed, at no point does it appear that Charnock is setting forth the proofs as part either of a positive demonstration of the existence of God or of general revelation; their function is rather to demonstrate the absurdity of atheism and its terrible social consequences. Indeed, he certainly does not sound any triumphalist note in terms of the devastating and irrefutable nature of his proofs – and his articulation of a form of 'Pascal's wager' would seem to indicate that he is well aware that his proofs are less than completely watertight as apologetic tools: they might persuade one of the dangers of atheism, but in practice they clearly do not finish the debate entirely. In fact, I would argue, what Charnock was actually *doing* when he preached this sermon was exhorting his people, his separated, despised flock, to a particular course of action, i.e. the maintenance of their basic theological stand; and that the proofs should therefore be interpreted as playing a small but important part within this larger purpose. Surrounded by a world that was going to the dogs, and where the unrighteous seemed to be prospering, Charnock was presenting a *persuasive* case for his people to remain faithful and not be lured away by the fleshpots of Egypt as personified in part by the sceptics in society but supremely by the practical atheists – in other words, all those who did not conform to Puritan notions of piety and who seemed nonetheless to be in overall control.

That in Charnock's discourse we are not dealing in the first instance with proofs as prolegomena to the theological exercise but rhetorical persuasions to particular actions and commitments is evident from my third point on this issue: the style of language and form of argumentation that Charnock uses. The discourse abounds with rhetorical questions which serve to hammer home his case time and again, and these, rather than the watertight logic of the proofs, are what distinguish the discourse and make the arguments so powerful. Indeed, this style of rhetorical argumentation pervades the treatise, so I provide below some select examples as demonstrations of his basic approach.

First, when noting the universal consent of humankind to the existence of a deity, Charnock demonstrates the impossibility of alternative explanations by showing them to be absurd and underlining this with a series of questions which require no answer. In the case of the governmental conspiracy theory, he says the following:

> It is unaccountable how this should come to pass. It must have been either by a joint assembly of them or a mutual correspondence. If by an assembly, who were the persons? Let the name of any one be mentioned. What was the time? Where was the place of this appearance? By what authority did they meet together? Who made the first motion, and first started this great principle of policy? By what means could they assemble from such distant parts of the world? Human histories are utterly silent in it, and the Scripture, the ancientest history, gives an account of Babel, but not a word of any design of this nature. What mutual correspondence could such have, whose interests are for the most part different, and their designs contrary to one another? How could they, who were divided by such vast seas, have this mutual converse? How could those who were different in their customs and manners, agree so unanimously together in one thing to gull the people?[43]

The litany of questions continues for another half a page after this, but the sample serves to show the sought of argumentative style with which we are dealing. The relentless barrage of questions is designed not simply to silence any gainsayers but to demonstrate that their position involves them in a myriad of absurdities such that their position is, quite literally, ridiculous. Indeed, the technique of the well-placed rhetorical question occurs again and again throughout the argument. For example, in proposing the classic argument that the first human being had no sufficient reason to create themselves at one point in time rather than another, Charnock presents his case in terms of loaded questions, constantly throwing the onus on his imaginary opponents and implicitly making their position appear absurd:

> If the first man did produce himself, why did he not do it before? It hath already been proved, that he had a beginning, and could not be from eternity. Why then did he not make himself before. Not because he would not. For having no being, he could have no will; he could neither be willing nor not willing. If he could not then, how could he afterwards? If it were in his own power, he could have done it, he would have done it; if it were not in his own power, then it was in the power of some other cause, and that is God. How came he by that power to produce himself? If the power of producing himself were communicated by another, then man could not be the cause of himself. That is the cause of it which communicated that power to it. But if the power of being was in and from himself and in

---

43   *Existence*, p. 38.

no other, nor communicated to him, man would always have been in act, and always have existed; no hindrance can be conceived. For that which had the power of being in itself was invincible by anything that should stand in the way of its own being.[44]

The argument is familiar. The presuppositions underlying the argument are familiar. But the power of the argument derives from the manner in which it is here framed as a series of questions which drive inexorably toward the conclusion that God must have created the first human and must therefore exist. Any other position invites nothing but ridicule.

One final example comes from the heart of the metaphysical proof section. At the one point where he quotes Aquinas, on the production of good, is it the metaphysics of Aquinas which provide the power of the argument? No. It is the series of rhetorical questions which accompany it which give the argument its persuasive force:

> Who ever saw statues or pictures but presently thinks of a statuary and limner? Who beholds garments, ships, or houses, but understands there was a weaver, a carpenter, an architect? Who can cast his eyes about the world, but must think of that power that formed it, and that the goodness which appears in the formation of it hath a perfect residence in some being?[45]

These are just three examples, but they are typical of the method of argument and emphasis in the work as a whole, right down to the applications, where Charnock uses rhetorical questions to show the crass moral results of rejecting God's existence and pointing to his own position as the only tenable one. One might observe at this point that this is scarcely surprising: after all, what we are dealing with here is not the opening chapter of a scholastic *summa* but something which originally, at least, started life as an oration, an oral text, a piece of rhetoric, into which the medieval proofs – along with a variety of others – were built in order to convince or persuade his audience of the basic correctness of his – and, he would have hoped, their own – position.

Conclusion

By way of conclusion, then, I return to the question I raised some time ago with reference to Charnock's discourse: 'Is this not a return to the mediaeval theological tradition of theistic proofs?' It should be clear by now that one can only give an unequivocally affirmative answer to this question if one is prepared to extract those passages which contain the so-called medieval proofs from the treatise, isolate them completely from the wider context, and examine them as nothing more than metaphysical artefacts, free from any historical contamination or admixture. Then, indeed, one might be able to say that yes, the arguments which depend upon causality, teleology, perfection, and the impossibility of infinite regression do have their precise counterparts in the Middle Ages.

44　*Existence*, p. 49.
45　*Existence*, p. 43.

If, however, one acknowledges the historical situatedness of all literary productions – including the theological – then one starts to ask questions of another kind which prevent the simple affirmative answer which the pure philosopher might give to the above question. Turning to sources, it soon becomes apparent that, while many of the arguments used have good pedigrees in the Middle Ages, Charnock's immediate chosen authorities are often not medieval schoolmen but Renaissance figures, indicating that he is not *returning* to anything but is rather standing in what has been a fairly continuous and developing tradition of theological and philosophical thought. This must immediately temper any judgements about the use of proofs as evidence of historical discontinuity or even retrogression between earlier and later Protestant orthodoxy – as must the use of the 'consent of the nations' proof which underlies so much of Charnock's treatise and finds an obvious antecedent in Calvin's *Institutio*. If we see Protestant theology in the seventeenth century as one part of a much wider intellectual world, such things as the proofs do not perhaps seems as extraordinary or significant as they might do otherwise.

Moving from sources to genre, it is clear that Charnock's discourse cannot be regarded as, in the first instance, the formal prolegomena to a *summa* of scholastic theology, and that for the very simple and obvious reason that it is simply not part of a *summa*. It is rather the written, probably expanded, form of a sermon, part of a series of sermons on the doctrine of God preached during the day-to-day ministry of Charnock's pastorate in London. Thus, it is the sermonic genre and the pastoral context which provide the key to understanding both the style of the piece and the underlying intention of the author behind the piece. As to the former, the rhetorical style of the overall argument is obvious from beginning to end in both form (rhetorical questions, purple passages) and content (argument from the consent of the nations, 'Pascal's wager etc). As to the latter, Charnock's intention, that, I believe is clearly neither to prove God's existence to the unbeliever, nor to analyse the possibility, scope, or place of natural theology in the theological scheme, nor to demonstrate the universal accountability of humanity to God. It is rather to *persuade* his believing audience, made up of a separated, persecuted, disillusioned body of non-conformists, of the fundamental correctness of their cause and of the disastrous consequences that follow from the atheism (absolute, sceptical and especially practical) which they see all around them and by which some, perish the thought, may have been tempted. This latter conclusion, of course, derives not simply from a knowledge of the discourse's literary form, but of Charnock's position as a non-conformist minister, labouring under the albeit slightly moderated strictures of the Clarendon Code in the 1670s. Thus, we see the importance to intellectual history not just of a sound knowledge of texts and genre but also of the very concrete historical circumstances within which such texts were produced.

My last words of conclusion are, perhaps, of an even more general nature but arise from what I have said so far. One of the criticisms which needs to be made against the reading of Reformed Orthodoxy offered by the Barthian tradition of T.F and J.B Torrance, Ernst Bizer and company is that texts which are only asked Barthian questions will tend only to give Barthian answers. The danger for those who reject this outworn and barren approach is that one limited perspective, with its restricted range of questions, might yet be replaced by another that prejudices or impoverishes the results of inquiry precisely through a similarly reductionist or ideologically driven approach.

Taking Charnock's first discourse as an example, it is clear that if we approach the text and ask merely metaphysical or doctrinal questions, then we will find only metaphysical or doctrinal answers; and yet, in so doing, we miss not simply Charnock's own intended purpose in writing the treatise but also the original significance of precisely those metaphysical and doctrinal aspects of the treatise that are only there, in the first instance, because they subserve the larger pastoral purposes for which the treatise was written. In other words, we may have analysed and expounded, albeit accurately and precisely, the nature of something which was, in fact, of little or no importance to Charnock himself in this context, concerned as he was in this text not primarily with framing a coherent ontology for theological construction but rather with overwhelming his believing audience with so many persuasive arguments for theism that their faith and their identity would be thoroughly reinforced. We must realize that such theological texts are not simply theological phenomena. They are also historical phenomena, shaped by many factors that are not theological or metaphysical in the strict sense of the word. We cannot simply excise the theology and philosophy for separate analysis – historical phenomena require some form of historical explanation and if Puritan theology is not simply a theological even but also an historical event, we cannot answer the various scholarly problems it raises simply in terms of purely theological categories. Historical context, literary genre, and authorial intention, to name but three, must all be taken into account if we are to move towards a rounded understanding of the place of Puritan theology and Reformed Orthodoxy in the larger history of ideas. Only then will we be able to avoid having our analyses openly hijacked or subtly subverted by yet one more unhistorical and ideologically driven theological or philosophical method of analysis. Charnock's discourse demonstrates, I believe, both the necessity and the advantages of this approach. Despite using the classic proofs, he is not really trying to *prove* God's existence but to *persuade* his hearers of the fundamental soundness of their theism – and that is an insight available only to those prepared to look further than the verbal content of a few key passages.

Chapter 3

No Way Out?

Christopher Hughes

Along with Arthur Prior and Richard Swinburne, and in opposition to Alvin Plantinga, Norman Kretzmann, and many others, Paul Helm maintains that whatever God knows is (now) necessary. Although I am not sure whether he is right, I am convinced that formidable difficulties beset any account on which God has (infallible) foreknowledge of not yet necessary truths. Accounts on which God timelessly has infallible knowledge of not yet necessary truths avoid at least some of those difficulties; but they seem incompatible with other beliefs about God that theists (or, at any rate, Christians) have traditionally held.

3.1 Plantinga on Ockham's Way Out

Necessarily, squares have four sides. Indeed, it has always been, and always will be necessary that squares have four sides. It appears, though, that not everything that is (now) necessary has always been necessary. For example, if you have read this far, it is (now) necessary that you have at read at least some of this piece. After all, if someone enjoined you not to read a single word of it, you could truthfully reply: 'that is no longer possible'. And if your not having read a single word of it is not (now) possible, then your having read some of it is (now) necessary. But although your having read some of this piece is necessary, it wasn't always so: inasmuch as your reading none of this piece is no longer possible, your reading some of this piece was once not yet necessary. Your having read some of this chapter is, we might say, an ex-contingency; and your having read none of it is an ex-possibility.

Consider the following (venerable)[1] argument:

1. Where S is an arbitrarily chosen subject, and P an arbitrarily chosen proposition, suppose S knew yesterday that P.
2. If S knew yesterday that P, then it is now necessary that S knew yesterday that P.
3. So it is now necessary that S knew yesterday that P.
4. *S knew yesterday that P entails P.*
5. Whatever is entailed by what is now necessary is itself now necessary.
6. So it is now necessary that P.
7. So if S knew yesterday that P, it is now necessary P.

---

[1] The argument set out here is essentially the same as one discussed by Aquinas (cf. *Summa Theologiae*, Ia, 14, 13, and *De Veritate*, 2, 12) and Jonathan Edwards (*Freedom of the Will*, 12), *inter alios*.

8. Given that *S* and *P* were chosen arbitrarily, anything anyone ever knew to be the case yesterday is now necessary. Generalizing the reasoning in (1)-(7), anything anyone ever has known or knows to be the case is now necessary: and anything anyone ever will know to be the case will be then necessary. No one's knowledge – not even God's – ever has extended, or ever will extend, past what is (then) necessary.

Is this argument sound? Ockham would say:

> No. Let *S* be God, and let *P* be a proposition that is true, but not yet necessary – say, that it will rain tomorrow. God has always known all truths. So God knew yesterday that it would rain tomorrow. Since it is not yet necessary that it will rain tomorrow, but true that God knew yesterday that it would rain tomorrow, it is false that if God knew yesterday that it would rain tomorrow, then it is now necessary that it will rain tomorrow.

But, supposing that the argument goes wrong when *S* = God, and what *S* knows is a not-yet-necessary truth, where exactly does it go wrong? (1) is an assumption to be discharged at the end of a conditional proof, and (3) follows by *modus ponens* from (1) and (2). (4) is a conceptual truth about knowledge, and (5) is a conceptual truth about necessity. (6) straightforwardly follows from (3)-(5), and (7) from (1)-(6). The upshot is that if the argument goes off the rails, it goes off the rails at (2). And this is indeed what Ockham would say.[2]

But can we make sense of the idea that, say, it is true, but not-yet-necessarily true that God knew yesterday that it would rain tomorrow? As Alvin Plantinga sees it, we can, once we take on board a distinction Ockham draws between propositions that are genuinely and strictly about the past or present, and those that are – at least verbally (*vocaliter, secundum vocem*) – about the past or present, but are (partly or entirely) about the future. It may seem initially plausible that any truth about the past (or present) is now necessary. But, upon reflection, we see that there is no reason to think that all truths that are only verbally about the past (or present) are now necessary. Suppose it is in fact true that it will rain tomorrow. Absent an argument that it is now necessary that it will rain tomorrow, there is no reason to think *it was true yesterday that it would rain tomorrow* is now necessary, in spite of its being verbally about the past. Similarly, suppose it is in fact true that Kate correctly guessed yesterday that it would rain tomorrow. That is no reason to conclude that *Kate correctly guessed yesterday that it would rain tomorrow* is now necessary, in spite of the fact that *Kate correctly guessed yesterday that it would rain tomorrow* is (partly) about the past.

For Plantinga, a truth (or fact) about a time is a *hard* fact about that time only if it is genuinely and strictly (i.e. exclusively) about that time.[3] Even if hard facts about the past or present are now necessary, he maintains, the same does not hold for soft facts about the past or present: only hard facts about the past are plausibly

2   Cf. Ockham's *Tractatus de Praedestinatione et de Praescentia Dei et de Futuris Contingentibus*, especially Question I.

3   See Plantinga's 'On Ockham's Way Out' in J.F. Sennett, ed., *The Analytic Theist: An Alvin Plantinga Reader*, p. 271.

thought to be now necessary facts about the past.[4],[5] It is clear, though, that *God knew yesterday that it would rain tomorrow* is not a hard fact about the past, inasmuch as it is not both genuinely and exclusively about the past. So, Plantinga thinks we may conclude, it is not now necessary that God knew yesterday that it would rain tomorrow; and if God in fact did know yesterday that it would rain tomorrow, it is not-yet-necessarily true that God knew yesterday that it would rain tomorrow.

Plantinga's choice of terminology here might mislead. One might have supposed that 'hard fact' was synonymous with 'now necessary fact' – which would make it true by definition that

i)   Only the hard facts about the past are now necessary.

and *not* true by definition that

ii)   Only facts genuinely and exclusively about the past are hard facts about the past.

As we have seen, though, Plantinga uses 'hard fact' in such a way that (ii), rather than (i), is true *ex vi terminorum*.

Why does this matter? Well, the argument Plantinga sets out in favor of the non-necessity of *God knew yesterday that it will rain tomorrow*, and attributes to Ockham, goes something like this:

God knew yesterday that it will rain tomorrow is not a hard fact about the past.

Only the hard facts about the past are (plausibly deemed) now necessary.

——

God knew yesterday that it will rain tomorrow is not (plausibly deemed) now necessary.[6]

---

4   There is a complication. Plantinga doesn't say quite what I have said. He says: 'Not all facts about the past, then, are hard facts about the past; and only the hard facts are plausibly thought to be accidentally necessary' (*ibid.,* p. 272). But what Ockham means by 'necessary *per accidens*' or 'accidentally necessary' is what I mean by 'now necessary'. And, at least as of section II of 'On Ockham's Way Out', Plantinga is using 'accidentally necessary' to mean what Ockham means by it. Later on, he offers his own account of accidental necessity, on which being accidentally necessary turns out to be different than being now necessary (the former, unlike the latter, is not closed under conjunction).

5   In whatever sense the past is necessary, the present also seems to be necessary. (If my not having been working on this piece five minutes ago is no longer possible, my not working on it right now is likewise no longer possible.) This suggests that a fact which is not a hard fact about in the past in Plantinga's sense (that is, a fact that is not genuinely and strictly about the past) might still be now necessary, because it is genuinely and strictly about the past-and-present. It would accordingly be safer for Plantinga to say that only the hard facts about the past-cum-present are (plausibly thought to be) now necessary. For the sake of simplicity, I shall ignore this complication in what follows.

6   When Plantinga speaks *in propria persona*, rather than saying flat out that only the hard facts about the past are necessary, he says more cautiously that only the hard facts about the past are 'plausibly thought to be' accidentally necessary (*ibid.,* p. 272 and 287). On the other hand, he attributes to Ockham the (unhedged) view that only the hard facts about the past are necessary, and endorses the intuitive plausibility of this view (p. 276). I take it, then, that he would be inclined to accept the unhedged version of the argument that would result from deleting the parenthetical qualifying phrases in its second premiss and conclusion.

If we construe 'hard fact' in the way Plantinga does, it seems that *God knew yesterday that it will rain tomorrow* is not a hard fact about the past. For it seems plausible that if P is genuinely and strictly about the past, and Q is analytically or definitionally equivalent to P, then Q is genuinely and strictly about the past. (If it is a fact genuinely and strictly about the past that Tom used to be a bachelor, and *Tom used to be a bachelor* is analytically or definitionally equivalent to *Tom used to be an unmarried man,* then it is a fact genuinely and strictly about the past that Tom used to be an unmarried man.) Moreover, no conjunction can be genuinely and strictly about the past, unless all its conjuncts are genuinely and strictly about the past. But *God knew yesterday that it will rain tomorrow* is presumably analytically equivalent to a conjunction (one gotten by applying the correct analysis of knowledge – whatever it is – to *God knew yesterday that it will rain tomorrow*). And at least one of the conjuncts of that conjunction will be *it will rain tomorrow*, which is surely not genuinely and strictly about the past. So, since *God knew yesterday that it will rain tomorrow* is analytically equivalent to a conjunction one of whose conjuncts is not genuinely and strictly about the past, *God knew yesterday that it will rain tomorrow* is not a fact that is genuinely and strictly about the past.[7]

If, however, we construe 'hard fact about t' as 'fact genuinely and strictly about t', it is by no means obvious that only the hard facts about the past are now necessary. Suppose you think that God, or the number 7, are – as a matter of metaphysical necessity – sempiternal. Then you will think that *God will exist tomorrow* (or *The number 7 will exist tomorrow*) is a now necessary fact, as is a conjunction such as *God existed yesterday and God will exist tomorrow* (or *The number 7 existed yesterday and the number 7 will exist tomorrow*). But although both of these conjunctive facts are (partly) about the past, it is hard to believe that either one is strictly and exclusively about the past. Again, suppose you believe that, as a matter of metaphysical necessity, for anything that happened yesterday, God will believe tomorrow that it happened yesterday. Then if it is, say, now necessary that it was sunny yesterday, it is also now necessary that tomorrow God will believe that it was sunny yesterday, and now necessary that it was sunny yesterday, and tomorrow God will believe that it was sunny yesterday. But it certainly looks as though only the first of these propositions is genuinely and strictly about the past. Naturally, these (alleged) cases of now necessary facts that are not genuinely and strictly about the past depend on controvertible premises (that necessarily, the number 7 or God will exist tomorrow; that necessarily, if it was sunny yesterday, then God will believe tomorrow that it was sunny yesterday); someone who rejected these premises might accordingly deny that there are any *plausible* cases of now necessary facts ((at least partly) about the past) that are not genuinely and strictly about the past. But given Plantinga's views on God's sempiternity, necessity, and necessary omniscience, he is

---

7   Plantinga offers a similar argument in Section II of 'On Ockham's Way Out'. But his argument relies on the premiss that if fact F is genuinely and strictly about the past, and fact F' is true in exactly the same possible worlds as F, then F' is also genuinely and strictly about the past. As we shall see, this principle seems more doubtful than the one I relied on. It implies that if *It was warm yesterday* is true in all the same possible worlds as *God will believe tomorrow that it was warm yesterday*, then both or neither are genuinely and strictly about the past.

not in a position to take this line. More generally, those who maintain that necessarily, God has infallible knowledge of now-contingent, as well as now-necessary truths, won't be able to take this line.[8]

So it is neither obvious, nor obviously in harmony with Plantinga's other beliefs, that among facts about the past, only the ones genuinely and strictly about the past are (plausibly deemed) now necessary facts. Suppose, though, that it true. Would that imply that the argument set out at the beginning of the chapter was unsound? Not by itself. If, among the facts about the past (and/or present), only those genuinely and strictly about the past (and/or present) are now necessary, *it is now necessary that S knew yesterday that P* is false, whenever *P* is (genuinely) about the future. But even if that is so, the argument at issue could still be sound – as long as the conditional, *if S knew yesterday that P, then it is now necessary that S knew yesterday that P* is true, irrespective of who and what *S* and *P* are. Absent a reason to doubt that that conditional is true, irrespective of who and what *S* and *P* are, we have no reason to doubt the soundness of the argument.

That said, the claim that only facts genuinely and strictly about the past (and/or present) are now necessary (which claim, for brevity, I shall call (C)) might figure crucially in an attack on the argument set out at the beginning of the chapter. That argument aims to show that there is no such thing as knowledge of the not-yet-necessary. If (C) is true, then all propositions genuinely (partly or entirely) about the future are not-yet-necessary. So if (C) is true, our initial argument is sound only if there is a sound argument (relying on the premises of the initial argument, and (C)) whose conclusion is that there is no such thing as knowledge of the future. But, an opponent of the initial argument might say, it is a Moorean fact that there is such a thing as knowledge of the future: nobody sane takes seriously the hypothesis that there isn't. So the argument for the non-existence of knowledge of the future – relying on the premises of our initial argument, and (C) – is unsound. Assuming that (C) is above suspicion, that must be because there is something wrong with the initial argument for the non-existence of knowledge of the not-yet-necessary.

So, if we could establish the claim that Plantinga deems intuitively plausible (viz., (C)), that would certainly call into question the soundness of the argument set out at the beginning of this chapter. But I doubt we are in a position to establish that claim. How else might we cast doubt on that argument?

One approach would be to challenge the argument's crucial second premiss. Why suppose that whenever it is true that *S* knew yesterday that *P*, it is now necessary that *S* knew yesterday that *P*? After all, when *P* has implications for the future, so does

---

8   I think the scholastics countenanced a different sort of now-necessary fact not genuinely and strictly about the past than the candidates mentioned here. Although they recognized there was a philosophical difficulty about how anyone (even God) could have foreknowledge of future contingents, they did not in general think there was a philosophical difficulty about how anyone could have knowledge of the future. Even we, they generally supposed, could have knowledge of 'future non-contingents'. Aquinas, for example, holds that we can have certain knowledge of, say, a future eclipse of the sun, inasmuch as that eclipse is not a future contingent state of affairs. In spite of the fact that *The sun will be eclipsed* is not genuinely and strictly about the past, for Aquinas, that the sun will be eclipsed is (in the sense of 'now necessary' at work in his discussion of the problem of future contingents) now necessary.

S knew yesterday that P; and all except those who deny that there are any not-yet-necessary truths about the future will admit that some truths with implications for the future are not yet necessary. Why couldn't *S knew yesterday that P* be among them?

An illustrious defender of that argument (Arthur Prior) would respond along these lines:

> It is intuitively very plausible that (for all *S* and *P*) if *S* knows something at a time, it is no longer possible that *S* doesn't know it then. If at time *t* it is still possible that *S* doesn't (then) know that *P*, then *S*'s (alleged) 'knowledge' at *t* that *P* is just a (more or less) educated) correct guess.[9]

I think we can unpack Prior's defense of *if S knows (knew) that P, it is now necessary (then necessary) that S knows that (knew that) P* as follows:

> i) (For all *S* and *P*) if *S* knows that *P*, it is now necessary that *S* has not got it wrong about whether *P*. For if it is still possible that *S* has got it wrong about whether *P*, then *S*'s belief that *P* is no more than a (more or less) educated guess, even if it turns out to have been correct. Similarly, if *S* knew that *P* at some past time *t*, it was then necessary that *S* hadn't got it wrong about whether *P*.

> ii) (For all *S* and *P*) if *S* 'knows' that *P*, and it is still possible that not-*P*, then it is still possible that *S* got it wrong about whether *P*. Similarly, if *S* 'knew' that *P* (at *t*), and it was still possible (at *t*) that not-*P*, then it was still possible at that time that *S* had it wrong about whether *P*.

> (iii) So (for all *S* and *P*) if *S* 'knows' that *P*, but it isn't now necessary that *S* knows that *P*, *S* doesn't know that *P*. And if *S* 'knew' that *P* (at a past time *t*), but it wasn't then necessary that *S* knew (then) that *P*, *S* didn't know (then) that *P*.

Someone could take issue with this argument by challenging (i), or (ii), or both. Against (i), she might say:

> *Pace* Prior, a correct 'guess' about the future that is educated enough may not *proprie loquendo* be a guess, because it is knowledge, even if it is still *possible* that the person 'guessed' wrong – if, say, it is extremely improbable (impossible for all practical purposes, as it were) that the person 'guessed' wrong.

I am suspicious of the idea that *S* can know that *P*, even though it is still possible that not-*P*, as long as the falsity of *P* is sufficiently improbable. Imagine that someone is about to draw a ball from an urn containing one billion balls, all but one of which are white, and one of which is black. Before a ball has been drawn, a white ball's being drawn is possible, and extremely likely; a black ball's being drawn is likewise possible, though extremely unlikely. If I predicted that a black ball won't

---

9   See Prior's wonderful 'The Formalities of Omniscience' *Philosophy* 38 (1963), pp. 114-129 (also reprinted in A. Prior, *Papers on Time and Tense*, Oxford: Oxford University Press, 1968).

be drawn, I would, so to speak, be making a hyper-educated guess: it's impossible for all practical purposes that my prediction is wrong (because it's impossible for all practical purposes that a black ball will be drawn). But could I claim to *know* that a black ball won't be drawn? On the face of it, I don't *know* that a black ball won't be drawn, in just the same way those who buy lottery tickets for fair lotteries don't *know* they won't win the grand prize (however astronomical the odds against their doing so). On the other hand, someone might concede that in cases like the ones just described, a hyper-educated but fallible guess about the future is not knowledge, and insist that in other cases, a hyper-educated fallible 'guess' about the future is knowledge.[10]

But suppose for the sake of argument that we may plausibly deny (i), and hence plausibly maintain that sometimes *S* knows that *P*, even though it is not necessary that *S* knows that *P*, and hence plausibly maintain that there is such a thing as knowledge of the not-yet-necessary. That would not help us defend God's knowledge of future contingents, as standardly conceived. For the (only) sort of knowledge of future contingents we shall have made room for is fallible knowledge – what Aquinas calls knowledge *per conjecturam* – and God's knowledge, traditionally conceived, is certain and infallible. A defender of the doctrine that God's (certain and infallible) knowledge extends beyond the now necessary, must accordingly challenge (ii) as well as or instead of (i).

If (ii) is false, then sometimes, *S* 'knows' that *P*, it is not possible that *S* has got it wrong about whether *P*, but it is still possible that not-*P*. In that case, sometimes *S* 'knows' (and believes) that *P*, even though it is still possible that *S* doesn't believe that *P*. If this is not evident: suppose it is not possible that *S* has got it wrong about whether *P*, and it is not possible that *S* does not believe *P*. Then we can show that *P* is necessary, via the following argument:

> It is now necessary that: if *S* believes that *P*, and *S* is not wrong about whether *P*, then *P*. It is now necessary that: *S* believes that *P*, and *S* is not wrong about whether *P*. So: it is now necessary that *P*.

Whenever it is necessary that *S* believes that *P*, and necessary that *S* is not wrong about whether *P*, it is also necessary that *P*. So, whenever it is necessary that *S* is not wrong about *P*, but not necessary that *P*, it is not necessary that *S* believes that *P*. In particular, when *S* 'knows' that *P*, and it is not yet necessary that *P*, but it is necessary that *S* is not wrong about whether *P*, it is not yet necessary that *S* believes what *S* in fact 'knows' (and believes).

---

10 Suppose my knowing that *P* is incompatible with its being now possible that I'm wrong about *P*. Then, it seems, we may infer that either (a) it is not a necessary condition of its being now necessary that *P* that *P* be entailed by the set of truths genuinely and strictly about the past-cum-present, or (b) there is virtually no knowledge of the future. (We are supposing that if I know that *P*, it is now necessary that I'm not wrong about *P*. But in almost any case in which I judge that it will be the case that *P*, the set of truths genuinely and exclusively about the past-cum-present will not entail that I didn't get it wrong about *P*. So either I don't know that it will be the case that *P*, or my knowing that it will be the case that *P* is now necessary, in spite of not being entailed by the set of truths about the past-cum-present.)

The denier of (ii) must accordingly maintain that the facts about what *S* believes (or believed) are sometimes 'open'. The difficulty, as Prior would no doubt have said, and Swinburne has said, is that they seem not to be.[11]

Suppose that, as I know, you used not to believe that *Q*. Since then, you have come to believe that *Q*, though I am unaware of this fact. Suppose I think that your believing that *Q* would be very bad (*Q* might be, say, Mackie's claim that moral beliefs are systematically erroneous). In such a circumstance, I might say to you:

You mustn't ever believe that *Q*.

If I did, you could truthfully answer:

That's no longer possible. I've made up my mind about, and in favor of, *Q*, although of course I might change my mind about in the future.[12]

Here is a different way to argue more or less the same point. If a proposition is not now necessary, and not now impossible, then its truth-value depends on how the open future goes – in other words, on which now-possible future turns out to be actual. So if *S believes that P* (or *S believed that P*) is not now necessary (and not now impossible), then its truth-value depends on which now-possible future turns out to be actual. But it seems clear that the truth-value of *S believes (believed) that P* does not depend on which now possible future turns out to be actual. If you buy a lottery ticket at 9.00, on the basis of your belief about what the winning number will be, and the drawing takes place at exactly 10.00, whether or not you guessed the winning number depends on which of the things that might happen after 9.00 do happen; but it surely does not depend on which of the things that might happen after 10.00 do happen.[13]

Plantinga would not find these considerations persuasive. He would, I think, respond to them along the following lines:

11   See A. Swinburne, *The Coherence of Theism* (Revised Edition), Oxford: Clarendon Press, 1993, pp. 173-183, and *The Christian God,* Oxford: Clarendon Press, 1994, pp. 130-134.

12   When I was a child, someone once said to me, as a joke, something like, 'Don't think of elephants today!' This command can only be a joke, because it cannot be obeyed. It cannot be obeyed, because an order cannot be obeyed until it is received (and understood). But once I have received (and understood) the order not to think of elephants today, the state of affairs it enjoins me to bring about (my not thinking of elephants today) is no longer possible, hence beyond my power to bring about. What goes for thinking-of goes for thinking-that.

13   Suppose that it is 10.05; you know the lottery has already taken place, but you don't know whether or not you guessed the winning number. Suppose also that (bizzarely enough) all you care about is whether you guessed the winning number of the 10.00 lottery; whether or not you'll ever actually collect the money, whether you'll still be alive tomorrow, etc matter not a whit to you. In that case, you might well be anxious about whether you guessed the winning lottery number, but you won't be anxious about what happened or is happening or will happen after 10.00. Post-10.00 events will be of no concern to you, because (you'll assume) the only thing in the world you care about is independent of those events.

It is initially plausible that the facts about what anyone believed (or believes) are hard facts about the past (or present), and thus now necessary.[14] But there is – or at any rate, there might be – an essentially omniscient being. If there is such a being, not all the facts about what someone believed (or believes) are hard facts about the past (or present), and not all the facts about what someone believed (or believes) are now necessary. So there are – or at any rate, there might be – facts about what someone believed (or believes) that are not yet necessary.[15]

As for the second argument, it is at first sight plausible that the facts about what someone believed (or believes) concerning the future are hard facts about the past (or present), and as such never depend on which of the (now possible) ways the future could go, the future does go. But there are or at any rate might be infallible predictors of the future. If there were, the facts about what predictions they made concerning the future would not be hard facts, and would depend (counterfactually, if not causally) on which of the (now possible) ways the future could go, it did go. So the facts about what someone believed (or believes) do sometimes, or at any rate might sometimes, depend on which of the (now possible) ways the future might go, it actually will go.[16]

I am not sure that an essentially omniscient being really is possible.[17] But suppose that it is. We can move from

(a) It is possible that there is an essentially omniscient being.

to

(b) It is possible that the facts about what someone believed (or believes) are not yet necessary.

given the conditional, (necessarily) if (a), then (b). But why should we accept this conditional? Edwards and Helm would argue that since the facts about (anyone's) past and present beliefs are now necessary, and there is an essentially omniscient God, everything that God (ever) knows is (then) necessary. So they would accept (a) and reject (b). Prior and Swinburne – in spite of their differences from Edwards and Helm on whether there are propositions that are not yet necessary and not yet impossible – would likewise accept (a) and reject (b). The possibility of an essentially

---

14 See 'On Ockham's Way Out', p. 273, where Plantinga says 'it seems natural to think' that propositions of the kind, *eighty years ago S believed that p*, are hard facts about the past, and thus plausible candidates for accidental necessity.

15 Plantinga does not address the particular arguments I have sketched in favour of the thesis that the facts about (anyone's) past (or present) beliefs are now necessary. But he does suggest that Nelson's Pike's argument for the incompatibility of God's infallible foreknowledge of our actions with our freedom – which depends crucially on the necessity of the facts about what God believed – is blocked (seen to be incogent) once we accept the possibility of an essentially omniscient being (*ibid.,* p. 275). So the reply I have put in Plantinga's mouth is, I hope, consonant with his views.

16 See Plantinga's discussion of Newcombe's paradox (*ibid.*, pp. 280-282).

17 I discuss some of my reasons for doubting that essential omniscience is possible in 'Negative Existentials, Omniscience, and Cosmic Luck', *Religious Studies* 34, 1998, pp. 375-401. I am also unsure whether it makes sense to think of a being without the possibility of states that *mis*represent the world, as having states that represent the world.

omniscient being does not, by itself, provide us with grounds to accept the possibility of not-yet-necessary facts about someone's past (or present) beliefs.

What would provide us with grounds to accept that possibility? Perhaps

(a') There are not-yet-necessary facts, and it is possible that there is an essentially omniscient being.

But, upon reflection, this seems doubtful. If there are not-yet-necessary facts, and there is (actually) an essentially omniscient being, then – arguably – some of the facts about what that being believed or believes are not yet necessary.[18] But just because there are not-yet-necessary facts, and there might be an essentially omniscient being, it doesn't follow that there might be not-yet-necessary facts about what someone believed or believes. Perhaps there are not-yet-necessary facts, but there wouldn't be if there were an essentially omniscient being.

What would show that there might be not-yet-necessary facts about what someone believed or believes, is

(a'') It is possible for an essentially omniscient being to have knowledge of not-yet-necessary facts.

In fact, we wouldn't need anything quite so strong. It would be enough if

(a''') It is possible for a being to have certain and infallible knowledge of not-yet-necessary facts.[19]

Fair enough; but why should any of this be thought to cast doubt on the claim that the facts about what anyone believed or believes are necessary? Call that claim (NPB) (for 'necessity of (the facts about) past (or present) beliefs'). If, (a'') (or (a''')) is true, then (NPB) is false. But this lessens the plausibility that (Plantinga appears to concede) (NPB) has initially, only if (a'') (or (a''')) is itself plausible.

In fact, I don't think either (a'') or (a''') is initially plausible. Judging from my experience with undergraduates, most people are strongly inclined to believe that (as a matter of conceptual necessity) knowledge is limited to the (then) necessary, even before being given an argument such as the one set out at the beginning of this chapter. That is, they are strongly inclined to regard it as a conceptual truth about certain and infallible knowledge, and possibility, that if it's still possible that not-P, nobody knows now (*certitudinaliter* and *infallibiliter*) that P, and nobody has ever known in the past (*certitudinaliter* and *infallibiliter*) that P. Plantinga says that 'divine foreknowledge and human freedom, as every twelve-year-old Sunday

---

18 I say 'arguably', because at least one philosopher (Swinburne) would maintain that even though God is omniscient, He doesn't know all the facts, inasmuch as He doesn't know the not-yet-necessary facts. See *The Coherence of Theism* (revised edition), pp. 177-183. Someone who construes omniscience in Swinburne's way can accept both that God is essentially omniscient, and that the facts about what anyone's past or present beliefs are necessary.

19 To establish the possibility of not-yet-necessary facts about what someone believed or believes, we wouldn't need the possibility of an omniscient knower of not-yet-necessary truths; it would be enough to establish the possibility of an infallible Newcombe predictor of people's not-yet-necessary choices.

School student knows, can seem to be incompatible'.[20] The reason for this, I take it, is that we are inclined to believe both that if I am free with respect to performing some future action, it is still possible that I won't perform it, and that if someone knows or knew (certainly and infallibly) that I will perform that action, it is no longer possible that I won't perform it.[21]

To recap: (NPB) is initially plausible. (a) may also be initially plausible, but it's no good discrediting the plausibility of (NPB) by appeal to (a), because someone can perfectly well accept both (a) and (NPB). The same holds for (a'). Nor can one discredit the plausibility of (NPB) by appeal to (a'') or (a'''): although each of these principles is incompatible with (NPB), they are also very counterintuitive, or at least, very doubtful.

In the same way, I don't think one can discredit the (initially plausible) principle that the facts about present and past beliefs don't depend on how the openness of the future is resolved, by appeal to the possibility of infallible predictors of not-yet-necessary choices. It is far from clear that there could be such predictors. On the face of it, if an infallible predictor predicts that I am, say, going to take two boxes (in the Newcombe's Problem case), then whether or not he so predicts does not depend on which of the (now possible) ways that the future might go, it does go; if the predictor has predicted that I shall take two boxes, and he really is infallible, then it's no longer possible that I won't take two boxes.

This concludes my defence of (NPB). If (NPB) is true, then, for any *S*, and any *P*, if *S* (infallibly) knows or knew that *P*, it is now necessary that *S* (infallibly) knows that *P*. If that is true, then – by the reasoning of the venerable argument set out at the start of this chapter – nobody can ever have (infallible) knowledge of the not then necessary. If what is wanted is (in Plantinga's words) an 'intuitively plausible' way of defending God's (infallible) knowledge of the not yet necessary, in the face of the venerable argument, the Ockhamist line considered so far does not appear to provide us with one.[22] If Ockham's way out is blocked, where else might we look?

---

20 'On Ockham's Way Out', p. 258.

21 Sometimes the difficulty is put this way: if I will perform a certain action freely, it is not necessary that I will perform it; if someone knows or knew that I will perform a certain action, it is necessary that I will perform it; so if someone knows or knew that I am going to perform a certain action freely, it both is and is not necessary that I will perform it. But putting the difficulty that way invites the response that the argument breaks down, once we realize that the first premiss is true, only if we give the necessity operator a narrower scope, while the second premiss is true, only if we give the necessity operator a wider scope.

22 Incidentally, I think that Plantinga's claims on behalf of Ockham's way out go beyond those that Ockham himself would be willing to make. Ockham holds that we have it on the authority of the Bible and the saints that God has infallible knowledge of future contingents. So, he concludes, (NPB) is false, and (a'') and (a''') are true. But I don't think that Ockham holds that either (a'') or (a''') is intuitively plausible, from a philosophical point of view. From a purely philosophical point of view, he seems to think, there is a deep mystery about how anyone *could* have infallible knowledge of future contingents. See my 'Ockham on an argument against God's knowledge of future continents', in A. Cirino and J. Reisch (eds), *Canterbury Studies in Franciscan Thought*, 2 (2008).

3.2 Plantinga on Boethius's Way Out

According to a tradition perhaps as old as our venerable argument, God and His knowledge are extratemporal. Although the supposition that God is extratemporal does not give the classical theist a way of blocking the venerable argument, it appears to give her a way to live with it. The conclusion of that argument is that no one can have knowledge, at any time, of anything that is not necessary at that time. A philosopher such as Boethius, who thinks God is outside of time, can apparently accept this conclusion with equanimity, without abandoning the claim that, for any time *t*, God (timelessly) has knowledge – infallible knowledge – not just of those true propositions that are necessary at *t*, but also of those true propositions that are not necessary at *t*.

Early on in 'On Ockham's Way Out', Plantinga mentions that a Boethian might attempt to defend God's knowledge of the not now necessary, in the face of the venerable argument, by appeal to God's extratemporality. But, he suggests, if the venerable argument shows that God doesn't have foreknowledge of the not now necessary, a variant of that argument shows that God doesn't have timeless knowledge of the not now necessary. The original argument crucially depends on the premiss, *If S knew yesterday that P, it is now necessary that S knew yesterday that P.* The variant argument would depend on the premiss, *If it was true yesterday that S timelessly knows that P, it is now necessary that it was true yesterday that S timelessly knows that P.* Both the original premiss, and the variant premiss, could be supported by appeal to the necessity of (propositions about) the past. Of course, one might object to the variant premiss on the grounds that *It was true yesterday that S timelessly knows that P* is not genuinely and strictly about the past. But, Plantinga thinks, one might with equal justice object to the original premiss, on the grounds that (when *P* concerns the future) *S knew yesterday that P* is not genuinely and strictly about the past. So, Plantinga concludes, the variant argument is no worse (though no better) than the venerable one.[23]

I disagree. For the reasons adduced in section 3.1, someone who wants to defend God's infallible 'timely' knowledge of the not now necessary from the venerable argument must say that it can be true at a time that *S* has a belief at that time, even though it is still possible at that time, that *S* does not have that belief at that time. And he must say that it can be true at a time that *S* infallibly knows something at that time, even though it is still possible at that time that *S* doesn't infallibly know that something at that time. Both of these are hard sayings; neither is a saying the Boethian is committed to. In order to defend God's infallible timeless knowledge of the not now necessary from the variant argument, the Boethian needs only to suppose that it can be true at a time that *S* has a belief at some 'un-time', even though it is possible at that time that *S* doesn't have that belief at that un-time; and that it can be true at a time that *S* infallibly knows something at some un-time, even though it is still possible that *S* doesn't infallibly know that something at that un-time. Neither of these sayings seems especially hard. Unless we think that only inevitably true propositions about what people believe are true, we shall accept that

---

23 *Ibid.*, pp. 262-264.

it can be true at an earlier time that S will have a belief at a later time, even though it is still possible at that earlier time that S won't have that belief at that later time; and that it can be true at an earlier time that S will infallibly know something at a later time, even though it is still possible at that earlier time that S won't infallibly know that something at that later time. If there can be not-yet-necessary truths at one time about what someone believes or knows at a different (later) time, why couldn't there be not-yet-necessary truths at a time about what someone believes or knows at a different un-time?

In short: the Ockhamist must take issue with the venerable argument; the Boethian needs only to take issue with Plantinga's variant of that argument. The fact that the original argument is harder to find fault with than the variant one, is a consideration in favour of a Boethian, rather than an Ockhamist, account of God's knowledge of the not-yet-necessary. Nor is it the only one, as we shall see in the next section.

3.3 Ockham's Way Out, Plantinga's Way Out, and Boethius's Way Out

Ockham holds that some true past-tensed statements ascribing knowledge to God are not yet necessary. But, he thinks, no such statements are genuinely and strictly about the past.[24] Now, for each true statement that is genuinely and strictly about the past, there is a corresponding (actually obtaining) purely past state of affairs. If, for example, 'The Dead played at the Muir Beach Acid Test in the mid-sixties' is true, then *the Dead's playing at the Muir Beach Acid Test in the mid-sixties* is an (actually obtaining) purely past state of affairs. Let S be a purely past state of affairs that includes every actually obtaining purely past state of affairs, and no non-purely-past state of affairs whose obtaining is not yet necessary.[25] Let P be the proposition that S obtains. If Ockham is right to suppose that all true statements genuinely and strictly about the past are now necessary, then P is now necessary. Moreover, accepting that P is now necessary is tantamount to accepting the necessity of the past. (We can think of S as the past (plus the necessary part of the future, if any part thereof is necessary).) It follows that Ockham is committed to the necessity of the past.

Plantinga, by contrast, appears not to be. In 'On Ockham's Way Out', he writes:

Let's suppose that a colony of carpenter ants moved into Paul's yard last Saturday. Since this colony hasn't yet had a chance to get properly established, its new home is still a bit fragile. In particular, if the ants were to remain and Paul were to mow his lawn this afternoon, the colony would be destroyed. Although nothing remarkable about these ants is visible to the naked eye, God, for reasons of his own, intends that they be preserved. Now as a matter of fact, Paul will not mow his lawn this afternoon. God, who is essentially

---

24 Cf., for instance, the passage from Ockham's *Tractatus De Praedestinatione* cited by Plantinga in 'On Ockham's Way Out', p. 270.

25 I might more straightforwardly have characterized S as a state of affairs which includes all and only purely past states of affairs. But suppose we follow Plantinga's lead in *The Nature of Necessity,* and say that a state of affairs S includes a state of affairs S' only if it is a (broadly) logically necessary truth that if S obtains, then S' does as well. In that case, if there are truths about the future that hold in every possible world, then any state of affairs that includes all the purely past states of affairs will also include non-purely-past states of affairs.

omniscient, knew in advance, of course, that Paul will not mow his lawn this afternoon; but if he had foreknown instead that Paul *would* mow this afternoon, then he would have prevented the ants from moving in. The facts of the matter, therefore, are these: if Paul would mow this afternoon, then God would have prevented the ants from moving in. So if Paul were to mow his lawn this afternoon, the ants would not have moved in last Saturday. But it is within Paul's power to mow this afternoon. There is therefore an action he can perform such that if he were to perform it, then the proposition

(34) That colony of carpenter ants moved into Paul's yard last Saturday.

would have been false. But what I have called 'the facts of the matter' certainly seem to be possible; it is therefore possible that there be an agent who has the power to perform an action which is such that if he were to perform it, then (34) would have been false.[26]

Plantinga goes on to say that inasmuch as (34) is genuinely and strictly about the past, there are or at least could be hard facts about the past whose factuality depends on which of the actions an agent could perform, that agent does perform.[27] As Plantinga sees it, this is not simply a point about logical or metaphysical possibility: we know very little about which true propositions about the past are such that we can so act that they would have been false.[28]

Plantinga concludes that facts such as (34) are not 'accidentally necessary', on at least one way of understanding accidental necessity (though he goes on to suggest that they are accidentally necessary, on a different way of understanding it). If Plantinga is right about the case of the carpenter ants, then there are or at any rate might be propositions that are genuinely and strictly about the past, but are not now necessary. In the hypothetical case, there is something that still could happen (Paul's mowing his lawn this afternoon), about which we can say: if it did happen, then it would be false the ants moved into Paul's yard last Saturday. But something which would be false, if something which still could happen, did happen, is something that could still be false. So it's not something whose falsehood is no longer possible; in other words, it's not something that is now necessary. Moreover (Plantinga concedes) 'The colony of carpenter ants moved into Paul's yard last Saturday' is genuinely and strictly about the past, if anything is. So Plantinga holds – or at least should hold, given his beliefs about the ants – that it is metaphysically and epistemically possible that there are true statements genuinely and strictly about the past, that are not-yet-necessarily true, and purely past states of affairs whose obtaining is not yet necessary. He is not – or at least should not be – committed to *P*; he should not accept the necessity of the past.

For reasons already adduced, I am with Ockham on the necessity of the past. Like him, I think that if we are happy to say that a given past-tensed statement is not-yet-necessarily true or not-yet-necessarily false, it is only because we think that the entire actual past could have happened, without the statement's being true, and the entire actual past could have happened, without the statement's being false. It's not

---

26   *Ibid.*, p. 279.

27   So, although Plantinga endorses Ockham's view that only hard facts about the past-cum-present are necessary (or, at any rate, endorses its plausibility), he does not endorse Ockham's view that all hard facts about the past-cum-present are necessary.

28   *Ibid.*, p. 284.

necessarily true that Smith smoked the last cigarette of his life yesterday, and it's not necessarily false that Smith smoked the last cigarette of his life yesterday; but that's only because the entire actual past could have happened, without its being true that Smith smoked the last cigarette of his life last night, and the entire actual past could have happened, without its being false that Smith smoked the last cigarette of his life last night. What I find very difficult to believe is that anything that actually has happened could still not happen (in the way that some things that actually will happen could still not happen), or to believe that any or all of the actual past could still turn out not to be actual (in the way that some of the actual future (the non-necessary part) could still turn out not to be actual). *Quod fuit non potest non fuisse.*

Whatever the attractions of the view that the past is necessary, Ockham's committment to it raises problems for his account of God's knowledge of future contingents.

The following principle is (I think) very plausible:

> If A is not yet necessarily false, then whatever is in fact now necessary (or now impossible) would still be now necessary (or now impossible), even if A were true.

If, for example, it is not yet necessarily false that Eel Pie Island will be flooded tomorrow, but it is now necessary that Trowlock Island was flooded last year, then it would still be now necessary that Trowlock Island was flooded last year, even if Eel Pie Island were flooded tomorrow.[29]

Suppose it is in fact neither necessarily true nor necessarily false that Eel Pie Island will be flooded tomorrow. Could it be that if Eel Pie Island were flooded tomorrow, it would not be the case that P? Not if P is necessary, and the above principle is true. After all, suppose it were true that:

(α) Were Eel Pie Island flooded tomorrow, it would not be the case that P.

Then it would also have to be true that:

(β) Were Eel Pie Island flooded tomorrow, it would not be necessary that P.

But if P is necessary, and (β) is true, then something which is in fact necessary, wouldn't be necessary, if something which is not necessarily false, were true – in contravention of our principle. So, the champion of the necessity of the past should conclude:

(γ) Were Eel Pie Island to be flooded tomorrow, it would still be true that P.

– and indeed (by the same reasoning) that

(δ)   Were Eel Pie Island not to be flooded tomorrow, it would still be true that P.

Whether or not Eel Pie Island is flooded tomorrow makes no difference to the past: if it will in fact be flooded tomorrow, the past would have been just the same as it

---

29 How could Trowlock Island's having been flooded last year *owe its necessity* to the (still contingent) flooding of Eel Pie island tomorrow?

actually is, if it hadn't been flooded tomorrow; and if it won't in fact be flooded tomorrow, the past would have been just the same as it actually is, if it had been flooded tomorrow.[30]

If we start with a true conditional, and replace its antecedent with an antecedent that is true at all the same times and possible worlds as the original antecedent, we end up with a true conditional. Given Ockham's views on God's necessary existence and essential omniscience, Ockham holds that *Eel Pie Island will be flooded tomorrow* and *God knew yesterday that Eel Pie Island will be flooded tomorrow* are true at all the same times and possible worlds. He likewise holds that *Eel Pie Island won't be flooded tomorrow* and *God knew yesterday that Eel Pie won't be flooded tomorrow* are true at all the same times and possible worlds. So Ockham is committed to

(ε) If God hadn't known yesterday that Eel Pie will be flooded tomorrow, it would still be true that *P*.

and

(ζ) If God had known yesterday that Eel Pie will be flooded tomorrow, it would still be true that *P*.

Which particular things God knew about the future makes no difference to how the past went, in just the same way that which particular way the future goes makes no difference to how the past went. Given that Ockham takes the present to be as necessary as the past, he is also committed to the claim that which particular things God knows about the future makes no difference to how the present is.

If, however, we say that the entire past and present, and, *a fortiori*, God's entire past and present, would have been exactly as it is, whether or not God knew yesterday that Eel Pie will flood tomorrow, then we seem to end up with an unacceptably 'thin' notion of what it is for God know something.[31] How could God's past or present knowledge of (and beliefs about) future contingents make no difference to the past or present? The strangeness of the suggestion that they could make no difference comes out particularly vividly if we suppose that the future is endless, and that at every time, there will be some things that are not yet necessarily true, and not yet necessarily false. In that case (assuming that truth does not entail (current) necessity), there will be some proposition that is actually true, but will never become necessarily true. (One could think of the proposition as: *h is the actual history of the world*, where *h* is one of an infinite number of 'branching' possible histories of the world.) On the view under consideration, it always has been, and always will be (not-yet-necessarily) true that God knows that proposition. But it's also guaranteed that at any time – past, present, or future – the whole history of the world up to and including then will be

---

30   We could get the same result if we supposed that if *P* is not necessarily false, whatever is in fact now necessary, would still have been *true*, even if *P* had been true. See Bas van Fraasen, 'Report on Tense Logic', in *Modern Logic: A Survey*, ed., Evandro Agazzi (Dordrecht, D. Reidel, 1981).

31   Cf. John Martin Fischer's 'Freedom and Foreknowledge', *Philosophical Review*, XCII, 1983, pp. 67-79, and Richard Swinburne's *The Christian God* (Oxford: Clarendon Press, 1994, pp. 130-134).

exactly as it would have been, if God hadn't known that proposition (and had known its negation instead). God always has and always will know the proposition, but the way things have been and are, for us and for God, will at any time be exactly the way they would have been, if God hadn't known the proposition. In that case, I lose my grip on what the difference could be between the never-necessary proposition's being not only true, but known by God, and its being true, though God will never know whether or not its true. We seem to be left with what Hume calls a distinction without a difference.

Ockham is faced with these difficulties, because his way out of what we might call 'epistemic necessitarianism' (the view that whatever anyone infallibly knows is necessary) involves holding onto the necessity of the past (and present). Inasmuch as Plantinga's way out of epistemic necessitarianism does not involve commitment to the necessity of the past or present, he is not threatened by what (if I remember correctly) Calvin Normore once called 'the disappearance theory of divine knowledge'.[32] But if, as I have suggested, the past is necessary (and the disappearance theory of divine knowledge is false), then neither Ockham nor Plantinga has found a way out.

If, however, we suppose that God and His knowledge are extratemporal, we can say:

> The past is 'fixed', and counterfactually independent of the open future. Since the past does not depend counterfactually on the open future, and God's knowledge of the open future is counterfactually inseparable from the open future, the past does not depend counterfactually on God's timeless knowledge of the open future. But that doesn't saddle us with the disappearance theory of God's knowledge of the open future. If anyone knows something, the way the world is when they know it is different from the way the world would be then, if he or she didn't know it. And this goes for extratemporal as well as temporal knowers. 'When' (at the un-time that) God knows that Eel Pie Island will be flooded tomorrow, the world is a certain way. It would not be the same way 'then', if God didn't 'then' know that Eel Pie Island will be flooded tomorrow.

It again looks as though the Boethian is in a better position than the 'temporalist' to maintain that God has infallible knowledge of non-necessities. Or rather, the Boethian is in a better position than the temporalist to maintain that God has infallible knowledge of non-necessities, on one way of understanding that claim. The proponent of the venerable argument holds that nobody ever has had or ever will have knowledge of non-necessary truths. By this she does not mean that nobody ever will have knowledge of things that are *now* not necessary; she means that nobody ever will have knowledge of things that are *then* (when they are known) not necessary. The temporalist must deny this, since (he thinks) God will have infallible knowledge tomorrow of what won't be necessary tomorrow. But the Boethian can agree that

---

32 Notice, though, that the only way Plantinga will avoid the problems Ockham encounters is if he supposes that how the openness of the future is resolved will make a (counterfactual) difference not just to what God's past beliefs were, but also to God's past. If he goes that route, he will have to say that the counterfactual dependence of the past on the open future is an actuality, and not merely a possibility.

whatever God knows is necessary, when God knows it;[33] she can agree that *being an object of infallible knowledge* implies *being necessarily true*, so that whenever (or 'when'ever) a proposition has the first property, it also has the second. If *being the object of infallible knowledge* implies *being necessarily true*, then God's (infallible) knowledge must, as the proponent of the venerable argument insists, be limited to the necessary. But that limitation, properly understood, is perfectly compatible with God's being infallibly omniscient, and the future's being genuinely open.

So far, so good. But theists (or, at any rate, Christians) traditionally suppose that God's knowledge of the world is of practical as well as theoretical value; God makes use of what He knows about the world, in acting upon the world. And – I shall argue – the Boethian (as much as the temporalist) may have trouble making sufficient room for the practical value of God's knowledge of the not yet necessary.

I dimly remember from my childhood hearing or reading about discussions of the usefulness of history. The *advocatus diaboli* would say: since the past is over and done with, and too late to do anything about, what is the use of knowing about it? The defender of Clio would counter that knowledge of history enables us to learn from our past mistakes: knowledge of the past is useful, in spite of our inability to influence the past, because we use that knowledge to influence (and improve) the future. What we know about the past makes a difference to what we do, which in turn makes a difference to how the future goes; so our knowledge of the past, via its effects on our actions, makes the future better (for us, or for others) than it would have been, if we hadn't had the knowledge.

In much the same way, *per conjecturam* knowledge of the future is useful. My *per conjecturam* knowledge that it will rain this afternoon is responsible for my bringing my raincoat with me this morning, which is in turn responsible for my being dry and comfortable this afternoon. So my knowledge of the future, via its effects on my actions, makes the future better (for me) than it would have been, if I hadn't had that knowledge.[34]

Suppose *per impossibile* that there are two Gods. One is what we may call a Swinburnean God. He always has existed, and always will exist. Moreover, He always has known (and He always has believed) all and only those propositions that

---

33 See Prior's explication of Anselm's idea that God's timeless knowledge of all of time in some ways resembles our knowledge of the past: 'Looking back over what *has* happened, we can distinguish what was bound to happen as it did from what could have happened otherwise, though of course none of it *can now*, by the time we look back on it, have happened otherwise. It is in some such way as this that God distinguishes necessities and contingencies even though there is no contingency left in the latter in the form in which they reach His gaze' ('The Formalities of Omniscience', p. 38 (in *Papers on Time and Tense*)). It is perhaps unfortunate that Prior speaks of their being no contingency 'left' in a state of affairs when it reaches God's gaze, since it suggests that God, rather than being timeless, inhabits a kind of ω-time later than all ordinary times.

34 Or at least, better than it would have been, if I hadn't had the corresponding belief. (If I hadn't known *per conjecturam* that it would have rained, but I had still firmly believed it, I would still have taken my raincoat this morning, and I would have been just as dry this afternoon. I shall ignore this complication because, in the theological case, God's believing something and His knowing it are counterfactually inseparable.

were then necessarily true. Also, He always will know (and He always will believe) all and only those propositions that will then be necessarily true. The other God is an Ockhamist God. He always has existed, and always will exist; and for any (past, present, or future) time, He knows at that time whatever is then necessarily or not-yet-necessarily true.

(Assuming that there are not-yet-necessary truths) the Ockhamist God knows more than the Swinburnean God. And the Ockhamist God's 'marginal knowledge' might, one should have thought, be of practical value to Him in His dealings with the world. If, say, the Ockhamist God now knows that it is not-yet-necessarily true that something bad is going to happen, or that a certain opportunity is going to arise, He can (before the event occurs, and before the event's occurrence is inevitable) take what a bureaucrat might call 'appropriate proaction'. Naturally, the Ockhamist God could still have been proactive, if He had known only what the Swinburnean God knows. But if the Ockhamist God had known only what the Swinburnean God knows, it seems, He might have made a different – less informed, sub-optimal – choice about how to 'proact'. This seems an especially strong possibility, if the Ockhamist God proacts with respect to a situation in which either X or Y might happen, X is extremely likely, but won't actually happen, and Y is extremely unlikely (and will remain so for as long as it is future), but actually will happen. Why suppose that the choice of proaction an Ockhamist God makes in that situation, on the basis of full information – including the information Y will happen – is the same choice He would have made under partial information – if all He had known was that although either X or Y might happen, X was very probable, and Y was very improbable? (An analogy: suppose you choose whether or not to take an umbrella this morning on the basis of your knowledge that it won't actually rain this afternoon, even though its raining this afternoon is now extremely likely. Would the choice you make be the same as the choice you would have made, if all you had known is that it was possible that it wasn't going to rain this afternoon, but extremely likely that it would?)[35]

Notice, though, the Ockhamist cannot say that the Ockhamist God has made certain things happen now, or in the past, only because of what He knows about the open future, so that if He hadn't had that knowledge, He wouldn't have made that thing happen. As we have seen, because the Ockhamist thinks that the past and

---

35 A similar case involving God might be the following: suppose that Larissa is going to have make a choice soon, and will be sorely tempted to choose the sinful rather than the sinless option. The Ockhamist God wants to give Larissa all the help she needs to resist temptation, but no more. He knows that if Larissa is not given special help, it is (currently) very unlikely that she will resist temptation, and it will remain very unlikely right up to the moment she actually makes her choice. But He also knows that, if she is not given special help, when she actually makes the choice, she will confound the probabilities, and do what is right. (I am assuming that the Ockhamist God has not only knowledge of future contingents, but also 'middle knowledge.') In that case, He will not give Larissa special help, since He knows she will in fact do the right thing 'off her own bat'. If, however, He had known only what the Swinburnean God knows (that Larissa might or might not resist temptation without special help, but is very unlikely to) He would have made a different choice, since He would rather that Larissa be specially helped and sinless, than un-specially-helped, and sinful, and not providing special help would involve too high a risk of getting His dispreferred option.

present are counterfactually independent of the open future, and God's knowledge of the open future is counterfactually inseparable from the open future, he must say that the past and present are counterfactually independent of God's knowledge of the open future. Suppose it is not-yet-necessarily true that the Ham Lands will be under water next week. If something happened in the past, or is happening now, it would still have happened, even if God hadn't known that the Ham Lands will be under water next week.[36] Moreover, If God made something happen in the past, or is making something happen now, He still would have made that thing happen, even if He hadn't known that the Ham Lands will be under water next week.[37] By the same reasoning, if God will make something happen in the part of the future in which it will still be open whether or not the Ham Lands will be under water next week, then He still would have made that thing happen, even if He hadn't known that Ham Lands will be under water next week. Suppose that, where *P* is a proposition that is not-yet-necessarily true up to a certain time *t*, and necessarily true at *t* and ever after, we call the part of history before *t* the *P-open* part of history. Then we may put the point this way: on Ockhamist assumptions, God never makes use of his knowledge of *P* in acting upon the *P*-open part of the history of the world; as far as those dealings are concerned, it is exactly as though He were in the dark about *P*, or knew that *P* was false.

As long as the Boethian accepts the counterfactual independence of the past from the open future, and the counterfactual inseparability of the open future from God's knowledge thereof, he will have to say the exact same thing. A timeless Boethian God knows all sorts of things that a temporal Swinburnean God does not know. Nevertheless, a Boethian God always acts upon the *P*-open part of the history of the world in exactly the same way He would, if He didn't have that extra knowledge. As far as His interactions with the *P*-open part of the history of the world are concerned, it's exactly as though He were in the dark about *P*, or knew that *P* was false.

Now it seems to me that most theists – or at least, most Christians – who think that God has knowledge of the open future, think that God's knowledge that *P* is of practical value to God in His dealings with the *P*-open part of history: it can and often does make a difference to how the world is while *P* is open, by making a difference to how God makes the world be during that interval.

An example: suppose you think that only those who freely turn to God can be saved, and no one can freely turn to God (in the future), if their turning to God is already necessary. Then you'll conclude that it is not yet necessary that all Israel will be saved. Suppose also that you believe that, just as St. Paul says (*Romans*, 11, 26), all Israel will be saved. Suppose finally that you are convinced that the salvation of all Israel is not just something St. Paul believed, but something God revealed to him (and us). Then you will probably believe that God's knowledge that all Israel would

---

36   More pedantically but less ambiguously: if some purely present state of affairs is obtaining now, or some purely past state of affairs obtained in the past, it still would have obtained, even if God hadn't known that the Ham Lands will be under water next week.

37   Again: if God in the past actualized a purely past state of affairs, or God now actualizes a purely present state of affairs, then God would have still actualized that state of affairs, even if He hadn't known that the Ham Lands will be under water next week.

be saved has already made a difference to what God has done, and thus to how the world was and is. For – you will think – many persons have believed (and believe) that all Israel will be saved, millions of Bibles say that all Israel will be saved, and so on, because God revealed that truth to Paul; and God wouldn't have done that if He hadn't known that all Israel would be saved. Unless you thought that God wouldn't have communicated to St. Paul that all Israel would be saved, if He hadn't believed it would be, you would not (unhesitatingly) describe the salvation of all Israel as something God *revealed* to St. Paul.

In sum: Boethius's way out enables us to accept the venerable argument, and still say that God has infallible knowledge of not-now-necessary truths.[38] But – if the past and present are counterfactually independent of the open future – it allows God to have such knowledge, only by guaranteeing that He'll never make use of it to influence the world as it is before what God knows has become necessary. For many theists, this will be too high a price to pay.[39]

3.4 Symmetries and Asymmetries

Some philosophers and theologians have been inclined to endorse all of the following theses:

(A) At the alethic level, there is a symmetry between statements about the past and present, and statements about the future. Say that a proposition is true at a (possible) time on a (possible) history just in case, if that possible history were the actual history of the world, that proposition would actually be true at that time. Say that a (present-tensed) proposition P is determinate (not subject to vagueness) just in case, for any possible time belonging to any possible history, P is either true or false at that time on that history. If P is determinate, then, just as exactly one member of the pair <It was the case that yesterday that P, It was the case yesterday that not-P> is true, exactly one member of the pair <It will be the case tomorrow that P, It will be the case tomorrow that not-P> is true. If the present-tensed proposition, *there is a sea-battle*, is determinate, then – *pace* Aristotle and Pierce – exactly one member of the pair <*There will be a sea-battle tomorrow at noon, There will be no sea-battle tomorrow at noon*> is true, just as exactly one member of the pair <*There was*

---

38 There are, of course, deep and difficult questions about the ultimate coherence and defensibility of the Boethian account. Plantinga is inclined to believe that it is incoherent ('On Ockham's Way Out, p. 262). Prior is inclined both to believe that a timeless being could not be omniscient (because He couldn't know what is happening now), and that a timeless being could not so much as exist (because existing just is existing at the present time). But whether or not the idea that a timeless God has infallible knowledge of not-yet-necessary truths is ultimately defensible, it is not in any obvious way incoherent.

39 Knowledge of future contingents is often thought of as crucially involved in God's providential government of the world.

a sea-battle yesterday at noon, There was no sea-battle yesterday at noon>
is true.[40]

(B) At the modal level, there is an asymmetry between the past (and, perhaps, the present), and the future. The past (and perhaps the present) are completely necessary, while the future is (at least partly) open. As a result of this, (purely) past states of affairs are always counterfactually independent of not-yet-necessarily actualized future states of affairs, although the converse does not hold.

(C) At the epistemic level, there is a symmetry between God's knowledge of the past and present, and His knowledge of the future. God's knowledge of the future is every bit as comprehensive, and every bit as infallible, as His knowledge of the past and present.

As the venerable argument brings out, (A)-(C) are at least apparently in tension. Philosophers and philosophical theologians have responded to this apparent tension in different ways. Some have concluded that the theses are incompatible, and accordingly denied at least one of them. Swinburne, for example, rejects (C). Prior and John Lucas reject both (A) and (C). Edwards and Helm hold on to (A) and (C), and deny (B). Other philosophical theologians have insisted that (A)-(C) are compatible: Boethius and Ockham are particularly illustrious examples.[41] Plantinga sides with the 'incompatibilists'. Like Edwards and Helm, he accepts (A) and (C), and denies (B) – though his denial of (B) involves 'softening' the past, rather than 'hardening' the future. What emerges from 'On Ockham's Way Out' (and, I hope, from this piece) is that a philosopher who thinks that God is in time will have a very hard time defending the claim that each of (A)-(C) is true. A philosopher who thinks that God is extratemporal may be better placed to do that, but only if she accepts that God never makes use of His (timeless) knowledge of a not-yet-necessary truth *P* in acting upon the *P*-open part of the history of the world.[42]

---

40 Though I have expressed (A) as a semantic thesis about the truth-values of statements, it is often thought of as following from, or at least linked with, a metaphysical thesis to the effect that the future is 'just as real' and 'just as determinate' as the past and present.

41 Aquinas is an interesting case. Although he sometimes sounds like a defender of the truth of each of (A)-(C), I am inclined to think that – at least some of the time – he construes the necessity of the past in such a deflationary way that he in effect endorses (A) and (C), while rejecting (B). See my 'Aquinas on God's Knowledge of Future Contingents', in J. Haldane, ed., *Mind, Metaphysics and Value in the Thomistic and Analytical Traditions* (Notre Dame Ind., Notre Dame University Press, 2002), pp. 143-159.

42 Thanks to Marilyn McCord Adams, Bob Adams, Andrew Bottani, Pietro Casalegno, Joseph Jedwab, Elisa Paganni, M.W.F. Stone, Peter van Inwagen, and Sandra Zucchi.

Chapter 4

The Argument from
Laws of Nature Reassessed

Richard Swinburne

In his many writings Paul Helm has charted and commented on various views of the relation between faith and reason, but his sympathy for natural theology seems very limited. My contribution to this volume is written in appreciation of what he has done and in the hope that it may encourage him to be more sympathetic to natural theology in the future.

I have campaigned for many years for the view that most of the traditional arguments for the existence of God can be construed as inductive arguments from phenomena to the hypothesis of theism (that there is a God) which best explains them.[1] Each of these phenomena gives some probability to the hypothesis, and together they make it more probable than not. The phenomena can be arranged in decreasing order of generality. The cosmological argument argues from the existence of the universe; the argument from temporal order argues from its being governed by simple laws of nature; the argument from fine-tuning argues from the initial conditions and form and constants of the laws of nature being such as to lead (somewhere in the Universe) to the evolution of animal and human bodies. Then we have arguments from those humans being conscious, from various particular characteristics of humans and their environment (their free will, capacity for causing limited good and harm to each other and especially moulding their own characters for good or ill), various historical events (including violations of natural laws), and finally the religious experiences of so many millions of humans.

I assess these arguments as arguments to the existence of 'God' in the traditional sense of a being essentially eternal, omnipotent, omniscient, perfectly free and perfectly good; and I have argued that his perfect goodness follows from the other three properties.[2] God's omnipotence is his ability to do anything logically possible. God's perfect goodness is to be understood as his doing only what is good and doing the best in so far as that is logically possible and in so far as he has the moral right to do so. So he will inevitably bring about a unique best possible world (if there is one), or one of a disjunction of equal best possible worlds (if there are such). But

---

1   See especially my *The Existence of God*, Clarendon Press, 1979. (For the detailed argument from laws of nature, see Chapter 8 of that work.) See also the simpler version of this *Is there a God?*, Oxford University Press, 1996. (See Chapter 4 for the argument from laws of nature.) The present paper is based on Chapter 8 of the second edition, 2004, of *The Existence of God*, Oxford: Clarendon Press, 2004.

2   See, for example, my *The Coherence of Theism*, Clarendon Press, revised edition, 1993, pp. 149-152 and 207-209.

if for every good possible world, there is a better, all that God's perfect goodness can amount to is that he will bring about a good possible world.[3] So God will bring about any state of affairs which belongs to the best or all the equal best or all the good possible worlds. If there is some state of affairs which is such that any world is equally good for having it or not having it, then we can say that there is a probability of ½ that he will make it. God will exercise this choice among worlds (and so states of affairs) which it is logically possible for him to bring about and which he has the moral right to bring about. There are some very good possible worlds and states thereof which God cannot for logical reasons guarantee to bring about – e.g. worlds where agents with a choice between good and evil always freely choose the good.[4] (When I write about 'free choice' I mean libertarian free choice, that is, a choice which is not fully determined by causes which influence it.) Also, God can only bring about a world if he has the moral right to do so. There are in my view limits to his moral right to allow some to suffer (not by their own choice) for the benefit of others – limits of the length of time and intensity of suffering which he may allow.

The traditional arguments to the existence of such a God, which I list above, are, I claim, cumulative. In each case the argument goes that the cited phenomena are unlikely to occur, given only the phenomena mentioned in the previous argument. That is, the existence of the Universe is improbable *a priori* (i.e. if we assume nothing contingent at all); the Universe being governed by laws of nature is improbable, given only the existence of the Universe – and so on. The argument then claims that if there is a God, these phenomena are much more to be expected than if there is no God. For God, being omnipotent, has the power to bring about a Universe and to endow it with the various listed characteristics, that is, to sustain a Universe in being with these characteristics either for a finite or for an infinite period. And, I have argued, all of these characteristics are good and so, in virtue of his perfect goodness, there is some probability that he will bring them about.

This is basically because, among the good worlds which a God has reason to make are ones in which there are creatures with a limited free choice between good and evil and limited powers to make deeply significant differences to themselves, each other, and their world by those choices (including the power to increase their powers and freedom of choice). The goodness of significant free choice is, I hope, evident. We think it a good gift to give to our own children that they choose their own path in life for good or ill, and influence the kinds of persons (with what kinds of character and powers) they and others are to be. But good though this is, there is the

---

3   For a fuller account of what God's goodness must amount to when there is no best or equal best possible world, see my *The Existence of God*, second edition, Clarendon Press, 2004, pp. 112-123.

4   In Plantinga's terminology God can only weakly actualize such a world, not strongly actualize it. See Alvin Plantinga *The Nature of Necessity*, Clarendon Press, 1974, p. 173. God can, however, make free agents strongly inclined (though not determined) to choose the good; if he makes such agents, he makes it very probable that they will do good. Or God can make them not so strongly inclined which will make it less probable that they will do good. But the second sort of freedom may be a freedom more worth having. For the different worths of the different kinds of free will God could create, see my *Providence and the Problem of Evil*, Clarendon Press, 1998, pp. 82-89.

risk that those who have such free will will make bad choices, form bad characters for themselves, hurt others and influence their characters for evil. For this reason I suggest that it would not be a good action to create beings with freedom of choice between good and evil and unlimited power to put such choices into effect. If God creates beings with the freedom to choose between good and evil, they must be finite, limited creatures. Even so, the risks are – as we know very well – considerable; and so, I suggest that God would not inevitably bring about such a world. For any world which God could make containing such creatures would be no worse for not containing such creatures. But I suggest that the converse also holds: any world which God could make to which you add such creatures would be none the worse for such an addition. For this reason there is a probability of ½ that he will make such a world. But my arguments do not depend on giving such a precise or such a high probability to God (if there is a God) making such a world. All that I am claiming is that there is a significant probability that a God would create such a world.

Let us call creatures with limited powers of the above kinds free rational creatures. If humans have (libertarian) free will (as is not implausible),[5] evidently our world is a world containing such creatures. We humans make deeply significant choices, affecting ourselves, each other, and our world; and our choices include choices to take steps to increase our powers and freedom, and form our characters for good or ill. But our powers in these respects are limited ones. Our world is a world of a kind which God can (with significant probability) be expected to make. Free rational creatures will have to begin life with a limited range of control, and the power to choose to extend that range or – alternatively – not to bother to do so. That limited range is their bodies. In order for them to be able to extend their range of control, there must be some procedure which they can utilize – this bodily movement will have this predictable extra-bodily effect. That is, the world must be subject to regularities, simple natural laws, which such creatures can choose to try to discover and then choose to utilize to make differences to things distant in space and time. You can learn that if you plant seeds and water them, they will grow into edible plants which will enable you to keep alive yourself and others; or that if you pull the trigger of a gun loaded in a certain way and pointing in a certain direction, it will kill some distant person. And so on. We can choose whether to seek out such knowledge (of how to cure or kill) or not to bother; and we can choose whether to utilize this knowledge for good or ill. In a chaotic world, that would not be possible – for there would be no recipe for producing effects.

So, given that – as I argued – there is a significant probability that a God would create free rational creatures (as defined earlier), there is a significant probability that he will create this necessary condition for the existence of such creatures – a world regular in its conformity to simple natural laws. It is not sufficient that there be natural laws; they must be sufficiently simple to be discoverable by rational creatures. This involves their being instantiated frequently, and that the simplest extrapolation from their past instantiations will often yield correct predictions. There could be a world with a trillion unconnected laws of nature, each determining that an event of a

---

5   For my arguments in favour of the view that they do have such free will, see my *The Evolution of the Soul*, Clarendon Press, revised edition, 1997, Chapter 13.

certain kind would be followed by an event of a certain other kind, but where there were only one or two events of the former kind in the history of the Universe. No rational creature could discover such laws. Or there could be laws governing events of a type frequently instantiated, but of such enormous mathematical complexity that the simplest extrapolation from the past occurrences would never yield correct predictions. The laws must be sufficiently simple and frequently instantiated to be discoverable from a study of past history at least by a logically omniscient rational being (one who could entertain all possible scientific theories, recognize the simplest, and draw the logical consequences thereof). (The laws, I must add, must not be of a totally deterministic kind, and cover all events. They must allow room for free will. However, I shall not discuss that aspect in this chapter.) Also the conformity of a material world to such laws is beautiful and a good in itself. The simple elegant motions of the stars and of all matter conforming to discoverable laws form a beautiful dance. And that is another reason why, if there is a God, we might expect a law-governed Universe, that is, a reason which adds to the probability of there being such a Universe, if there is a God.

In order to keep this chapter to a reasonable length, I shall assume that if gods are at work, monotheism of the traditional kind is far more probable than polytheism (that is, the view that many independent gods of finite powers provide the ultimate explanation of things).[6] I shall regard the alternative with which we are contrasting theism as naturalism, the view that any ultimate explanation of the Universe and its properties is of a scientific kind, that is in terms of matter-energy and its properties.[7] In this chapter I seek to investigate further my claim that, given naturalism, even if there is a Universe, it is most unlikely that it would be governed by simple laws of nature. My argument in the past has been that if we are confined to scientific explanation, while we can explain lower level laws by higher level ones, there can be no explanation of the conformity of nature to the most fundamental laws. Yet this conformity consists simply in everything in the Universe behaving in exactly the same way. Such a vast coincidence of behaviour, as a vast brute fact, would be *a priori* extremely improbable. Hence, while simple laws of nature are quite probable

---

6   Mark Wynn has pointed out that there are very many different possible hypotheses, each postulating different numbers of gods with different powers, whereas there is only one hypothesis postulating one God of infinite power. Hence, he claims, although each of the former hypotheses might be less probable *a priori* than the hypothesis of theism, the disjunction of the former is plausibly more probable than the hypothesis of theism, as an explanation of the world's order. (See his 'Some Reflections on Richard Swinburne's Argument from Design', *Religious Studies* 29 (1993), 325-335.) But if the order of the world is to be explained by many gods, then some explanation is required for how and why they co-operate in producing exactly the same patterns of order throughout the Universe. This becomes a new datum requiring explanation for the same reason as the fact of order itself. The need for further explanation ends when we postulate one being who is the cause of the existence of all others, and the simplest conceivable such – I urge – is God.

7   I also ignore the claims of John Leslie and Hugh Rice, considered seriously by Derek Parfit, that there is at work an inanimate principle producing states of affairs because they are good. For my reasons for ignoring this see my 'Response to Derek Parfit' in (ed.) P. Van Inwagen and D.W. Zimmerman, *Metaphysics: The Big Questions*, Blackwell, 1998.

if there is a God, they are very improbable otherwise. So their operation is good evidence for the existence of God.

I stand by my argument that, given naturalism, it is vastly improbable that the Universe (that is, the one in which we live) would be governed by (simple) laws of nature. But what I had not appreciated before and what I wish to bring out in this chapter is that the argument should be phrased as an argument from simple laws of nature (that is, ones discoverable in the sense defined earlier) and that their strength depends on what laws of nature are, and on whether – if the Universe had a temporal beginning – on what that beginning was like.

The argument is an argument from 'the Universe' being governed by discoverable laws of nature. By 'the Universe' I mean that system of physical bodies spatially related to (i.e. at some distance in some direction from) ourselves. I do not rule out the possibility of there being other universes, systems of physical bodies not so related, and we will need to consider that possibility in due course. It is a well-justified extrapolation from study of the spatio-temporal region accessible to our telescopes, a region vastly wider than the region in which we live, that the whole Universe is governed by the same laws. They may be the laws of General Relativity, Quantum Theory and a few other theories; or the laws of a Grand Unified Theory, or of a Theory of Everything. But what is meant by the claim that it is so governed; what is the truth-maker for there being laws of nature? One view, originating from Hume's views on causation, is, of course, the regularity view. 'Laws of Nature' are simply the ways things behave – have behaved, are behaving, and will behave. 'All copper expands when heated' is a law of nature if and only if all bits of copper when heated always have expanded, now expand, and will expand. We need, however, a distinction between laws of nature, and accidental generalizations such as 'all spheres of gold are less than one mile in diameter'; and we need to take account of probabilistic laws such as 'all atoms of C_{14} have a probability of decaying within 5,600 years, of $\frac{1}{2}$'. Regularity theory has reached a developed form which takes account of these matters, in the work of David Lewis.

For Lewis, 'regularities earn their lawhood not by themselves, but by the joint efforts of a system in which they figure either as axioms or theorems'.[8] The best system is the one which has (relative to rivals) the best combination of strength and simplicity. Strength is a matter of how much it successfully predicts (that is, that it makes actual many events, past, present or future – whether observed or not – probable; and very few actual events improbable); simplicity is a matter of the laws fitting together, and no doubt, each having internal simplicity in a way which Lewis does not, but no doubt could, spell out. The true laws are the laws of the best system. So 'all spheres of gold are less than one mile in diameter' is probably not a law, because it does not follow from the best system – as is evidenced by the fact that it certainly does not follow from our current best approximation to the ultimate best system – a conjunction of Relativity Theory and Quantum Theory. Laws may be probabilistic as well as universal; if 'there is a 90% probability of an A being B' is a consequence of some theory, it will confer strength on that theory in so far as

---

8   David Lewis, *Philosophical Papers*, vol 2, Oxford University Press, 1986, 'A Subjectivist's Guide to Objective Chance – Postscript', p. 122.

90% actual A's (past, present, and future) are B. Lewis's account of laws of nature is part of his campaign on behalf of 'Humean Supervenience', that everything there is supervenes (logically) on 'a vast mosaic of local matters of particular fact', which he interprets as a spatio-temporal arrangement of intrinsic properties, or 'qualities'.[9] Laws of nature and causation are for Lewis among the things thus supervenient.

Now there do seem to be overwhelming well-known objections to any Humean account, including Lewis's, if laws of nature are supposed to explain anything – and in particular to explain why one thing causes another, as Humeans suppose that they do. The reason why laws explain causation, according to Humeans, is because causality reduces to components which include laws of nature. Hume's famous regularity definition of a 'cause' was as 'an object precedent and contiguous to another, and where all the objects resembling the former are placed in a like relation of priority and contiguity to those objects that resemble the latter'.[10] 'Objects' for Humeans are events or states of affairs, and are constituted by instantiations of bundles of purely categorical properties (such as, perhaps, being 'square' or 'red'), in contrast to dispositional properties whose nature it is to cause or to permit other objects to cause certain effects (such as is perhaps being 'soluble'). For a present day Humean such as Lewis, as I noted earlier, only certain kinds of regularities are laws and so function in an account of causation. Then the heating of a particular piece of copper causing its expansion is a matter of the former being followed by the latter, where there is a law that events like the former are followed by events like the latter. But since whether some lawlike statement constitutes a law depends, on this account, not merely on what has happened but on what will happen in the whole future history of the Universe, it follows that whether A causes B now depends on that future history. Yet, how can what is yet to happen (in maybe two billion years' time) make it the case that A now causes B, and thus explain why B happens? Whether A causes B is surely a matter of what happens now, and whether the world ends in two billion years time cannot make any difference to whether A now causes B? And hence none of this can make any difference to what is the true explanation of why B occurs (viz. that A occurred and caused it) – though, of course, it might make a difference to what we justifiably believe to be the true explanation.

It is because of their role in causation, that laws of nature are said to generate counterfactuals. Suppose that I don't heat the copper; it is then fairly evidently the case that 'if the copper had been heated, it would have expanded'. But if a law simply states what does (or did or will) happen, what grounds does it provide for asserting the counterfactual? It would only do that if there were some kind of necessity built into it.

These seem to me conclusive objections to the regularity account. If, however, despite them, we were to adopt this account, the conformity of all objects to laws of nature being just the fact that they do so conform, would have no further cause except from outside the system. If there were no God it would be a highly improbable coincidence if events in the world fell into kinds in such ways that the simplest extrapolation from the past frequently yielded correct predictions. There are innumerable logically possible ways in which objects could have behaved today, only

---

9   *Philosophical Papers*, vol 2, pp ix-x.
10   David Hume, *A Treatise on Human Nature*, 1. 3. 14.

one of them being in conformity with the simplest extrapolation from the past. If, on the other hand, God causes the behaviour of physical things, then the coincidence is to be expected for reasons given earlier. We would, however, need to give some non-Humean account of God's intentional causation – otherwise its universal efficacy would itself constitute a brute coincidence!

So, dismissing Humean accounts of laws for good reason, let us consider alternative accounts of laws of nature, that is accounts which represent talk of 'laws' as talk about a feature of the world additional to the mere succession of events, a feature of physical necessity which is part of the world. This feature of physical necessity may be thought of either as separate from the objects which are governed by it, or as a constitutive aspect of those objects. The former approach leads to a picture of the world as consisting of events (constituted perhaps by substances with their properties) on the one hand, and laws of nature on the other hand; and this approach can be developed so as to allow for the possibility of there being universes in which there are no events, but merely laws of nature.[11] Laws of nature are thus ontologically concrete entities. The version of this account which has been much discussed recently is the version which claims that laws of nature are logically contingent relations between universals – either Aristotelian instantiated universals (Armstrong) or Platonist not-necessarily-instantiated universals (Tooley). For Armstrong there being a fundamental law of nature that all F's are G consists in there being a connection of physical necessity between the universal F and the universal G. It being a fundamental law of nature that 'all photons travel at 300,000 km/sec relative to every inertial reference frame' consists in there being such a connection between the universal 'being a photon' and the universal 'travelling at 300,000 km/sec relative to every inertial reference frame', which we can represent by N (F, G). This relation between universals is itself a (logically) contingently existing universal. The instantiation of F thus inevitably brings with it the instantiation of G. One can perhaps begin to make sense of this suggestion if one thinks of the causing of states of affairs as making properties, which are universals, to be instantiated; and this involving the bringing of them down to Earth from an eternal Heaven, together with whatever is involved with those universals – viz. other universals of (physical) necessity connected thereto. But for Armstrong, there is no such eternal Heaven – 'there is nothing to the law except what is instantiated ... The law ... has no existence except in the particular sequences'.[12] But then – does the relation between universals exist before the law is instantiated for the first time, or not? If yes, there is an eternal Heaven in which it exists. If not, what causes it rather than some alternative to exist? Tooley thinks of the relations between universals as existing in an eternal Heaven prior to their instantiation in this world. This will meet the problem of why they are instantiated on the first occasion, and also allow from the plausible possibility of there being laws which are never instantiated:

---

11   Thus 'I hold ... that many empty [possible] universes exist. As I see it, there is a world devoid of all material objects and events in which the general principles of Newtonian mechanics are laws; there is another empty world in which the general principles of Aristotelian physics are laws' – John W. Carroll *Law of Nature*, Cambridge University Press, 1994, p. 64 n. 4.

12   D.M. Armstrong, *A World of States of Affairs*, Cambridge University Press, 1997, p. 227.

Imagine a world containing ten different types of fundamental particles. Suppose further that the behaviour of particles in interactions depends upon the types of the interacting particles. Considering only interactions involving two particles, there are 55 possibilities with respect to the types of the two particles. Suppose that 54 of these possible interactions have been carefully studied, with the result that 54 laws have been discovered, one for each case, which are not interrelated in any way. Suppose finally that the world is sufficiently deterministic that, given the way particles of the types X and Y are currently distributed, it is impossible for them ever to interact at any time, past, present, or future. In such a situation it would seem very reasonable to believe that there is some *underived* law dealing with the interaction of particles of types X and Y.[13]

If there is such a law, and it consists in a relation between universals, they can only be ones in a Platonist heaven.

But Platonist heavens are very mysterious. God, as an intentional agent, could exercise power over the Universe in the way in which we exercise it over our bodies.[14] If there is a God, his causal agency is of a familiar type. But how do universals act on the world? This is a very mysterious causal relation between the non-spatio-temporal world and our world for which we have no analogue. Thus Lewis: 'How can the alleged lawmaker impose a regularity? Why can't we have N(F, G) and still have F's that are not G's.'[15]

If, despite these difficulties, we adopt a relation-between-universals theory, the question then is – if there is no God – why should there be any connections between universals at all, and why should there be universals instantiated frequently enough and the mathematical connections be sufficiently simple so as to yield discoverable regularities. There might be universals which were instantiated without bringing any other universals with them, so that there was no predictable effect of the instantiation. But on this account virtually all universals are connected to other universals. And there might be universals, but only ones of kinds instantiated once or twice in the history of the Universe, rather than ones like 'photon' or 'copper' which are instantiated often, and so can be used for useful prediction. And again, the mathematical connections between the universals – e.g. between the masses of bodies, their distance apart, and the gravitational attraction between – might be of such complexity as never to be inferable from past behaviour. Although *a priori* it is for reasons of simplicity more probable that there will be a Universe in which a few particular universals are instantiated, connected in a few particular simple ways, than that there will be a Universe in which a certain vast number of particular universals are connected in a particular complicated way, there are so many possible

---

13   Michael Tooley, 'The Nature of Laws', *Canadian Journal of Philosophy* 7(1977), 667-698. See p. 669.

14   Or rather, since we do this by exercising power over our brains, in the way in which we exercise power over our brains. In so doing, we normally think of the power over the brain only in terms of the effect which it causes. But clearly we could, and some people do, train themselves to produce brain states of a kind defined by their internal nature – e.g. to produce α-rhythms – and not in terms of the effects which they normally cause.

15   Op. cit., p. xii. A similar objection is raised in John Foster, 'Regularities, Laws of Nature, and The Existence of God', *Proceedings of the Aristotelian Society* 101 (2000-2001), pp. 145-161 – See pp. 154-156.

universals and kinds of connection between them, most of which will not yield discoverable laws, that my intuition is that there is a rather low probability that if there is no God, the Universe will evince discoverable regularities. Whereas, if there is a God, there is a considerable probability that he would cause the instantiation of a few universals connected in simple ways, if laws of nature consist in connections between universals, for the reasons given earlier. My intuition on the extent to which the simplicity of a theory makes for the prior probability of its truth derives from my assessment of the extent to which we allow it to play a role in determining the relative probability of scientific theories equally good at predicting the data.

However, the probability of the existence of God is in no way dependent on this 'intuition'. If you think that *a priori* simplicity makes for probability to a far greater extent than I have supposed, then you will indeed suppose that it is a priori probable that in a godless universe there will only be a few universals connected in simple ways. Still, that leaves a number of concrete entities (universals) and a number of connections between them. And if the simplicity of a supposition makes it as probable as we are supposing, then the simplicity of the supposition that there is a God will make it even more probable *a priori* that there is a God than that there are a few universals simply connected in a Godless Universe. For God is *one* personal being with infinite degrees of the properties which are essential to persons; and the notion of an infinite degree of some property is a simpler notion than that of a large finite degree of the property. (It is the notion of zero limits.) To be a person you need to have some power to perform intentional actions, and some knowledge of how to do them. God is supposed to have power and knowledge with zero limits. Persons have some degree of freedom as to which actions to do – God is supposed to have freedom with zero limits. The supposition that there is a God is thus simpler than the supposition that there are a few particular universals connected in particular ways. The more you suppose the relative simplicity of the Universe is to be expected if there is no God, the more you must suppose that the existence of God is to be expected *a priori*. And that will diminish the *a priori* probability that there is a Godless universe at all. So the more you expect a Godless universe to be orderly, the less you expect there to be a Godless universe at all. Intuitions stronger than mine about the extent to which simplicity is evidence of truth, make it *a priori* probable that there is a God and so make *a posteriori* arguments from the character of the Universe in favour of the existence of God otiose. So I revert to my 'intuition' that while a particular simpler theory is more probable than a particular complicated theory, we cannot claim that it is *a priori* probable (i.e. more probable than not) that a simple theory is the true one.

The alternative to thinking of the physical necessity involved in laws of nature as separate from the objects governed by it, is to think of it as a constitutive aspect of those objects. The way in which this is normally developed is what we may call the substances-powers-and-liabilities account of laws of nature. The 'objects' which cause are individual substances – this planet, those molecules of water. They cause effects in virtue of their powers to do so and their liabilities (deterministic or probabilistic) to exercise those powers under certain conditions. Powers and liabilities are thus among the properties of substances. Laws of nature are then just (logically) contingent regularities – not of mere spatio-temporal succession (as with Hume), but of causal succession, regularities in the causal powers (manifested and ummanifested) of substances of various kinds. That heated copper expands is a law is just a matter of every piece of copper having the causal power to expand, and the liability to exercise that power when heated. As a matter of contingent fact substances fall into kinds, such that all objects of the same kind have the same powers and liabilities. The powers and liabilities of large-scale things (lumps of copper) derive from the powers and liabilities of the small-scale things which compose them (atoms; and ultimately quarks, electrons etc). And all ultimate particulars have some powers and liabilities exactly the same as each other (e.g. the power to cause an effect proportional in a certain way to their mass, charge, spin etc, and the liability to exercise that under conditions varying with the mass, charge, spin etc, of other objects and fall into a few kinds whose members have all the same powers and liabilities as each other). This account of the ultimate determinants of what happens as merely substances and their causal powers and liabilities does provide explanation of what happens, and in familiar terms. (We ourselves have causal powers which we, unlike inanimate objects, can choose to exercise.) It was the way of explaining things familiar to the ancient and medieval world, before 'laws of nature' began to play their role in the sixteenth century. It was revived by Rom Harré and E.H. Madden in *Causal Powers*.[16] 'Laws of nature' were originally supposed to be God's laws for nature, and thus have their natural place in a theistic world-view. The naturalist would seem to me to have difficulty, as was illustrated earlier, in making sense of their operating without a lawgiver. He would do better to adopt the substances-powers-and-liabilities account; and the theist too, unless he is an occasionalist, had better – in my view – endow substances with powers and liabilities so that they act on their own, and think of God's 'laws' as determining which powers and liabilities substances have, and conserving those powers and liabilities in substances. On this account, causation is an essential component of laws rather than laws being an essential component of causation.[17]

The question then becomes – why do all substances have some powers and liabilities exactly the same as each other (e.g. the power to attract each other in accord with a force proportional to $mm'/r2$, and the liability always to exercise that power), and why in respect of other powers and liabilities do they fall into a small number of kinds (photons, protons etc). The answer provided by this model is in terms of ancestry. A substance has the powers and liabilities it does because it was produced by another substance exercising its power to produce a substance with just those powers and liabilities. If a proton is produced (together with an electron and an antineutrino) by the decay of a neutron, then the proton's powers and liabilities

---

16   Blackwell, 1975.

17   This allows the logical possibility of singular causation, that is causation which does not exemplify a pattern captured in a law. I have argued elsewhere that human agency is such causation. When, to take a simple example, I try to lift a weight and succeed, this cannot be represented as an instance of a lawlike succession in virtue of exemplifying some regularity of my trying lawlikely causing my success. This is because to try to do x just is to exert causal influence in favour of x occurring. 'Trying' isn't something separate from 'causing'; if it is successful, it just is causing. There is no law at work connecting independent states. Or so I have argued. See my 'The Irreducibility of Causation', *Dialectica* 51 (1997), 79-92.

are caused by the neutron, in virtue of its powers and liabilities. How improbable it will be *a priori* that all substances fall into kinds in the way described will depend on whether this process had a beginning, and of what kind that beginning was.

Suppose, first, that the Universe did have a beginning, a 'Big Bang' of some sort. There are two different kinds of theories of a beginning. The first state might have been a spatially extended state, or a spatially pointlike state. In the first case, we still have a lot of substances, no doubt crammed into a very small space, but all of them falling into a few kinds in virtue of their different powers to produce the few different kinds of substances we have now. In terms of the Big Bang model, there was not literally a singularity; it was just that as you approach the first instant in the temporally backward direction, you find denser and denser states; but it really all started in a very but not infinitely dense state. That state would then still consist of innumerable substances of very few kinds. The alternative first state would be a literally pointlike one. In the first instant on this theory, there was an unextended point, endowed with the power to decay into innumerable substances, of very few kinds, and liability to exercise that power at some time or other.

How is a scientific choice to be made between the two theories? We set up a physics which accounts in the simplest way for the present data. Is evolution from a point compatible with that theory? It is not if our theory does not allow infinitely dense matter, or the force necessary for expansion from an infinitely dense state. We then have the choice of complicating a physics to allow for this possibility, or not. A theory of the latter kind is going to be probable only if not too much complication is required.

What is the *a priori* probability of the Universe beginning uncaused by God in each of these alternative states? Clearly, if the first state was simply a very condensed version of our present state, there is still the vast coincidence of all the substances falling into few kinds having exactly the same powers and liabilities. Given theism, the coincidence is explained. Suppose now that science supports the theory that the Universe began at a point. What is the prior probability that if it did, it would begin with a power to produce the total regularity in the behaviour of observed substances which we find? There are many alternative powers and liabilities with which an initial singularity might be endowed. It might have no powers, or powers with no liability to exercise them unless interfered with, or merely the power and liability to keep itself in being, or the power and liability to produce other substances which themselves had no power to sustain themselves in being for long, or the power and liability to produce other substances which themselves would have all kinds of different and unconnected powers and liabilities. And so on. Which is the most probable *a priori*? Simplicity alone can determine this. My intuition here, parallel to my earlier intuition with respect to hypotheses about the instantiation of universals with certain connections and based on what I see as the weight which we give to simplicity in science, is that the most probable state is the zero state (no powers at all); but that a power and liability to produce objects all with the same particular powers (including powers to produce similar objects which would produce similar objects) and liabilities is more probable than any particular hypothesis of powers and liabilities to produce objects with chaotic and erratic powers. Yet, since there are so many ways of producing objects with chaotic and erratic powers, for each way of producing objects with all the same powers, there is a very low probability *a priori* that the singularity would have built into it the power to produce innumerable objects all with the same powers and liabilities to go on producing similar objects for billions of years so as to produce discoverable regularities. As before, if you give simplicity a much greater weight than I give it in determining prior probability, the need for *a posteriori* arguments for the existence of God begins to disappear. However, I suggest that the very low probability of the singularity having the character just described is not as low as the *a priori* probability of all of very many substances beginning their existence uncaused in a Godless universe with the same powers and liabilities. For the former involves a beginning from only one point-like substance. And so the naturalist should prefer a real to a nominal singularity if he can have it. (My suspicion is that he cannot – all matter-energy occupying an unextended point is, I suggest, not a possibility allowed by the current theory of matter-energy, and so not a state which we could justifiably postulate as the cause of the evolution of the Universe. But I could well be mistaken about this. And not an enormous amount turns on it.)

Suppose now that the Universe has an infinite age. The properties (of powers and liabilities) of every substance are then caused by those of a preceding substance. So there are substances with exactly the same such properties (including the power to produce substances of the existing kinds) because there always have been. But then *a priori* this is just as unlikely as that all the substances at an initial moment should have all the same powers and liabilities. A theistic explanation of all substances having all the same such properties will claim that God conserves substances with their properties from moment to moment – which he can do in virtue of his omnipotence – and which he does for the reasons described earlier.

I have been assuming so far that there is only one Universe. But there may be many universes. Our only grounds for believing that there are such will be either that this supposition is a consequence of the simplest explanation of how things are in our Universe, or that it is *a priori* probable. But here we come to an interesting disagreement about which kind of explanation would be the simplest explanation of how things are in our Universe. In my view, and in my view of what almost all scientists, detectives etc, have supposed, the simplest explanation is one which postulates as few entities as possible behaving in mathematically simple kinds of ways.[18] The most probable explanation of the data is the simplest one which yields the data with high probability. On that view of simplicity, our only grounds for believing that there are other universes would be if by extrapolating back from the present state of our Universe in accord with the mathematically simplest supposition about what are its laws, leads us to a state at which there was a Universe split, a state in which those laws will have dictated that another Universe would 'bud off' from our Universe. But in that case the other Universe would be governed by the laws which govern our Universe, and so we can consider the two universes (or however many universes we learn about) as one multiverse, and the whole preceding structure of argument gives the same results as before.

---

18   For a fuller account of what makes a scientific theory simple, see my *Epistemic Justification*, Clarendon Press, 2001, Chapter 4.

But it has been suggested that the simplest theory is the one expressible in the shortest number of computational syllables,[19] from which it follows that the simplest theory of universes (compatible with there being at least one universe) is the one which claims that all logically possible universes exist. This claim has been put forward by Max Tegmark,[20] but he does not draw out the full consequences of his bold claim. He discusses only universes governed by laws; but clearly the vast majority of logically possible universes are not law-governed, or – if they are law-governed – the laws are not simple. And he *assumes* that 'self-aware substructures', that is, in my terminology 'rational beings', are embodied. But since, in my view fairly clearly, rational beings may be disembodied, if we make Tegmark's assumptions, then it remains very improbable that rational beings such as ourselves should find ourselves embodied in a physical universe governed by simple laws. And, even if rational beings had to be embodied, we live in a Universe far more orderly than is needed for our continued existence for a few years. Beyond the area of, say, a small country the world might be totally chaotic; and what happened more than a few years ago might be undiscoverable. But as far as the telescope can reach and a long way back in history, our Universe is totally and discoverably orderly. This sort of Universe is not typical of the universes in which we could have existed (whatever our account of laws), and so *a priori* it is improbable that we would. But theism can explain why there is *so much* order – viz. we can progressively discover more and more order and extend our range of knowledge and control if we so choose – travel to distant planets and learn about our remote ancestors. I argued earlier that God has a reason to put us in a Universe like this.

So – even on Tegmark's (to my mind) totally mistaken understanding of simplicity, his 'simplest explanation' of the existence of our Universe is in fact very improbable, because on his account it is very improbable that we would find ourselves (as we do) in this Universe. But theism can explain why we are in a Universe with vast discoverable order. Hence I suggest that there is no good reason for believing in the existence of other universes, except perhaps ones governed by the same laws as our own. So it does not affect the issue of why things are law-governed if we suppose that there is more than one Universe. And I have argued that whether talk of 'laws' is talk of regular successions of events, of concrete entities determining the behaviour of substances, or of the powers and liabilities of substances, it is *a priori* improbable that a Godless Universe would be governed by simple laws, but there is quite a significant probability that a God-created Universe would be governed by simple laws. Hence the operation of laws of nature is evidence – one strand of a cumulative argument – for the existence of God.

---

19   R.J. Solomonoff, 'A formal Theory of Inductive Inference', *Information and Control* 7 (1964), 1-22.

20   Max Tegmark, 'Is "The Theory of Everything" merely the Ultimate Ensemble Theory?', *Annals of Physics* 270 (1998), 1-51.

Chapter 5

Where and How does God Speak? Faith, Reason and the Question of Criteria*

Alan J. Torrance

That the *recognition* of where and how God speaks is intrinsic to the Self-Communication of God belongs to the very heart of the Christian Gospel. Yet the history of theology has too often failed to recognize this. Indeed, the very suggestion continues to be regarded in some quarters as dangerously exclusivist and isolationist, if not sectarian. It will be the contention of this chapter that first, confusion on this matter places in question the very integrity and viability of the theological enterprise and second, clarity on this matter requires us to redress fundamental confusions in how we have treated the relationship between faith and reason.

The question 'Where and How does God speak?' is a question about criteria – that is, if it is not merely an invitation to list subjectively those places and ways in which one happens to think that God is speaking. To suggest that God speaks *here* or *there* and in *this* or *that* way is to adopt criteria. It is to endorse those specific critical controls underlying one's claims which are presumed in one's answer to the question: How and where does God speak? All truth-claims as to where, how and what God speaks seem to assume or presuppose further, logically prior, truth-claims. The suggestion that critical criteria are presupposed in such claims, however, is a seductive one. Their logical priority suggests some kind of historical priority – that they come first, that they are '*pre*-suppositions' of the recognition of revelation and thus that they must necessarily be *temporally* prior to the revelation event. If they are given in advance of the Self-Communication of God then we can assume that these criteria (with their truth claims) are 'prior givens'. To the extent that these criteria are assumed to be prior 'givens', they are 'assumed to be valid in advance of God's Self-disclosure and this assumption will, of course, be ratified by it. But the inescapable question that emerges from any reference to 'given' criteria is 'given by what or by whom?'. In other words, the question we have been set immediately becomes a question relating to these criteria, namely, 'Where and How are these criteria 'given'? Does 'given' mean 'given by our culture'? Or does it mean 'given by the language-games that constitute and condition our thinking', that is, the way we interpret, divide up and construct our world? Or does it mean 'given in our natures

---

* A condensed and revised version of this chapter first appeared in Paul J. Griffiths and R. Hütter (eds), *Reason and the Reasons of Faith* (T. and T. Clark International, 2005), pp. 27-52.

as rational and/or linguistic[1] and/or moral beings'? The critical question which then emerges here is whether what is 'given' can be false, can be distortive, whether our 'given' systems of processing, prioritizing and assessing can be assumed to be veridical – whether, that is, *they* are 'given' *by God*. If this is something we are entitled to assume, *from where the entitlement*?

It might appear that we are simply playing an infinite regress game of a kind that can never be resolved and therefore ought to be ignored. However, to assume that there is no resolution while continuing to make theological statements is, as a matter of fact, to assume a resolution, to stop the buck by making a fideistic commitment to some particular set of presuppositions. Christian revelation, I shall suggest, commits us unambiguously to the recognition that the buck does stop and must stop and that the question of criteria and suppositions begins in the irreducibly *ecclesial* event of God's Self-communication in and through the incarnate Logos recognized and affirmed by the reconciling presence of the Spirit. If this is not affirmed as the ground of theology, Christian thought can only undergo what Aristotle (and Lessing) term a *metabasis eis allo genos*, a transformation into something of a radically different kind. No other alternative is available to us. *Tertium non datur!*[2]

---

1   Cf. Noam Chomsky and Jerry Fodor's innatist concept of language – what Richard Rorty refers to as a 'wired-in language (and metalanguage) of thought'. The easy development from this to a rationalist, Cartesian epistemology is illustrated in Zeno Vendler's *Res Cogitans* (Ithaca, New York, 1972) in which he writes of our 'native ideas', 'As for the content of this native stock of concepts, we can at the present time do no more than make educated guesses. Yet, I think, the task of spelling it out in detail is not an impossible one: Aristotle, Descartes, Kant, and recently Chomsky have succeeded in marking out domains that must belong to this framework... There are, then, the "clear and distinct" ideas which lend intelligibility to the rest. They are "a priori" in origin and self-contained in their development: experience cannot change their content. No experience is relevant to one's idea of ... what it is to believe... what is truth... what is a person... If these ideas need clarification, the way to obtain it is to reflect on what we all implicitly know and show forth in the correct use of language...' pp. 140-141, (cited in Richard Rorty, *Philosophy and the Mirror of Nature*, Blackwell, Oxford, 1980, 251-252). The theological ramifications of such a position are clear!

2   A common tactic by which to take the edge off the challenge here is to reduce theological statement to amorphous abstraction such that it ceases to offend a wide variety of different criteria of assessment. The 'discipline' of theology tolerates here what no other academic institution or 'discipline' would. The reason why this is allowed to happen is not only that its subject-matter is itself deemed to be inherently and essentially amorphous but, worse, that it *requires* to be regarded as such in the name of the inclusivity of its object!

In other words, the epistemological implication of inclusivity becomes indiscriminate access! The political correctness that disallows one from questioning the authenticity of another's spirituality involves the refusal to question the theological claims of others *vis-à-vis* God – unless, of course, they are deemed to be 'exclusivist'. What should become clear, is that intrinsic to these suppositions is a host of complex truth claims and criteria – that the inclusive answer to the question 'Where and How does God speak?' is 'Here, There and Everywhere' or, 'In whatever ways you determine to be affirmative of your identity, spiritual insights, convictions, orientations etc.'. But how 'inclusive' is an approach whose truth-claims involve, for example, the *de facto* rejection that God is the *Ens concretissimum* and where God's Being is inseparable from God's Being-in-Act and Being-as-Word. Is it really 'inclusive' of the faith

The Epistemological Implications of Nicaea

I have suggested that it is a fundamental claim of Christian orthodoxy that *the conditions for the recognition and affirmation of Christian truth are* intrinsic *to the event of revelation.* In other words, to the extent that the Holy Spirit is the means of the perception of the revelation of God in Christ, the event of revelation includes within itself the essential grounds for the recognition of Christian truth. Its essential criterion, therefore, includes that specific self-authenticating perception that *is* the presence of the Spirit. It is thus inherent within the very nature of Christian revelation that it is neither anticipatable nor endorsable from any prior or independent set of conditions or foundations. It can neither be demonstrated nor affirmed, therefore, from any external Archimedean point.[3] The condition of the perception of the person of Christ, as God's inclusive and affirmative Word to humanity, is none other than the free and creative presence of God as the Holy Spirit. And it is for these reasons that Athanasius, in his *Letters to Serapion,* was so emphatic in stressing the epistemic significance of the Holy Spirit. Either we recognize the Spirit together with the Word as reconciling all things and joining and presenting all creation to the Father, or we are party to the 'irrational' (*alogistikos*),[4] to the 'unreason', to the fabulous invention (*muthoplastia*)[5] and false notions (*kakonoiai*)[6] which characterize the approaches of those who seek to interpret God's purposes from outside the context of this reconciliation. Those who hold such views cannot, therefore, be interpreted as being neutral but actively opposed to the Spirit (*pneumatomachountes*).[7]

The thrust of this position is that only God can reveal God to creatures who are alienated in their capacity to think through to the reality of God – *echthroi te dia-noia,* to use Paul's phrase. For this reason, theological *noein* requires the transformation (*metanoia*) by the Spirit of our *noein*. It requires a noetic transition or paradigm shift. Why? Because it cannot be generated by the subject from a standpoint within a foreign paradigm.[8] What is required is that we are reconciled with the 'Spirit of Sonship' who is the Spirit of Wisdom and Truth. The alternative to the reconciled

---

of Christians to evacuate God's concrete and ergo *eph'hapax* presence from all that the church determines to be the foundation of its existence and its *raison d'être*?

3   Cf. Fergus Kerr's critique of Karl Rahner where he draws on Wittgenstein and Heidegger in exposing the 'megalomania' inherent in the theological desire to find an 'Archimedean point'. 'Rahner Retrospective III: Transcendence or Finitude', in *New Blackfriars* 62 (September 1981), p. 378f.

4   St. Athanasius, *Letters to Serapion,* (trans., C.R.B. Shapland), Epworth, London, 1951, 147.

5   *Ibid.*

6   *Ibid.*, 106.

7   *Ibid.*, 147.

8   In Athanasius' words, matters of faith cannot be 'measured by human wisdom, but by the hearing of faith'. (105). What is being referred to here is not some irrational leap of faith, but a paradigmatic discrepancy between the two forms of perception. From within the new paradigm, unreconciled human wisdom is perceived to be in error.

objectivity which this brings is opposition – for Athanasius, indeed, the madness (*mania*) of those who are engrossed in themselves (*eis heautous straphentes*).[9]

That the underlying thrust of this argument is not an imposition on the New Testament witness is suggested, for example, in the account of Simon's recognition of Jesus as the Messiah in Matthew's Gospel (chapter 16). To offer second hand theories as to who Jesus is said to be is well within Simon's grasp but to answer the question 'Who do you say that I am?' demands an event of revelation which is epistemically (and thus ontologically) transformative. In response to Simon's recognition, identification and affirmation of God's presence in 'the Christ', Jesus comments first, that 'flesh and blood did not reveal this to you but my Father in heaven'. Second, Jesus renames Simon 'Peter' (Cephas). In sum, he is now reconstituted as participant within a new humanity in union with the Second Adam, and ergo participant within the *ekklesia* – the presence on earth of the Kingdom of God, the New Creation. Hans Urs von Balthasar comments on this text, 'Simon the fisherman, before his meeting with Christ, however thoroughly he might have searched within himself, could not possibly have found a trace of Peter... In the form "Peter" Simon was capable of understanding the word of Christ, because the form itself issued from the word and was conjoined with it.'[10]

Second, there is the very extensive utilization of the eye/sight and ear/hearing metaphors throughout Matthew, Mark, Luke-Acts, John and the Pauline corpus – the unambiguous thrust of these is that we require to be *given* the eyes to see as also the ears to hear. Revelation involves and includes this provision.

Third, other metaphors in the Pauline material speak of a *metamorphosis* of our minds for the sake of the *discernment* of truth – the reconciliation of our minds from a state of epistemic alienation whereby they cease to be schematized (*suschēmatizesthai*) by the secular world.[11]

And, finally, this emphasis on an epistemic *metanoia* as intrinsic to the event of revelation and the *sine qua non* of veridical perception clearly underlies the thinking of the author of the fourth gospel. Nothing less is required, indeed, than that we be reconstituted 'from above' or 'born again'. Unfortunately, the metaphorical force of such language has not only been weakened but effectively destroyed by approaches which suggest either that we can bring this state about by an act of decision or that this has to do with moral self-transformation. The force of these metaphors seems to be to suggest that God-talk (*theologein*) finds its ultimate grounds in the recognition of the *Logos theou*, the Word of God, and that this takes place in and through the reconciling, indeed, reconstitutive presence of the Spirit of God. Such perception does not, therefore, result from a natural evolution of processes immanent within the self and is not grounded in prior (innate and veridical) epistemic conditions and propensities. It requires a paradigmatic reorientation of our whole apperception. It involves a transformative reschematization of our epistemic affiliations and allegiances

---

9   *Ibid.*, 151. For Athanasius, the unwarranted projection of creaturely self-understandings on to the transcendent is a form of insanity. It is this which characterizes the method of the 'Arian madmen' (*op. cit.*, 147).

10   Hans Urs von Balthasar, *Prayer,* S.P.C.K., London, 1973, 48-49.

11   Romans 12:2.

– the reconfiguring of our epistemic base through the creative presence of the Spirit. As von Balthasar's comments suggest, this involves an element of discontinuity (a shift) which means that *prospectively*, such a perception is unanticipatable. At the same time, however, it denotes *retrospectively* an event which constitutes a radical fulfilment in transformation – and thereby a profound *continuity*.

In sum, the recognition and perception of God's presence in Christ seems to be conceived to be the result of an event of paradigmatic *metanoia*, transformation (*metamorphosis*[12]), reschematization and reconciliation – and not, indeed, one that can be generated by the knowing subject off his or her own bat. For the same reasons, the new paradigm is not one that can be appreciated from within the frame of reference of the Greek mind for which its affirmations are folly. As to the goal of this? It is summed up in the expression *logikon latreian* – rational participation in the mind of Christ, in the Son's epistemic and, indeed, semantic (rhematic[13]) communion with the Father.

In short, as in the case of the hackneyed tale of the traveller to Connemara, the Body of Christ and the Kingdom of God are not places to which we can plot a continuous journey from some external or foreign point of reference.[14] Providing reasons for the faith that is in one (which is integral to the theological task), therefore, does not and cannot mean providing rationalistic demonstrations which plot any such direct route. The supposition of so much Christian apologetics, as also of Christianity's critics, that 'reason' offers occupancy of some Archimedean country – and whose occupants can rest confident in the inherent reliability of immanent truth criteria – would appear to be at odds with the Gospel witness to the extent that at its heart is a transformed and all-transforming event of recognition.

The Timeless Challenge of the Socratic. Criterial Immanentism and the Pursuit of the 'Given'

Through the argumentation of the agnostic Johannes Climacus, Søren Kierkegaard sought to articulate how what we shall refer to as 'criterial immanentism' inevitably collapses revelation into a form of self-knowledge (the Socratic *Gnothi seauton!*). I should now like to consider two related case studies which have not only been highly influential in their impact on the shape and direction of contemporary theology but which illustrate the inevitability with which criterial immanentism translates theological statements into anthropological statements or, indeed, autobiographical statements.

The developments leading to David Strauss's hermeneutics and introduction of 'myth theory' are too well-documented to require reiteration in any detail here.[15]

---

12 Cf. Romans 12:2. Given that we are not to be schematized by this world, our thinking requires to be reschematized in and through our being brought to be '*en Christo*'.

13 Cf. John 17:8. The Son gives us the '*rhemata*' (words/participative speech-acts) which the Father gave him.

14 A local inhabitant was once asked the way to Connemara. The reply ran, 'If I were going to Connemara, I wouldn't be going from here!'

15 For a recent, scholarly analysis see Timothy J. Lawson, 'The Influence of Benedict D. Spinoza's Philosophy on the Theology of David Friedrich Strauss' Ph. D. thesis, King's

Suffice to say, behind Strauss's theological approach stands a) the epistemology of Leibniz with its dichotomization between necessary truths of reason (to which epistemic access is *a priori*) and contingent truths (known by sense perception) together with b) Spinoza's emphasis that the truth of a historical narrative cannot provide knowledge of God, which derives alone from general ideas possessing epistemic certainty. These provided, in turn, the background to Lessing's famous insistence that events and truths belong to radically different and logically unconnected categories – and which led, in turn, to the devaluation of the significance of the historical and 'contingent' in favour of necessary truths of reason. In consequence, theology came to be perceived as belonging to the domain of the *a priori* determinations of 'reason' together with all that 'reason' counts as its dictates.[16] The consequence of these developments was a renewed concern to reformulate Christian doctrine in the light of the immanent predeterminations and confident prescriptions of the sphere of subjective reasoning.[17] That the influence of idealism in the theological sphere thrived in this climate is evidenced by the natural synthesis in Strauss' methodology of the influences of Leibniz and Spinoza, on the one hand, and Hegelian idealism on the other – Strauss was, of course, a student of the Hegelian F.C. Baur and went on to study under Hegel himself. These influences led him to interpret the primary interest of the Gospels as lying in the evidence they provided of the workings of consciousness in the sphere of religious experience.[18] Utilizing Hegel's concept of 'unconscious invention', the Gospels were interpreted as poetic evidence of the 'purely human desire to realise the immanent goal of Spirit in its journey toward the Hegelian Being-in-and-for-itself'.[19] The Gospels came to be interpreted in terms of an assumed synthesis or coincidence of the *human* idea, reason and spirit with *God* who, in turn, was identified as the absolute Idea, as absolute Reason and Spirit. With the benefit of historical hindsight it is clear how dangerous the resulting transfer of christological and theological attributes on to the human race, as advocated in the famous dogmatic conclusions of his critical examination of the life of Jesus, can be. That this follows naturally from the immanentism which characterizes (or sustains) idealist approaches should be equally plain.[20]

College London, 1994.

16   Cf. *Über den Beweis des Geistes und der Kraft*, 1777 in which we find his famous affirmation that 'Accidental truths of history can never become the proof of necessary truths of reason'.

17   This can be seen in Lessing's early paper (c. 1753) 'The Christianity of Reason' (*Das Christentum der Vernunft*) which foreshadowed the speculative restatements of the doctrine of the Trinity using Leibnizian ideas in *The Education of the Human Race* (*Die Erziehung des Menschengeschlechts*), 1780. Cf. Henry Chadwick, *Lessing's Theological Writings*, Palo Alto, California, 1956 and also his article 'Lessing, Gotthold Ephraim' in Paul Edwards (ed.) *Encyclopaedia of Philosophy*, Vol 4, Collier and Macmillan, New York, 1967, 443ff.

18   Paul Edwards, Vol. 8, 25.

19   *Ibid.*, 26.

20   The following quotations are taken from the section entitled 'Dogmatic Import of the Life of Jesus' in *The Life of Jesus Critically Examined* (*Das Leben Jesu kritisch bearbeitet*) (trans. George Eliot, London, 1848) 779-780 (italics mine).

Thus by a higher mode of argumentation, from the *idea* of God and man in their reciprocal relation, the truth of the conception which the church forms of Christ appears to be confirmed... here, the veracity of the history is deduced from the truth of those conceptions. That which is rational is also real... Proved to be an idea of reason, the unity of the divine and human nature must also have an historical existence.

But does this, Strauss asks, mean that we must attach exclusive value to that particular piece of history associated with the life of Jesus?

This is indeed *not* the mode in which Idea realizes itself; it is not wont to lavish all its fullness on one *exemplar*, and be niggardly towards all others – to express itself perfectly in that one individual, and imperfectly in all the rest: it rather loves to distribute its riches among a multiplicity of exemplars which reciprocally complete each other – in the alternate appearance and suppression of a series of individuals. And is this no true realization of the idea? Is not the idea of the unity of the divine and human natures a real one in a far higher sense, when I regard the whole race of mankind as its realization, than when I single out one man as such a realization? Is not incarnation of God from eternity, a truer one than an incarnation limited to a particular point of time?

He then summarizes as follows:

This is the key to the whole of Christology, that, as subject of the predicate which the church assigns to Christ, we place, instead of an individual, an idea... In an individual, a God-man, the properties and functions which the church ascribes to Christ contradict themselves; in the idea of the race, they perfectly agree. Humanity is the union of the two natures – god become man, the infinite manifesting itself in the finite, and the finite spirit *remembering* its infinitude; it is the child of the visible Mother and the invisible Father, Nature and Spirit; it is the worker of miracles, in so far as in the course of human history the spirit more and more completely subjugates nature, both within and around man, until it lies before him as the inert matter on which he exercises his active power; it is the sinless existence, for the course of its development is a blameless one, pollution cleaves to the individual only, and does not touch the race or its history. It is Humanity that dies, rises and ascends to heaven, for from the negation of its phenomenal life there ever proceeds a higher spiritual life... This alone is the absolute sense of Christology... The phenomenal history of the individual, says Hegel, is only a starting point for the mind.[21]

The affirmation of the veridical status of 'rational' criteria immanent within the mind can do no other than interpret the history of Jesus, together with all other history, as exemplifying these prior suppositions which are absolute. The result is inevitably none other than a selective process of value-transfer from Jesus (or whoever else is deemed as exemplifying the criteria one applies) to the human race as a whole (or as one thinks it should be). The obligatory conclusion is the ascension and deification of the universal (humanity as a whole) and the denigration of the particular, the material and the 'phenomenal' (the spatio-temporal). The critical control on the process is *anamnesis* – our 'recalling' our infinitude/transcendent

---

21   Whether Hegel would have been happy with Strauss's interpretation of his thought is a matter for debate. There is clearly, however, more than sufficient continuity to illustrate the point we wish to make here.

capacities – and our criteria are those ideas immanent within the human spirit which are deemed 'eternal'.

Strauss's approach exemplifies how the supposition of 'criterial immanence' inevitably leads to the material identification of God's Self-communication with the universalization of our own interpretative criteria and self-understandings.[22] The theological ratification of our criteria identifies self-knowledge with knowledge of the divine, that is, the universal, the 'rational', the timeless, the immaterial. Given that the historical (the spatio-temporal) can do no more than exemplify, only one response to the Where question is possible. 'Where' God speaks is answered exclusively in terms of that which is assumed to be universally immanent.

Neo-Kantian Immanentism and the Transfer of the 'Given' to Thought Itself

A further illustration of precisely this dynamic (and the idealist agenda in which it was couched) may be found in the thought of the so-called 'existentialist' Rudolf Bultmann who had such a major impact on theology in the 1960's and 1970's.

In his own lucid summary of his theology written toward the end of his career, *Jesus Christ and Mythology*, Bultmann begins his exposition of 'modern' Biblical interpretation[23] by emphasizing the extent to which exegesis is always guided by principles and conceptions which act as presuppositions. Accordingly, he asks 'Which are the adequate presuppositions?'[24] or again, 'which is the adequate method, which are the adequate conceptions?'. His answer is defined in terms of the '"life-relation", which we have in advance'[25] to the subject-matter (*Sache*) of the text. It is this which provides the prior understanding (*Vorverständnis*) 'from which our questions and our conceptions arise',[26] this is to be interpreted in the light of our prior 'knowledge of God in advance'. The human being, he argues, 'has a relation to God in his search for God, conscious or unconscious. Man's life is moved by the search for God because it is always moved, consciously or unconsciously, by the question about his own personal existence. The question of God and the question of myself are identical.'[27]

Here, again, an affirmation of theological criteria as immanent within us is seen not simply to be a matter of merely methodological import but one which concerns the 'matter' (*Sache*) of theology. As Bultmann comments, 'to understand human existence in its relation to God can only mean to understand my personal existence...'[28] It is this element, together with his reduction of consideration of divine action to 'the meaning of God as acting' – that 'I cannot speak of God's action in

---

22   It is not surprising that Strauss's *Das Leben Jesu kritisch bearbeitet* would so influence Feuerbach in his concern to explore further human consciousness and the psychological mechanisms underlying myth-making.

23   Rudolf Bultmann, *Jesus Christ and Mythology*, S.C.M., London, 1960, 45ff.

24   *Ibid.*, 49.

25   *Ibid.*

26   *Ibid.*

27   *Ibid.*, 53.

28   *Ibid.*, 58.

general statements; I can speak only of what He does here and now with me, of what He speaks here and now to me'[29] which has led to D.M MacKinnon's famous comment that Bultmann can do no other than translate theological statements into autobiographical statements. In other words, despite his genuine concern to speak of the otherness of God and the divine Address from beyond, his underlying methodology ('You obtain the conceptions from your own psychical life'[30]) means that he fails sufficiently to free himself from the Socratic insistence on the primacy of self-knowledge.[31]

But is this existentialism? Certainly, Heidegger saw existential phenomenology as grounded in analysis of the particular '*existenziell*' understanding constitutive of the individual Dasein – suggesting that the self-relation constituted the essential context of phenomenological 'dis-covery' (*a-letheia*).[32] Moreover, as the *Cartesian Meditations* of Edmund Husserl (to whom Heidegger's *Being and Time* was dedicated) make clear, the Heideggerian phenomenology which so influenced Bultmann, to the extent that it is grounded in the self-relation can be interpreted as a 'higher order' Cartesianism.[33] However, it is Roger Johnson's analysis of the background of Bultmann's thought which most effectively exposes the idealist roots of Bultmann's programme of demythologization in Marburg Neo-Kantianism and it is his analysis which I should like to consider briefly as illustrating the methodological challenge and reach of the 'Socratic'.[34]

During Bultmann's formative years in Marburg (first as a student and then as professor), the university was, to no small extent, committed across faculty divides to Neo-Kantian philosophy.[35] The essential thrust of this was articulated in the journal of the Marburg school which was launched by Cohen and Natorp with the express

---

29   *Ibid.*, 66.

30   *Ibid.*, 50.

31   Cf. *ibid.*, 59 where he argues that 'the acknowledgement that I cannot find God by looking at or into myself' is itself 'the expression of my personal knowledge of myself'.

32   'Dasein always understands itself in terms of its existence... Only the particular Dasein decides its existence... The understanding of oneself which leads along this way we call "existentiell" (*existenziell*). (*Being and Time,* eng. trans. John Macquarrie and Edward Robinson, S.C.M., London, 1962, 33). For his discussion of *aletheia* see, *ibid.,* 56-57.

33   See Heidegger's discussion 'The Concept of Phenomenon' (*ibid.*, 51-56) in relation to his discussion of existential analysis.

34   In the following section I am drawing both on Roger Johnson's *The Origins of Demythologising. Philosophy and Historiography in the Theology of Rudolf Bultmann*, E.J. Brill, Leiden, 1974 and A.C. Thiselton's *The Two Horizons: New Testament Hermeneutics and Philosophical Description with special reference to Heidegger, Bultmann, Gadamer and Wittgenstein*, Paternoster, Exeter, 1980 as also on Lewis White Beck's excellent discussion of Neo-Kantianism in Paul Edwards, Vol. 5, 468 ff. Unfortunately, there is comparatively little written in English on this extremely important and influential philosophical school.

35   This is not to imply that Bultmann was explicitly and consistently committed to this philosophy. It is rather to suggest that he had absorbed its framework of thinking and its essential categories – as Johnson, Thiselton and others have shown. Paradoxically, it is the fact that Bultmann was not a philosopher, that he was not consistent and that he really wrestled with the tension between what he wished to affirm as a Christian theologian and what he thought he could affirm with intellectual and academic integrity that makes him so

aim of pursuing the transcendental method even further than Kant himself.[36] To this end Cohen offered a determined critique of Kant's 'givens'. 'Here is the fundamental weakness of Kant: that thinking has its beginning in something outside of itself. We begin with thinking itself. Thought does not need to have its origins outside of itself.'[37] As evidence for this he set out to expound the mathematical differential as the necessary device for the creation of nature *qua* object of possible experience concluding that the 'mathematical generation of motion (by the integration of the derivative) and thereby nature itself is the triumph of pure thought.' As Lewis White Beck comments, 'Cohen saw in the method of the calculus a paradigm of the category of origin (*Ursprung*) and the logical process of production (*Erzeugung*) to which every fact owes its reality; that is, its position in a logically necessary scheme'.[38] Consequently, 'through the work of thought on its own materials, Cohen believed he could dispense with all independent "givens" in knowledge. Nothing is given (*gegeben*)... Fact is that which is completely determined by thought. The thing-in-itself is not a thing at all. It does not exist, but is only a thought of a limit (*Grenzbegriff*) to our approach to a complete determination of things as they are; that is, as they would fully satisfy systematic thought.'[39] For Cohen, 'Only thinking may produce that which may be regarded as Being (*Sein*).'[40]

The 'given' now ceases to be the 'given for thought' or the 'conditioned by thought' and becomes thought itself. As Ernst Cassirer was later to describe his teacher, he was 'one of the most resolute Platonists that has ever appeared in the history of philosophy'.[41] What soon becomes clear is that the effect of Cohen's panlogism is the transformation of Kantian idealism into a form of Hegelianism.[42] In the light of Johnson's penetrating analysis of the Neo-Kantian influence on Bultmann, we see that the philosophical background to Bultmann's programme of demythologization

---

interesting. For others, like Karl Jaspers, this inconsistency is simply a cause of frustration and much rude comment – as found, for example in his essay entitled 'Myth and Religion'!

Because Bultmann confines philosophy to one book by Heidegger, and, as I suspect, misunderstands that book when he emphasizes its "scientific", objective, scholastic aspect, he in effect cuts himself off from all philosophy. His writings reveal this in other ways as well. Whenever Bultmann refers to the history of philosophy in his studies, he is concerned with statements that can be quoted with the superficial correctness of historical data; he is not concerned with philosophy itself. *Kerygma and Myth*, Vol. II, 138.

36 In launching the journal they wrote, 'Whoever is bound to us stands with us on the foundation of the transcendental method'. 'Philosophy, to us, is bound to the fact of science, as this elaborates itself. Philosophy, therefore, to us is the theory of the principles of science and therewith of all culture.' *Philosophische Arbeiten,* Vol. 1, No. 1, 1906 (cited by Beck in Edwards, Vol. 5, 470).

37 Accordingly, 'thought may regard as "given" (*gegeben*) only that sort of thing which it may discover itself Cohen, *Logik der reinen Erkenntniss*, Berlin, 1902, 68.

38 Beck, *op. cit.*, 471.

39 *Ibid.*

40 Cohen, *Logik der reinen Erkenntnis*, Berlin, 1902, 67 (cited in Johnson, 48). The effect of this movement was that the word '*Objekt*' would have less and less prominence and the concepts of '*objektivieren*', '*objektivierend*' and '*Objektivierung*' would take its place.

41 Cited by Beck, 471.

42 Cf. Beck, *ibid.*

parallels significantly the background and context of Strauss's introduction and promulgation of 'myth theory' within the field of New Testament research. The philosophical background in both cases is idealism – indeed, remarkably similar forms of idealism.

The following quotation from Natorp summarizes the Gospel of Neo-Kantianism and anticipates something of the impact it would have on derivative theological debates.

> In the beginning was the act, the creative act of the formation of the object, in which alone man built up himself, his human nature, and as he objectified himself in this, the stamp of his spirit was fundamentally and in a completely unified manner impressed upon his world. Rather, a whole world of such worlds, all of which he may call his own. The creative ground of such a deed as the formation of the object is the law: that fundamental law which one still designates as *Logos, Ratio, Vernunft.*[43]

As Johnson's extended analysis leads him to conclude, the influence of the Marburg school led Bultmann to interpret knowledge as 'objectification in accordance with the principle of law'. Indeed, law provided the norm in the assessment of all cultural phenomena.[44] The culture of the primitive-religious period was thus to be interpreted precisely in terms of the objectifying activity of Spirit. The *knowing subject* requires to be conceived, whatever the field of knowledge, not as an historical individual but as *Geist* – where *Geist* is a logical ideal paralleling mathematical *Vernunft*.[45] For the Neo-Kantians, as also for Bultmann, therefore, not only the 'natural sciences' (*Naturwissenschaften*) but the human sciences (*Geisteswissenschaften*) required to be interpreted in terms of the law-governed process of objectification.

But this dimension of Neo-Kantianism posed a problem. What was to be done with those 'realities' which could not be 'objectified', namely, the self conceived as an individual 'I' and, indeed, God and, for Bultmann, the divine Address? The clear implication of the Kantian system for interpreting God was anticipated in Kant's own comment, 'God is not a Being outside me, but merely a thought within me'.[46] So what could Neo-Kantianism offer religion and the spiritual realm of the self given its determination to rid the realm of thought of any 'givens' for thought? The answer is presented as 'a new kind of *Gegenstand*' – a '*Gegensatz* against the structure of the whole system',[47] namely, the category of the individual (*Individuum*). This recognized the fact that a) we need to make room for the life of the individual as

---

43   Paul Natorp (a quotation from August Messer, *Die Philosophie der Gegenwart*, 1920, 106, cited in Johnson, 48). The primary thrust of this quotation, when abstracted from the constraint of 'law', illustrates how Kantianism opened the door to post-modernism, together with the individualistic isolationism that attends so much of it!

44   Roger Johnson, *The Origins of Demythologising*, 1974, 53.

45   As Bochenski describes the knowing subject of Neo-Kantianism, 'All that belongs to the body, to the particularity of the self is excluded. What remains is consciousness pure and simple, which has no more reality than a mathematical point.' M. Bochenski, *Contemporary European Philosophy*, 1956, 92.

46   *Opus Postumum*, Kant's handschriftlicher Nachlaß (Berlin, 1936) Vol. 8, p. 145 (cited in Dalferth, *Theology and Philosophy*, 166).

47   Natorp, *Religion innerhalb der Grenzen der Humanität*, J.C.B. Mohr, Leibzig, 1894, 59, cited by Johnson, 66.

a participant within the spheres of art, literature[48] and religion; and b) as Natorp emphasized, it is axiomatic that we must not objectify the 'I'.[49] Consequently, there emerged a new kind of dualism between two spheres: that of the *Individuum* – conceived significantly as the sphere of *Religion* – on the one hand; and that of the objective (*objektive Gestaltung*), the rational (law-governed reason), on the other. These were to constitute two modes of reality qualitatively distinct from each other and therefore not analysable within one mode of philosophical analysis.

The resulting dualism led to an irreducible dichotomy between non-objective (that is, 'non-objectified') feeling or experience (*Gefühl* or *Erlebnis*) or 'faith' on the one hand, and objective knowledge (cognitive perception) on the other. Revelation and divine address were located accordingly within the former and thus within the sphere of the *Individuum*. Why? Because neither God nor God's Word of Address may be regarded as 'generated' or 'produced' by the processes of objectification in accordance with law. The consequence of this for Bultmann's programme of demythologization was his emphasis on the sphere of *Existenz* as the location of the divine Address together with his non-cognitive concept of *Erlebnis* and faith, on the one hand and his endorsement of the laws of objectification (the generation of objects), reason, science and the modern world-view on the other – leading to the dualist dialectic and theology of paradox at the core of his theology. The sphere of *Erlebnis* could not be conceived as a sphere of objective knowing since that which is *known* can only denote that which is *objectified* in accordance with the laws of thought. It is this leads to the paradox whereby faith 'understands'[50] an event or facet of reality in a manner incompatible with objective, scientific knowledge of that same reality. Faith 'understands' an action to be free, for example, when it is known to be causally determined – since every event is necessarily objectified in accordance with the universally determining laws of thought. As should be plain, Bultmann's view that the 'modern' or 'scientific' world-view *requires* that reality be perceived as a closed, causal, law-governed continuum is in actual fact the product of Neo-Kantian epistemology.

---

48 'We are the heirs of Goethe as well as of Kant', Natorp, *Religion innerhalb der Grenzen der Humanität,* 59.

49 As Cohen had argued 'the individual appears to contradict every system, every connection, and every relation'. He continues, 'What is fundamental to the understanding of the individual is the isolation of the individual from any system of connections in which the *Gegenstand* might be considered'. Cohen, *Logik der reinen Erkenntnis,* 300-301 (cited in Johnson, 67).

It is here also that we see the remarkable parallels between Cohen and Natorp and the phenomenological method of Husserl as it was taken over by Heidegger. Beck writes, 'Just as Cohen's antipsychologistic panlogism brought him close to Husserl's *Logische Untersuchungen,* Natorp's linking of psychology and panlogism brought him close to Husserl's *Ideen*; and it is easy to see how Nicolai Hartmann, Natorp's pupil, could move over into the phenomenological camp...' *ibid.*, 471. In short, Bultmann's synthesis of Marburg Neo-Kantianism and Heideggerian phenomenology was a quite natural one.

50 One wonders what can be meant by 'understand'. Is our 'understanding' not similarly conditioned by the laws of thought as these determine the nature of reality?

It is against this background that the following pivotal statements in *Jesus Christ and Mythology* require to be interpreted: 'our relation to the world as believers is paradoxical' in that whereas, I see 'worldly events as linked by cause and effect not only as a scientific observer but also in my daily living' which means 'there remains no room for God's working', 'faith "nevertheless" understands as God's action here and now an event which is completely intelligible in the natural or historical connection of events'.[51] That the same dualistic philosophy shaped his conclusions in the field of ethical interpretation (in accordance with the laws of practical reason) is made plain elsewhere: 'The pious man may wish to attribute the rational law of his conscience to God. That, however, does not change the fact that, in the sphere of reason, God does not speak to him.'[52]

It is significant to note here, with A.C. Thiselton,[53] how the individualistic understanding of living by faith in contrast to living under law inherent in nineteenth-century Lutheranism fused with the parallel Neo-Kantian dualism between a) the 'open' realm of the *Individuum* and b) the *Gesetzlichkeit* of rational and ethical knowledge. In short, the Lutheran faith-works or grace-law dichotomy, grounded as it was in a misconstrual of Judaism, the nature and the function of the law, and the tension between Judaism and Paul[54] substantially strengthened the appeal of Neo-Kantianism. This is made apparent in Bultmann's comment, 'Our radical attempt

---

51 *Jesus Christ and Mythology*, 65. He adds that what he means by the 'nevertheless' (the German *dennoch* of Psalm 73:23) parallels Paul Tillich's 'in spite of'.

The underlying problems and inconsistencies are widely discussed and, interestingly, most vehemently by those to the 'left' of Bultmann (Jaspers and Buri, for example). Karl Jaspers comments, 'Bultmann speaks neither as the nihilistic spellbinder nor as the authentic man of faith. He speaks as a scientist, and his intentions are of the best. But because he advances theological propositions in the name of "abstract scientific consciousness", steeped as he is in false notions of modern science and misled by his belief in an allegedly scientific philosophy, his words lack palpable conviction.' 'Myth and Religion' in *Kerygma and Myth*, Vol. II, 157.

David Fergusson offers further perceptive criticism of Bultmann's interpretation of science – albeit with a more Anglo-Saxon flavour! 'The scientist does not make the assumption that God cannot intervene in the course of nature. The only assumption the scientist makes is that, in the search for the natural explanation of types of event, considerations of divine intervention are largely irrelevant. This resembles more a working assumption about the proper domain of natural science than a philosophical conviction about the impossibility of miracles.' He then adds, 'Bultmann's tendency to overlook this reflects his rather Kantian isolation of the self from the social and natural world'. *Bultmann*, Chapman, London, 1992, 122. (Cited by Anthony C. Thiselton in the context of his highly significant analysis of the influence of Kant on the development of Postmodernism, *Interpreting God and the Postmodern Self: On Meaning, Manipulation and Promise*, T&T Clark, Edinburgh, 1995, 102.)

52 *Religion und Kultur*, col. 420 (Johnson, 62).

53 See Thiselton's impressive analysis of this in the subsection of *The Two Horizons* entitled, 'Bultmann's Fusion of Neo-Kantian Epistemology with Nineteenth-Century Lutheranism: Objectification in Accordance with Law', pp. 212-217.

54 This facet of Lutheranism has now been shown by E.P. Sanders and others to involve a misconstrual of Judaism and an inappropriate polarization between Judaism and the Gospel. See, for example, Sanders's critique of Bultmann's use of the 'nevertheless' in interpreting Paul's concept of the law in *Paul, the Law, and the Jewish People,* S.C.M., London, 1985,

to demythologise the New Testament is in fact a perfect parallel to St. Paul's and Luther's doctrine of justification by faith alone apart from works of the law. Or rather, it carries this doctrine to its logical conclusion in the field of epistemology. Like the doctrine of justification it destroys every false security... Security can be found only by abandoning all security.'[55] 'There is no difference', he insists, 'between security based on good works and security built on objectifying knowledge.'[56]

It is no surprise to find that the 'paradoxical identity'[57] which characterizes the life of faith for Bultmann echoes the paradoxical nature of existence as it was conceived by Kant – what led Kant, indeed, to be interpreted by Hans Vaihinger as an 'as if' (*als ob*) philosopher.[58] We live and act *as if* we are free despite the fact that scientific reason dictates that this cannot be the case. In direct parallel to this, Bultmann concludes *Jesus Christ and Mythology* by citing the Pauline exhortations to live 'as though...'[59] and then he adds, 'Let those who have the modern world-view live *as though* they had none'.[60]

Summary

As we saw earlier, the idealist influence on Strauss led to the unqualified transfer of Messianic predicates to the human race, to humanity *per se*. 'It is Humanity that dies, rises, and ascends...' In the negation of the phenomenal, the particular and the individual there proceeds higher spiritual life – progress towards 'union with the infinite spirit of the heavens'. In the consequent liberation from the individual and the material and the resultant subjugation of nature is to be found nothing less than perfection. The immanent progress and ascension of humanity (the 'race') is interpreted as the sinless appropriation of divinity – an immanentist *theosis*. What is

---

footnote 48, 119-120. 'The present point is that, when Paul stated the "nevertheless" (nevertheless still obligated), the law functioned as law' (120).

55   'Bultmann replies to his Critics' in *Kerygma und Myth 1*, pp. 210-211 (cited in Thiselton, 213).

56   *Jesus Christ and Mythology*, 84.

57   'Faith insists not on the direct identity of God's action with worldly events, but, if I may be permitted to put it so, on the paradoxical identity which can be believed only here and now against the appearance of non-identity' – that is, what requires to be understood 'as a link in the chain of the natural course of events', *Jesus Christ and Mythology*, 62. Cf. John Macquarrie's famous statement of the dilemma posed by Bultmann's paradox in the opening paragraph of *The Scope of Demythologising. Bultmann and his Critics* (S.C.M., London, 1960) where he describes a car heading for 'a precipitous fall into an abyss of some sort'. 'Almost at the last moment, as it appears, he has pulled strongly on his wheel, the car has slewed violently round, and instead of going over the dip it now follows a different road in quite a new direction' (11).

58   Hans Vaihinger, *Philosophy of the As-If.* S. Körner describes Vaihinger as 'one of the most acute and careful of Kant's commentators'. S. Körner, *Kant*, Penguin, Harmondsworth, 1955, 34.

59   *Jesus Christ and Mythology*, 85.

60   *Ibid.* (italics mine). Cf. Schubert Ogden's related critique of Bultmann's distinction between a 'possibility in principle' and a 'possibility in fact' in *Christ without Myth. A Study based on the Theology of Rudolf Bultmann*, Harper, New York, 1961, 111ff.

illustrated by this is the extent to which a confusion of the human and the divine is the inevitable outcome of 'criterial immanentism'.

In the case of Bultmann, his admirable but tragic struggle to sustain a theology of revelation which spoke of God in personal terms in the context of an essentially idealist interpretation of epistemic criteria led him into irreconcilable ambiguity and dualism. The realms of knowledge, ethics, culture as also the human and natural sciences were interpreted in terms of the immanent processes of objectification and, thus, the constructs of categories immanent within the self. Not only the 'objective' but also the 'subjective' were interpreted accordingly in terms of the constructs and outworkings of the laws of thought – the processes of objectification and subjectification.[61] The resulting postulation of the realm of the individual (identified as the sphere of religion) had the effect of further compounding confusion between the divine and the human – the question of God and the question of myself become identified and the Word of God that occupies this procrustean bed constitutes neither knowledge of God[62] nor knowledge of the contingent, created order. Consequently, the very concept of the Self-communication of God necessarily falls casualty to the dualistic dichotomy between two controlling givens: a) *Thought – objectification* (the construction of the objective) in accordance with *law* (the eternal immanent principles of thought governing the processes of objectification); and b) *Individual existence* – where God is 'given' neither to thought nor to human knowing nor to ethical perception but to some supposed domain of non-cognitive, non-objective 'experience' of 'faith'.[63] Consequently, what is actually 'given' in and through the divine Address to the self is an exhortation to live *as if* one had no world-view.

In sum, the idealist predetermination of the answers to the How and Where of the divine Self-communication by way of an immanentist epistemology effectively

---

61 For Neo-Kantianism, the objective and the subjective realms were not to be conceived as two realms. As Beck points out, 'they were two directions of knowledge, objectification and subjectification, each starting from the same phenomenon and each employing the transcendental method of categorial constitution, resolution into *Ursprung* (origin) and *Erzeugung* (production).' Beck, *op. cit.*, 471.

62 As Ingolf Dalferth says of the Kantian understanding of God, 'God is not a reality over against us which could in any way be known by theoretical reason. Rather, the notion of God is to be construed relative to the conditions of the possibility of experience, knowledge and moral fulfilment: God is not an objective reality but an 'Ideal of Reason', a regulative principle necessary for the systematic unity of our knowledge about the world of experience; and he is – in the realm of practical reason – a postulate of practical reason necessary for the achievement of the highest good. But this amounts to saying that there is no knowledge about God that could be true or false: all theoretical knowledge is limited to what can be experienced, yet God is not a *dabile.' Theology and Philosophy*, Basil Blackwell, Oxford, 1988, 174-175.

63 The Neo-Kantians were more consistent than Bultmann in describing this as *Gefühl* (feeling). Bultmann's desire to talk of 'experience' rather than 'feeling' is bound up with his eagerness to speak of God as a personal Being. That Bultmann does this, constitutes, in Fritz Buri's eyes 'a remnant of illogically retained mythology' (*Kerygma und Mythos* Vol. 2, 92 (Thiselton, *Interpreting God...*, 103). Ogden cites Buri's comment that, in this respect, Bultmann is 'falling back into mythology... into contradiction with his own presuppositions'. *Christ without Myth. A Study based on the Theology of Rudolf Bultmann*, Harper, New York, 1961, 107.

predetermines the evacuation of the divine Self-communication of its content. What should also be plain is how all forms of criterial immanentism must ultimately lead to either a) a monist fusion and identification of the divine and the human or b) irresolvable dualism rendering God irrelevant to human knowing and understanding or, worst of all, c) to the confused adoption of 'middle axioms'.[64]

The Givenness of God and Criterial Immanentism: 'Better well hanged than ill wed'

No theologian has explored the underlying issue here with greater clarity and profundity than Søren Kierkegaard. In his pseudonymous *Philosophical Fragments*[65] he distils the debate with idealism to the question of the nature and status of the criteria in terms of which we determine what is true.[66] Accordingly, he opens by asking the question with which Plato wrestled in the Meno, namely, 'Can the truth be learned?' Here he addressed the 'pugnacious proposition' that underlies the appeal of idealism: 'a person cannot possibly seek what he knows, and, just as impossibly, he cannot seek what he does not know, for what he knows he cannot seek, since he knows it, and what he does now know he cannot seek, because, after all, he does not even know what he is supposed to seek'.[67] In short, if we do not already possess within us the necessary criteria for the recognition of the truth (criteria, that is, which themselves actually contain the truth) we can neither search for the truth nor, indeed, recognize it when it comes our way. The seductive appeal of idealism is that it solves the problem of discovery, by affirming that the truth, and thus the criteria for the recognition of truth are already immanent within us. To the extent that the truth is within it cannot be introduced to us, it can only be dis-covered as something we have known from eternity. For this reason, Socrates interprets all learning and seeking to be forms of recollecting. All teaching becomes, therefore, a form of midwifery whereby learners (*mathetai*[68]) are enabled to give birth to the knowledge already

---

64   It is not insignificant that John Baillie the 'Christian Platonist' who has had such an influence on the moderate tradition advocating 'middle axioms' studied under Cohen and Natorp. In his 'Confessions of a Transplanted Scot' in *Contemporary American Theology: Theological Autobiographies* (Round Table Press, New York, 1933, 33-59) he comments on having attended the lectures of Eucken, Cohen and Natorp and adds that 'the course of my reflections was notably affected by them' (43). This influence was combined with that of the British idealists – Bradley, Bosanquet, Pringle-Pattison and Sorley.

65   Significantly, he chose to do so, under the pseudonym of an agnostic (Johannes Climacus) who occupies a position outside the faith and makes no Christian assumptions.

66   That his discussion relates to Hegel in particular does not make it any less relevant to the Neo-Kantian school of thought which would come later – as we have seen, Cohen was Platonist and ultimately Hegelian in his formulation of idealism.

67   Johannes Climacus (Søren Kierkegaard), *Philosophical Fragments* (trans. Howard V. Hong and Edna H. Hong), Princeton University Press, Princeton, 1985, 9.

68   The term 'learner' translates the term *mathetes* which we normally translate as 'disciple'. Kierkegaard is contrasting two different kinds of 'discipleship'.

immanent within them.[69] For this reason, Socrates would pose questions to slaves (questions of geometry, for example) which the slaves would answer as they were helped to become aware of what they already knew. He would then, recognizing his own insignificance as a mere midwife, quietly disappear from view and move on – concerned to do nothing that might attract attention to himself and thus distract the learner from that highest relation, namely, his relation to the Truth that is within. 'In the Socratic view, every human being is himself the midpoint, and the whole world focuses only on him because his self-knowledge is God-knowledge.'[70] Thus the teacher can and must never be anything other than a mere facilitator – 'if I were to imagine myself meeting Socrates, Prodicus, or the maidservant in another life, there again none of them would be more than an occasion, as Socrates intrepidly expresses it by saying that even in the underworld he would only ask questions, for the ultimate idea in all questioning is that the person asked must himself possess the truth...'.[71]

Integral to this is the consequence that if Socrates were to allow himself to become associated in any way in the mind of the learner with his relation to the truth, that would be to distort his relation to the truth. For the teacher to undermine that relation would signify that, far from being the friend of the learner, he was the learner's enemy in that he would be eclipsing or distorting the highest relation which a human being can possess, namely, the learner's relation to the Truth. It is necessarily the case, therefore, that the identity of the teacher be seen to be ultimately and absolutely insignificant whoever that teacher might be. And the learner's temporal 'point of departure' in remembering the truth (like the teacher and the occasion) is similarly 'a nothing'. In short, the moment I discover the truth I recognize the temporal point of departure as also the teacher to be of no significance, lost to the eternal, having no bearing on my relationship to the truth which is a timeless and eternal one. Indeed, I could not find the temporal moment of discovery again 'even if I were to look for it, because there is no Here and no There, but only an *ubique et nusquam* (everywhere and nowhere)'.

In sum, if the source of knowledge, discovery and the recognition of the truth is immanent within the enquirer, then the teacher and the temporal occasion have and can have *absolutely* no significance. Whether it is Jesus, Gandhi, the Dalai Lama, or a dead dog who facilitates my birthing of my immanent understanding of God and reality, this is and can be of no relevance because there can and must be no association or confusion of the Truth and my relation to the Truth with those 'individuals' or 'spatio-temporal' histories and any relation I might have to them. They can be nothing more than accidental (or incidental) exemplars, as D.F. Strauss saw so clearly.

---

69   This was the divine commission to Socrates which constrained him to be a midwife but forbade him to give birth 'because between one human being and another *maieuesthai* (to deliver) is the highest, giving birth indeed belongs to the god'. *Ibid.*, 10-11.

70   *Ibid.*, 11.

71   *Ibid.*, 13.

'If the situation is to be different...'

'If the situation is to be different, then the moment in time must have such decisive significance that for no moment will I be able to forget it, neither in time nor in eternity, because the eternal, previously non-existent, came into existence in that moment.'[72] That is, if the theological scenario is to differ epistemically from the idealist one then there must be an *intrinsic* relationship between the truth, our relation to the truth and the specific 'moment in time' or 'occasion'. Given this alternative presupposition Kierkegaard goes on to reconsider the relations involved in the question 'Can the truth be learned?'.

The Preceding State

Clearly, if the moment possesses decisive significance in the learner's relation to the truth 'then the seeker up until that moment must not have possessed the truth, not even in the form of ignorance... Consequently, he has to be defined as being outside the truth... He is, then, untruth.' But this brings us back again to the question of the *Meno*. How then is the learner to recognise the truth? If he is in untruth he clearly cannot be 'reminded' of it.

The Teacher

Since the teacher cannot remind the learner who is 'outside the truth' of what the truth is, then, if the learner is to obtain the truth, 'the teacher must bring it to him, but not only that. Along with it, he must provide him with the condition for understanding it, for if the learner were himself the condition for understanding the truth, then he merely needs to recollect, because the condition for understanding the truth is like being able to ask about it – the condition and the question contain the conditioned and the answer. (If this is not the case, then the moment is to be understood only Socratically.)'[73]

Here Kierkegaard presents the single most pertinent challenge to dogmatic, hermeneutical and theological method, the fundamental question to which the question set as our topic directs us. The criteria for the recognition and appropriation of the Self-communication of God as Truth, cannot be extrinsic to that event of Self-communication without our committing ourselves to the Socratic position *in toto*.

As Climacus goes on to establish, if we are not to return to the Socratic, then the teacher is not a midwife but a 'deliverer' who delivers us from error and the unfreedom integral to it by constituting in himself the condition of our being in relation to the truth. Such a teacher, Kierkegaard suggests, would require to be interpreted not only as deliverer but as reconciler eternally inseparable from the learner's relation to the Truth. As for the 'moment', it is short and temporal and

---

72   *Ibid.*, 13.
73   *Ibid.*, 14.

therefore passes, yet it is 'filled with the eternal' – that is, intrinsically linked to the eternal. Consequently, he suggests, we might call it the 'fullness of time'![74]

The Learner

If the moment is of 'decisive significance' and, again, if we are not to return to the Socratic, then the change which takes place denotes a transition from 'not to be' to 'to be'. There is a reconstitution, a rebirth, a conversion. 'In as much as [the learner] was untruth, he was continually in the process of departing from the truth; as a result of receiving the condition in the moment, his course took the opposite direction, or he was turned around. Let us call this change *conversion*...'[75] The effect of this is to expose the profound contrast between *metanoia* as the condition of our relation to the truth, and the Socratic *anamnesis*. Whereas *anamnesis* denotes the confirmation and ratification of the epistemic criteria immanent within us, *metanoia* denotes, by contrast, a profound transformation of the epistemic orientation of the whole person. As the New Testament scholars, J. Behm and E. Würtheim, explain, *metanoia,* as conceived in the proclamation of Jesus 'affects the whole man, first and basically the centre of personal life, then logically his conduct at all times and in all situations, his thoughts, words and acts...'[76]

It is imperative to appreciate here, however, that this kind of epistemic reorientation does not denote an irrational 'leap in the dark'. As Murray Rae observes, 'it involves neither the abandonment of reason (*contra rationem*) nor an addition to reason (*supra rationem*) but rather reason's redemption'. He comments,

> The canons of reason are not as neutral as is often supposed but are themselves the product of a particular world-view, typically a dualist one, whether it be the cosmological dualism between the *cosmos noetos* and the *cosmos aisthetos* of Plato, the Cartesian dualism between *res cogitans* and *res extensa* or the Kantian dualism between *phenomena* and *noumena*. However much Hegel, with his phenomenology of spirit, attempted to escape such dualisms his philosophy does not attain the hoped for reconciliation of the eternal and the temporal but is simply the sublation of the latter by the former. Hegel thus retains the prejudice of his above mentioned forbears against the Biblical notion that history is the locus of divine self-disclosure. Kierkegaard, on the other, considers that those who have eyes to see and ears to hear are those who by God's grace have been able to let go of such limited frameworks and to perceive the world anew under the condition which is called faith.[77]

Kierkegaard's concept of conversion as a radically discontinuous transition (involving a transformation of apperception, orientation and understanding) is thus considerably more than a mere 'Gestalt switch' (a suggestion which M.J. Ferreira

---

74 *Ibid.,* 18.

75 *Ibid.*

76 '*Metanoeo* and *metanoia*' in *T.D.N.T., Vol. IV*, ed. Gerhard Kittel, Grand Rapids, Eerdmans, 1967, 1002. I owe this reference and the thrust of the following discussion of Kierkegaard's interpretation of 'conversion' to Murray Rae, *Kierkegaard's Vision of the Incarnation: By Faith Transformed*, Oxford, Clarendon Press, 1997.

77 Rae, *ibid.,* 113.

considers at length[78]), where we can switch between one way of looking at the world and another and where each 'seeing as' is as valid as the other. Rather, Rae argues, it shares more in common with a 'paradigm shift' which recognizes that progress in knowledge (as in scientific knowledge) is not a matter of continuous evolutionary advancement or some kind of deductive progression. There is a radical discontinuity between the old and new paradigms and there is nothing which can be done from within the old paradigm that may constitute a propaedeutic for the new. To quote Rae again, 'By the standard of the new paradigm those who continue to operate within the old exist in untruth and employ structures of understanding which compel them to dismiss the claims of those who have undergone a paradigmatic transition'.[79] What it is important to appreciate here is that 'reason cannot itself be regarded as a framework or paradigm, much less an absolute or neutral one, but must rather be understood as a tool, very likely among others, which makes possible the heuristic functioning of a particular paradigm... Reason is constrained by the paradigm within which it operates and cannot be the means by which that same paradigm is undermined and replaced.'[80] This is precisely what is implied by Kierkegaard's comment concerning Hegelianism, that 'it is impossible to attack the System from a point within the System'.[81]

This is not to suggest, however, that that *metanoia* on which our being in relation to the Truth – and thus to God's Self-communication – depends, can be subsumed within some wider category of 'paradigm shifts'. As Eberhard Jüngel argues, 'theology has to do with a paradigm change *sui generis*: the existential change in human understanding conveyed by the phrases *ta tes sarkos phronein* and *ta tou pneumatos phronein* (Romans 8:5)'.[82]

As Climacus appreciates, a 'system of existence cannot be given'. To the extent that the Gospel bears witness to our deliverance to a new form of existing, we do not have a system given to be thought or appropriated or even appreciated. Rather, the *metanoia* at its heart speaks of a recreation for an 'authentic existence' which demands subjectivity, passion and commitment to a particular way of viewing and understanding the world.[83]

---

78   *Transforming Vision: Imagination and Will in Kierkegaardian Faith*, Clarendon, Oxford, 33ff.

79   Rae, *op. cit.*, 119.

80   *Ibid.*, 120.

81   *The Point of View for My Work as an Author*, p. 131n. Sikes comments, 'The System is invulnerable if one grants it the two essential elements of any system – its methodology and its presuppositions. It was then the task of Climacus to refute it on these two grounds.' Walter Sikes, *On Becoming the Truth*, St. Louis, Bethany Press, 1968, 64 (cited in Rae, 121fn).

82   Eberhard Jüngel, 'Response to Josef Blank' in *Paradigm Change in Theology* (1989), 297f.

83   As such it may be seen to involve commitment to what Evans describes as a particular 'plausibility structure'. Cf. C. Stephen Evans, *Kierkegaard's Fragments and Postscript*, 264ff.

How does God Speak? Moving beyond Vestibules

The effect of Climacus' argumentation is to place in question approaches to theology which begin by establishing, *a priori*, foundational prolegomena to theological perception or understanding. This generally takes the form of a propaedeutic, endorsing *pre*suppositions, *pre*conditions, *pre*-understandings,[84] *pre*-apprehensions[85] etc. These address the 'how' of God's speaking by reference to the *a priori* determinations of human capacities (or, indeed, incapacities) and prior orientations. The very acknowledgement of Transcendence involves the displacement or critical suspension of questions which assume that the relevant criteria of judgement are internal. To recognize the Transcendent (where Transcendence does not reduce to *apophasis* – arguably the most seductive form of human self-assertion!) involves the perception that questions posed from a ground within the self must themselves be questioned – just as that ground in the self requires to be questioned, as it continued to be for Peter. (As Peter sought to interpret what was and was not to be expected of Jesus in the light of his pre-understandings of Messiahship, the Counter-logos reprimanded him suggesting that this was nothing less than demonic!)

It is precisely this insight which characterizes Bonhoeffer's reference to Kierkegaard in addressing the 'christological question' in his lectures on *Christology*.[86] Opening with the assertion 'Teaching about Christ begins in silence' he cites Kierkegaard's insistence that we be silent before the Absolute. This *silence,* Bonhoeffer comments, 'has nothing to do with mystical silence which, in its absence of words, is, nevertheless, the soul secretly chattering away to itself. The church's silence is silence before the Word.'[87] In short, christology demands a *methodological* silence. The Logos *qua* divine Logos cannot be subsumed ('crucified') by the requirements of our prior, predetermined and predetermining *logoi*. To this extent, the Logos requires to be interpreted from our perspective as the Anti-Logos/Counter-Logos – the one who stands to judge, question and revise all our presuppositions (methodological, epistemological and otherwise) *vis-à-vis* God and God's purposes for humanity. There can thus be no Hegelian assimilation of the Anti-Logos within the human Logos[88] – and there can be no assimilation of the one Christ within a general interpretation of the race.

---

84   That is, the Heideggerean concept of the *Vorverständnis* which has influenced modern theological debates – together with some of the other preparatory conceptualities (the *vorontologisch*, the *vorphänomenal*, the *vorphilosophisch*, the *Präparat* which characterize the phenomenological method of *Sein und Zeit* and which we have seen to have been taken over in Bultmann's exposition of hermeneutical method.

85   Cf. Rahner's concept of the human subject's *Vorgriff* as discussed in *Foundations of Christian Faith. An Introduction to the Idea of Christianity* (trans. William Dych), Darton, Longman and Todd, London, 1978, 33ff, as also in chapters 5 and 12 of *Hearers of the Word*, Seabury, New York, 1969.

86   It is not insignificant that these were given in 1933 – the year in which Bonhoeffer set out courageously to oppose anti-semitism and the assimilation of Christianity within the prior demands and agendas of German culture.

87   Dietrich Bonhoeffer, *Christology*, trans. John Bowden, Collins, London, 1966, 27.

88   *Ibid.*, 29-30.

In sum, the 'how question' in our title is addressed in and through asking the 'who question'. As Bonhoeffer puts it: 'The question "Who?" is the question of transcendence. The question "How?" is the question of immanence.'[89] This excludes, therefore, from christological thought the question as to 'how the fact of the revelation can be conceived. This question is tantamount to going behind Christ's claim and providing an independent vindication of it. Here the human Logos presumes to be the beginning and the Father of Jesus Christ.'[90]

Here we see that there is ultimately no distinction to be drawn between idealist approaches which interpret objective knowledge as objectification, that is, the construction or generation (*Erzeugung*) of its objects and those which uphold prior subjective criteria (often in the name of 'Fundamental Theology') which *merely* operate censorship and discrimination in and through the process of discernment. The selective predetermination of what *does* and *does not* count in determining the content of God-talk and revelation is equally invalid in both cases with regard to the 'Sub-stance' or *Fundamentum* of theology. In the final analysis, *both* construct the *Sache* and dictate the terms of its 'speech' by identifying themselves and their claims with the 'how' and 'where' of God's Self-communication. This is *not*, of course, to deny that any considerations offered could *ever* be pertinent or appropriate. What it is imperative, however, to note here is that it is *emphatically not* our concern to advocate *a priori* that we rule out as invalid any *a priori* determination of criteria![91] Our concern is, rather, a radically *a posteriori* one, namely, that we recognize that the very nature of Christian revelation or Divine Self-disclosure implies that the propriety and impropriety of critical criteria are to be determined *out of the event of God's Self-communication itself* and, second, that consideration of the nature of this event suggests that the determination to 'rule in' independent, immanent criteria of assessment in advance of the revelation event is quite simply incompatible with the nature and content of that event. Any such move constitutes a *de facto* denial of the event.

The Divine Self-communication as Constituting Its Own Vestibule

If Kierkegaard's utilization of the agnostic Climacus to undermine criterial immanentism (together with the methodological and epistemological vestibules associated with it) takes the form of a *via negativa*,[92] Karl Barth's critique, like Dietrich Bonhoeffer's, takes the form of a *via positiva*. It operates out of Christian affirmation and not by way of any general demonstration of mutual incompatibilities. In offering

---

89   *Ibid.*, 30.

90   *Ibid.*, 33. It is interesting to note Athanasius's parallel suspicion of the How question. 'Having learned these things, they ought not to be so bold as to ask doubting, how these things could be...' *Letters to Serapion*, 106.

91   Our concern here is not a *philosophical* one, like that of Derrida!

92   It is imperative to realise that Kierkegaard is not seeking to offer a demonstration of the truth of Christianity – if he were, his approach would, of course, be guilty of internal inconsistency! It is for this reason that Kierkegaard uses the agnostic pseudonym and opens with a one sentence preamble: 'The question is asked by one who in his ignorance does not even know what provided the occasion for his questioning in this way' (p. 9).

a 'church dogmatics' he seeks to establish the nature of theological knowledge by way of a *Nachdenken* or a 'backward look' – outlining the methodological, criterial and epistemological conditions of God's Self-communication to human creatures – where these are conceived as 'post-suppositions' carried and established in, through and with the event of the divine Address itself.

Seven inter-related facets of Barth's discussion are pertinent to this.[93]

The Ecclesia as Constituting the 'Where' of Divine Self-communication

Barth categorically refuses to begin with the question, 'How is human knowledge of revelation possible? For the theologian to ask such a question would imply either a) that there is, or can be, doubt as to whether revelation is known or b) that 'insight into the possibility of knowledge of divine revelation' can be expected from the 'investigation of human knowledge' in abstraction. The first involves a *de facto* repudiation of revelation's having taken place. The latter constitutes, at best, a form of disobedience in the face of revelation – in that it seeks to validate the particularity of the revelation event with recourse to universal structures which are deemed to be *more* foundational. It is to turn one's back on God's grounding of our knowledge of him in his Self-presentation to us in Christ.

If the Body of Christ is the place of the discernment of God, we do not stand outside it either to confirm or to test this revelation. When we speak of or acknowledge revelation we are using what J.L. Austin would term a 'success word'. To acknowledge Christian revelation is to speak of something *that has taken place.* It is to speak in the light of that reality.

To cite Bonhoeffer again, 'In the church in which Christ has revealed himself as the Word of God, the human Logos puts the question: Who are you, Jesus Christ, Word of God, Logos of God? The answer is given, the church receives it new every day.'[94]

The Holy Spirit as the 'Point of Connection' between God and Human Hearing

'According to Holy Scripture God's revelation occurs in our enlightenment by the Holy Spirit of God to a knowledge of His Word. The outpouring of the Holy Spirit is God's revelation. In the reality of this event consists our freedom to be the children of God and to know and love and praise Him in His revelation.'[95] The condition for the appropriation and thus realization of God's Self-communication is the Holy Spirit alone. It is the Spirit who constitutes the point of connection (*Anknüpfungspunkt*) between God and the human hearer and who is the condition of our having the ears to hear. The 'Revealedness' of revelation is to be understood in terms of the creative presence of the Spirit alone – and not some innate, immanent and static intersection

---

93   This brief discussion of Barth is largely a précis of part of the first chapter of my book, *Persons in Communion: an Essay on Trinitarian Description and Human Participation*, T&T Clark, Edinburgh, 1996.

94   Bonhoeffer, *Christianity*, 32.

95   *C.D.* 1.2, 203.

between the divine and the human conceived as self-selected and self-endorsed human capacity.

The Non-neutrality of the Christian Theologian

To be 'absolutely neutral' in relation to God is to be 'absolutely hostile' to God ('schlechterdings gegen ihn').[96] Non-commitment before the revelation event or the prioritizing of other criteria or grounds as foundational to the reality of the Self-giving disclosure of God is not an appropriate theological option. In short, the very facticity of revelation involves a correlation between theological truthfulness and obedience. To acknowledge the event of Christian revelation is to acknowledge that we begin *there*. If we refuse not only to interpret God but to allow our approach to interpreting God to be 'informed' by revelation, we deny revelation. In the language of Kierkegaard, we are endorsing as foundational or fundamental a form of existence that is outwith the truth and requires to be understood, therefore, as 'error'.

The Inseparability of the Formal and the Material

It is radically inappropriate, therefore, to separate formal and material considerations and to introduce prior or 'foundational' philosophical prescriptions at the methodological, epistemological or ontological levels.[97]

As Eberhard Jüngel summarizes Barth here '...das Sein Gottes geht und eben so allem menschlichen Fragen zuvorkommt'[98] ('the Being of God proceeds, and thus precedes all human questioning'[99]). Christian theology is, therefore, a reflecting (lit. 'after-thinking') on the proceeding of God toward the contingent created order as the Logos and in the Spirit. God's being-as-such or God's being-in-this-way *precedes* and thus determines truly theological questioning (the Who question addressed to God) *ab initio*. The significance of this for theology is that it 'realises that all its knowledge, even its knowledge of the correctness of its knowledge, can only be an event, and cannot therefore be guaranteed as correct knowledge from any place apart from or above this event'.[100] Theological prolegomena must invariably be *post-legomena*.

---

96   *C.D.* 1.1, 47-48 *(K.D.* 1.1, 48). '(I)f the eternal presence of Christ is to be revealed to us in time, there is a constant need of that continuing work of the Holy Spirit in the Church and to its members which is always taking place in new acts.' *Ibid.*, 513.

97   It is this feature to which Jüngel refers when he argues that 'Barth's doctrine of the Trinity as dogmatic interpretation of God's self-interpretation possesses an anti-metaphysical and anti-mythological significance'. Jüngel, *The Doctrine of the Trinity: God's Being is in Becoming* (eng. trans. by Horton Harris), Edinburgh, 1976, 29.

98   Eberhard Jüngel, *Gottes Sein ist im Werden. Verantwortliche Rede vom Sein Gottes bei Karl Barth: Ein Paraphrase*, J.C.B. Mohr, Tübingen, 1976, 10.

99   Jüngel (eng. trans. by Horton Harris) xx.

100 *C.D.* 1.1, 42 *(K.D.* 1.1, 42).

Semantic Metanoia

Intrinsic to the event of God's Self-communication is the *a posteriori* revision of the meaning of the terms we use and the provisionality of the suppositions which accompany them. The impropriety of an *a priori* foundationalism relates no more to our interpretation of method and our ways of knowing than to the functioning of the terminology we use. Whenever we make theological statements or ask theological questions, suppositions are made with respect to the meanings of the terms we use. These suppositions, which are inevitable and potentially innocent, become less than innocent if we fail to appreciate their provisionality or 'sketch-like' quality.[101] Hence, semantic reformation or reconciliation is thus *intrinsic* to revelation – not least because thought and language are irreducibly inter-related.

The Identity in God between Word and Act and the Irreducibly Personal Nature of God's Word

Barth also stresses the identity (rather than mere correspondence) in God between God's Word and God's Act. 'God's Word is itself God's act.'[102] God's Word is 'enacted Divine event'.[103] Consequently, whenever God speaks to humanity its content is a *concretissimum*[104] – it is an act, and an act, moreover, which includes its hearing. There can be no dichotomy, therefore, between God's act of communication as Word and God's being communicated as Word. When revelation takes place the church has come into being. Neither can there be any dichotomy between God's *work* and God's *being*. Consequently, when we are talking about the perception of God's Word, we are not engaging in an anthropological discussion about human capacity, we are talking about *God.* And to the extent that we are doing this we are the church in communion with the *Being* of God. As Barth comments, when we

---

101 Suppositions here can too easily become, in Collingwood's language, 'relative presuppositions' or more sinisterly 'absolute presuppositions' which are so fundamental to one's frame of reference that one is not even aware of what one is presupposing *(Essay on Metaphysics*, Oxford, 1940).

102 *C.D.* 1.1, 147 (*K.D.* 1.1, 153). It is this that gives rise to Horst Pöhlmann's comment that Barth is committed to an 'actualistic ontology'. Cf. Horst Georg Pöhlmann, *Analogia entis oder Analogia fidei?, Die Frage der Analogie bei Karl Barth*, Göttingen, 1965, 119. He suggests also, 'Man kann deshalb ohne Übertreibung von einem Panaktualismus Barths sprechen' *ibid.,* 117. As I argue in chapter four of *Persons in Communion. Trinitarian Description and Human Participation*, it is certainly not Barth's intention to seek to universalize an actualistic concept of being. His emphasis on the *a posteriori* nature of theological articulation precludes this kind of ontological agenda. For his criticism to work Pöhlmann requires to show that Barth's grounds for his refusing to operate theologically with a dualism between God's being and act are foreign to an *a posteriori* theological description of the New Testament notions of the divine Presence, Glory, Word and the identification of the Redeemer as 'Immanuel'.

103 *C.D.* 1.1, 59 (*K.D.* 1.1, 60).

104 *C.D.* 1.1, 140 (*K.D.* 1.1, 145).

speak of the Holy Spirit, 'we are always speaking of the event in which God's Word is not only revealed to the human person but also believed by her'.[105]

This brings us to the essentially *personal* nature of God's Self-communication. There can be no conceptual reduction of God's Word. It is the truth *precisely* by virtue of its being God's speaking person – *'Dei loquentis persona'*.[106] This implies again that revelation in Christ is not *an* objective reality – where ultimate reality is thereby attached to *oneself* as subject. It is *the* objective reality in that *the* Subjective Agent in the event is God. God's Word is thus as unanticipatable and unrepeatable by human beings as God's Being is unanticipatable or unrepeatable. We can no more anticipate the Word than we can be its authors. This means, moreover, that what God speaks can never be known or true anywhere in abstraction from God Himself. 'It is known and true in and through the fact that He Himself says it' and 'that He is present in person in and with what is said by Him'.[107]

Eschatological Provisionality

To the extent that the eschatological qualification 'not yet fully realized' relates to the human act of God-talk we must also recognize the time-governed and provisional nature of our terminology and forms of expression. One implication of this is that there is no place, therefore, for any conceptuality which constitutes a 'natural' bridge between the times, between the *regnum gloriae* and the *regnum gratiae*. If a concept is provided which possesses a realized eschatological function then this must be affirmed *subsequent* to the event of revelation by grace and must not be presupposed by it. Moreover, its meaning and rules of use will always require to be reformed – it is a conceptuality which is 'on the way', undergoing a process of semantic reconciliation.

---

105   Again, we see that to attempt to speak about God on the basis of some predetermined set of epistemological criteria or independent grounds, is simply not to speak about the same God! Why? Because without the divine proceeding which is the Holy Spirit and the Incarnate Logos, God is not God – God is not the God whose being is in this becoming. The point here is not the affirmation of any *logical* necessity of the divine utterance being heard but simply a theological one concerning the coinherence of the person of the Word in Jesus Christ and the Holy Spirit.

106   *C.D.* 1.1, 136 *(K.D.* 1.1, 141). Barth uses the same Latin phrase later on (p. 304) where he again stresses the irreducibly concrete particularity of the divine address in revelation as this is to be identified with the being of God. Here he writes, 'According to Scripture God's revelation is God's own direct speech which is not to be distinguished from the act of speaking and therefore is not to be distinguished from God Himself, for the divine I which confronts man in this act in which it says Thou to him. Revelation is *Dei loquentis persona*'.

107   'The personalising of the concept of the Word of God, which we cannot avoid when we remember that Jesus Christ is the Word of God, does not mean its deverbalising.' *C.D.* 1.1, 138. It is its personal nature which underscores its verbal quality. To emphasize the former serves to strengthen, rather than to detract from, the latter.

God's Self-Communication and 'Properly Basic' Beliefs

The implication of Kierkegaard's, Bonhoeffer's and Barth's arguments (not to mention those of Athanasius and the New Testament writers mentioned earlier) is that the event of God's Self-communication in the Word perceived by the Spirit conditions and establishes 'properly basic' beliefs, to adopt Alvin Plantinga's conceptuality.[108] These are beliefs that do not require to be justified or accounted for with reference to other *more basic* beliefs or suppositions. That is because they are basic and warranted – although their warrant is not demonstrable by making recourse to universally accessible evidence. The suggestion I am making is that the perception of God in his Self-communication as Word requires to be articulated in these terms. This is not unrelated to Bonhoeffer's statement that, 'Jesus' testimony to himself stands by itself as self-authenticating... The fact of the revelation of God in Christ cannot be either established or disputed scientifically.'[109] To deny that this is the case is to rule out the validity of God's Self-communication in Christ *tout court.* Moreover, any denial of this on theological grounds will require to make recourse to basic beliefs of some other kind – which will themselves be ascribed to divine action of some kind.

This is emphatically not to say that *everyone* is justified in claiming their particular religious beliefs to be 'properly basic'. Neither is it to say that one cannot articulate why one regards it appropriate to claim one's beliefs to be properly basic – the function of the above arguments is to do precisely that. However, it is also the case that one may not be able to demonstrate one's reasons to be valid to people operating on the basis of other incompatible basic beliefs. To expect this to be possible would itself be a contradiction of the perception that God's Self-disclosure includes his Self-identification. It would be to deny that not only the propriety but the *perception* of the propriety derive from and are carried by the divine Self-communication itself. In other words, the very nature of our 'properly basic' beliefs is that they do not acknowledge the assumption that other suppositions constitute a more basic Archimedean point from which we can assess the proper basicality of the beliefs 'communicated' in and through God's Self-communication. To insist that any 'information' communicated requires to be ratifiable, confirmable *and hence discernible* with recourse to basic beliefs quite independent of any divine address is, of course, to return to the Socratic!

Unfortunately, the desire to do precisely this is deeply rooted within the European tradition and is exemplified not only in Descartes and the concern in his *Meditations* to establish the roots of the tree of knowledge – where these roots are, not surprisingly,

---

108 For his most recent discussions of 'proper basicality' see his *Warrant the Current Debate* (Oxford University Press, Oxford, 1993), chapter 4 and *Warrant and Proper Function* (Oxford University Press, Oxford, 1993), chapter 10. In *Warrant the Current Debate*, he suggests that for Calvin 'certain beliefs about God are... properly basic' and mentions his doctrine of the *sensus divinitatis* in this regard (86). This is ambiguous since, for Calvin, our *sensus divinitatis* does not remain properly functional as it would have done 'si integer stetisset Adam' (if Adam had remained whole). Plantinga comments, however, that he shall explore Calvin's views further in *Warranted Christian Belief.*

109 *Christology*, 32.

to be found within the self conceived as a self-affirming *res cogitans*[110] – but, more significantly, in the form of classical foundationalism that we find in Locke for whom a belief is justified when, in Locke's language, I have 'done my best' to fulfil my intellectual duties.[111]

In his famous book, *An Essay Concerning Human Understanding,* (1690), John Locke established classical evidentialism by asserting that 'all beliefs need to be based on evidence' and that and we have duties not to believe anything for which we do not have evidence.[112] Consequently, 'belief cannot be afforded to anything, but upon good reason'. Not only must we base our beliefs on evidence, we must also have degrees of 'firmness' of our holding of beliefs in direct proportion to the quality of the evidence. As Stephen Evans summarizes this position, we have an epistemic duty to examine all the grounds of probability and then proportion our degree of belief to the degree of probability which the evidence provides.[113]

Three obvious problems result from this widely influential assumption:

First, any assessment of any belief must itself presuppose other beliefs. Second, how could we begin to determine the evidential support for a belief? By stepping outside them? Clearly, this raises endless problems. Finally, all this assumes that we have some kind of voluntary control over our believings – that I can decide to believe something less firmly by an act of self on self.

This means, for example, that I have an epistemic duty to determine how much evidence I have to believe I am not a brain in a vat on Alpha Centauri. Once I have carried out my duties by working this out (one wonders how!) I then have a duty not to believe that I am not a brain in a vat to a greater degree than my evidence warrants.

Endless further issues emerge relating, for example, to the status and justifiability of moral beliefs – that malformed babies should not be given a lethal injection at birth, for example, as I once heard a former theological colleague argue. How is it possible to determine that such a belief is sufficiently evidenced to be justified? The conclusion we are forced to draw is that, as Alston, Wolterstorff and Plantinga have argued 'being justified in believing something is not identical with being able to justify a belief'.[114]

God's Self-Communication, 'Proper Functionality' and the Ekklesia

To know something is for one's beliefs to be true and warranted. Warrant or justification involve a concept of proper epistemic function. Given that an individual's thought processes are irreducibly bound up with the semantic functionality of the community of which she is part and which conditions and constitutes the way she interprets and understands reality, there can be no dichotomy between the proper functionality

---

110   Descartes was, of course, influenced by the Platonist dimension of St. Augustine's thought to whom he owes the *cogito ergo sum* argument. Epistemic certainty is to be found within the self.

111   C. Stephen Evans, *The Historical Christ and the Jesus of Faith*, O.U.P., 1996, 213. I.

112   Evans, *op. cit.*, 208ff.

113   Evans, *ibid.*, 209.

114   Evans, *ibid.*, 216.

of the knowing subject and the proper functionality of the semantic community of which she is part. Here again, one perceives the significance of the inseparability of the perception of God's Self-communication from participation not in the old, noetically ('dianoetically') dysfunctional humanity, but in the New Humanity, in the Body of the '*eschatos Adam*'. Properly basic, justified true belief requires to be seen emerging in and through reconciled participation in the community of the redeemed. The question 'where' and 'how' God speaks requires to be answered ecclesially.[115]

Where does this leave our understanding of the relationship between faith and reason?

Duplex Cognitio?

It has long been held in Reformed[116] and Catholic circles that there are 'two separate sources of justified or warranted belief'.[117] 'Reason' or 'philosophy' constitutes one source of knowledge, faith provides another. Something of this is reflected in the encyclical, *Fides et Ratio* which reiterates the affirmation of the First Vatican Council that 'there exists a knowledge which is proper to faith surpassing the knowledge proper to human reason, which nevertheless by its nature can discover the Creator'. He writes, 'there exists a two-fold order of knowledge, distinct not only as regards their source, but also as regards their object' (9) The deliverances of reason and faith are assumed to be in harmony and lead to 'truth in all its fullness': The truth 'which God reveals to us in Jesus Christ, is not opposed to the truths which philosophy perceives' (34). As Alvin Plantinga has commented, 'That much is truistic, no truth of any kind can contradict any truth of any kind. What is not truistic is the pope's further claim: since God is the author both of faith and of our reason, God would not bring it about or permit it to be that faith and reason were in conflict.'[118]

So do we go with John Paul or Alvin Plantinga? Do we affirm that God would not permit it to be that faith and reason were in conflict or do we allow that he might? This depends in part on our definitions of 'faith' and 'reason'. If we define 'faith' and 'reason' in such a way that they become 'success words' (J.L. Austin) and thus, by definition, must lead veridically to their proper objects, then, indeed, it is appropriate to suggest that they will not be in conflict. But if reason refers to human processes of reasoning and what actual human reasoning delivers and can be seen to deliver, then it is not at all clear that God would not permit them to be in conflict. This is doubly the case, of course, if faith can also be confused as to its object.

---

115   This would not be considered new by those Greek fathers who emphasized the self-authenticating nature of the Word (the *Autologos*) manifest to the *ekklesiastikon phronema* (the ecclesial mind) in a context of worship (*eusebeia*).

116   Cf. for example, Charles Hodge's *Systematic Theology* which describes 'reason' as God's primary revelation to humankind and regards it as 'the prerogative of reason to judge the credibility of a revelation'; *Systematic Theology*, Vol.1 Grand Rapids, Eerdmans, org. 1871, p.50.

117   Alvin Plantinga's review of *Fides et Ratio, Books & Culture*, Jul/Aug, 1999.

118   Plantinga, *ibid.*

Four questions/issues emerge here.

a) On what grounds might it be suggested that reason can deliver a body of knowledge and that God would not allow it to go astray? Are the grounds of this supposition reason itself? If so, then this suggests a circularity – to argue that reason confirms that reason can be trusted to generate a non-*a priori* body of knowledge seems suspect. If this claim is made on the basis of faith then we have in fact affirmed the priority of the insights of faith and its necessity in informing our reasoning!

This would seem to undermine Pope John Paul's advocacy of a 'truly propaedeutic path' (90) and, indeed, of fundamental theology.

b) Second, suppose we argue that reason really *can* establish the validity of its function within its own terms (as seems to be implied), then this raises a further problem. Bertrand Russell's set theory and property paradoxes illustrate how reason applied in its most rigorous form finds itself demonstrating logically incompatible conclusions from innocent premises.[119] In short, the most rigorous applications of human reason generate deductive conclusions which are in tension with themselves and are required to be by the law of the excluded middle. In short, reason itself seems to suggest that reason, left to its own resources, may be inherently flawed.

c) Third, reason invariably operates from an epistemic base, a series of affiliations, allegiances or 'canons' on the basis of which its deductive processes do their work. These generally cannot be demonstrated by virtue of reason's rationally contemplating its own products or operating *ab initio* on its own grounds. Even in the most exact sciences, reason necessarily assumes a series of assumptions taken on faith, as these include one's own memory, testimony, the collective testimony of the scientific community (and we might include non-demonstrable heuristic intuitions, subliminal awareness and the like). Indeed, it is hard to conceive of anything other than the most trivial operations of reason which do not operate from an epistemic base – that is, which do not assume affiliations grounded in 'faith' of one kind or another. This is not to

---

119   'Russell's paradox represents either of two interrelated logical antinomies. The most commonly discussed form is a contradiction arising in the logic of sets or classes. Some classes (or sets) seem to be members of themselves, while some do not. The class of all classes is itself a class, and so it seems to be in itself. The null or empty class, however, must not be a member of itself. However, suppose that we can form a class of all classes (or sets) that, like the null class, are not included in themselves. The paradox arises from asking the question of whether this class is in itself. It is if and only if it is not. The other form is a contradiction involving properties. Some properties seem to apply to themselves, while others do not. The property of being a property is itself a property, while the property of being a cat is not itself a cat. Consider the property that something has just in case it is a property (like that of being a cat) that does not apply to itself. Does this property apply to itself? Once again, from either assumption, the opposite follows. The paradox was named after Bertrand Russell, who discovered it in 1901.' *Internet Encyclopaedia of Philosophy*.

undermine or undercut the operations of reason, it is rather to suggest that this is how reason functions.

d) The purpose of my chapter has been to emphasize the importance of what Pope John Paul refers to as the *auditus fidei* and which, I have suggested, involves our being given the ears to hear. Is it not clearly the case that the *auditus fidei* does indeed have something to say *vis-à-vis* our engagement with philosophy and the assumptions of philosophers, as well as those of ethicists, political scientists etc.? The question with which the age-old concern with the relationship of faith and reason is confronted boils down to this: should I really seek to put the *auditus fidei* and its deliverances to one side and appeal, rather, to autonomous reason operating from some basis which contains no non-demonstrable beliefs?

This raises three questions: a) Would it be possible, in the name of an appeal to 'reason' and philosophy, to separate from my thinking, all those believings constitutive of my epistemic base and which relate to God's purposes *vis-à-vis* all that is, the meaning of life, who God is etc.? b) Even if this were possible, why would I want to do this if I believed that faith offered me insight into the nature of ultimate questions and the meaning of life? c) Even if it were possible, and if I did want to do this, would it be an appropriate response to the creating and reconciling God who (one might deduce from the very facticity of revelation) desires that I operate from 'believings' generated by the Holy Spirit and the recognition of who Christ is when it comes to interpreting God, the world and humanity? Indeed, would such an approach not constitute, as I have suggested above, a *de facto* denial of revelation (and disobedience to the extent that it suggests God's endorsement of a need to reveal himself) if the implication of revelation is that we are not able to know as we should, that we are not able to understand the meaning of life aright, that worldly philosophies and their products are not to be relied upon? Finally, if the Light of the world is presented to the Body, if the incarnate *Word* is *homoousion to patri*, why would we and why should we wish to find our way by what, by comparison, can only be regarded as the created light of the stars? Why should we wish to circumscribe the incarnation in this way – or relocate it to some exclusive sphere of 'salvation'? Moreover, why should we wish to ground our understanding of it in a fundamental theology or predetermine its interpretation by way of a *praeparatio* or propaedeutic path?

As a violinist, I use all four fingers of my left hand.[120] Now it is conceivable that I could choose to use only three fingers or possibly two.[121] But what good reason could there possibly be for choosing not to use all the resources at one's disposal when performing a Brahms sonata? Is it and can it be rational, let alone an appropriate response to revelation, for Christians to choose *not* to bring all their best epistemic resources to bear on the interpretation of reality, the meaning of human life and so on right from the start? Furthermore, what kinds of grounds could there

---

120　This example is adapted from a similar climbing analogy used by Alvin Plantinga.

121　Paganini sought to impress audiences playing pieces using only one string, but it did not always enhance his interpretation of the music!

be for not wishing to do this in the light of God's Self-disclosure as this includes the reconciliation and reschematization of our minds in and through which we are given eyes to see and ears to hear what, otherwise, we would not see or hear aright, if at all!

Chapter 6

Science, Chesterton and the Will of the Creator

Stephen R.L. Clark

The Contingency of Creation

The man of science says 'Cut the stalk, and the apple will fall', but he says it calmly as if the one idea really led up to the other. The witch in the fairy tale says, 'Blow the horn and the ogre's castle will fall'; but she does not say it as if it were something in which the effect obviously arose out of the cause. ... The scientific men ... feel that because one incomprehensible thing constantly follows another incomprehensible thing the two together somehow make up a comprehensible thing. ... A tree grows fruit because it is a *magic* tree. Water runs downhill because it is bewitched. The sun shines because it is bewitched.[1]

Chesterton here addresses, with characteristic panache, a theme all too familiar to philosophers: 'too familiar' because familiarity has bred inattention. David Hume popularized the argument that, as far as *logic* goes, anything at all could be the cause of anything. We are used to seeing apples fall, but – experience aside – nothing prevents their taking wing instead. One thing leads to another, but not because there would be any *logical* absurdity in its leading somewhere else entirely.

Hume drew the conclusion that we had no strictly rational argument to defend our actual belief that the future was predictable at all. If there is no law of logic to require that apples fall, then our reason for supposing that they do is only that, so far, they have. But there is no better *logical* reason to suppose that future events 'resemble' past events than to suppose that apples always fall. Our expectation that they will is only an ingrained habit.[2] Of course, if everything always happens in the same way as it has before, then we can conclude that, if apples fell last year, they will again – but the major premise is no more a *logical* necessity than the lesser claim that apples always fall, and far less plausible. Everything *doesn't* always happen in the same way as before.

Even our notion of what *counts* as a resemblance, or what will count as 'doing the same thing', has no basis in any merely logical understanding. The argument

---

1   G.K. Chesterton *Orthodoxy* (Fontana: London 1961; 1st published 1908), p. 50f. Chesterton's philosophy of science is examined by Stanley Jaki, *Chesterton: a seer of science* (University of Illinois Press: Urbana 1986).

2   I am aware that some recent commentators have sought to tame Hume's scepticism with the pretence that he 'really believed' in causality, identity, induction and so on. Oddly, those commentators do not usually attempt to prove that he was 'really' an orthodox theist, though they would have far better textual evidence for that conclusion.

has made its way into contemporary philosophical literature in the guise of Nelson Goodman's 'grue'.[3] Grass is grue just if it was green when it was examined before some arbitrary future time t, and will be blue thereafter. Any evidence before time t that it is *green* is just the same as the evidence that it is *grue* (and therefore, as *we* say, will turn blue at t). In fact the argument preceded Goodman. Robert Chambers, writing in *Vestiges of the Natural History of the Creation,* employed Charles Babbage's argument in his *Ninth Bridgewater Treatise.*[4] The 'very same computer program' (as we would now call it) may conscientiously progress from 1 to 2 to 3 to every number up to 100,000,001. The obvious inference is that it will continue 'in like fashion' – yet the numbers that follow are instead 100,010,002; 100,030,003; 100,060,004; 100,100,005; 100,150, 006 'and so on' until the 2672nd term. Babbage suggests that the rule has changed unpredictably. Alternatively, the original rule was not what it seemed – but until we passed the hundred million mark there could be no way to distinguish the actual rule from the 'obvious' one. Either way, inductive inference fails.

So our inductive habit is grounded in habitual identifications, habitual ways of following rules or programs, that have no fully rational defence. They are simply the ways 'we' use, and which (if Darwinists are right) may have given our ancestors some slight advantage over creatures using different descriptions, rules and habits. It is probably easier to operate the rule 'Add One' than the rule which issues in Babbage's Sequence, and creatures will not usually be required to move far enough to reveal the error, any more than they need to feel that space is not Euclidean. Actually, the simplest rule of all will be 'to do – or seem to oneself to do – what worked last time'.[5] Creatures who thought that apples flew, or that fire burnt only upon second Tuesdays, lost (unless, of course, they managed to ensure that nothing happened to disabuse them). But nothing in Darwinian theory, any more than in logic, shows that they will always lose, or that they lost for really obvious reasons, or that some other creatures, living different lives, might not have adopted different habits too. Our habits don't equip us for life beyond the fields we know, or those our ancestors once knew. After the event, perhaps, we may find some pattern, but cannot rationally expect to know of it beforehand, nor to believe that it will be 'the final pattern'.

---

3   Nelson Goodman, *Fact, Fiction and Forecast* (Athlone Press: London 1954): I am deliberately citing the version that includes a temporal reference rather than the mere 'green & unexamined or blue & unexamined'.

4   Robert Chambers, *Vestiges of the Natural History of Creation* (1844: reissued by Leicester University Press: Leicester, and by Humanities Press: New York, in 1969), after Charles Babbage, *Ninth Bridgewater Treatise Fragment* (Frank Cass: London 1967; 1st published 1837), pp. 34ff.

5   See K.Z. Lorenz, *Foundations of Ethology,* trs. K.Z. Lorenz and R. Warren (Springer: New York, 1981). Lorenz points out that even learning from experience requires an inbuilt, axiomatic rule which cannot itself be 'learnt from experience'. As stated, of course, the rule also validates superstition – and many medical prescriptions that turn out not to be well-founded.

Speculative physicists, since at least the Stoics,[6] have been unhappy with that conclusion. Everything, they think, must really be entirely as it is. There must, after all, be intellectually discoverable rules, as absolute as those of logic or simple arithmetic, to 'explain' why apples fall, the grass is green, and only sparrows hatch from sparrow eggs. Modern physicists have sometimes been prepared to alter the laws of logic, or suggest that there are after all no reasons why *this* particle decays at exactly *that* point in space or time, any more than *this* man's character explains why he was crushed by *that* collapsing building.[7] But the aim is still the same: to show that everything that can happen does, and that what doesn't happen is impossible. Rather than admit a world that operates like Chesterton's, 'by magic', speculative physicists have preferred to suggest that even when there is no logical or mathematical or even physical reason why things should go exactly as they apparently do, true logic rules. If either A or B is possible, and there is no reason why one should happen *rather than the other*, then it must be *that both A and B occur*, in separate worlds arising from the momentarily open instant. If there is no logical or mathematical reason why the initial conditions of creation should have been just so, then it must be that every possible set of such conditions is or has been real. We live, unsurprisingly, in a universe fine-tuned for life, because no universe not fine-tuned has any inhabitants like us. Why this should strike anyone as more plausible than the conclusion that the universe *has* been fine-tuned for life (and there are no others), is a matter for psychologists rather than philosophers![8]

Even if all possible universes somehow did exist, that fact itself, the brute fact of existence, should remain to trouble us. 'It is one thing to understand the underlying order of the universe, it is another to propose that this understanding is logically sufficient for the real existence of what this is an understanding of. If any cube must, of necessity, have six sides, it does not follow that there must be cubes.'[9] That fact – that anything at all exists – is widely ignored or fuzzily explained away. There is certainly a sense, at the edge of reason, in which it is possible for nothing at all to be – though it would not then be *true* that nothing was (it cannot *be* the case that nothing at all is the case). I have argued elsewhere that if it were genuinely possible for nothing at all to be, and if – accordingly – the mere existence of anything is an absolutely inexplicable fact, there can be no limits on what 'might' come into existence. If 'the universe' just 'happens' to exist, then any universe at all is just as likely – including ones in which our intellectual habits only apply within arbitrarily defined regions. It is not only 'the speed of light' that might be different elsewhere: anything at all might be, or might be 'the same' according to some unheard-of

---

6   Even since Aristotle: 'the proper object of unqualified scientific knowledge is something which cannot be other than it is' *(Posterior Analytics* 1.71b15) – but Aristotle was also aware that precision is not always possible.

7   Plotinus, *Enneads* 4.3.16, 8ff

8   On which see William Lane Craig, 'The Teleological Argument and the Anthropic Principle: *The Logic* of *Rational Theism: Exploratory Essays*, eds W.L. Craig and M. McLeod *(Problems in Contemporary Philosophy* 24. Lewiston, N.Y.: Edwin Mellen, 1990), pp. 127-153.

9   Paul Helm, *Faith and Understanding* (Edinburgh University Press: Edinburgh 1997), p. 92.

reading of the rules we use. A universe that 'just is' is rationally inexplicable, and rationally indescribable as well.[10]

I conclude that – if we are to retain our confidence in scientific reason – we must acknowledge that there is something that must be (without ever having *come* to be), and that it somehow contains – whether by rational necessity or will – whatever forms or rules or principles now govern the world we live in. It does not follow that everything is now exactly as it must be (or, conversely, that only the 'strictly impossible' is unreal). It is one thing to agree, or to insist, that Something Is and Must Be, and quite another to imagine that *everything* is as it must be. 'Rational' discourse, so it seems to me, must find a middle way. There is at least one necessary existential truth.[11] There may be – indeed there *must* be – many such truths that aren't necessities.

Necessity and Personal Explanation

And so to return to Chesterton.

When someone asks why A has followed B, it is not reasonable to answer, 'Well, As always follow Bs', as if this were an explanation. That As *always* follow Bs is what demands an explanation in the first place. That this A follows that B, on this occasion but no other, is perhaps just one of those things, exciting no particular puzzlement. Certainly, if it is true that As always follow Bs then it follows at once, by logic, that *this* B will be followed by an A. But there are at least two difficulties. First (as before), we cannot possibly know by experience that As *always* follow Bs. Second, if they do it is because this A has followed a B, and so has that, and that, and that, and so indefinitely. The instances of the 'law' aren't as they are because of any such generalization. Rather the reverse: the generalization is true, if at all, because all the particular cases are like that. And *why* are they? It follows that 'laws of nature' aren't explanations, but only instances of what needs to be explained.[12] The more often that an A follows a B the more we have to explain. It is also true that the more often this occurs the less we *wonder* at it: but that is merely the weakness of our grip on

---

10   See my *God, Religion and Reality* (SPCK: London 1998).

11   Another route to what is, functionally, the same conclusion is to observe that we cannot explain existence by referring to anything that *exists* (which would leave us with the same problem): instead, the only possible explanation of existence is a transcendent 'non-existent' one – as theists have always supposed (see 'The Cosmic Priority of Value': *Tijdschrift voor Filosofie* 62.2000, pp. 681-700). In what follows, I have chosen to use the more familiar language of 'necessary existence': a larger examination of the two traditions, or the two verbal formulations, would require another chapter.

12   'At the basis of the whole modern view of the world lies the illusion that the so-called laws of nature are the explanations of natural phenomena' (L. von Wittgenstein, *Tractatus Logic-Philosophicus*, eds. D.F. Pears and B.F. McGuinness (Routledge & Kegan Paul: London 1972, 2nd ed); see M.O'C. Drury *The Danger of Words* (Routledge and Kegan Paul: London 1973).

reason.[13] If we could show that 'As follow Bs as a matter of logical or arithmetical necessity' we would have an answer to our puzzlement – though this too would hardly be an *explanation* rather than a proof that nothing needed explaining. 'Of *course* As follow Bs, because that's what being A or B amounts to.' All manner of unexpected arithmetical relationships turn out, on closer examination, to be obvious, requiring no particular 'explanation' – as if they could conceivably have been different. So an *explanation*, in our ordinary way of speaking, is something less than logical necessity. On the one hand, there is still something that needs explanation because it might have been otherwise. On the other hand, we now know *why* it is *not* otherwise. An explanation does not compel, but does – precisely – *explain* the explanandum.

So what does this amount to? What is it 'to explain'? The goal of scientific speculation is often thought to be explanation. But if scientists hope to roll everything up into a single, necessary theorem, from which everything that happens follows, there is a sense in which they will then have abandoned 'explanation'. Nothing then will need explaining, unless it is – as before – the brute fact of existence. If there is only *one* possible world, because there is only *one* possible theorem, then everything is only as it must be. 'Explanation' is only an end to puzzlement, though it seems likely still that 'the brute fact of existence' will remain as the final mystery. *Something* 'breathes fire into the equations'. 'That something exists' can only be a necessary truth if there is something whose nature it is to exist, such that its existence follows from its essence (in short, if Anselm was correct). If he was not correct to think that there was anything that *must* exist, then the actual existence even of the one and only world or meta-world must be brute fact – and it follows, as before, that, literally, *anything* might turn out to be true (since we don't know what the *actual* world is, beyond the truism that it does contain us).

A familiar way of avoiding that destructive implication is to agree that something necessarily exists: not as one brute option amongst indefinitely many, but as the only, ultimate context of all explanation. The scientific dream (though not all scientists necessarily share the dream entirely) is to derive all lesser theorems from that ultimate necessity. Something must exist, and everything else follows from that fact. Knowing this, the wise man will be surprised or puzzled by nothing whatsoever. The apple falls by necessity.

The conviction of the logician that nature is a logical whole for the intellect, as opposed to the feeling of the voluntarist that nature, if it may be said to exist at all, is a collection of independent entities with the characteristics of individual wills, sums itself up in the

---

13   Lev Shestov puts the point well: if beet seeds suddenly began to produce oranges, bananas, calves, or even rhinoceroses, we should at first be astonished, but in a few generations be utterly accustomed to the event. 'For the fact that a small grain produces an enormous beet is as incomprehensible, despite all the explanations of the botanists, as the birth of a rhinoceros from the same grain' (*Potestas Clavium*, tr. Bernard Martin (Henry Regnery: Chicago 1970; 1st published 1923) p. 173).

doctrine adopted by Spinoza from Maimonides of the unity of nature, or the unity of substance.[14]

But that dream is not the only possibility, and not what the Founders of our modern science supposed:

'Without all doubt this world could arise from nothing but the perfectly free will of God. ... From this fountain ... [what] we call the laws of nature have flowed, in which there appear many traces indeed of wise contrivance, but not the least shadow of necessity. These therefore we must not seek from uncertain conjectures, but learn them from observations and experiments. He who is presumptuous enough to think that he can find the true principles of physics and the laws of natural things by the force alone of his own mind, and the internal light of reason, must either suppose that the world exists by necessity, and by the same necessity follows the laws proposed; or if the order of Nature was established by the will of God, that himself, a miserable reptile, can tell what was fittest to be done.' The first thrust is levelled at the Greeks, the second at Descartes.[15]

If there are to be explanations, then, there must be something that has no need to come into existence, since it always, of its nature, *is*. Alternatively, it does not strictly *exist* (in the way that you and I exist) at all. But the relation of that Thing to everything else is not that of logical entailment, as though the actual totality of things were all that ever could be. That would be as much as to say that there *is* no actual totality of things, since everything we *call* a thing (including our own selves) is no more than a fragment of the universal Ens, a single theorem of the universal science, without any chance of ever having been otherwise.[16] So the only available sort of explanation, bridging the gap between Necessary Being and actual beings, is that Necessary Being is of a sort that *chooses*. The mere nature of that Necessary Being will constrain the abstract possibilities to some indefinite but real extent. That, after all, is why we are driven to admit its Being in the first place: if there were no such necessity then, literally, *anything* could happen and *reasoning* our way to truth would be impossible.[17] But its nature cannot be the only explanation for all that is: we must also suppose that its nature could be realized in an indefinite number of ways, and that the *actual* world stands to it as our own chosen lives may stand to us. This is not to say that the choice is arbitrary. 'The universe is contingent, not because God is rationally indifferent to which universe he chooses but because its existence

---

14   Leon Roth, *Spinoza Descartes and Maimonides* (Clarendon Press: Oxford 1924), p. 87; see also Paul Helm *Eternal God* (Clarendon Press: Oxford 1988), p. 186.

15   Isaac Newton represented by Hooykaas, after Cotes' preface to second edition of *Principia*: R. Hooykaas, *Religion and the Rise of Modern Science* (Scottish Academic Press: Edinburgh 1972), p. 49.

16   The variant thesis, that all possible outcomes are equally real, is just as vacuous: to say that everything possible occurs is to deny the need for explanation. If everything must happen somewhere, it is no surprise if it happens *here*.

17   There are some speculative writers who imagine that they can agree to this (that 'reason' is only a set of passing habits). Their folly in saying this is equalled only by their strange timidity in failing to act upon it.

is not deducible from a set of logical truths.'[18] And part of His choice is apparently to let Himself be chosen.

Or to put the same point in more Plotinian fashion: the intelligible world, which is also the divine intellect in which all intelligibles are gathered into unity, derives its existence not from any demand of logic or necessity, but from its own turn towards the One. That One lies beyond both being and understanding. Whether we speak of its 'necessary existence' or deny that it 'exists' in any ordinary way at all (as Plotinus did), we need to acknowledge it. And though it is inevitable that the One engenders Being, this is not because it *needs* to. Our choice here-now is to turn towards or away from the One revealed to us in Beauty.

Epistemology and Incarnational Theology

So in the beginning God *made* the heavens and the earth. And also in the beginning the Word, through which all things were made, *was* God.[19] In all the great monotheistic traditions it has been orthodox to agree that this our actual world is only one possible world among many, and also that there is something eternally the same in all the worlds that God has made or might make. Not all the worlds we might think 'possible' are actual (though many may be). Not even all the worlds that are compatible with God's own being are actual (though many may be). That aspect or element of the actual world, and of any truly possible world, that is required by God's own nature has been identified as the Torah, the Koran, or else the 'Son' of God. Some sects have judged that Moses or Mohammed were close copies of that 'Son': though they might themselves have been quite different, they managed – by God's grace – to show us what the shape of things must be.[20] Even some Christian sects have thought the same of Jesus: that there was a first-century Jewish hasid who managed, by God's grace, to show us the shape of things, and especially the shape that God desires of people. In other possible worlds those same individuals (Minos,

---

18   Helm, *Eternal God*, op. cit, p. 187. Helm himself seems inclined to regard the chosen universe as one required by God's *nature,* in that he is 'bound' to prefer the better. It is less clear to me that there is a uniquely 'better' world amongst many possible worlds, but I would concede that God's choice can only mythologically be likened to the wilful selection of one world amongst many possible. Strictly, there are no other possible worlds than this, any more than there are infinitely many possible but non-existent people. That the actual world is only one possible world among many is only a figure of speech, a way of saying that things don't *have* to be this way. Nor was God's choice preceded by a period of indecision. *This* is the world God makes, but he doesn't have to, and needs no reasoning to 'make up his mind'.

19   *Genesis* 1.1; *John* 1.1 ff. Neither 'the beginning' nor the use of the past tense should be taken to imply that this occurred at some time long ago: there are good reasons (both empirical and logical) to suppose that the world has a finite history, but its earliest moments are no *more* dependent on God's will and reason than the later ones. That the array of ordinary events must have been finite (that is, that this world *came to be*) is a further reason to distinguish what *must* be (God) and what is merely contingent on His will.

20   In Plotinus's version, the role is partly filled by Minos, 'filled full of lawgiving by the divine touch' (*Enneads* VI.9.7).

Moses, Jesus or Mohammed) ended their lives quite otherwise, and maybe some *other* individuals bore the burden instead.

That one's made Christ, this other, Pilate, And This might be all That has been.[21]

But Christian orthodoxy has preferred to insist that Jesus was not just an individual human being who happened to be God's messenger and message. Instead, it is supposed that Jesus *is* the Word, and that there is no other. That single individual has a dual nature: he is at once all that God's nature demands, as of necessity, and also something *chosen*. 'Begotten, not Made' as touching His Godhood, but also a *made* thing as a human creature.

This strange doctrine has been criticized for centuries, by theists as well as secular philosophers. My present concern is not with its theological or religious development,[22] but only with its relevance to human knowledge, and the natural world we seek to understand. My concern is with the possibilities, rather than with any detailed study of the actual Jesus (though that distinction could itself be criticized). In the earlier part of this chapter I argued that there *must* be something that exists (or transcendentally *is*) *of and by itself*, that never needed to *begin* and cannot *end*. I further argued that the relation of that 'Necessary Existent' to the actual world cannot be wholly necessary: its nature explains some aspects or elements of the world, but many such elements or aspects are, as it were, *chosen*, products of will and not necessity. Employing traditional language, we can say that God's Will and Reason is not itself a product of His Will and Reason, or not a product that could intelligibly be otherwise. There is a difference between the offspring of His nature and of His will (though this is not to say, or even imply, that any offspring of His nature is an automatic 'emanation' from the One). Some things, if we had the 'mind of God', we could see were as they must be. Much we would only see that they might be, or that in fact they are. Even if the Incarnation is necessary (as Anselm and Duns Scotus both supposed, for rather different reasons), 'it is not necessary for a valid Incarnation that the Godman is employed as a carpenter; it is not necessary for the atonement that the cross on which Christ hung was made of oak, say, and not cedar'.[23]

But Newton's barb remains:

> He who is presumptuous enough to think that he can find the true principles of physics and the laws of natural things by the force alone of his own mind, and the internal light of reason, must either suppose that the world exists by necessity, and by the same necessity follows the laws proposed; or if the order of Nature was established by the will of God, that himself, a miserable reptile, can tell what was fittest to be done.

How could we expect to fathom God's necessities or understand His choices? Only if it is possible, by God's grace, for a human being (or for any creature) to

---

21   R. Browning, 'Christmas-Eve and Easter-Day', $16: *Poems* (Oxford University Press: Oxford 1912), p. 511.

22   On which see my *God's World and the Great Awakening* (Clarendon Press: Oxford 1991), pp. 118ff.

23   Helm, *Faith and Understanding*, op. cit, p. 144, after Anselm.

achieve, by human means, a grip on God could we suppose it possible to do either. The Stoics spoke bluntly: Dion, supposing he is wise, is equal to Zeus Himself.[24] If that sort of wisdom were impossible it would also be impossible to hope that we, being miserable reptiles, could discover truth. Newton was wrong to think that mere *experience* or the description of it could be counted on: without God's guidance we cannot even identify the true description of a present fact. Only if there is, somewhere, a real identity between what a human being can think and see, and what is actually true of the world God makes, do we have any chance at all of knowledge.

So just as it is a necessity of thought that God exist and that the world is founded upon His Will and Reason, so is it also necessary to suppose that somewhere, and somehow, God's knowledge can also be *our* knowledge. That this was achieved in Jesus is not a thesis to be proved by reason. That it *could* have been can only be denied by those who have despaired of intellect. If it is strictly impossible for a mortal mind and heart to be the complete expression of God's Will and Reason, that is as much as to say that *our* world can never be *God*'s world. God, and the World He sustains, must always be a grand unknown, with purposes and descriptors that must be opaque. It is not enough to reply that our world might significantly *mirror* God's. If there is no-one with access to them both, how could we ever confirm that they were even similar? Nor will it do to say, as might seem easier, that a mortal intellect might *house* the immortal. In cases of possession the god's view displaces and suppresses any merely mortal mind: it is, exactly, as if Someone Else were moving that body's parts. In cases of inspiration it may be that the mortal mind can overhear the god's advice, without ever *being* the god, and without any assurance that it is a god at all. But neither possession nor inspiration allow that any human contrivance could be adequate. Only if God's Word is *also* and unfeignedly a human person can we have any confidence that what we do and think as people can also be what God and His Word require.

But how can that be possible? We are ourselves familiar with the gap between *our* perception of things and how things *really* are. *My* world is, perforce, a world of discrete, middle-sized objects glimpsed on a human time-scale and with humanly-contrived significance. My imagination may flesh out the gaps in my perception, piecing together a phantom of my body's inner parts, the room next door, the house across the street, the roads and railways leading away from town. I may even have some vague notions of this world's position in an imagined galaxy or local cluster, or this age's relationship to the long-ago destruction of the dinosaurs, the formation of the planets, or the emergence of second-generation stars. But that larger world, as well as the immensely *smaller* worlds of virus, atom and superstring, is something that I learn or guess about, not something that I readily experience. If I were instead to be immediately aware of *all* those other worlds, and conscious of *this* moment and locality as one amongst immensely (infinitely?) many, how could I still be human? Being human *is* to live amongst uncertainties, from one location only, at one particular age. A circle whose centre is everywhere and whose circumference

---

24 Plutarch, *On common conceptions*, 1076a, reporting Chrysippus' view: A.A. Long and D.N. Sedley, eds, *The Hellenistic Philosophers* (Cambridge University Press: Cambridge 1987), vol.1, p. 380: 61J.

nowhere (which is, God) cannot at the same time be one whose centre *only* travels between Judaea, Egypt and Galilee.

The Incarnate Word's particular mode of consciousness, of course, is hardly for us to decipher. By one account the Word must 'empty' itself for the duration of that single human life – but how then can that life have been *more* than human? On another, it retained omniscience and omnipresence – but how then can it have been *human*? Once again, my object is only to address the epistemological and metaphysical issues about our grasp of scientific truth. And in that context it seems that there must be an answer. After all, we have to believe that knowledge is available to us. One thought *can* fill immensity. We can hope to know *everything* because there is a pattern to events which is their matrix, governor, source or what you will. We cannot reasonably expect to infer that pattern merely from the finite series of events with which we are ordinarily acquainted, since any such series is compatible with infinitely many patternings (as Charles Babbage realized). But it does not follow that we might not have that pattern through another route. Those who follow the outward expression of the pattern, its letter, are too easily misled. Only those who have internalized its spirit can expand the series as the pattern wills. It may be true that only a finite sequence of the pattern was available to the Incarnate Word (and certainly it could only *express* a finite sequence). But the rest of the infinite sequence could still have been contained in it, and readily available to those who were infected by its spirit (or the spirit of the One from whom it springs).

Consider another, sadder allegory. Some forms of brain damage leave the victim 'blind' (so far as any conscious visual experience goes), but capable – surprisingly – of *guessing* correctly where things are. The information is available, in one mode, even though it is not represented visually. The Incarnate Word cannot, in one way, contain the worlds. But in another it can 'guess' rightly about anything it chooses to attend to. Its guesses and extrapolations can't be wrong, whereas ours often are. We don't discover that infallibility by experience, of course: however long the series that it successfully predicts, it *might* – as far as our experience goes – go wrong next minute. Success may strengthen a conviction, but is not its proper source. For that we need 'the testimony of the spirit'.

If the Stoics were right to think that there were no contingencies, then Dion and Theon alike could be God's 'equal': each knows implicitly what must be, even though their explicit and conscious knowledge may be limited by their locale and circumstances. Each will guess right about each other's world, but neither has conscious access to it. If there were contingencies then, equally, neither could *know* what they do not themselves, individually, perceive. Neither would know everything implicitly. Only the one who is involved in every choice could *know* exactly what is chosen, since it is in those choices that the pattern itself is willed. So two theses of orthodox Christianity do hang together. On the one hand, there is no rationally discoverable formula which dictates all and only real events, and so there is no chance of severally acquiring that. No *separate* individual can know everything, since their separation, exactly, places many contingencies apart from them. Nor can we work out the truth merely from our own flawed experience and logical intuition. On the other hand, if there were – as there must be – *someone* who knows everything it can only be the one original maker. If the Word is God's *Will* and Reason, then it knows, it contains, all happenings by its share in what occurs. So the Incarnate Word does not guess right *by formula* but, as it were, by memory. He *remembers*, when He needs or wills to, what is variously and by His permission willed. It follows that there can only be one Incarnate Word, not many.

Briefly, there are three options. In the first, no finite being can actually know all things – and in that case, we cannot even know *some* things, since all our seeming knowledge can be subverted by the next event. In the second, we can know all things, since they are determined by a single formula whose essence can contain the whole, and there may be many sages. In the third, there is only one who knows, by formula and by participation, and it is against His knowledge, guided by the spirit, that we check our own.

By Lev Shestov's account, Spinoza was, or might have been, just such a Stoic sage, fitting the second option: one who 'carefully pruned away from his "being" all "sensible" elements, so that he succeeded better than anyone else in transforming his soul into a general idea. He ceased to be Spinoza *hic et nunc*; he became *philosophus*, that is, a being not only bodiless but "without senses", like the God whom he worshipped'.[25] For that reason, Shestov suggested, Spinoza 'provoked in his contemporaries so superstitious a repugnance': by being a philosopher he abandoned humanity. 'It is the essence of reason to perceive things from the aspect of eternity'.[26] Shestov's dream, and Chesterton's, was different, and focused on one who was at once divine and truly, paradigmatically, human. The only actually possible world is one in which God is become human.

Maybe Spinoza, Aristotle and the rest were right, in theory: *reason*, or *the divine reason*, contains things whole. But all *our* efforts in that direction end in failure and idolatry: our only hope is to encounter the divine here-now, as something that we could not have imagined, and cannot now comprehend. We do indeed have glimpses of the world beyond our immediate vision, but such glimpses are at once expanded into theories that take us further away from the place where God has placed us. So science, as we now practise it, rests on theology: on the faith that there is a discoverable pattern, to be identified not merely by ratiocination but by loving involvement in an historically grounded community of the faithful. The One, the Word and the Holy Spirit are One God; the Word is both God and finite being; and the Spirit lives in the hearts of all faithful people. Without those convictions, science – and all human reasoning – are no more than a set of habits.

---

25   Shestov, op. cit, p. 265.
26   Spinoza, *Ethics*, 2p44c2, cited by Shestov, op. cit., p. 364.

Chapter 7

Can We Make Sense of the Idea that God's Existence is Identical to His Essence?

Howard Robinson

7.1 Introduction

The last thirty years or so have seen an extensive revival of sympathetic discussion of those questions in the philosophy of religion that concerned the scholastics. Very little sympathy has been directed, however, to the topic chosen for this essay.[1] Analytical philosophers seem to fear that any metaphysical talk of 'being' is redolent of the jargon they associate with Heidegger, and represents abandonment of the first principles of rigorous philosophy. This feeling persists despite the fact that there has been a growing scepticism about the Kantian dismissal of 'existence' on the grounds that '"exists" is not a predicate'. Even more paradoxically, discussion of analogical predication flourishes, though the main reason for thinking that univocal talk about God is not possible is that there are no distinct properties in Him, corresponding to predicates, and this is because He is pure undifferentiated being – *ipsum esse subsistens*: it is due, that is, more or less to the doctrine I shall be discussing. I hope to show that, though there is no shortage of problems, there is something important and plausible in the doctrine that the divine essence is identical with the divine existence.

The proper way to begin discussing a topic which employs arcane and abstract jargon, such as 'essence' and 'existence', might seem to be to attempt a definition of these terms. This, unfortunately, would guarantee that there was no space to discuss the topic itself, so controversial are both concepts. Furthermore, I do not think that this would be the best away of approaching an understanding of the gist of the doctrine. My strategy instead is, first, to look at some of Aquinas' arguments for this doctrine, then to reformulate the strongest version and spend the rest of the paper investigating it.

---

1 Brian Davies, O.P., in one of the relatively few articles that has taken it seriously, cites the dismissive comments of otherwise sympathetic analytic philosophers, such as Kenny, O'Hear, and C.J.F. Williams.

7.2 Aquinas's Arguments, S.T. 1a.3.4.[2]

It is natural to begin our discussion by looking at the arguments Aquinas uses in the *Summa Theologiae*. The relevant passage is as follows:

> *I* answer *that*, God is not only His own essence, as shown in the preceding article, but also His own existence. This may be shown in several ways.
>
> First, whatever a thing has besides its essence must be caused either by the constituent principles of that essence (like a property that necessarily accompanies the species – as the faculty of laughing is proper to man – and is caused by the constituent principles of the species), or by some exterior agent., – as heat is caused by fire. Therefore, if the existence of a thing differs from its essence, this existence must be caused either by some exterior agent or by its essential principles. Now it is impossible for a thing's existence to be caused by its essential constituent principles, for nothing can be a sufficient cause of its own existence, if its existence is caused. Therefore that thing, whose existence differs from its essence, must have its existence caused by another. But this cannot be true of God; because we call God the first efficient cause. Therefore it is impossible that in God His existence should differ from His essence.
>
> Secondly, existence is that which makes every form or nature actual; for goodness or humanity are spoken of as actual, only because they are spoken of as existing. Therefore, existence must be compared to essence, if the latter is a distinct reality, as actuality to potentiality. Therefore, since in God there is no potentiality ... it follows that in Him essence does not differ from existence. Therefore, His essence is His existence.
>
> Thirdly, because, just as that which has fire, but is not itself fire, is on fire by participation; so that which has existence but is not existence, is a being by participation. But God is His own existence, as shown above [1a. 3. 3.]; if, therefore, He is not His own existence He will be not essential but participated being. He will not therefore be the first being – which is absurd. Therefore God is His own existence, and not merely His own essence.

These three arguments can be stated as follows.

A

(1) Any property of a thing not identical with the essence of that thing is either caused by the essence or comes from outside.

(2) Essence cannot produce its own existence or it would be prior to itself.

Therefore

(3) If existence is not identical with essence, it must come from outside.

(4) God's existence does not come from outside.

Therefore

(5) God's existence is identical with His essence.

---

2   There are at least two other places in which Aquinas discusses this topic. They are *Summa Contra Gentiles*, Bk.I, ch.22, and *De Potentia Dei*, Bk.3, Qu.7, Art.2. I discuss such arguments as are found in these sources and are different from those in *S.T.* in an appendix.

B

(1) Existence is what makes something – including essence – actual.

Therefore

(2) Considered separately, essence is potential relative to the actuality of existence.

Therefore

(3) If God's essence is not identical to His existence, He would have potentiality in Him.
(4) God has no potentiality in Him. (1a. 3. 1)

Therefore

(5) God's essence is identical to His existence.

C

(1) Something which has a property, but is not identical to that property, has it by participation.

Therefore

(2) Something which has existence but is not identical with existence has it by participation.

Therefore

(3) If God has existence but is not identical with His existence, then He participates in existence.
(4) Anything which participates in existence cannot be the first or primary existent.
(5) God is the primary existent.

Therefore

(6) God is His own existence. (That He is His own essence is already proved, 1a. 3. 3)

7.3 Initial Discussion of Aquinas's Arguments

Of the three arguments, the one that can most usefully be developed is *A*. All the arguments draw heavily on scholastic conceptual apparatus, but *A* is the one that can most easily be cast in a way that frees it from too contentious a dependence on that apparatus. Before developing it we will look at *B* and *C*.

B can be made formally valid by adding two premises. To move from (1) to (2) one needs

(1a) If something *x* is made actual by something *y*, then *x* is potential.

And to move from (2) to (3)

(2a)   Anything potential prior to being actualized remains potential after actualization.

The generation of (5) from (3) and (4) is a simple move of *modus tollens*.

(1a) is probably uncontroversial, and, *ex hypothesi* so is (4). (1) treats existence as a genuine property and so is controversial. (2a) seems to be very deeply immersed in a particular understanding of the concepts of potentiality and actuality. Matter, when actualized by a form, is still spoken of as potential, but does it follow that essence or form, considered as a universal, is still potential when realized? In other contexts, the form, though only contingently realized, is thought of as the actualizing component. We shall return to discussing (briefly) the contrast between the form-matter and essence-existence dichotomies in section 7.4, but for the moment the moral is that this argument is too entangled with the scholastic apparatus to be put to independent use.

C has three contentious components. (1) seems to embody a Platonic conception of the relation between properties and their instances; the move from (1) to (2) involves treating existence as a property; and (4) seems a rather opaque doctrine. (4), like (2), involves treating existence as a property, but also depends on what Plantinga calls the *sovereignty-aseity assumption*.[3] This is the idea that it is inappropriate that there should be any properties logically prior to God, and that this would be so if He had to be described as *participating in* properties. We shall be discussing this in section 7.7.

For all these reasons, *C* does not constitute a good jumping-off point for a modern argument.

To make *A* valid, the move from (1) to (2) requires

(1a) Existence is a property.

Therefore

(1b) If the existence of a thing is not identical with the essence of that thing, it is either caused by the essence or comes from outside.

The other steps are uncontroversial. (2) seems to be true (though we will discuss a variant of it when considering *A'*) and (4) is not in dispute. The main problem with *A* as it stands is that it is opaque what one is committing oneself to in the talk of 'essence'. I think the argument can be restated simply in terms of *properties*, and it is in that form we shall discuss it.

A'

(1) For any property F possessed by an object *a*, *a* is F either in virtue of some other properties it possesses, or from outside, or [*a*'s] F = *a*.
(1a) Existence is a property.

Therefore

(1b) If anything, *a*, possesses existence, then *a* exists either in virtue of some other property it possesses, or from outside, or *a*'s existence is identical to *a*.
(2) Existence of *a* can never be in virtue of any other properties *a* possesses (for no properties are self-instantiating).
(3) God's existence cannot come from outside.

---

3   *Does God Have a Nature?*, 31-32.

Therefore

(4) God's existence = God.

To complete the argument we need to add:

(5) God's essential properties – being omniscient, omnipotent and morally perfect – are not a consequence of other properties, nor do they come from outside.

Therefore

(6) God is identical to His essential properties

Therefore

(7) God's existence = His essential properties.

This argument is valid. The assumptions are (1), (1a), (2), (3) and (5). (3) and (5) are not in dispute here. (2), rightly understood, should be uncontroversial. The objection to it has been raised that existence can be possessed in virtue of *any* property, because, for any F, if x is F, x must exist.[4] Whilst this is true, it misses the point, which is that the existence of something (that is, that it exists, or why it exists) can never be *explained* simply by reference to its possession of some other property. This is what the ontological argument tries to do and why it falls under suspicion. So in the relevant sense of 'in virtue of', (2) is correct.

The two controversial premises are (1a) and (1). The contentious nature of (1a) – which, we have already seen, is common to all the arguments from Aquinas we have considered – is well-known, and usually invoked as if it were the heart of the problem with all metaphysical uses of the concept of existence. We will discuss it in the next section. (1) is problematic in two ways. One is the question of whether the options presented in (1) are exhaustive. In particular one may challenge whether it may be (or it may be most rational to treat it as) a brute fact that an object has a certain property; that is, one may doubt whether there need be an account of how an object comes to possess its properties, *including existence*. The other is whether the option that *a*'s F is identical to *a* really makes sense, or whether it is a category mistake to identify an object with one (or any) of its properties. The first of these questions will be dealt with in section 7.5: the second governs our change of direction in the latter part of the paper.

7.4 'Existence is not a property'.

As is often now remarked, it is not clear at first sight what it means to say that existence is not a property, or that 'exists' is not a predicate. Following Frege, it is usually interpreted to mean that one can always paraphrase legitimate first order existential claims as quantified expressions. Thus 'horses exist' is more perspicuously cast as 'there are horses', and 'unicorns do not exist' as 'there are no unicorns' and 'the Queen of England exists' as 'there is some unique thing which is the Queen of England', and 'the King of France does not exist' as 'there is no unique thing which

---

4   This point was raised in discussion by Professor Alex Orenstein.

is King of France'. Existence claims with names as their subjects – such as 'Tony Blair exists' – are deemed ill-formed on the grounds that positive assertions are tautologous and negative ones ('Tony Blair does not exist') are self-contradictory. In neither case are they informative, for if you can name it, its existence is presupposed, and if it does not exist, one cannot name what one is talking about.

Two issues arise here. First, are first-order existential claims really redundant? Second, is it obvious that quantification does not attribute a property?

It is not obvious that there is no informative use for first order existential claims. Brian Davies, who defends the Fregean line in 'Aquinas, God and Being', considers the sentence 'Queen Elizabeth II does not know that Brian Davies exists'. This seems to be a straightforward assertion. Davies replies we shall only be able successfully to convey what the Queen's ignorance amounts to by disposing of the expression '– exists' and saying such things as 'Queen Elizabeth II does not know that someone wrote *The Thought of Thomas Aquinas* and that the same person was born in London, is the son of Lillian and Brian Davies, is a philosopher, etc' (507).

In other words, denial of the first order existential use commits one to the descriptive theory of proper names. As this theory is generally rejected on strong grounds, this is a risky commitment. Nor is this kind of case the only one. G.E. Moore considered '– no longer exists' and '– might not have existed' as instances where the first order use is not plausibly eliminable. I do not think that these cases have been convincingly answered. Christopher Williams challenges these cases by what is meant to be a *reduction*.[5] The purpose of invoking these embedded attributions of existence is that, if they make sense, so must '*a* exists'. Williams says that this implication cannot be correct, for '*a* exists' is defective for the reasons given above, namely that '*a* exists' is a referential tautlogy and '*a* does not exist' is a contradiction, so the attribution of existence adds nothing to the act of reference itself. It is not possible here to go into this question adequately, but there are two ways in which one might resist it. First, it rests on the contemporary dogma that reference is an extensional relation: I can think about, fear, hate or love what might not exist, but I cannot refer to it. Put this way, it seems almost self-contradictory (how can I fear etc something without being able to identify it sufficiently for it to be proper to say I am referring to it?) but commitment to the extensional nature of reference lies at the heart of modern philosophical logic.[6] But, second, even if this approach to reference were correct, it would not follow that existence were not a property, but only that bare assertions or denials of existence were existential tautologies or contradictions, rather like 'I am a thinking being' and 'I am not a thinking being'. For the reference to work, the positive predication must be true, and without the reference there is no proposition, but '– is a thinking being' is a perfectly good predicate. The natural response to this is to point out that '– is/is not a thinking being' occurs mainly in contexts which are neither tautologies nor contradictions, whereas '– exists/does not exist' is always in such contexts. But the relevance of this depends on how one draws the relevant field of discourse. 'Exists' figures non-redundantly in 'no longer exists' and 'might not have existed', but not in present tense uses. '– is a thinking being' is non-redundant in everything except first

---

5 In *Being, Identity and Truth*, 28-33.
6 I discuss this in the second half of 'The ontology of the mental'.

person present tense uses. This is only a difference of degree.[7] Even without these considerations, it is not obvious that existence is not a property. I conclude that there are good reasons for thinking that there are ineliminable uses of 'exists' as a first order predicate, and, therefore, for thinking of existence as a first order property.

It tends to be assumed that if one can reduce all uses of 'exists' to the quantifier, then one has shown that existence is not a property. This does not obviously follow. The existential quantifier could be thought of as attributing the property of existence, which is the common feature of all objects in the domain of discourse, as normally understood. The quantifiers are normally explained as abtractions created by replacing names by variables. Thus we understand

Ex (x is a horse)

via its derivability from something of the form

a is a horse

If we think of the latter, in its standard (that is, non-fictional etc) use as equivalent to

a is a horse and *a* exists

then we can see the quantifier as drawing on the ubiquitous presence of the first order predicate.[8]

It is to avoid this natural reading that the classic interpretation of existence as attributing something to the concept is devised. What is attributed is usually thought to be relational. Thus 'there are horses' glosses as 'the concept *horse* is instantiated' where instantiation is obviously a relation between a universal and a particular. Initially, this strikes me as no more plausible than other second order explanations of meaning – for example, explaining identity statements such as 'Hesperus is Phosphorus' as 'really meaning' 'the name "Hesperus" refers to the same thing as the name "Phosphorus"'. Implausibility apart, the considerations raised above suggest that the quantificational analysis cannot accommodate all uses of 'exists'. But there is a way of taking the second order analysis which is not incompatible with regarding 'exists' as a first order predicate, and that can be approached by treating existence as a *monadic* predicate of concepts.

The view that assertions of existence attribute a monadic property to concepts provides an approach to the scholastic doctrine we are considering. Existence added

---

7   There have been philosophers, usually influenced by 'ordinary language' and Wittgenstein, who think that each idiom alone must demonstrate that it has a significant use. On this account 'I am a thinking being' (and 'I know I am in pain') are deemed without use and therefore without sense. I take it that any grasp on the distinction between semantics and pragmatics, or 'conversational implicature' shows this to be nonsense.

8   This answers the problem raised by Penelope Mackie in her entry 'Existence' in *The Routledge Encyclopaedia of Philosophy*. She says

... if existence is a genuine property, an account must be given of the relation between this property and the existential quantifier, since it is undeniable that some general existential sentences are closely related to, if not equivalent to, existential quantifications (vol. 3, p. 492).

to essence constitutes the first-order individual. Existence is not simply a property of the individual, in the ordinary sense; it is more a metaphysical component of it, along with form or essence. So the monadic property of the concept – its instantiation – is the same thing as the existence of the individual. These are two compatible philosophical perspectives on the same situation. This way of looking at existence parallels the two accounts of individual substance that Aristotle presents in *Met. Z* and *Categories*. According to the latter, one can take the existence of the individual substance as ontologically primitive: on the other, this can be understood as the individualization of a form.

One might be worried because the essence-existence (or concept-existence) partnership seems suspiciously close to the form-matter pairing.[9] In both cases that which endows the general nature of something is individualized by the other component. On the other hand, the two dichotomies stand in opposite relations to the actuality-potentiality dichotomy. Form actualizes the in-itself-merely-potential matter, but existence actualizes the in-itself-abstract (and so only potentially concrete) essence. But there need not be a contradiction here. Form (and essence) are actual in the sense that they have a determinate nature, in contrast with matter as such. But they do not have actuality, in the sense of actual existence, from themselves. Nor do they derive it from matter, for it is not matter that determines that a form is realized, though it is a necessary condition. Nor does matter make existence redundant in its role as particularizer. Matter is *kinds* of stuff. Flesh and bones, or water, are kinds. Even prime matter is a type of thing, not a bare individuality. This is why essence, which includes reference to matter, as form does not, is still universal.

My tentative conclusion is as follows. (i) There can be no harm in saying that existence is a property of all actual objects, and the difficulty in eliminating certain first-order predications of 'exists' strengthens this conclusion. (ii) Existence can be thought of as what realizes or individualizes kinds: it may do this through realization in matter (for most things) or possibly without in the case of some.

7.5 Existence is not Best Treated as a Brute Fact

A' (1) requires that there be some account of why it is that a thing exists. But could it not simply be a brute fact: there is a God, although there might not have been? In responses to this objection, one might argue that it is not clear what force we can attach to the suggestion that He might not have existed. If there is a God then it is plausible to conclude not merely that without Him nothing would have existed, but that without Him nothing *could* have existed. This is not meant just causally, but metaphysically: if there is a God of the traditional kind, it has consequences for what it is for finite things to exist, not merely for why they do. Once one accepts that God is the source of things, one has to accept that there is no other way they might have come to exist. Just as water, when it exists, could not have failed to be H_2O, existent beings, when they exist, could not have failed to be dependent on God: in other words, it shows us something about the nature of existence itself. There could

---

9   See *De Pot.* III, 7, ii, 9th objection and reply for Aquinas's comments on this.

not have been any world in which anything existed and He did not.[10] Furthermore, if God exists, then it is not metaphysically possible that He should not have existed, though it may be conceivable, in the sense that we can coherently describe a world in which He is not. Does it follow from this that, if God exists, it is not just a brute fact that He does, but a fact that has some kind of account? If there are no genuinely possible worlds in which He does not exist, and if anything that does exist derives its existence from Him, then His existence can hardly be described as an accident.

I do not wish to pretend that the parallel with natural kind terms is exact. Although there cannot be water that is not H_2O, there can be waterish stuff that is not: the restriction is more semantic than metaphysical, because it does not restrict what combinations of properties are possible, only what you are allowed to call them. Existence, however, is like pain: there cannot be painish stuff that is not pain, and there cannot be existence-ish stuff that is not existent. The parallel with natural kinds is this: just as science tells you what the real or inner nature of a natural kind is, so a correct metaphysics will – or perhaps one should say *might* – tell you what the real nature of existence is. In both cases, given that they have this real nature, it could not have been otherwise. (How far the metaphysics that can give this answer, if there is one, is purely *a priori* and how far it draws on the empirical, is another question.)[11]

---

10   David Chalmers in 'Does conceivability entail possibility?' denies that there is such a thing as 'deep necessity' – that is, as any kind that cannot be given the purely semantic interpretation to which Kripke's is subject. A proper treatment of this would require a full discussion of modality. In brief, my view is that *objective possibility* must be a function of the potentialities of the world as it actually is. This might seem to suggest a *combinatorial* theory of possibility, but it does not: recombinations are not, or are not necessarily, potential in the actual (see Robinson, 'Some problems with the combinatorial theory of possibility'). The full range of what we call 'logical possibilities' are objectively possible only if reality contains some force which really could have actualized any of them. It looks as if this would have to be God. Otherwise such possibilities will not be real, but only *subjective possibilities* – ones that are conceivable by us without surface contradiction – perhaps with certain indeterminacies. (We can conceive of them as what a God, if there had been a God, could have done, and this may be indeterminate in a way that what He can actually do would not be, if He actually exists.) If there is a God, there never was any potentiality for anything without Him, and existence could not have failed to be something wholly dependent on Him.

11   Brian Davies, in 'Aquinas, God and Being', takes God's creatorship and uncreatedness as an adequate gloss on what it means to say that God is *ipsum esse subsistens*. See his remark that:

'God, [Aquinas] says, is the source of the *esse* of things...Considered as such...God is *ipsum esse subsistens*...in saying that God is *ipsum esse subsistens* Aquinas means that God is not created (515)'. But one might have hoped that His being *ipsum esse subsistens* was what enabled Him to be – or was an explanation of the fact that He is – the uncreated source of the being of everything else, not merely a label for the fact that He is. Certainly *A'*(1) requires that it be taken in this way, for it lists the various accounts that might be given of the fact that something exists: the upshot is that either it derives it existence from elsewhere, or is identical with its own existence. This latter ought not to mean simply that it does not in fact derive its existence from elsewhere, but to be a kind of explanation of why it has no need to. My addition to Davies's view is that God is metaphysically necessary and that this throws light on the nature of existence as a property of other things.

One might want to say that it is a brute fact that God exists in one sense and not in another. There are coherently describable worlds in which God does not exist and it is a brute fact that none of them is the actual world. On the other hand, there never was any way in which it could have *turned out* that God did not exist. So it is not brute in fact, only relative to what we can conceive. Metaphysically, His existence had to be. So the options in (1) are exhaustive.

My tentative conclusion from these last two sections is that existence is probably a property, God's relation to it is more intimate than anything else's, and one should look favourably on any coherent theoretical articulation of this, if there is one.

7.6 The Argument So Far

The conclusion we are approaching is that *A'* has some force. If we are right about existence being a property, (1a) is true, and the further option in (1), that God's existence is just brute, does not seem plausible, so (1) is probably reasonable as it stands – provided that the idea that an object might be identical to one (or more) of its properties makes sense. This was our second reservation about (1) and it is a natural one. *Being blue* or *being dizzy* are perfectly good properties, but that would not suggest that it means anything to say that a non-abstract object is *pure blueness itself* or *pure dizzyness*, without any other distinct properties. What this suggests is that the question of whether existence is a property is not the crux of the problem: as with the ontological argument, the Kantian objection misses the main point.[12] What is really worrying is that the conception of God as pure being makes Him look like a self-predicating Form of Being, which seems to involve the crudest kind of Platonism. This picture is perhaps also reinforced by the apparent parallel with form and matter. It is as if, though 'being' is something we all possess, most things are made of finite matter, circumscribed by form. God, on the other hand, is 'made' solely of pure 'being', uncircumscribed by anything.

It would be a help if one could give a broader theoretical context to the peculiar intimacy of God to His existence, for nothing so far said shows that existence is the sort of thing that might constitute the whole nature of an object. To sort out this question – in so far as we can – it will be profitable to approach the issue from another angle. This can be done via the idea of divine simplicity.

7.7 Simplicity and the 'Neoplatonic' Model

A major motive behind the doctrine that God's essence is identical with His existence is belief in divine simplicity. There is a strong tendency to associate complexity with the possibility of nonexistence. This is one of the arguments that Aquinas uses for identifying essence and existence in the *Summa Contra Gentiles*, Bk I, chs 13 and 22. Such a possibility has a weaker and a stronger form. The stronger form is the possibility of generation and decay. This makes intuitive sense when the complexity

---

12 For the argument that existence as a predicate is not the real issue in the ontological argument, see Robinson, 'Varieties of Ontological Argument'.

in question is a matter of physical parts: that such parts might *come apart* is clearly plausible. The seeds of decay are not so obviously present in the case of logical complexity. It is not obvious that God's omniscience and His omnipotence need holding together by some external force. Because of the analogy between essence and existence and form and matter, however, one can perhaps see how an essence that is other than its existence might lack, or even come to lack, it. But logical complexity might be vulnerable to the weaker form of the possibility of nonexistence: maybe logical complexity, or, perhaps, just the complexity that results from the distinction of being and essence, might leave open the metaphysical possibility of God's nonexistence.[13] It might, that is, lead to His existence being just a 'brute fact', as I argued it probably was not in the last section. I will return to this at the end of this section.

The doctrine of God's simplicity has three elements.

(i) All God's properties are identical with each other.
(ii) He is Himself identical with the properties: that is, the individual is identical with the essence.
(iii) The *existence* of this unity is not something further: that is the individual, essence and existence are all the same.

Discussion of the doctrine of divine simplicity often centres on (i). If this does not make sense, then (ii) and (iii) (and (iii) is essentially the same as the topic of this chapter) are hardly worth pursuing, for their objective – the absolute unity of God – will already have been undermined. (Unless, that is, one regards the unity of essence and existence, because of its similarity with form and matter, to be a more substantial issue of unity than property distinctness.) We shall look, therefore, at the claim that all God's properties are identical.

Plantinga has the following objection. We can think of the properties either as universals or as instances of universals. If we think of them as universals there are two objections. First, it is manifestly false that goodness *is* knowledge, etc. Second, this interpretation, when combined with the doctrine that God is identical with His essence, would make God to be a property, and a property cannot act, and generally be the right kind of thing to be God. If, on the other hand we think of them as instances, there are also two objections. First, it would make God into a state of affairs, which, like a property, is too abstract. Second, it would not satisfy what Plantinga calls the 'sovereignty-aseity assumption'. We must look into this, because this assumption is what motivates the doctrine that God must be identical with His essence – that is, (ii) in the account of simplicity.

The sovereignty-aseity assumption.' ... if God were good or blessed, or knowledgable or wise by *particpation* in the properties goodness, knowledge, blessedness, or wisdom, then he would be *subsequent* to these properties; and if he *had* an essence (or nature), as opposed to being *identical* with it, then that essence would be his cause' (*Does God Have a Nature?*, 31-2).

---

13 In the case of the other properties, the threat is that He might have had some without the others; for example, that He could have been omnipotent and omniscient but not morally perfect.

The idea, therefore, is that, if He were not to be identical to his essence, then there would be an abstract entity – a nature – determining what he was like.[14]

It seems plausible that this is a problem for the Platonist, for then the universal is something distinct from God. But if one thinks of the universal as existing only in (or as) its instances, it is not so obvious that there is anything co-eternal with God and independent of Him. We do not need, however, to pursue this, for I think Plantinga misunderstands the idea that all God's properties are identical. In a sense, he takes it too literally. The idea is not that all God's properties are really one property, but that God has a nature that contains all the positive features of the properties ascribed to Him, without possessing them as separate features. This can be expressed in what I will call:

> *The neo-platonic model of God.* (i) There is a way of being such that that way of being lacks nothing positive of the properties attributed to Him in His traditional predicates, but without these properties being realized in the separately individualized way that they are realized in other cases and which constitute the paradigms of their intelligibility to us. (ii) This requirement is satisfied only if (a) the requisite way of being is thought of as *absolute, pure,* or *unlimited being,* or *pure act,* so that nothing positive is omitted; and (b) the various properties we attribute to God can be thought of as preeminently in Him.[15]

This contrasts with what one might call:

> *The limited 'efficient causal' model of God.* God possesses the 'three absolutes' – moral perfection, omnipotence and omniscience – and causally produces and sustains everything else in the universe.

This latter more modern and 'common-sensical' model seems to make God a 'Being amongst beings', as well as leaving unresolved the question of His relation to the properties He apparently instantiates. The 'neo-platonic' conception, on the other hand, faces the problem of showing how such unfamiliar ways of talking are intelligible.

Let us consider the elements of the neo-platonic model in turn.

---

14   There are two problems in this area which it is necessary to distinguish. First there is the relation between God and the properties – like wisdom and goodness – which we attribute directly to Him and in which He might therefore be said to participate. Second there is His relation to abstract objects, including properties or universals, in general. With these there arises a problem parallel to the *Euthyphro* problem in ethics, namely, can they or can they not be said to depend on God's will: either way there are problems. As will be seen from footnote 15, what I call the neo-platonic approach has ambitions to solve both, but in this chapter I am only concerned with the former.

15   If we were to use this model to try to solve the more general problem of God's relation to abstract objects, as described in note 13, then we would need the further condition that God contains in preeminent form, as part of the plenitude of His being, all positive properties found in the world, not just those attributed to Him. This raises serious difficulties for empirical and sensory qualities, at least.

(i) rests on two thoughts. One is that in the normal case of the possession of a property there is in the object that possesses it what one might describe as a distinct outline of that property which distinguishes it from the other properties the object possesses. In a certain sense, it cuts the object at its joints. In scholastic terms, there is a distinct form present. It is not just that, somehow or other the predicate truly applies, but that there is a distinct feature – a kind of particular real essence – that grounds it, and each property has a different ground (though perhaps not wholly distinct or non-overlapping from all others). The second thought is that this is not the case with God: the grounding of all properties is 'God as a whole', and that this means, not that He fails to satisfy the predicates or possess the properties, but that He satisfies them preeminently.[16] The two natural questions are, is the former account of how properties such as wisdom, knowledge and goodness apply to humans correct, and, if it is, does it make sense to apply them in the deviant way to God? The answer to the first appears to be that it is correct. The underlying complex structures – psychic or neurological – that makes someone wise or knowledgeable or virtuous, though, no doubt possessing common elements, are distinct: or it is very plausible to claim so. The second question is the issue of analogical predication, and I shall not discuss it here, but will assume that a positive answer is possible.[17] So it seems that the first condition of the neo-platonic model is not implausible.

The claim of (ii), that we can call this nature of God *pure being*, has already been discussed to some degree in section 7.5. We there concluded that the fact that His existence is not brute, but metaphysically necessary and the source of all other being, gives some sense to the notion that He is *esse ipse subsistens*. We could also draw on a distinction between a *thick* and a *thin* concept of existence. The thin concept is the logical property that everything existent shares. A thick concept would be one that provided a metaphysical analysis of what it is to exist. What this is, and even whether there is such, will depend on substantive metaphysical truth. For example, according to Berkeley, *esse est percipi vel percipere*. This is not presented as a contingent truth, but as the correct philosophical perspective on what existence is. If he is right, it could not have been otherwise. According to Plotinus, being is what emanates from the One in its act of self-understanding. In both cases (and I do not wish to imply that they cannot be reconciled), a correct analysis of the source of existence throws light on the nature of existence for all existent things. This is not just a feature of idealist or theistic metaphysics. If certain sorts of arguments correctly showed that everything was spatial curvature, or spatio-temporally located causes – or even water – then they would show what the real as opposed to nominal essence of existence was. We could conceive it might be otherwise, but it could not.

---

16 In 'A Modern Defence of Divine Simplicity', Brian Davies presents a largely apophatic view of our talk about God. Although I agree with much of what he says, I think that too 'negative' a line makes it difficult to understand how God can possess *preeminently* – a very positive notion – the properties we attribute to Him.

17 It must be admitted that this may be too quick. Perhaps what a successful account of analogical predication would do, would be to show that *if* a being of the nature I am attributing to God is possible, then it is possible to talk about it analogically, rather than that the possibility of the analogical talk would show that it is possible. I do not at the moment see how to pursue this further.

I think that we can conclude that there are three conditions that together make defensible sense of the doctrine that can be expressed by saying either that God's existence is identical with His essence, or that He is *ipsum esse subsistens*. They are: (i) God's nature is such that everything that exists depends upon Him in a strong sense, so that it is not metaphysically possible that there should have been anything without Him and not even metaphysically possible that He should not have existed. (ii) It is the case that God lacks the kind of structure that makes predicates applicable to other things, whilst appropriate predicates still apply to Him. (iii) A metaphysics which throws some light on how a being of the sort invoked in (ii) can play the role of God in (i) also throws light on what existence for anything is and how it is possible.

This enables us to return to the discussion with which this section started, namely, would divine complexity, particularly the complexity resulting from a distinction between existence and essence in God, leave greater room for His nonexistence and make it not metaphysically necessary? One might try the following argument.

(1) If something is the source of the being of everything else and has no source of its own being, then it is not metaphysically possible that that thing should not exist, if it exists in fact.

(2) God is the source of the being of everything else and has no source of His own being.

Therefore

(3) It is not metaphysically possible that God should not exist, if He exists in fact.

(4) If something's essence is not identical to its existence then it is metaphysically possible that it should not exist, even if it does in fact.

Therefore

(5) God's essence is identical to His existence.

This argument is valid. The arguments immediately above seem to carry us to (3), for they concern reasons for thinking that God's nonexistence is not metaphysically possible, if He exists. (4) seems to be supported by the arguments for A'(1). There the options were that God's existence come from outside, follow from His other properties, be a brute fact, or be identical with Him. The first two are obviously impossible and the last is almost the same as the essence-existence identity claim. So the only available option for someone who denies this identity is to accept that God's existence is a brute fact. What this means, however, is that it was a real metaphysical possibility that He should not have existed, which is what (4) asserts. So we seem to have another sound argument for the doctrine.

7.8 Appendix (I): Essence, Existence and the Ontological Argument

It has often been alleged that the identification of essence and existence would validate the ontological argument and that Aquinas's attempt to distance himself from the ontological argument by distinguishing what is *per se notum* and *notum quo ad nos* is weasel words. I want to end this paper with a brief defence of Aquinas.

That the identification of essence and existence leads to the ontological argument could be expressed in the following argument.

(1) There is a coherent verbal definition of the divine essence.

Therefore

(2) There is such an essence existing as an abstract entity of some kind.
(3) It is provable that the divine essence is identical with its existence.

Therefore

(4) The divine essence is actualized.

(1) and (3) (most relevantly, (3)) are *ex hypothesi*, and the move from (2) and (3) to (4) seems to be valid. If the argument is to be unsound, the transition from (1) to (2) must be invalid. In fact it is clearly invalid as it stands. To complete the enthymeme we need
(1a) To any coherent definition there corresponds an essence existing as an abstract object of some kind.

This would be disputed both by a nominalist and by someone who thought that the range of genuine universals was narrower than that of coherent concepts. We can concede that the nominalist option is not open to someone who deploys the concept of essence as it is employed in our topic. Even Plato himself accepts that the range of forms is narrower than that of concepts or meanings: mud and hair are too mean, and, probably, he would not accept any privative forms. Sometimes he seems to agree with Armstrong that the only forms one needs are those necessary for one's account of the world, from which other concepts can be derived. We could then express Aquinas's position in the following argument.

(5) As (1) above.
(6) For any coherent concept, there is a corresponding essence if such an essence is necessary for the correct account of reality.
(7) Various arguments – for example, first cause arguments – show that there must be a God to account for the world.

Therefore

(8) There is a divine essence.
(9) It is provable that this is identical with the divine essence.

In this pattern of argument, God's existence is not proved *a priori* – not *notum quo ad nos* – but is proved by some version of the cosmological argument. On the other hand, divine necessity – that is, the metaphysical impossibility of God's nonexistence – is *per se notum*, because it follows from the identity of His essence and existence.

7.9 Appendix (II): Other Arguments in Aquinas for the Doctrine

As well as in the *Summa Theologica*, Aquinas discusses this topic in at least two other places, *De Potentia Dei*, III, 7, ii, and *Summa Contra Gentiles*, I, 22. For our purposes, the discussion in *S.C.G.* is not significantly different from those we have discussed above. The arguments I called *B* and *C* are present in more or less the same form; *A* is rather different, though not enough to merit separate attention here. In addition, there is the argument based on the impossibility of divine complexity, which, though not present in *S.T.*, we have already considered. The argument in *De Potentia Dei*, however, is quite radically different, and so, for greater completeness, I want to consider it briefly.

The argument in *De Potentia Dei* is as follows:

> I answer that in God there is no distinction between existence and essence. In order to make this clear we must observe that when several causes producing various effects produce one effect in common in addition to their various effects, they must needs produce this common effect by virtue of some higher cause to which this effect properly belongs. The reason for this is that since a proper effect is produced by a particular cause in respect of its proper nature or form, different causes having different natures and forms must needs have their different proper effects: so that if they have one effect in common, this is not the proper effect of any one of them, but of some higher cause by whose virtue they act: thus pepper, ginger and the like which differ in characteristics have the common effect of producing heat; yet each one has its peculiar effect differing from the effects of the others. Hence we must trace their common effect to a higher cause, namely fire to whom that effect properly belongs. Likewise in the heavenly movements each planet has its peculiar movement, and besides this they have all a common movement which must be the proper movement of a higher sphere that causes them all to revolve with the daily movement. Now all created causes have one common effect which is *being*, although each one has its peculiar effect whereby they are differentiated: thus heat makes a thing *to be* hot, and a builder gives *being* to a house. Accordingly they have this in common that they cause *being*, but they differ in that fire causes fire, and a builder causes a house. There must therefore be some cause higher than all other by virtue of which they all cause being and whose proper cause is *being*: and this cause is God. Now the proper effect of any cause proceeds therefrom in likeness to its nature. Therefore *being* must be the essence or nature of God...

This is a valid argument, as follows.

(1) If various things that mainly have different effects also have a common effect, this must be because of some higher cause to which that common effect is appropriate or proper.

(2) All causes produce *being* of some kind, though in other respects their effects are different.

Therefore

(3) There is some higher cause to which production of being is appropriate or proper – and this is God.

(4) The effects of a thing that are proper or appropriate to it proceed from their likeness to its nature.

Therefore

(5) Being is the nature of this thing – that is, of God.

The first comment is that we here seem to have a 'sixth way' of proving God's existence, for we appear to move from the fact that there are causes to the conclusion that there is a God who is 'pure being'. It is not, however, a very impressive argument. It might be plausible to claim that, if various diverse causes have a common effect then there probably is some common property that they share which explains their common effect, but the reification of this property as a 'higher thing' – a separate entity – seems unjustified. The second premise conflates the 'is' of predication with the 'is' of existence. *Perhaps* this is permissable, given that existence is a property, on the grounds that possession of some property *F* involves *existing* in a certain mode. But we need not pursue that. (3) does follow from (1) and (2). (4) rests on the Aristotelian theory of causation as the transmission of form. The conclusion appears to be too strong. All that would follow would be that being is *part of* the nature of God, not identical with it. Fire is not identical to heat, though heat is essential to it.[18]

Bibliography

Aquinas, St Thomas, *Summa Theologica, First Part*, London, 1912.

Aquinas, St Thomas, *On the Power of God*, vol. 3, London, 1934.

Aquina Aquinas, St Thomas, *Summa Contra Gentiles*, Bk 1, New York, 1968.

Chalmers, David, 'Does Conceivability Entail Possibility?', forthcoming.

Davies, Brian, 'Aquinas, God and Being', in *The Monist*, vol. 80, 1997, 500-520.

Davies, Brian, 'A Modern Defence of Divine Simplicity', in *Philosophy of Religion: a guide and anthology*, ed. Brian Davies, Oxford, 2000, 549-565.

Mackie, Penelope, 'Existence' in *Routledge Encyclopaedia of Philosophy*, vol. 3, ed. Edward Craig, 490-493.

Plantinga, Alvin, *Does God Have a Nature?*, Milwaukee, 1980.

Robinson, Howard, 'Varieties of Ontological Argument and the Relevance of Kant's Objections', *Annales*, vol. 24, Budapest, 1992, 57-76.

Robinson, Howard, 'Some Problems with the Combinatorial Theory of Possibility', *Acta Analytica*, 21, 1998, 147-161.

Robinson, Howard, 'The ontology of the mental' in *The Oxford Handbook of Metaphysics*, eds M. Loux and D. Zimmermann, Oxford, 2003, 527-555.

Williams, C.J.F., *Being, Identity and Truth*, Oxford, 1992.

---

18 Versions of this paper have been read at the Butler Society, in Oriel College, Oxford, and at a private seminar in Oxford. I am grateful for the comments of various people including Lesley Brown, Christopher Kirwan, Penelope Mackie, Alex Orenstein and Richard Swinburne.

Chapter 8

Self-Determination and Moral Responsibility from Calvin to Frankfurt[1]

Thomas Pink

Responsibility and Self-determination

It is natural to suppose that we have a special moral responsibility for our actions and omissions and their consequences. We can be directly to blame for how we act as we cannot be directly to blame for what happens quite independently of anything we do or fail to do.

But why should it be for our actions and omissions that we are responsible? After all, the restriction of moral responsibility and blame to agency is not uncontroversial. From David Hume in the eighteenth century to Robert Merrihew Adams and T.M. Scanlon in our time there have been thinkers who have denied the action-responsibility tie.[2] They have supposed that we are as much responsible for the beliefs, desires and other attitudes which precede our actions as we are for our actions themselves. Even if their views may appear counterintuitive, they do demand reply. If our agency – our actions and omissions – is distinctively our responsibility, there must be something special about action and the capacity for it which explains why.

The obvious explanation is that our capacity for action is a capacity for self-determination. Many of our beliefs may be imposed on us by the evidence; desires and feelings may simply come over us. But where action is concerned, it can be we ourselves who determine what we intentionally do. It seems to be this belief that human action can be self-determined which underlies our ordinary understanding of our moral responsibility. We can be held morally responsible for how we act, because how we act is something that we can determine for ourselves as we determine nothing else.

The idea that human action is distinctively self-determined; and that because human action is self-determined, we have a special moral responsibility for how we act – these ideas are controversial. As we have noted, some philosophers deny them. But they are familiar ideas, widely understood and assented to by many ordinary people, and I want to assume them for the sake of argument. I want to consider further what this responsibility-basing self-determination might involve,

---

1   More on the subject of this paper is to be found in my *Free Will: A Very Short Introduction*, Oxford, 2004 and in my *The Ethics of Action*, volume 1 *Self-Determination*, volume 2 *Normativity*, Oxford forthcoming.

2   See Robert Merrihew Adams's 'Involuntary sins', *Philosophical Review* 1985 and Scanlon's *What We Owe to Each Other*, Harvard 1998.

and how such self-determination might occur in human action. We shall be making our enquiry, not at the level of any special psychology or science of the mind, but at the level of common sense belief – the same level at which we ordinarily deploy the conceptions of moral responsibility and blame. This is an inquiry into the 'common sense psychology' of moral responsibility.

There are two ways in which western philosophers have tried to understand the self-determination which we exercise in and through our action. The first way is as an inherently two-way power over whether or not we perform a given action – the power of *freedom* or, as I shall also term it, the power of control. But for a long time the existence of freedom, even its very possibility, has been the object of much philosophical dispute and scepticism. So a second way of conceiving self-determination has been developed. Self-determination has been conceived as a very different kind of power – a power which, as we shall see, is not two-way in nature at all; and this is the power which I shall term *voluntariness*.

The project of replacing freedom with voluntariness in the theory of moral responsibility unites thinkers as diverse as John Calvin in the sixteenth century and Harry Frankfurt in our day. In what follows I shall argue that, whatever its other attractions, this project faces a serious difficulty. It is in deep conflict with common sense psychology – and in particular with our ordinary conception of our own agency. For we ordinarily conceive of our agency occurring in forms which, though intuitively self-determined and fully our responsibility, are clearly non-voluntary. Self-determination, as we ordinarily conceive it, certainly cannot be voluntariness. It looks as though it must instead be freedom.

Freedom

By freedom I mean its being up to us – within our control – which actions we perform. If I possess freedom, it can be up to me whether I raise my hand or let it fall, open my eyes or close them, go for a walk or stay at home. Which I do is within my control; and whichever I end up doing, I was free to do otherwise. The idea of freedom or control is the idea of a power over our action – a two-way power which makes alternative ways of acting available to us.

One feature of freedom seems clear; and that is the essential link between the exercise of freedom and intentional agency. If I am to be exercising control, that must be through something which I am intentionally doing or intentionally refraining from doing. I cannot be exercising control through things which are merely happening quite independently of my own agency. Freedom is a power which is exercised over and through our capacity for action. So if we are morally responsible for how we exercise our freedom, that would explain why it should be for our actions and omissions and their consequences that we are responsible.

This idea of freedom is familiar. We naturally think that we actually do possess this freedom in relation to much of our action. Within certain limits – those limits set by our strength and resources – we think that it really can be directly up to us what actions we perform, whether we raise our hand or let it fall, whether we go for a walk or stay still. And it is very natural to explain our moral responsibility for how we act in terms of freedom. On this view, we are responsible for how we act in so far as how we act is within our control.

Freedom may be the most natural way of understanding why it is for our actions and their consequences that we are responsible. But the idea of freedom presents many problems and puzzles – the problems and puzzles which make up the free will problem. For example, there is the familiar question of whether freedom is compatible with causal determinism: if how I act is causally determined in advance by prior events outside my control, can it really be up to me – within my control – which actions I perform?

If, for whatever reason, suspicion grows that we may not really possess a freedom to act otherwise, then understanding moral responsibility in terms of freedom can start to look bad news. We may be tying moral responsibility and blame – central features of our ethics and of our social organization – to a freedom which simply does not exist.

This worry was once felt particularly deeply within western Christianity. For Christianity in the west had to live with the legacy of Augustine. And Augustinianism, in its most extreme form,[3] combines a deep belief in our status as blameworthy wrongdoers with an equally deep belief in our lack of any freedom whatsoever to do right. Extreme Augustinians such as Calvin had, therefore, to make coherent sense of moral responsibility without freedom. And it is importantly in their attempts to do this that we find the first developed attempts to conceive the self-determination which we exercise in our action in terms that are explicitly opposed to freedom.

Voluntariness

Voluntariness is doing what is one's will because it is one's will. It is doing what one has decided because one has so decided, or (alternatively) doing what one wants because that is on balance what one wants. And as much as does freedom, voluntariness too looks like a characteristic peculiar to action. For intuitive non-actions such as ordinary desires and beliefs are not formed voluntarily, since – it seems – our desires and beliefs are not subject to our will. We cannot generally form particular desires and beliefs just on the basis of deciding to form them. But our actions are subject to our will, or so it is often thought; and this may be why it is for our actions and omissions that we are responsible.

For voluntariness furnishes what looks very much like a form of self-determination, or a basis for it. The agent is to be identified with his will – with his own decisions, or with the balance of his desires or preferences. Self-determination then consists in that will causing its own content, what is willed, to be executed. Moral responsibility, then, is for the commission or omission of voluntariness. We find this notion of voluntariness being appealed to as an alternative to freedom by thinkers from John Calvin to Harry Frankfurt. We might not be free to act otherwise than as we do. But our actions can still be our responsibility because in them we are

---

3   A form which may not be found, at any rate with the same clarity, in Augustine himself.

doing what we ourselves will. Action can be self-determined because when we act, we are exercising a capacity to act as we will – as we ourselves decide or prefer.

Voluntariness is clearly consistent with the causal predetermination of action. After all, voluntary actions arise precisely through the effect on what we do of our prior motivations. Indeed voluntariness was originally used to explain how the predetermination of our actions is really consistent with moral responsibility – even given the admitted incompatibility of such predetermination with freedom. Thus Calvin argues that, thanks to the Fall, we are predetermined to do wrong by necessity, and lack any freedom to do right. As sinners, our actions are no longer within our control. But even in the absence of a freedom to do right, we can still be morally responsible for our inevitable wrong-doing because our wrongdoing is done voluntarily, out of a preference for or will towards doing it:

> The chief point of this distinction, then, must be that man, as he was corrupted by the Fall, sinned willingly, not unwillingly or by compulsion; by the most eager inclination of his heart, not by forced compulsion; by the prompting of his own lust, not by compulsion from without. (p.296)…he who sins of necessity sins no less voluntarily (p.317). *Institutes of the Christian Religion* ed. McNeill vol 1, Westminster Press 1960.

Harry Frankfurt's account of moral responsibility is a variation of Calvin:

> It is a vexed question just how 'he could have done otherwise' is to be understood in contexts such as this one. But although this question is important to the theory of freedom, it has no bearing on the theory of moral responsibility. 'Freedom of the will and the concept of the person' in *The Importance of What We Care About*, p. 24.

It is enough for moral responsibility that

> …a person has done what he wanted to do, that he did it because he wanted to do it, and that the will by which he was moved when he did it was his will because it was the will he wanted. Ibid. p. 24.

Just like Calvin, Frankfurt is seeking to displace freedom as the self-determination on which our moral responsibility is based, and to put voluntariness in its place. Notice, though, one difference between Frankfurt and Calvin. Frankfurt appeals not only to the action's being performed because it is willed, but also to the actions's being so willed because the agent wants it to be so willed. And by this Frankfurt means that the action should not only be performed because the agent wants to perform it; but that these desires to perform it should be motivating the agent into action because the agent wants to be motivated by them. We shall return to consider this further element in the story, and why Frankfurt adds it.

It is very important to remember just what different notions freedom and voluntariness really are. Freedom is inherently a two-way power. It links the doing of A to the alternative of refraining, and says that each alternative is available. To say that A is done through exercising this freedom is to say that it was also up to the agent not to do A. But nothing is said about how the doing of A was caused. Whereas matters are quite the other way round with voluntariness. To say that A is done voluntarily is to say something about A's cause: A is done as an effect of wanting or deciding to do A. On the other hand, nothing whatsoever is said about any capacity on the agent's part to refrain from doing A, or about the equal availability of not doing A as an alternative.

Voluntariness, of course, is not just a notion used in theories of moral responsibility. It is also used in theories of action. What I shall call the *voluntariness-based model* of action says that to perform an intentional action, on this theory, just is to act voluntarily – to do something in response to the desirability of doing it, on the basis of and as an effect of a desire or decision or intention to do it. This is a model of human action which goes back to Thomas Hobbes, and which we find defended nowadays by, for example, Donald Davidson and his many followers.[4]

If we identify action itself with voluntariness, why not identify self-determination with voluntariness too? For then we can explain why action and self-determination should go together – why self-determination should be something which we exercise in our intentional action. For self-determination and action are now both being explained and defined in terms of one and the same idea – the idea of voluntariness. So it is easy to see why action and self-determination should be associated. This model of action turns voluntariness into a very attractive explanation for how action is distinctively self-determined. We are appealing to a property which non-actions lack – but which all actions have.

On the other hand, this, of course, does raise a worry. For, if anything, voluntariness looks as if it might prove too general a feature of action. Not all action that is voluntary is plausibly self-determined. Not everything we do because we want to is really our responsibility. Desires might be compulsive, or imposed from without, or in some other way alien to the agent. To be motivated into action by such desires is not to be self-determining. Accounts of self-determination that rely on voluntariness will therefore need to beef the notion up. We may need to isolate those desires and other motivations which are properly the agent's – with which the agent really can be identified: self-determination must involve acting voluntarily on the basis of these motivations in particular.

And this, clearly, was part of the intention behind Harry Frankfurt's appeal to our wanting to be moved by the desires that move us. If we are acting on certain desires because we want them to motivate us, then perhaps those desires are ones with which we can be identified – so making the action which they motivate one which is genuinely self-determined.

It might be thought that Frankfurt's theory of identification is straightforwardly incoherent for a very simple reason. Motivating attitudes such as desires are not formed and held voluntarily or at will. As we have already noted, we surely cannot form and hold particular desires at will, just on the basis of deciding that we shall hold them. But when Frankfurt stipulates that

> ...the will by which he was moved when he did it was his will because it was the will he wanted

---

4   See Davidson's *Essays on Actions and Events*, Oxford 1980.

is he not really assuming the opposite? Is he not supposing that fully responsible action is motivated by desires that are held voluntarily?

But Frankfurt's position is in fact more nuanced. Frankurt explicitly refrains from claiming that the very existence in us of a desire, or even its strength, need be voluntary. What is supposed to be voluntary, at least on occasion, is whether the desire, once possessed with a given strength, constitutes our will in the sense of actually moving us to act as desired (see 'Freedom of the will and the concept of a person' p. 16). And that certainly can be voluntary; though, very importantly, we can make sense of the voluntariness involved as really nothing more than a first order voluntariness – a voluntariness at the point of the action desired. The principle remains that motivating attitudes themselves are inherently non-voluntary; I cannot form a desire or increase or decrease its strength at will.

For example, I may be aware that I hold a particular desire to do A – say a desire based on the stylishness of so acting. I may also know that if I did do A, I would be motivated in so doing by, *inter alia*, this desire to act stylishly. Suppose that, knowing all this, I also want to be motivated in my action by this desire. Then I will hold a second and further desire to do A – this time a desire to do A as a means to, or constitutive of, my acting out of the first desire to be stylish. And the second desire can then perfectly well add its weight to the first, to get me to do A out of both motivations. If this happens, that the desire to be stylish has motivated me into doing A is something which has occurred voluntarily; it has occurred on the basis of a desire that that desire motivate me. But the voluntariness is really first order, in relation to my actions. It is entirely explained in terms of my doing A in response to the apparent desirability of so doing – a desirability which reflects my beliefs about how A would be motivated were I to do it, and the desirability of doing A thus motivated. My desire to act stylishly in doing A, and the strength with which it is held, is itself entirely non-voluntary, formed as it is in response not to the desirability of holding the desire, but to the desirability of its object – doing A considered as something stylish.

The motivating force of some desires can be voluntarily reinforced by further desires – desires to act out of those desires – without the first motivating attitudes being in any way formed or held voluntarily themselves. And though much of Frankfurt's language may suggest more, it is only to the possibility of so much that he strictly commits himself.

But Frankfurt's theory faces two other objections. First, as has often been pointed out, the theory threatens to be viciously regressive, since it only raises the further question of our identification with the reinforcing motivations – with the desires to act out of other desires. What if these reinforcing motivations are not relevantly 'ours'? It seems that to be ours, these further motivations would in turn have to be reinforced by further motivations to act out of them. In which case a vicious regress is bound to ensue.

Secondly, it is most implausible to suppose that such reinforcing desires are very commonly held. Consider the voluntary actions with which I am normally concerned – such as whether I get to the station in time, or pay my bills. What motivates me to perform them? Certainly not a desire to act out of any particular motivation. I want to get to the station on time simply in order to get to work. I want to pay my bills simply in order to retain my credit. The desires which generally motivate actions such as these – what appear to be perfectly good, morally responsible and fully self-determined actions – are entirely unreinforced by any desires to act out of certain desires rather than others. Frankfurt's theory is wholly implausible in the concerns which it foists on morally responsible agents.

Voluntariness and Classical Compatibilism

Voluntariness, then, has been used to provide an account of self-determination to rival that of freedom. But it has also been used to state what freedom is, with the immediate aim of explaining freedom rather than replacing it. The project here is to solve the traditional free will problem – which is, of course, a problem about the compatibility of freedom with causal determinism. Is freedom compatible with the causal determination of our actions by conditions outside our control? Incompatibilists deny the compatibility; Compatibilists maintain it. And from Thomas Hobbes in the seventeenth century onwards, many Compatibilists have tried to use voluntariness to characterize freedom – and in terms that leave freedom clearly compatible with determinism.

I shall call a version of Compatibilism which uses voluntariness to characterize what freedom is *classical Compatibilism*. The hope of classical Compatibilism is to save freedom by rendering it a less problematic notion – and in particular, to leave freedom entirely consistent with causal determinism. But I shall suggest that classical Compatibilism has only further removed freedom from playing any distinctive role in moral theory. Attempts to explain freedom in terms of voluntariness have the inevitable effect of tying moral responsibility to voluntariness alone, and not to freedom at all.

Freedom, according to classical Compatibilism, is constituted by a sort of complex two-way voluntariness – by a capacity to act however one wants to act. To have control over whether one does A is for it to be true both that one would do A if one wanted to, and that one would refrain from doing A if one wanted to. Such a conception of freedom of action is plainly Compatibilist. It is fully consistent with one's actions being entirely determined, via one's desires, by conditions outside one's control.

We can now easily see how classical Compatibilism prevents freedom from remaining a serious condition on moral responsibility. For defining freedom in terms of voluntariness profoundly changes our view of what is going on when an agent exercises freedom.

The distinctive feature of freedom or control is that it is inherently a two-way power. It precisely involves alternate courses of action. To be free is to be free to do A or not – to have control over whether one does A or not. It is therefore to possess one and the same capacity which could be exercised in either of two ways – either to do A, or to refrain. To say that A is done freely, is to say that A is done on the basis of a capacity – control of which action one performs – that could equally have been used to refrain from doing A. To possess that capacity of freedom or control with respect to an action's performance is, equally, to possess it with respect to the action's omission.

Whereas voluntariness is quite different. To do A voluntarily is to do A because one decides or wants to. But this capacity to do A on the basis of wanting to do it would in no way be involved in refraining to do A. Voluntarily to refrain from doing A would involve the quite distinct capacity to refrain from doing A on the basis of wanting to refrain. And the capacities really are distinct, in that each capacity can be possessed without the other. To use Locke's example: I can possess and be exercising a capacity to stay in my room on the basis of wanting to; but, unbeknown to me, the door may be locked, and I altogether lack the capacity to leave should I so want.[5] Moreover, as distinct, the two capacities are exercised quite separately: each of these two capacities is exercised without any exercise of the other – we obviously cannot at one and the same time both be doing A and refraining.

Voluntariness can only be used to provide an account of freedom, then, by appealing to an agent's possession of both these two distinct capacities for voluntariness – both a capacity to do A voluntarily and also a capacity voluntarily to refrain; and by then claiming that the agent is exercising his freedom whenever he is exercising one of these capacities. But if freedom is indeed nothing but a combination of two distinct capacities for voluntariness, then voluntariness is going to be the only capacity for self-determination ever exercised. And then freedom must surely drop out as a distinct condition on moral responsibility.

Suppose I exercise my power to do A on the basis of wanting to, while lacking any power to refrain from doing A were I to want to refrain. (I would end up doing A in any case.) How could the mere lack of a power voluntarily to refrain affect the question of whether I was morally responsible for doing A? The only power of self-determination I could ever be exercising in doing A is a power to do A on the basis of wanting to. And I am exercising that power in any case. The presence or absence of an unexercised voluntary power to refrain must be irrelevant to my moral responsibility for doing A. And that is because it is quite irrelevant to the power of self-determination which I actually exercise in doing A.

Our moral responsibility for action depends on the fact that we ourselves determine how we act. The question then is what kind of self-determining power we really exercise. For that will provide the true basis of our moral responsibility. Is it that we are exercising a power to act otherwise? Or is it that we are acting as we will and because we so will? Which matters – control or voluntariness? The idea of freedom as two-way voluntariness is an attempt to combine both conceptions. But it is a deeply unstable compromise, and control is surely going to be the loser. And this is because when we are said to be exercising our freedom, no power to act otherwise is ever actually exercised by us to determine how we act – only a power to act as we will. The power to act otherwise may be present, but only as an entirely inert factor. Why make moral responsibility depend on it, if it is irrelevant to any power that the agent actually exercises over how he acts?

---

5   *An Essay Concerning Human Understanding*, Book 2, chapter 21 'Of power', §10 – p. 238 ed. Nidditch, Oxford 1975.

If we reduce freedom to a complex form of voluntariness, then we shall displace freedom from the theory of moral responsibility. It will be voluntariness and not freedom which explains how action is something self-determined. To the extent then that common sense really does want to adhere to freedom as a condition of moral responsibility, it must reject classical Compatibilism. Freedom cannot be reduced to a mere set of capacities for voluntariness.

It was inevitable, given its inherent logic, that the classical Compatibilist account of freedom as two-way voluntariness would eventually lead many moral philosophers to abandon any interest in freedom as such. Our freedom to do otherwise has ceased for many moral philosophers to be a central question within ethical theory, and become instead a problem that is primarily of interest to metaphysicians.

Indeed, for many modern Compatibilists, freedom is no longer properly recognized as a distinctive conception of self-determination in its own right. Freedom has begun to disappear as a clear alternative notion to voluntariness. The terms 'free' and 'control' are now applied to the exercise of mere voluntariness, as if there was nothing else that they really could mean. Davidson gives clear expression to just this shift:

> It is natural to suppose that an action one is free to perform is an action that one is also free *not* to perform…isn't it an empty pretence to say a man is free to perform an action if he is not also free to perform it? Surely, freedom means the existence of alternatives.
>
> The difficulty (recently brought to the fore by Harry Frankfurt) is that if we say a man is free to do x only if his doing x depends on whether or not the attitudinal condition holds (he chooses to do x, decides to, wills it, has rationalising attitudes), then we find counter instances in cases of overdetermination. What a man does of his own free will – an action done by choice and with intent, caused by his own wants and beliefs – may be something he would have been caused to do in another way if the choice or motives had been lacking.
>
> Two intuitions seem at war…The intuitions are, on the one hand, the view that we cannot be free to do what we would be causally determined to do in any case, and on the other hand, the feeling that if we choose to do something and do it because we chose it, then the action is free no matter what would have happened if we *hadn't* chosen. 'Freedom to act' in *Essays on Actions and Events*, pp. 74-75, Oxford 1980.

Davidson wants to hold on the term 'freedom' to express the self-determination which action distinctively involves. But, at the same time, the self-determination that really attracts him is voluntariness – *doing something because we choose to do it*, as Davidson puts it. That surely provides all the self-determination which we could ever want – and, of course, it is a self-determination which we can perfectly well exercise even if we lack the freedom to act otherwise:

> …it is an error to suppose we add anything to the analysis of freedom when we say an agent is free to do something if he can do it *or not*, as he pleases (chooses, etc.), ibid., pp. 74-75.

Notice, though, how keen Davidson is to disguise his abandonment of freedom. Freedom is a highly intuitive conception of the self-determination underlying moral responsibility – far too intuitive to be abandoned openly. The language of freedom cannot be given up entirely, but is reapplied. Terms such as 'freely' are retained, but are used now to pick out voluntariness, not freedom.[6]

Davidson hijacks the terminology of freedom to pick out voluntariness – and he can get away with this because Compatibilism had already allowed freedom to evaporate to not much more than voluntariness anyway. And here we see a fundamental difference between inheritors of the traditions of classical Compatibilism such as Davidson and Frankfurt and an earlier thinker such as Calvin. Unlike Davidson and Frankfurt, Calvin preceded modern classical Compatibilism and shared none of its concerns. Calvin was intent, not on reinterpreting human freedom, but on denying it.

Calvin was engaged in an ideological battle. He rightly viewed freedom and voluntariness as quite different notions. The scholastic accounts of moral responsibility which he faced appealed to a human freedom to act otherwise. And that made them, in Calvin's eyes, the dangerous intellectual constructions of a false religion. Calvin saw himself as battling against a Pelagianizing version of Christianity – a version of Christianity which misguidedly sought to turn the exercise of moral responsibility into a human achievement that was independent of God's work, and which used the notion of a human freedom to act otherwise to conceptualize this independence. Calvin was not concerned to reinterpret these theories, but to define their error clearly and to reject it. For Calvin the appeal to voluntariness was designed clearly to oppose and supplant accounts of moral responsibility which appealed to freedom. So Calvin condemned as a dangerous fudge any attempt to redefine 'freedom' to mean the same as voluntariness. Such redefinition simply clouded the issue, leaving room for the continuation of Pelagian error:

> Man will then be spoken of as having this sort of free decision, not because he has a free choice equally of good and evil, but because he acts wickedly by will, not by compulsion. Well put, indeed, but what purpose is served by labeling with a proud name such a slight thing? A noble freedom, indeed – for man not to be forced to serve sin, yet to be such a willing slave that his will is bound by the fetters of sin! Indeed, I abhor contentions about words, with which the church is harassed to no purpose. But I have scrupulously resolved to avoid those words which signify something absurd, especially where pernicious error is involved. How few men are there, I ask, who when they hear free will attributed to man do not immediately conceive him to be master of both his mind and will, able of his own power to turn himself toward either good or evil? (p. 264) *Institutes of the Christian Religion* ed. McNeill vol. 1.

Whereas the modern attempt to rebuild moral responsibility on the foundation of voluntariness has arisen in a very different way. Davidson and Frankfurt are working within, not against, an already existing and well established tradition of thinking about freedom – the tradition which is Compatibilism in its classical form. This tradition was originally about, not rejecting freedom, but redefining freedom in terms of a complex combination of voluntariness. The move into explaining

---

6   For an example of the hijacking of the term 'control' to pick out, not two-way freedom, but a kind of one-way voluntariness, see Fischer and Ravizza's 'guidance-control' in their *Responsibility and Control*, Cambridge 1998.

responsibility simply in terms of voluntariness alone is really an inevitable end-stage of this Compatibilist tradition – a stage in which, as far as the theory of moral responsibility is concerned, we are passing, very softly but ineluctably, from the steady conceptual dilution of freedom into its final and complete abandonment. And so the language of freedom and control can continue to be used – but now to pick out voluntariness, and not freedom proper at all. Though we entirely lack the freedom to do otherwise, as voluntary agents we are still said to do A 'freely'. The language of freedom and control has effectively been stolen, and misapplied to voluntariness – without, it seems, even the thieves themselves being fully aware of what they are really doing.

There is also another factor in play – a factor that lulls us into accepting what is really an outright theft of terms such as 'freely'. Even in ordinary usage, where someone, through exercising freedom, through doing something that they were genuinely free not to do, brings about an outcome which in fact would have happened anyway, we still talk of that outcome as something they bring about *freely* – as occurring through an exercise of their control. And this despite the fact that the occurrence would have occurred anyway, and so is outside their control.

But this simply shows that we can be morally responsible not only for how we exercise our freedom, but also for the consequences of that exercise. It may indeed be true that had we exercised our freedom otherwise, those consequences would have arisen anyway, being produced by someone or something else. Nevertheless, in actual fact it is as effects of our own free doing that the consequences have resulted; and so they have arisen as our responsibility, and we are said have brought them about freely. In other words, terms such as 'freely' are being used here to track what is still a thoroughly freedom-dependent responsibility. There is nothing here that legitimizes Davidson's complete detachment of terms such as 'freely' or 'control' from genuine freedom or control. And certainly nothing here shows that freedom is not essential to human self-determination and responsibility.

Frankfurt Cases

Harry Frankfurt, it is true, has claimed to prove that moral responsibility does not depend on freedom. In 'Moral responsibility and alternate possibilities' he asks us to consider cases where, he argues, we are deprived of the freedom not to perform some action A by the mere possibility of someone else's intervention.[7] Someone, Black, is ready to ensure that we do A. Were our motivations not already causally determining us to do A, Black would intervene to change those motivations, making sure that we were moved to do A after all. But as things are, our motivations already causally determine that we will do A. We do A, then, because of our own pro attitude towards doing A, and not because of any actual intervention from outside. We are therefore morally responsible for doing A, even though we lacked the freedom to do otherwise.

---

7   See 'Moral responsibility and alternate possibilities' in *The Importance of What We Care About*, Cambridge 1988.

Such cases do not, in fact, establish very much. They may well involve our having a responsibility for doing A despite lacking the freedom not to do A. But we can still explain our responsibility for doing A as something freedom-dependent in just the way discussed above. Suppose, thanks to Black's readiness to intervene, we would do A whatever happened. Nonetheless, it may still be through our own free doing that we actually end up doing A – as an effect of some prior action which we were free not to perform. In which case we are clearly responsible for doing A – but responsible in an entirely freedom-dependent way. Moral responsibility has not really been detached from freedom after all.

For example, the determining motivations which actually cause us to do A might be motivations that have arisen out of our own prior decision to do A. For we do see decisions as actions which we can be free to perform or not. Going by ordinary belief, the point at which we first exercise freedom is the point at which we decide for ourselves what we shall do. Just as it is up to us whether, say, we cross the road or not, so it is up to us whether we first decide to cross the road. It is in deciding for ourselves and forming intentions about what we shall do that we determine for ourselves what we shall do. So the psychological events and states of decision and intention that explain our voluntary actions are themselves cases of self-determined action. Taking decisions and forming intentions seems itself to be a case of intentional or deliberate action.

In which case, our responsibility for doing A could be derived from our responsibility for having decided to do A – a responsibility based in turn on our having had control over whether or not we took that decision. And that means that our moral responsibility still depends on our having had, at the stage of our initial decision, a freedom to do otherwise.[8] It is still only for what we control, and for its consequences, that we have moral responsibility. Or at any rate, such a dependence has not been disproved.

What if some agent lacks the freedom not to take the initial decision to do A, perhaps because the same story of potential intervention applies in turn to it? Black would have intervened to ensure the decision's occurrence had the agent not already been determined in advance to take it – this time not by some yet earlier action on his part, but by prior motivations, such as desires, that are entirely passive. Again, Black does not actually have to intervene. The agent takes the decision off his own back, other than because of such intervention. Frankfurt will press the question: is the agent then not morally responsible for taking his decision?

It may well be objected to Frankfurt that in this case the agent cannot be responsible. For his decision has not arisen as or out of any exercise of freedom, but has been imposed on him by conditions outside his control – by mere passions. But of course, if we do make this objection, we must still be assuming that moral responsibility depends on freedom – which is just the idea that Frankfurt is trying to get us to abandon. It seems we have a stand-off.

---

8   This point has already been made against Frankfurt by e.g. David Widerker in his 'Libertarianism and Frankfurt's attack on the principle of alternate possibilities', *Philosophical Review* 1995.

Or perhaps not a stand-off. For at this point Frankfurt faces a fundamental difficulty. Frankfurt faces this difficulty if he wants us to accept that we can be responsible for the decision to do A – and that we can be responsible even given the *total* absence of any freedom to do otherwise. For no matter his dismissal of freedom, Frankfurt still wants to tie moral responsibility to agency.[9] So he must hold on to the idea that moral responsibility presupposes some sort of capacity for self-determination – a capacity for self-determination that is exercised by us in our agency and nowhere else. Suppose then that decisions are a form of intentional action for which we can be responsible and in taking which, therefore, this self-determination can be exercised. And suppose that, as Frankfurt would want to maintain, the responsibility-generating self-determination exercised in decision taking is not freedom. If not freedom, what else is it?

It is not enough that our decisions are taken 'off our own back', other than as a result of the interventions of others. Desires and other such non-actions can similarly be formed 'off our own back', without the intervention of others; but if moral responsibility is tied to agency, we are not directly responsible for those. We need a positive story about what we are doing when we take a decision – a story that explains how decisions, as actions, are self-determined as non-actions are not. Now Frankfurt does have an alternative account of the self-determination which action involves; that account is voluntariness. We are morally responsible for how we act because in action we are exercising a capacity to act as we decide or prefer – we are acting as on balance we want to act, because we want so to act.

The problem for Frankfurt is that if decisions really are actions, this alternative story of voluntariness cannot apply.

Non-voluntary Action and the Will

A number of modern English philosophers, such as Bernard Williams[10] and Galen Strawson[11] argue that if our experience of our own action is what gives us the idea of self-determination in the first place, then the idea of self-determination which we are given must be an idea of voluntariness. And that is because our action is essentially voluntary. To act is to do something on the basis of wanting or deciding to do it, and that is how we experience our own agency. The child wants to pick up that ball lying on the floor, and finds itself managing to pick the ball up just as it wanted to do. In managing to do what it wants, the child has had, if you like, its first experience of successful self-determination. And it is from later reflecting on this experience of being able to act as we want that the idea of self-determination first comes.

On this view, any association between self-determination and freedom is a later development – and nothing more than a philosophical make-believe or fable. For the only self-determination which in fact we experience in our actions is voluntariness.

---

9   See for example, 'What we are morally responsible for', p. 100 in *The Importance of What We Care About*.

10   See for example his *Shame and Necessity*, California 1993 and 'Saint-Just's illusion' in *Making Sense of Humanity*, Cambridge 1995.

11   See his *Freedom and Belief*, Oxford 1986 esp. pp. 109-110.

But is our experience of our own agency really an experience of voluntariness? Certainly not, I want to argue – at least on our ordinary understanding of action. Intentional action need not be voluntary; in fact it centrally occurs in forms which exclude voluntariness. In other words, I want to argue that the voluntariness-based model of action gets the common sense psychology of action badly wrong.

If decisions and intention-formations are self-determined actions – and that is what we ordinarily suppose them to be – what form does this self-determination take? What kind of self-determination is to be found within the will itself? Let us consider an example. Suppose I am faced with a choice. I can take either one of two decisions. I can decide to go for a walk. Or I can decide to stay home. Now if decisions are self-determined, it must in some sense be me who determines which I decide to do. If I decide to go for a walk, it must in some sense be me who determines that I take this particular decision. But what form does this self-determination take? Is it voluntariness or is it freedom?

One hypothesis, as we have seen, would be that the self-determination is voluntariness. It is me who determines that I take the decision in so far as I take the decision to go for a walk voluntarily, that is, on the basis of having decided to take it. But can my decision to go for a walk be taken voluntarily? It seems not. I cannot first decide that I shall decide to go for a walk, and then take the decision to go for a walk voluntarily, just on the basis of the prior decision to take it. As Thomas Hobbes put it, using 'willing' for 'deciding':

> I acknowledge this liberty, that I can do if I will, but to say, I can will if I will, I take to be an absurd speech. Hobbes *Of Liberty and Necessity*.

I cannot decide today that at 2pm tomorrow precisely I shall then take a decision to go for a walk – and expect as a result to take that decision tomorrow, at the time decided on, just on the basis of today's decision to take it then. And this does not seem a contingent matter.[12]

Why cannot my decision to go for a walk be taken voluntarily? Consider what decisions are like. First, any decision, such as a decision to go for a walk, is a content-bearing psychological attitude. It is a psychological occurrence which is directed at

---

12   That I take a specific decision to do A rather than B is not something I do voluntarily. But even if this particular decision is taken non-voluntarily, there is something else which may be done voluntarily. That I make up my mind at all, one way or the other, about whether to do A may be something that I do voluntarily, on the basis of a prior decision to make up my mind. Does this allow us to understand self-determination at the point of the will in terms of voluntariness? Clearly not.

Remember we need to make sense of self-determination, not simply in relation to my taking a decision at all, but in relation to which decision I take. What is self-determined as well, and the self-determination of which also needs explaining, is not merely that I take a decision at all – but what specifically I decide.

Suppose, when I do decide, my decision is to do A rather than B. We would ordinarily think that not only do I determine for myself that I take a decision at all. That I take this specific decision to do A rather than the alternative is also something which I deliberately and intentionally do – and which I determine for myself. The problem for Frankfurt is that my taking this specific decision to do A is not something which I can do voluntarily.

a content or object of thought – that I perform the voluntary action decided upon. For example, any decision to go for a walk has as its content or object *that I go for a walk*. Secondly, decisions occur as motivational responses to the desirability of this content – to the desirability of acting as decided. A decision to go for a walk motivates me to go for a walk; and it is taken in response to the desirability, real or apparent of going for a walk. If the decision is taken rationally, then that will be because going for a walk really would be a desirable thing to do. That means that the decision is going to be based on beliefs about its object – on beliefs about what going for a walk would involve, and why going for a walk would be desirable or a good idea. To argue or persuade someone into deciding to go for a walk, you need to persuade them that going for a walk would be a desirable thing to do.

Decisions to act are taken in response to the desirability of acting as decided. And that is because decisions to act have a central function – the function of applying practical reason as it concerns the voluntary actions decided upon. The whole point of taking decisions about what to do, is to ensure that I perform the right – the desirable – voluntary actions thereafter. I go to the trouble of taking a decision about whether to go for a walk or stay home, so as to ensure that whichever I end up doing, whether going for a walk or staying at home, really is the right or desirable thing to do. So of course my decision to go for a walk must be based on my beliefs about what going for a walk would involve, and on whether I find going for a walk desirable.

We now see why my decision to go for a walk cannot be taken voluntarily. What we do voluntarily, what we do on the basis of a prior desire or decision to do it, is done in response to the real or at least apparent desirability of doing it. For example, my going for a walk is done voluntarily because it is done on the basis that going for a walk would be a desirable thing to do. So, if my decision to go for a walk was taken voluntarily, it too would be taken in a similar way: on the basis that it – the *decision to go for a walk* – was a desirable decision to take.

But then the grounds on which the decision was based would no longer have to do with the desirability of acting as decided – they would no longer have to do with the desirability of going for a walk – and would instead have to do simply with the desirability of taking the decision itself, something which might have nothing at all to do with going for a walk. And that would be a major departure from our common sense conception of decision making.

It is one thing to take a decision, as in real life we actually always do take decisions, non-voluntarily, in response to the desirability of the decision's content or object – in response to the desirability of acting as decided. It is quite another to take a decision voluntarily, in response to the desirability of the decision itself. To see this, consider Gregory Kavka's decision prize.[13] Suppose someone offered me a prize – a huge sum of money, say £1mn – just for today at 2 o'clock deciding later on to perform some mildly unpleasant action – such as drinking a very mild toxin the following day, a toxin which is mildly unpleasant, but which will cause no permanent harm. This prize, we should note, is offered simply for taking that decision at 2 o'clock. The prize has nothing to do with my subsequently acting as

---

13   See Gregory Kavka, 'The toxin puzzle', *Analysis* 1983.

decided. The prize does not depend on my actually drinking the toxin. I win the prize just by taking the decision at the required time, and whether or not I ever carry the decision out. I can win the prize whether or not I ever actually drink the toxin.

The decision clearly is a desirable decision to take, because taking it wins a huge prize. Suppose then that the decision to drink the toxin could be taken voluntarily, just on the basis that taking the decision was desirable. Then at 2 o'clock I could surely take the decision voluntarily, having decided to take it in order to win the prize. But decisions do not really work like that. I could not take the decision just in order to win the prize. And that is because such a decision would no longer be doing anything like its proper job – which is to respond to reasons for and against its object or content, drinking the toxin. The only way I would ever actually decide to drink a toxin would be through somehow coming to see drinking the toxin as a desirable thing to do. In fact, it seems clear that if I find drinking the toxin wholly undesirable, both in itself – the toxin is mildly unpleasant – and because it clearly has no desirable effects – drinking the toxin will not win me any prizes – I shall decide not to drink the toxin.

It is the desirability of acting as decided that moves me to take a decision to act – not any independent benefits brought by the decision itself. Decisions must be taken non-voluntarily, in response to the desirability of their objects. They cannot be taken voluntarily, in response to their own desirability. And that is because deciding what to do is about ensuring that we perform the right – the desirable – voluntary actions thereafter. Which means that the function of decisions must be to respond to the desirability of their objects, the voluntary actions decided upon.[14]

Hobbes, we saw, denied that decisions are voluntary. His conclusion was to deny the possibility of self-determination at the point of the will. Precisely because decisions are not voluntary, Hobbes denied that decisions are self-determined. But our ordinary understanding of decisions is that though our decisions are not voluntary, they are still self-determined. It is we who determine for ourselves what we decide. And if that is so, the self-determination which we exercise when we decide what to do cannot be voluntariness. Common sense psychology is fundamentally opposed to the replacement of freedom by voluntariness in the theory of moral responsibility.

Perhaps then the self-determination which is found within the will itself must be freedom. And that is surely what we ordinarily suppose. We ordinarily think that our decisions and intentions are self-determined, not because we think that decisions are voluntary, but because we think that it is up to us, or within our control what we decide and intend to do. Whether I decide to raise my hand or let it fall – whether I decide to go for a walk this afternoon or stay in – this is entirely up to me, and I am free to decide otherwise. And it is only because of this control which I have over what I decide to do that my decisions count as self-determined – that I count as the person who determines which actions I decide to perform.

---

14 For further argument on this point, and a more detailed discussion of the toxin puzzle, see my *The Psychology of Freedom*, Cambridge 1996.

The Practical Reason-based Conception of Action

Self-determination begins then, not with voluntary action, but with the non-voluntary motivations, the decisions and intentions, which explain our voluntary actions. Self-determination begins in a kind of second order, action-generating intentional action – with decision and intention-formation, a kind of action which is inherently and essentially non-voluntary.

Hobbes and his followers might still challenge this. For they can deny that decisions really are intentional actions at all. The idea that our decisions are our own intentional doing – that they are actions which can be self-determined – this idea, they will maintain, is just a myth.[15] For, as Hobbes and Davidson and many others will insist, intentional actions are by nature what we do voluntarily; and decisions are not voluntary.

But we ordinarily suppose that decisions are actions – that, though non-voluntary, what we specifically decide to do is as much our own deliberate and intentional doing as is anything in our lives. In which case Hobbes, Davidson and many other English-language philosophers must be wrong about action. Intentional human action cannot consist in voluntariness – in doing what we decide or want – but in something else. So what does human action consist in?

At work is a quite different understanding of intentional action from the voluntariness-based model. At work is what I call a *practical reason-based theory* of action – a model which I would argue we can find in ancient Stoicism, in scholastic philosophy as in the work of Aquinas, Scotus and Suarez, and in Kant.[16]

On this view, deciding to go for a walk counts as an intentional action, not because it is something that we do voluntarily – it is not – but because such a decision occurs as special mode of exercising rationality in response to a content or object of thought: a mode of exercising rationality which is distinctively practical or action-constitutive. The voluntariness-based model, as we saw, takes action to be a voluntary effect of a prior exercise of rationality in becoming motivated to act – an exercise of rationality which, as non-voluntary, is itself passive. Whereas the practical reason-based model takes action to be a specifically practical exercise of rationality in its own right.

---

15 See for a recent statement of this view Bernard Williams's *Shame and Necessity* and also his 'Nietzsche's minimalist moral psychology' in *Making Sense of Humanity*.

16 The idea of a practical reason-based model was introduced in my 'Reason and agency', *Proceedings of the Aristotelian Society* May 1997, vol. 97 pp. 263-280. For an historical discussion, see my 'Suarez, Hobbes and the scholastic tradition in action theory', in *The Will and Human Action: from Antiquity to the Present Day*, ed. T. Pink and M.W.F. Stone, London 2003 and 'Action, will and law in late scholasticism' in *Moral Philosophy on the Threshold of Modernity*, ed. J. Kraye and R. Saarinen, Dordrecht 2004.

The two companion volumes *The Ethics of Action: Normativity* and *The Ethics of Action: Self-Determination* (Oxford forthcoming) will constitute a full defence and elaboration of the practical reason-based model – and an account of its considerable implications for moral theory.

Remember what decisions are like. In taking a decision to go for a walk I am exercising a capacity for rationality. I am forming a rationally appraisable psychological state – a content-bearing attitude which can be appraised as rational or irrational; and I am forming the attitude as a response to its content. I am taking my decision to go for a walk in response to the real or apparent desirability of going for a walk. My decision is rational only if going for a walk actually is desirable, or at least not undesirable.

This mode of exercising reason is practical or action-constitutive because it possesses a distinctive feature of action. This distinctive feature of action is goal-direction. For action, it is very plausible to suppose, is essentially goal-directed. To act is to pursue a goal; and to be pursuing a goal, to be adopting a means to an end, is to be performing an action. And a central point about decision making is that it is indeed goal-directed, just as any action is. Deciding, say, to go for a walk is something which we do as a means to an end. The whole point of my taking a decision to go for a walk is to ensure that its content comes true, and that as a result I do go for a walk.

We can see how decisions are goal-directed when we consider decision rationality further. For my decision to go for a walk to be rational, then, as we have said, going for a walk must be a desirable thing to do. But that is not enough. Deciding to go for a walk must also be likely enough to ensure that I do actually go for a walk. Which is why sensible, rational people don't take decisions about matters which their decisions clearly can't affect; since the function of decisions is to lead to their fulfilment, that a decision has no chance of doing this is a conclusive argument against taking it. I may, quite rationally, want and hope to spend my old age doing useful and interesting things, rather than in idleness. But there's no point my now deciding to spend my old age being useful if that decision will have no effect – if, for example, given the long time yet to pass, no decision I took now would make any difference to my motivations in old age.

Contrast decisions with a rather different kind of content-bearing motivation – a motivation which is intuitively passive, and which we do not ordinarily see as a self-determined action. Contrast decisions with mere desires or wants. If the object of a desire or want really is desirable, the fact that holding the desire would do nothing to make its object true is no argument against simply holding the desire – against simply wanting something to happen. Indeed, we can quite rationally and sensibly want something to happen while also not only expecting but wanting it to happen, if it does, quite independently of the fact that we want it. The very desirability of what we want might entirely depend on its happening other than because we want it to happen.

I might deeply want a grown-up son or daughter to do the right thing – but to do it autonomously, entirely on their own, because they have determined for themselves what they should do, and without my influencing them in any way. Suppose I fully expect and am quite sure that whatever they end up doing, they certainly will do it autonomously – they will do it quite independently of me. That does not make it irrational for me still to *want* them to do the right thing. What, in those circumstances I can't rationally do is *decide* that they will do the right thing.

And that is because a decision is an action with a goal. A decision is an exercise of rationality which is directed at its content or object as a goal – a goal which that exercise of rationality is to attain or effect; and that makes a decision an intentional goal-directed action – an action whose rationality depends on the likelihood of its effecting that attainment. And in this case, where my child is concerned, I know that what I decide will have no effect on what my child will do. So deciding what my child will do would be pointless.

A decision is the formation of a content-bearing attitude – a response to a content or object. But this response is practical in nature, being directed at its object as to an end or goal to be attained by it. Whereas though a desire is an object-directed motivation too, it is not practical in nature. A desire is directed at its object merely as something desirable – not as an end or goal to be attained thereby. So the rationality of desiring an event to occur does not depend on the desire's being able to cause that event to occur.

Moral Responsibility and Freedom

Since Hobbes, much English-language philosophy has tended to understand action in terms of voluntariness. And it has tended to understand self-determination in terms of voluntariness too. But common sense ordinarily thinks of decisions as self-determined actions. And, as we have seen, decisions cannot be voluntary themselves. They cannot be voluntary if – as common sense ordinarily supposes – the function of decisions is to respond to the desirability of their objects, the actions decided upon. Decisions cannot be voluntary if deciding what to do is about ensuring that we perform the right – the desirable – voluntary actions thereafter.

The idea of voluntariness may be less metaphysically problematic than that of freedom. But nevertheless, our common sense idea of self-determination cannot be an idea of voluntariness. And that is related to the fact that our common sense idea of action is not an idea of voluntariness either. Our decisions are actions not because they are voluntary – they are inherently non-voluntary, as we cannot take decisions at will or as we decide – but because they are goal-directed exercises of rationality. In taking decisions, our goal is to determine our voluntary actions. So if our decisions are self-determined, that cannot be because our decisions are voluntary. If our decisions are self-determined, that must be because it is up to us – within our control – what actions we decide to perform. Our moral responsibility for what we do – for our decisions to act, and for what we do through those decisions – must be based on freedom.

Chapter 9

Mystical Experiences of God and the Culture of Science

Jerome I. Gellman

Recent philosophy of religion has seen several attempts to defend the evidential value of apparent mystical experiences (or perceptions) of God. Most prominently Richard Swinburne has argued that mystical experiences of God give evidence that God is in real contact with human beings. He also believes that when this evidence is added to other evidence we can obtain a cumulative evidential case for God's existence (Swinburne, 1991).[1]

In addition, William Alston has argued for the 'practical rationality' of engaging in a mystical doxastic practice, one in which certain kinds of nonsensory input are taken to justify a belief that one has experienced God (Alston, 1991).

The Scientific Objection

Now one of the major objections to both enterprises is the 'scientific objection' that in our scientific age it is no longer justified to believe that people have genuine experiences of God. The objection comes in two forms. One form offers specific alternative naturalistic explanations for apparent God-perceptions, explanations allegedly enjoying clear advantages over saying that people do have genuine experiences of God. The second form does not have specific naturalistic conditions to point to as an alternative explanation. Instead it contends that *in principle* God should disappear from explanations of alleged God-sightings. That is because were we to recognize valid mystical experiences of God we would be acknowledging a supernatural explanation for them. However, in the name of scientific probity we should reject supernatural explanations, whether or not we already possess a viable naturalistic alternative explanation. On this view, whatever explanations might turn out to be adequate in the future, they will be naturalistic ones, and God will not figure in them. Thus, God should disappear now from our account of alleged mystical experiences of God.

Attempts to offer specific alternative explanations have not met with general consent, although currently a number of interesting candidates appear in the literature. (For a discussion of these, see Gellman, 2001.) The second form of the 'scientific objection' promises to succeed, however, even in the absence of a successful

---

1   Others who have argued in a related direction are Caroline Frank Davis (1989), Keith Yandell (1993) and Gellman (1997 and 2001).

alternative explanation. In what follows I wish to contribute to an assessment of the second form of the scientific objection.

The Second Form of the Scientific Objection

I will present a rationale for this objection by way of analogy to what happened in scientifically developed cultures to the idea that shamans or divines could perceive evil spirits that were causing a person to be ill, what led, that is, to a 'disappearance theory of demon-perceptions'. Consider a culture where the idea prevails that a variety of demons cause illness, and where shamans or divines supposedly are able to perceive the demons at work when the shamans prepare themselves properly for the occasion following a prescribed ritual.[2] In such a culture, demons play a dual role, one explanatory, and the other perceptual. People invoke demons to explain the presence of illness in a person and affirm demons to be objects of perceptual reports.

Nowadays, most people in Western cultures believe neither that evil spirits cause illness nor that divines really perceive them. Most Westerners have a different explanation of sickness and disease. They know about microbes, antibodies, and so on, and have developed medicines and treatments that cure many ailments and arrest the progress of others. Based on available scientific theories, Western science may not be able to predict just when a particular person will contract a specific illness. Yet, it can do quite a bit of successful predicting, and in many cases when an illness strikes, it knows what will happen in the organism and how to go about dealing with the illness. In addition, the scientific story gives us an idea of the mechanisms involved in the contracting of illnesses, providing ways to prevent outbreaks of sickness and plagues. The idea that spirits cause illness provides no such benefits. So scientifically influenced cultures have replaced the demon-explanation of illness with a scientific story with powerful theoretical (and practical) advantages over the demon story.

Now, as long as the demon-explanation was in force, when shamans or divines *seemed* to see demons near a sick person, there was good reason to think they really did see them, those very demons who, by common belief, were causing the malady. After all, the demons were in the vicinity. However, after the abandonment of the demon explanation, it was no longer compelling to think divines enjoyed reliable demon-perceptions. It became preferable to think shamans were hallucinating, that what they actually saw were demon-hallucinations and not real demons. There existed no need for demons in order to explain disease. Therefore, we looked for what we knew about self-induced trances and substances ingested in order to 'see' demons, hoping to find some alternative explanation there. In the absence of support for the demon-hypothesis as explanatory of illness, we were freed up to turn to possible alternative explanations for shamans seeming to see demons. We had good reason to prefer the hypothesis that divines were having demon hallucinations to saying they were really seeing demons. Demons disappeared from our explanations.

---

2   I have adapted the example and its application from Rorty (1965).

One version of the disappearance theory would simply remove demons from the explanation of disease and perceptions of shamans. It would not bother to deny the existence of demons. A person might embrace this version and yet continue believing in the existence of demons, perhaps on 'faith'. Another version would deny the existence of demons altogether, declaring that 'we are not in need of that hypothesis'.

Analogously, our second form of the scientific objection would start by noting how God's special actions used to be invoked to explain a splendid array of natural events. For example, when a child would become ill with fever, the parent might interpret this as an act of God, and pray to God to rescind the evil decree. Nowadays that same parent, even if of a religious mind, likely will attribute the fever to the child's exposure to microbes. The parent will see the fever as a nuisance, requiring a visit to the doctor, and the giving of medicine daily for a number of days. When these steps are taken, the nuisance will usually pass. In this way, scientific explanations have been steadily replacing theistic explanations of specific events.

As long as God was conceived of as acting here and now in special acts that intruded upon the natural world, that supported thinking God might be experienced while so acting. So when the Children of Israel thought God was splitting the sea for them, they could think they saw God's 'mighty arm' on the sea, then and there. A parent with a child with a dangerous disease, believing God was presently acting to help the child get well, might believe God's active presence could be felt at the child's bedside. The assumed circumstance of special providential activity created the occasion for supposing God really was perceived.

In addition, as long as people invoked God's special actions for explaining other events in the world, miraculous events, there would have been support for invoking God's special activity as well in God appearing to a person in a mystical experience. The background of supernatural intervening action in the world supported thinking God also could be acting in a special way to initiate a mystical experience of God.

The more we have replaced God's special providence with scientific explanations, the more we have lost the basis for thinking God was experientially available in conjunction with specific events at a certain place and time. The context, remember, underwrote the shaman's perception of the demons – the demons were detected near where they were assumed to be causing sickness. Claim to see the demons far from where sickness visits, and your claim would be weakened accordingly. Once God's specific causal activity recedes, accordingly we lose a basis for explaining why God has been perceived here and now. In addition, the steep decline in God's special miraculous activity in the world in general, decreases the attraction of thinking God would act in a special way to become revealed to someone in a mystical experience. We should now find it more attractive to believe some scientific explanation will explain it all. Relieved of the pressure of theistic explanations of particular events, now we are free to turn to other factors for alternative explanations of theistic experiences.

Matthew Bagger's Version of the Second Objection

Bagger's Argument

Matthew Bagger has provided a version of this objection (Bagger, 1999). I wish to examine this version closely.

Bagger argues that (p. 198):

> The modern ideal of a unified sphere of inquiry with no areas immune from naturalistic explanation renders supernatural explanation suspect and in need of defense.

Bagger proceeds to detail this assertion. He cites the 'centrality of institutions of inquiry' being 'completely independent of religious commitment' as a particularly crucial feature of 'modern life' (p. 218). Thus, the modern inquirer 'rejects any presupposition to inquiry not based on the natural evidence available to him and assumes everything ultimately explicable in terms of a unified casual structure' (p. 218). Not only does modern inquiry not invoke the supernatural to explain the natural, 'the supernatural itself becomes a subject of naturalistic explanations' (p. 219).

As a result, claims Bagger, in modern inquiry (p. 221):

> We never reach the point where we declare a naturalistic explanation of discrete events occurring within the natural order unattainable in principle. The success of modern modes of inquiry reinforces this tendency. The incredibly rapid pace of knowledge growth over the last several centuries confirms a hesitation to declare some phenomenon in principle inexplicable on natural principles.

Bagger compares the invocation of God to explain mystical experiences to the invocation of miracles to explain natural phenomena. Just as 'the intransigence of certain well-attested anomalies no longer leads to supernatural explanations, but rather to future insight into natural processes' (p. 223), so even if we lack a ready alternative explanation for God-perceptions, we should not settle for a supernatural explanation. Indeed 'The mere protracted inability to explain something naturalistically could never in itself legitimate a supernatural explanation' (p. 227). The elimination of miracles from our explanatory vocabulary should be matched by an elimination of a supernatural explanation of mystical experiences of God.

Bagger concludes by advising that 'Theism's cultural relevance relies on the fact that it does not detract from the modern ideal of epistemic flourishing'. Theism, therefore, should not present itself in 'reactionary and unacceptable forms' (p. 227).

If Bagger is right, here we have an in-principle objection to supposing that anyone ever has a genuine perception of God. So if Bagger is right, we do not need a live alternative explanation to the theistic explanation of mystical experiences of God in order to resist the latter. We should resist the latter in the name of our epistemic standards.

Bagger rejects a defence by William Alston (1991). On this defence, taking perceptions of God as evidentially worthy does not require invoking the supernatural as an 'explanation' of the perceptions. Instead, claiming direct perception of God, one is *prima facie* justified in relying straightaway on one's perceptual experiences. Alston presents an alternative 'perceptual construal' to the 'explanatory construal' of the justification of mystical experiences of God. Alston writes that on the 'explanatory construal', which he rejects (Alston, 1991, p. 66):

> The subject must have sufficient *reasons* for this supposition if it is to be justified, whereas on the perceptual construal there is at least the possibility of a direct knowledge of God, not based on reasons....

and that on the explanatory construal (1991, pp. 66-67):

> the subject is faced with the task of justifying a causal hypothesis before he can warrantedly claim to be perceiving God; whereas if the experience is given a perceptual construal from the start, we will at least have to take seriously the view that a claim to be perceiving God is prima facie acceptable on its own merits.

Alston wishes to contend that a direct perception of God can justify relying on it on the very grounds that it is *a perception* of God, and not because we invoke God in an *explanation* for why a person has an experience of a certain type. In that way, we detour around the issue about what kinds of 'explanations' are legitimate, relying on the presumed reliability, everything else being equal, of perceptual episodes.

Bagger's response to Alston consists in invoking a conception of experience on which 'experience is explanation' (1991, p. 200). As Bagger puts it, 'In the very making of a perceptual claim, one implicitly commits to the belief that the situation is best explained by the presence of the object allegedly perceived' (p. 200). Hence, a person who claims to have a direct perception of God is claiming implicitly that the best explanation for the experience is that God has appeared. Therefore, Alston cannot get around the inference to the best explanation.

Bagger's Conventionalism

Bagger presents his commitment to 'modern' modes of inquiry and explanation as following from his conventionalist approach to 'justification' and 'good explanation'. 'To justify a belief', writes Bagger, 'one must offer good explanatory reasons, reasons that, when viewed against the background of all one does not currently doubt, contribute to the best overall explanatory account of the phenomena in question' (1999, p. 83). Concepts of justification, therefore, vary for Bagger with conceptions of what are 'good explanations'.[3] Bagger writes that, 'We cannot enumerate any formal criteria of justified belief.... Any candidate for justification must conform to an ideal of human epistemic flourishing. Ideals of human flourishing, however, bear the distinctive marks of time and place, era and culture' (p. 86). We cannot enumerate any formal account of 'good explanation' either. In Bagger's view, 'To construct timeless canons of explanatory goodness for universal application overlooks both the pragmatic element (interest-relativity) in explanation and the historical and

---

3   One could question Bagger's way of linking justification to good explanation. I will not pursue that issue here.

cultural relativity of epistemic values' (p. 86).[4] What constitutes justification and a good reason is thus a matter of convention.

Bagger does not conclude that necessarily each culture or period is isolated epistemically from every other, but holds out the possibility, at least, of cultures sharing enough epistemic assumptions for cross-evaluation. Nonetheless, 'the justificatory status of a belief can vary from culture to culture, and from one historical epoch to another' (p. 87). Just so, goodness of explanation can vary from culture to culture, and from one historical epoch to another.

The point of Bagger making his argument a matter of the conventional meaning of 'explanation' is that he does not have to argue for the superiority of the current concept of explanation to which he appeals. To turn back alternative explanatory models it is sufficient to be able to show that they depart from the prevailing convention concerning what is a good explanation. It as though Bagger renders supernatural explanation not just wrong, but incoherent within the cultural-intellectual atmosphere in which it is raised. It is an alleged conceptual, not empirical, mistake to appeal to supernatural explanation in Bagger's culture in our day.

This conventionalist conception of good explanation, then, determines Bagger's endorsement of 'modern' modes of inquiry that preclude supernatural explanation. He shows how Teresa of Avila could have been justified in her time and cultural setting in placing a supernatural explanation on her mystical experiences. Her concept of good explanation allowed such an interpretation of her mystical episodes. We today in a scientific culture, however, are precluded from invoking supernatural explanation. The latter do not fit our present concept of justification and good explanation.

An Evaluation of Bagger's Argument

Perceptual Judgements

Bagger's thesis that a perceptual claim always involves an implicit judgement about a best explanation seems doubtful for a few reasons: Children, who do not yet have the concept of a 'best explanation', or even of 'perception' or cannot yet work with them, are able to make perceptual claims in confidence. They have no belief, implicit or otherwise, about the 'best explanation' of their 'perception'. In addition, it is implausible to think that everyone who makes a perceptual judgement must have an implicit belief about its best explanation. We should distinguish between unreflective and reflective perceptual judgements. In an unreflective perceptual judgement, if I believe that I see a tree, plausibly this belief is an immediate response formed in reference to the perceptual content present to me. I need not have any belief about the best explanation of my perception. When I reflect on the origins of my perception, for example when asked what I think the best explanation for it is, then I might form the belief that there having been a tree in front of me is the best explanation

---

4   According to Bagger, the pragmatic element of justification includes as well that justification has relevance only when justifying oneself to others (Bagger, 1999, Chapter 3).

for my having had the tree-like perception. Beliefs, implicit or otherwise, about best explanations seem to be a feature only of reflection on perceptual beliefs.

Bagger thinks otherwise. He writes that 'Experience includes tacit commitment as to how best to interpret a stimulus. These commitments rarely reach the light of day' (Bagger, p. 5). He claims that the process of sizing up an experience and deciding what is its best explanation 'functions through habit'. Bagger seems to maintain that every 'non-reflective' perceptual judgement really involves an extremely fast, subliminal, mental evaluation of the perceptual information and a quick forming of a conclusion about its best explanation, which then issues in a perceptual judgement. If that were the case, then indeed every such judgement would involve an implicit belief about best explanation.

Now whether there are implicit psychological reckonings of the sort in question is a claim for cognitive psychologists to examine, but on the face of it that calculations occur producing an implicit 'belief' about a 'best explanation' is quite implausible. In evolutionary terms, it is more plausible to think that organisms have reactive mechanisms that adapt them to their perceived environment, without the need for a belief in what is the best explanation of the perceptions. Those reactive mechanisms most in line with the environment have survival value. Those with less, eventually disappear along with their owners. This needn't involve any judgement. What these mechanisms have to do is correlate perceptual input with prudential behavioural output and at times with a belief about what the subject perceives, such beliefs no doubt usefully stored for later behavioural possibilities. For this there would be no need to posit anything more than reactive, belief-forming mechanisms that determine non-reflective perceptual judgements, sans subliminal calculations of best explanation.

Nevertheless, Bagger is correct about our having to utilize supernatural explanation when we come to the stage of explaining genuine God-perceptions. So if supernatural explanation falls, so will genuine perceptions of God.

Conventionalism

When Bagger contends that we cannot enumerate 'formal criteria' for justification and good explanation, if he means we find no explicitly formulated criteria 'timelessly' across cultures, he is no doubt correct. However, it would be a mistake to conclude from this that there are no conceptions of good explanation implicitly at work across various cultures and periods. Diversity can be a function of differing conceptions of good explanation, but also of starting from different justified beliefs, of different talents in applying criteria of good explanation, and of differing powers of imagination in framing ideas and testing them out. Perhaps the best theory about good explanation will turn out to be that there are some, at least, implicit rules to be found just about wherever we look. Thus, two different styles of thinking may be subsumable under a general conception of good explanation, with the differences accountable for otherwise. The issues here are large and difficult. They include issues such as to what degree our concepts prescind from their practical application to reach a high level of abstraction and to what degree our concepts are immanent in our working paradigms. If we think of a specific concept of good explanation depending strongly on specific moves paradigmatic of explanation on the ground, as Bagger does, we will be less prepared to recognize (some, at least) implicit standards of explanation than otherwise. In any case, the conventionalist conception of explanation, and justification, remains controversial in philosophy and by no means has won the day. Nevertheless, for the sake of argument, in what follows I will grant Bagger his conventionalist position.[5]

I wonder, though, to what extent people hold, as Bagger claims, to a 'modern ideal' of explanation, excluding the supernatural. Moreover, I wonder who are the 'we' in his statement that 'we never reach the point where we declare a naturalistic explanation of discrete events occurring within the natural order unattainable in principle'. My wonder arises because Bagger ignores the massive numbers of traditional religious believers in modern societies like the United States, in which he writes. For tens of millions of religious devotees supernatural explanation is alive and well. Bagger also ignores a mass culture that sociologists have documented as a new religious paradigm in Western countries, most especially the United States. This is the movement of 'new spirituality' that appeals to inner experience and devotion, yet is unconnected to traditional organized religion. The sociologist Phillip Wexler has written of this phenomenon as an emerging 'mystical society' with a new social vision (Wexler, 2000). 'The new society is mystical', writes Wexler, 'because it is about the quest for direct experience of the transcendental', invites an 'immediacy' that is the 'hallmark of a mystical consciousness and life' (p. 15). Here too supernatural explanation lives and thrives.

Here is how the sociologist, Robert Wuthnow, who has studied the new spirituality, describes the situation in the United States at the end of the twentieth century (Wunthow, 1998, p. 1, quoted in Wexler, 2000, p. 117):

> Judging from newspapers and television, American's fascination with spirituality has been escalating dramatically. Millions of people report miraculous interventions in their lives by such forces as guardian angels who help them avoid danger and spirit guides who comfort them in moments of despair. Faced with death, many people report seeing a brilliant tunnel of light that embraces them in its mysterious glory – and live to write best selling books about these experiences. When pollsters ask, Americans overwhelmingly affirm their faith in God, claiming to pray often to that God.

There is no denying, therefore, a prominent, pervasive cultural phenomenon of happily using supernatural explanation along with recognition of scientific modes of inquiry. Whether the two go well together is beside the point when trying to ascertain the conventionally recognized types of good explanation out there in the world. Out there in the world, it is far from true that scientific inquiry has supplanted supernatural explanation. Therefore, in empirical terms Bagger's case seems weak.

Bagger, of course, is right that many people in his Western culture, principally secularists, do exclude supernatural explanation in the name of modern modes of inquiry. Apparently two subcultures reside together in modern societies, one that thinks in terms of supernatural explanation and one that does not. The latter subculture might be more prominent than the former in the sense of having greater

---

5   Susan Haack has argued against conventionalism in Haack, 1993, Chapter 9.

access to political centres of power in Western countries. Yet it is hard to say which subculture reflects, in numbers and cultural significance, a dominant convention concerning 'good explanation' in modern Western societies.

Suppose Bagger somehow were able to show empirically the dominance of an exclusively scientific understanding of what makes for good explanation. Perhaps the religious and spiritual cultures signify no more than an 'under-culture' to the culture guided exclusively by scientific modes of enquiry (though I strongly doubt this). Even then, I would find unacceptable Bagger's rejection of supernatural explanation in the name of a conventionalist defence of contemporary modes of enquiry. Here is why. On Bagger's conventionalist position, shifts in 'good explanation' are not based on epistemic criteria, but are more like *zeitgeist* swings. We should suppose that new explanatory paradigms catch people's interest and set off a shift that carries a culture to a different way of thinking. Alternatively, we are to suppose that changing values push forward new or dormant ways of explaining. Of course, such changes do not take place overnight.

Philosophers of knowledge have described the complex processes involved in scientific paradigm shifts (see Kuhn, 1962, Lakatos, 1978a, and Lakatos, 1978b). Scientific paradigms arise, may lie dormant, compete between themselves, become dominant, wane, and sometimes return. Proposals are made. Some catch on, while others are dropped. Some linger until found attractive later on. Others burst into sight and fade quickly. In addition, dropped paradigms can stay around in a subdued voice alongside newly dominant ideas. There is every reason to believe that shifts of paradigms in explanation would be as fluid and dynamic, and surely as complex and winding as are scientific paradigm-shifts.

Since this is so, I find unacceptable an *a priori* rejection of supernatural explanation because of contemporary modes of enquiry. Nothing in the conventionalist story could possibly generate an *a priori* prohibition purely in the name of a dominant current fashion in explanation. To invoke dominant current vogues of good explanation as a roadblock to the advancing of alternatives contradicts the natural way in which ideas of good explanation arise, challenge, and flourish. To reject alternatives solely because they are not the dominant mode of explanation would be to unjustly wield conventionalism as a protective strategy of a most conservative kind. If this is what Bagger is up to, I find an inner inconsistency, if not incoherence, in Bagger's conventionalist argument against supernatural explanation.

Bagger does look for support from the 'success' of modern modes of enquiry and to the 'rapid growth of knowledge' afforded therein, as a reason for going modern and scorning supernatural explanation. By Bagger's conventionalist lights, however, that talk can reflect only the epistemic standards of 'modern' modes of enquiry themselves and does not support those modes from the 'outside' as it were. 'Success' and 'knowledge' do not have formal criteria, on conventionalism, any more than do justification and good explanation. Therefore, Bagger cannot invoke them in favour of modern modes of enquiry as a way of stifling possible alternative sources of good explanation. They themselves only reflect once again the dominant conception of what makes for good explanation.

Instead of vetoing it the way he does, Bagger might have addressed supernatural explanation directly by considering its potential or lack of it for 'epistemic flourishing'.

For example, he might have discussed theistic philosophers who have laboured to square divine activity with a modern scientific understanding of the world. For these philosophers and those like them, supernatural explanation belongs in the category of 'good explanation' along with Bagger's scientific, naturalistic explanations. One way to argue against supernatural explanation would have been to show that these theistic attempts failed, or must fail. This Bagger does not attempt to do. Bagger fails to give persuasive reason why a person for whom God's activity in the world is a live option should ignore the theistic understanding of mystical experiences of God.

Supernatural Explanation

What, though, of people for whom supernatural explanation is not a live option, those who think of good explanation exclusively as scientific explanation? These will include both Baggerian conventionalists as well as defenders of the analogy to demon-perceptions. For them, the idea that mystical experiences of God are genuine, implying supernatural explanation, would require a shift in their thinking and admit supernatural explanation as a category of explanation. In all likelihood, therefore, for a person for whom God's activity in the world is not a live option, neither will valid experiences of God be a live option. Can anything be done to influence their opinion? Here are a number of suggestions that a defender of validity of experiences of God might make:[6]

(1)   The defender of the validity of mystical experiences of God might point out that contemporary canons of explanation were formed not so much in full awareness of the rich historical phenomenon of mystical experiences of God, but rather by choosing to ignore it entirely. Hence, the current, non-theistic models of good explanation were born in sin, ignoring what many have and continue to consider a good explanation for these experiences, namely a supernatural explanation.

Why should this mode of explanation be unacceptable? The apparent reason, alluded to above, would be fear that the success of science would thereby be impeded, a clamouring for supernatural explanation competing with sober naturalistic ones. This is a very important point, and the defender of validity will want to provide a reasonable defence of supernatural explanation not hurting the advance of science. As I have already noted, Bagger does nothing to show this direction cannot be successful.

(2)   A defender of the validity of mystical experiences of God might be willing to offer, if pushed to the wall, a non-interventionist conception of genuine God-perceptions. That is, a defender might be willing to contend that genuine mystical experiences of God could be explained by non-interventionist supernatural activity. The explanation of genuine God-perceptions would be in terms of how God created and designed the world, a world that thereafter afforded experiences of God in accordance with its stable, ongoing laws and structures, and in accordance with God's

---

6   By a 'defender of the validity of mystical experiences of God', I mean someone who contends that at least some such alleged episodes are valid experiences of God.

original purposes and intentions. Perhaps God is always experientially available, our needing only the proper naturalistic conditions to succeed in perceiving God.

A naturalistic explanation would have to modify the notion that God initiates perceptual encounters with God, an idea implying interventionist metaphysics. God's 'making God available' to us in mystical perception would turn into a metaphor for the elusive and variable naturalistic conditions necessary for perceiving God in a mystical way. In particular, we would need a naturalistic story about how training in non-egocentrism was necessary, in most cases, for mystical success. An appropriate theory about brain activity and mystical experience might help matters along here. God's original acts, purposes and intentions would hover above all of that.

This move, of course, would rid us only of interventionist supernatural explanation, leaving us with the category of the supernatural nonetheless. However, the move might help ameliorate some of the resistance from worries over the integrity of science.

(3)   The defender of the validity of mystical experiences of God will want to marshal philosophical arguments against an exclusively naturalistic understanding of the world, forcing recognition in any case of the category of supernatural explanation. One important endeavour in this direction is Robert Adams's argument that natural science cannot explain the correlation between phenomenal qualia, such as flavours and colours, and physical states that obtain in perceptual experience. Adams argues that a theological explanation is required for this (Adams, 1987). A second important anti-naturalist argument is due to Alvin Plantinga. Plantinga contends against the idea that human knowledge could have come about from evolutionary development in a naturalistic way. The most we could expect from evolution is that we would have beliefs adaptive for survival. However, adaptive beliefs need not be true, and Plantinga argues that on purely naturalistic assumptions we should not expect them to be true. Thus, we should maintain that God guides the evolutionary process to bring about not only adaptive but also true, reliable beliefs about the world (Plantinga, 1993). Another way of trying to dispute naturalism would be to argue that it couldn't account for the existence of the universe.

When all is said and done, however, the defender of the validity of mystical experiences of God might not convince a person for whom supernatural explanation is not a live option. This is an important point, but falls short of Bagger's ambition. It does not show that anyone who considers Bagger's conventionalist argument should reject the possibility of supernatural explanation and thus of valid mystical experiences of God. It gives no reason why a person who countenances supernatural explanation should give it up.

Bibliography

Adams, Robert (1987), *The Virtue of Faith and Other Essays in Philosophical Theology*, New York: Oxford University Press.

Alston, William (1991), *Perceiving God: The Epistemology of Religious Experience*, Ithaca: Cornell University.

Bagger, Matthew C. (1999), *Religious Experience, Justification, and History*, Cambridge: Cambridge University Press.

Davis, Carolyn Franks (1989), *The Evidential Force of Religious Experience*, Oxford: Clarendon Press.

Gellman, Jerome (1997), *Experience of God and the Rationality of Theistic Belief*, Ithaca: Cornell University Press.

Gellman, Jerome (2001), *Mystical Experience of God, A Philosophical Inquiry*, London: Ashgate Publishers.

Haack, Susan (1993), *Evidence and Inquiry, Towards Reconstruction in Epistemology*, Oxford: Blackwell.

Kuhn, Thomas S. (1962), *The Structure of Scientific Revolutions*, Chicago: University of Chicago Press.

Lakatos, Imre (1978a), *The Methodology of Scientific Research Programmes*, in Worrall, John and Currie, Gregory (eds), Cambridge and New York: Cambridge University Press.

Lakatos, Imre (1978b), *Philosophical Papers*, in Worrall, John and Currie, Gregory (eds), Cambridge and New York: Cambridge University Press.

Plantinga, Alvin (1993), 'An evolutionary argument against naturalism', in Radcliffe, Elizabeth S. and White, Carol J. (eds), *Faith in Theory and Practice, Essays on Justifying Religious Belief*, Chicago and Lasalle: Open Court, pp. 35-65.

Rorty, Richard (1965), 'Mind-Body Identity, Privacy, and Categories', *Review of Metaphysics*, 19, 24-54.

Swinburne, Richard (1991), *The Existence of God*, Revised Edition, Oxford: Clarendon Press.

Wexler, Philip (2000), *Mystical Society, An Emerging Vision*, Boulder: Westview Press.

Wuthnow, Robert (1998), *After Heaven, Spirituality in America Since the 1950's*, Berkeley, Los Angeles and London: University of California Press.

Yandell, Keith (1993), *The Epistemology of Religious Experience*, New York: Cambridge University Press.

Chapter 10

Parts and Properties in Christology

Richard Cross

I

It is a theological commonplace that contradictory properties can be exemplified by an incarnate divine person, provided that such properties are exemplified in two different respects, as it were: in respect of his divine nature (or *qua* God), and in respect of his human nature (or *qua* man). Assume that 'Christ' is a proper name for an incarnate divine person. The theological commonplace is supposed to allow us consistently to make statements to the effect that (e.g.) Christ is impassible and passible – that is to say, properly, that he is impassible in respect of his divine nature, or *qua* God, and passible in respect of his human nature, or *qua* man.

'In respect of', here, is not to be construed as 'in virtue of (such-and-such a property)': this is the old 'reduplication' of the scholastics, and tells us merely why it is that a predicate is ascribed to its subject. Thus understood, the claim that Christ is impassible in respect of (in virtue of) his divine nature would entail that Christ is impassible *simpliciter*, just as the claim that a surface is coloured in virtue of its being red entails that it is coloured *simpliciter* – supposing that Christ is God *simpliciter* and that the surface is red *simpliciter*. By definition, if a property F is *simpliciter* a property of substance *x*, then it is not the case that *x* is not-F. Accordingly, if *x* is *simpliciter* not-F, then it is not the case that *x* is F. (I hope to provide reasons below that will justify the good sense of this understanding of '*simpliciter*': for the time being, I shall assume it without argument.[1] Given that '*simpliciter*' is supposed to

---

1   So by '*simpliciter*' I do not, of course, mean 'essentially'. It is essential to Christ that he is God, but it may not be essential to the surface that it is red. In what follows, I shall silently assume the ascription of time-indices: e.g. if at *t* the surface is red *simpliciter*, then at *t* it is coloured *simpliciter*. My proposed definition of '*simpliciter*' shows below that if *x* is *simpliciter* F, then it is not the case that *x* is qualifiedly not-F. One recent account, that of Peter van Inwagen, denies that the use of 'in respect of' is necessary for avoiding such Christological contradictions, claiming instead that an incarnate divine person has these contradictory properties *simpliciter*. Van Inwagen, however, understands 'in respect of' as the medievals' reduplication: hence his correct assessment that such qualifiers are irrelevant to the project of solving Christological contradictions: see Peter van Inwagen, 'Not by Confusion of Substance, but by Unity of Person', in Alan Padgett (ed.), *Reason and the Christian Religion: Essays in Honour of Richard Swinburne* (Oxford: Clarendon Press, 1994), 201-226 (esp. pp. 221-223). His account of how something can be *simpliciter* both F and not-F entails accepting relative identity, such that (roughly) something can be the same person as some person who is F and the same person as some person who is not-F. I shall here presuppose – I believe uncontroversially – that relative identity is false. So my account of the logic of these Christological propositions is correspondingly different. According to van Inwagen, *x*'s being *simpliciter* F entails the falsity of the claim that it is not the case that *x* is F, but not of

indicate that the relevant sentence is true if understood straightforwardly, and given the standard rules for negation in the predicate calculus, this conclusion should in any case hardly come as a surprise.) In effect, reduplication is a way of allowing one property to be exemplified by a substance in virtue of the substance's exemplification of some other property. Reduplication is explanatory, but appealing to it does not entail that there is a sense in which either property fails to be *simpliciter* a property of the substance. Thus, the reduplicative understanding would lead to the following unqualified Christological assertion: 'Both, Christ is passible, and it is not the case that Christ is passible', a blatant contradiction.

It may be thought that the case of the Incarnation is marginally different from the sort of non-theological case that I described in the previous paragraph, simply because humanity and divinity are names of natural kinds, or at least of things very analogous to natural kinds, whereas redness is just the name of an accidental property. But this makes no difference to the general rule. *Being human* and *being divine* are properties just as much as *being red* is. If something is possible in virtue of its being human, then it is *simpliciter* possible just as much as something that is coloured in virtue of its being red is *simpliciter* coloured (supposing that these things are, respectively, *simpliciter* human, and *simpliciter* red).[2]

But 'in virtue of (such-and-such a property)' is not the only possible interpretation of 'in respect of'. One obvious sense in which the theological strategy could be made to work would be if the two natures, divine and human, were to be understood to be *parts* of the incarnate divine person. (They could, for example, be individual essences, exemplifications of kind-universals, and related to Christ as parts to whole.) The medievals called this kind of qualification 'specification'. There is nothing contradictory in the thought that, for example, D.C. Williams's lollipop, Heraplem (the one with the red, round, peppermint head) is both red and beige – beige in respect of its stick, Paraplete, and red in respect of its edible lollipop top. It is thus qualifiedly red and qualifiedly beige, and this is a case of the medievals' specification. What renders the proposal uncontroversial is precisely the fact that Heraplem is constituted of two, smaller, concrete individuals – Paraplete and the edible lollipop top. Constitution is a relation between part and whole, and part of what makes Heraplem the individual is it is that it is constituted of these smaller parts, Paraplete and the edible lollipop top. At least some of the properties of the

---

the claim that *x* is *simpliciter* not-F. As I have indicated, I am inclined – for reasons that will I hope become clear below – to *define x*'s being *simpliciter* F in terms of its incompossibility with *x*'s being not-F: hence *x*'s being *simpliciter* F entails its not being the case that *x* is not-F. But *x* may be qualifiedly F and qualifiedly not-F. Hence, *x*'s being qualifiedly F does not entail that it is not the case that *x* is not-F. More succinctly, without the resources of relative identity, it is not possible to avoid an inference from *x*'s being *simpliciter* F to its not being the case that *x* is not-F, for reasons that will become clear below. Anyone who disagrees with the rejection of relative identity will, I think, find all Christological problems solved by van Inwagen.

2   *Being coloured*, of course, is a determinable of which *being red* is a determinate, whereas it is not the case that *being possible* is a determinate of *being human*. But *being possible* is generally thought to be entailed by *being human*, and no defender of Chalcedonian orthodoxy would want to deny that Christ is possible (in virtue of his human nature).

smaller parts are also – qualifiedly – properties of the whole, precisely in virtue of the constitution relation that exists here between part and whole.[3]

These parts are Williams's 'gross' parts, and it seems to me that, whatever theory of properties we adopt, there are principled ways of distinguishing these gross parts from properties as such. This distinction will be central, because I am going to argue that the theological strategy outlined in the first paragraph can be made to work *only* if we accept that the two natures of Christ are *parts* of him. (Of course, parts here do not have to be material parts: body and soul are, on some analyses of human nature, parts of a human being, and no one would claim that the soul is a material part of a human being.) My principal aim here is to show some of the implications of denying that the divine and human natures are parts of an incarnate divine person. But in a final section I shall try to suggest some reasons for denying that the natures could be parts.

Thus far, I have presented a parts Christology as though the only option is seeing the divine and human natures as parts of Christ. There is a second option: the human nature could be a part of the person of Christ, such that the other part is not the divine nature but an object that was, before the Incarnation, identical with the person of the Word. This position differs by a whisker from the view that the two parts of Christ (in a parts Christology) could be the two natures, and in what follows I shall simply assimilate it to this latter view. (While the two positions are not the same, it makes no difference to my argument about Christological qualification which of the two parts Christologies we consider.)

I am not able properly to substantiate the claim that parts and properties can be distinguished in *any* plausible theory of properties. But I am going to consider two theories of properties here that between them cover most of the options canvassed in modern philosophy. I shall assume that there are substances in the world, and that there is some principled way in which we can distinguish substances from aggregates – perhaps by invoking natural kinds, or something of that sort. The first theory of properties that I shall consider is that the mark of a property – whether universal or particular – is that it can be *exemplified*.[4] It is this that distinguishes properties from substances. Substances cannot be exemplified.[5] The second theory is that properties are tropes (supposing that it is false that tropes are instances of universals). On this view, it is usual to understand substances to be bundles of compresent tropes, though I shall give below some reasons for supposing that such a straightforward theory of

---

3   For an attempt to show which sorts of parts can have properties that are also properties of the whole, see Lynne Rudder Baker, 'Unity without Identity: A New Look at Material Constitution', *Midwest Studies in Philosophy*, 23 (1999), 144-165. I am grateful to Eleonore Stump for this reference.

4   It makes no difference here whether we think of properties as universal or particular. Exemplification is a relation, analogous to – perhaps even identifiable with – inherence. And we can clearly speak indifferently of universal properties and particular properties as inhering in their substances.

5   It makes no difference to my argument whether or not we decide to adopt a merely extensional account of properties, or whether we accept that there are extramental universals. Neither does it make any difference whether or not we accept a sparse theory of properties. All I need is the notion of exemplification.

substance requires some modification. I shall focus on the first of these two theories in the next section, and return to the trope theory in a third section. For, as we shall see, the trope theory raises mereological difficulties all of its own.

Before I proceed to the main argument of my paper, however, it is worth pausing to sort out some possible misapprehensions. For the topic turns out to need rather careful handling. The initial difficulty lies in the fact that not every seemingly contradictory pair of predicates in fact turns out to be so, and it is hard to see when such predicates are formally contradictory. The sense of the words we used is very often heavily context dependent. So the first task in any case of a seemingly contradictory pair is *disambiguation*. For any pair of predicates φ and ψ, it is an easy matter to test for formal contradictoriness. φ and ψ are contradictories if and only if φ and ¬ψ are logically equivalent. (I will not consider any Christological examples of this, because it would take too long to discuss them; but think for example about the pair 'spatial' and 'spaceless', which seems to be a good case of a pair that is not in fact formally contradictory. It is easy enough, too, to formulate an analogous test for contrariness, but since any genuinely contrary pair of predicates entails a formally contradictory pair, I will not worry further about contrariness here.)

Consideration of such cases allows us to see certain other ways in which apparently contradictory predicates turn out not to be so. Consider too the pair 'x is pleasant', 'x is unpleasant'. Someone could be pleasant when sober, unpleasant when drunk (or perhaps unpleasant when sober, and pleasant when drunk). But these are obviously not contradictories, because each predicate in this case implicitly contains a time-index, and the time-indices do not coincide: the respective predicates turn out on inspection to entail 'pleasant-at-t_1', 'unpleasant-at-t_2' respectively. Or it could be that someone is pleasant to person x, but unpleasant to person y. And in this case, the pair is not contradictory because the apparently monadic properties turn out in fact to be relational. So another good case of seemingly contradictory predicates that sometimes turn out not to be so is that of relational ones: 'is to the north of' and 'is to the south of' are not necessarily contradictory predicates, simply because the second term of each predicate is lacking; 'is to the north of London' and 'is to the south of Edinburgh' are not contradictories, though of course 'is to the north of London' and 'is to the south of London' are.

So, correspondingly, the relevant sorts of property are *intrinsic* properties. In what sorts of circumstances can we allow one and the same object to exemplify contradictory intrinsic properties? Clearly, there is no difficulty in one and the same object exemplifying contradictory properties at different times. For there is no problem with something's being white at t_1 and not-white at t_2. In what follows, I shall suppose that all of these conditions are met, and then consider whether there is any strategy that can be used to allow the ascription of genuinely incompossible properties (corresponding to formally contradictory predicates) to one and the same object at one and the same time. And I shall argue that the available strategy is one that is effective only in mereological contexts.

II

On the first theory of properties, it is a relatively straightforward matter to distinguish a part from a property. For parts are like substances (they may even be substances, but for the sake of convenience I shall reserve the term 'substance' to refer to a complete object, and suppose that there are principled ways of distinguishing complete from incomplete things). Parts are not the sorts of thing that can be exemplified. On the contrary, parts themselves exemplify properties: my heart is a part of the substance that I am, and it exemplifies certain primary qualities of its own, some of which are also properties of me.

My argument in this section is that the possession of a property by the whole of a substance is sufficient for the possession of that property *simpliciter*. A property is a property of the whole of a substance if it is not a property merely of a set of parts of that substance less than the whole substance. For my purposes here, I do not need to establish that possession of a property by the whole of a substance is *necessary* for the possession of that property *simpliciter*. My argument will be that, if we deny a parts Christology, then all of Christ's divine properties, and many of his human ones, will be properties of the whole Christ (i.e. not properties merely of a set of parts of Christ less than the whole Christ), and thus properties of his *simpliciter*. And I shall argue that it is impossible for a substance to have, *simpliciter*, contradictory properties. As we shall see, the claims that properties had by the whole of a substance are had by it *simpliciter*, and that a substance cannot have, *simpliciter*, contradictory properties, are so closely linked that the defence of one involves a defence of the other too.

One important preliminary. It is clear that mereological contexts are sufficient to allow the exemplification of a property *in a certain respect*. In many cases, properties of the different parts are not *simpliciter* properties of the whole substance. The reason is that such properties are incompatible with intrinsic properties of other of the substance's parts. This is clear enough from the fact that the parts of a substance are distinct from each other, and thus have largely different and contradictory properties. If we need to avoid a contradiction in ascribing such properties to the whole substance, we can add a qualifier such as 'in a certain respect'. I am blue with respect to my eyes, and white with respect to my skin; I have blue eyes and white skin, and these things are parts of me.

Having noted this preliminary point, let me begin with the second claim introduced at the beginning of this section – namely, the claim that it is impossible for a substance to have, *simpliciter*, contradictory properties. (Thus, I shall begin with an attempt to justify my definition of '*simpliciter*' offered at the beginning of this essay.) Consider a substance, either one that lacks parts altogether, or whose only parts are entirely homogeneous: a red surface, for example. Suppose that this surface has, apart from its extension, only two properties: its redness and its solidity. We should not say that it is red in one respect, and solid in another. Thus the surface is red *simpliciter*, and solid *simpliciter*.

One reason is that there is no sense in which the surface is not-red, or not-solid. To see this, consider what it could be that exemplifies the properties of non-redness and non-solidity. Not the properties, respectively, of solidity and redness, because on this sort of view of properties, these properties do not exemplify any properties other than the second-order ones of being exemplified, being inherent, and such like.[6] But not the surface, since we should naturally claim, for example, that the surface's being red is sufficient to prevent (*de dicto* modality) its being simultaneously not-red. So there simply is no plausible subject (other than the substance itself) for the contradictory property: and if there is no subject for the property other than the substance itself, it is hard to see how it could be false that the substance has the property *simpliciter*.

This looks to me sufficient to establish the point, at least in the case of mereologically simple things, and thus to provide some initial justification for my claim (made at the beginning of the article) both that, if a property F is *simpliciter* a property of substance *x*, then it is not the case that *x* is not-F, and that if *x* is *simpliciter* not-F, then it is not the case that *x* is F. But what if someone were stubbornly to deny that the surface's being red is sufficient to prevent its being not-red (such that, for example, it could be not-red in respect of its solidity)? In this case, we would have to allow, *pari passu*, that for any intrinsic property any mereologically simple individual exemplifies *simpliciter*, it also exemplifies simultaneously the complement of that property.[7] But this principle – which I shall label the 'complement principle' – looks massively implausible. If both properties are had *simpliciter*, then the complement principle would render impossible any coherent application of the principle of non-contradiction, at least in the case of mereologically simple things.[8] If the complementary property is had qualifiedly, such that e.g. the redness of the surface is exemplified *simpliciter*, but the complement of the property is exemplified qualifiedly, it would follow that a mereologically simple individual has, qualifiedly, the complement of every intrinsic property that it has *simpliciter*. This is insufficiently parsimonious as part of a general theory of properties. But there is a further problem with it too. According to the suggestion I am considering now, the surface is (e.g.) red *simpliciter*, and qualifiedly not-red. What is the subject of this non-redness? Not the solidity, for reasons already considered. So the surface is. But what is the

---

6   There are potential infinite regress problems with any talk of exemplification itself being exemplified, but philosophers who accept this sort of view of properties have answers to them, so I will not consider the matter further here. Properties perhaps exemplify too the determinables of which the properties are determinates, but this makes no difference to the point I am making: being coloured does not entail being not-solid, for example.

7   Not quite 'any' individual, at any rate if we presuppose a sparse theory of properties. On a sparse theory of properties, it is not the case that there is a property corresponding to every significant predicate. A sparse theory of properties allows for the possibility of an individual with just one property, and the rule that for any property any individual has, it also has the complement of that property would not obtain in the case of an individual with just one property, if such there be. And note too that the complement of the property would here need to be a genuine contradictory, such that the pair satisfied at least all the criteria outlined in section I.

8   Or else the complement principle would require us to accept relative identity, the route preferred by van Inwagen. In effect, relative identity would allow us to ascribe to an object under a certain description – even a mereologically simple object – the contradictory of any property that it has under any other description. The Christological usefulness of this is obvious, and ideally spelt out by van Inwagen.

force of claiming in this case that the surface is qualifiedly not-red? Presumably, that it exemplifies its non-redness in virtue of its exemplifying the further property of solidity. And this looks like a standard case of reduplication, and thus to entail that the surface, which exemplifies its solidity *simpliciter*, therefore exemplifies its non-redness *simpliciter*. The case that I am describing here, then, according to which a mereologically simple substance is *simpliciter* F and qualifiedly not-F, looks to generate a contradiction. More generally, I take it that every intrinsic property of a substance that lacks parts is *simpliciter* a property of that substance.

This entails that we cannot use qualifiers such as 'in a certain respect' to deal with putative contradictions in cases where substances lack parts. There is another point that needs to be grasped before we can turn to the theological application of all this. Clearly, I have been making a distinction between the exemplification of an intrinsic property in a certain respect, and the exemplification of an intrinsic property *simpliciter*. I have thus far discussed the issue largely in relation to mereologically simple substances, and I have argued that all of the properties of such a substance are had *simpliciter*. But I want to argue too that at least some of the intrinsic properties of the whole of a mereologically complex substance are such that they are exemplified *simpliciter*. Consider for example those intrinsic properties of the whole of a mereologically complex substance that are had by the substance not as the result of exemplification of the same property by one or more of the substance's parts. It would be odd to claim that such properties are had merely *qualifiedly* by their substance. They are properties *simpliciter* of their substance. Consider too those properties of the whole of a mereologically complex substance that are had by the substance as a result of the exemplification of the same property by all of the substance's parts. It would be odd to claim of such properties that they are had merely qualifiedly by their substance. They are properties *simpliciter* of their substance. (Examples of the first sort of case: my being 140lbs in weight; my being this human being. An example of the second: a homogeneous surface's being red.) In short, and roughly, something is *simpliciter* F if it is wholly F.[9] There are two relevant ways in which a substance can be wholly F. Assume that x is F, but that it is unknown whether x be wholly F. The first way for x to be wholly F is for no part of x to be F. The second way for x to be wholly F is for every part of x to be F.[10] (Again, examples of the first: my being 140lbs in weight; my being this human being; an example of the second: a homogeneous surface's being red.)

Clearly, in addition to the sorts of case I have been discussing so far, there are some properties that belong to a substance as a result of their belonging to one or more parts of the substance. Consider *being renate*, or *being one-eyed* (in a cyclops). It is not clear to me whether or not we should claim that such properties belong to their substances *simpliciter*. After all, any renate substance, or any one-eyed

---

9   I am assuming that a part-free object is *eo ipso* a whole thing, but the point could very easily be made less coarsely to take into account the objection of someone who did not concede this. (It is for this reason that I am saying 'roughly' here.)

10   The purpose of the last clause is to exclude properties such as 'being a part of x'.

substance, has parts that are not, respectively, renate or one-eyed.[11] Fortunately, I do not need to decide about these cases. As I shall show in a moment, it is easy enough to show that it is merely the *whole* Christ who has his divine properties, and likewise for some of his human properties too, and that properties possessed by a whole in the ways described above are possessed *simpliciter*.

Under what sorts of circumstances does a substance fail to exemplify a property *simpliciter*? The argument thus far entails that mereological contexts are the only relevant cases. After all, if a substance is *simpliciter* F if it is wholly F, then if a substance is F, it is qualifiedly F only if it fails to be wholly F. And it fails to be wholly F only if it has parts that are not F. Denying this entails accepting a version of the complement principle for mereologically complex things: if a substance exemplifies a property *simpliciter*, then for at least some of these properties, the substance exemplifies the complement of the property too – specifically, in those cases where the complement is exemplified by one or more parts. But this is insufficiently parsimonious as a theory of properties, since it entails that I, for example, have qualifiedly the property of (e.g.) not being able to see (because no part of mine that fails to include my optical system can see), and a theory of properties would certainly need to include a way of blocking such counterintuitive claims.

It could be objected that my application of the complement principle here relies on an unwarranted analogy between a simple, part-free, substance, and a mereological whole. Part-free substances exemplify *all* their intrinsic properties *simpliciter*; mereological wholes exemplify some of their properties *simpliciter*. But the analogy looks reasonable enough. An intrinsic property that is had *simpliciter* is

---

11   So it could be held that *being one-eyed* is *simpliciter* a property of a cyclops (there is no sense in which the cyclops is not one-eyed), even though this property is exemplified by the cyclops in virtue of his possession of a certain part (namely, his one eye). But – even if we accept this, as I am inclined to do – the crucial distinction is that *being one-eyed* is not a property of the cyclops's eye. *Being blue* is (as we may suppose) a property of the cyclops's eye; and it is only qualifiedly a property of the cyclops, because the cyclops is brown too, in respect of his skin. On my definition, if the cyclops is *simpliciter* one-eyed, he cannot qualifiedly have the property contradictory of *being one-eyed*, viz. *not being one-eyed*. It is true that any arbitrarily chosen part of the cyclops that does not include his eye has the property of not being one-eyed. The cyclops's leg, for example, is not one-eyed. But we should not want to assert of the cyclops himself that he is not one-eyed, whether qualifiedly or *simpliciter*. What makes the whole cyclops one-eyed, on this account, is that he includes just one eye. Not being one-eyed is just a privation. So if we intend to hold that the cyclops is *simpliciter* one-eyed, we will need to claim that, as soon as something includes just one eye, it is one-eyed, even if it has parts that do not include this one eye. Thus, on this view, the whole cyclops, even though he includes all his not-one-eyed parts, is not even qualifiedly not-one-eyed, since he includes a part sufficient for being unqualifiedly one-eyed. Put another way, not even a mereologically complex thing could be *simpliciter* F and qualifiedly not-F. In fact, I do not need this strong principle in what follows. After all, if my argument is correct, the only case in which something could be qualifiedly F is if F-ness is *simpliciter* a property merely of a set of its parts less than the whole they compose. This could have relevant Christological purchase only if it should turn out to be the case either that the human nature is a part of Christ, or that the divine nature is a part of Christ – and I am supposing here that neither nature is a part of Christ.

simply identified as one that is not had merely as the result of its exemplification by a set of parts less than the whole they constitute – and as thus defined it makes no difference whether the substance is mereologically complex or not.

All of this has an obvious theological application. Suppose that the divine and human natures are not parts of Christ. This supposition does not entail that Christ has no parts. After all, he has all the parts usually had by human persons: a head, eyes, a heart, and so on. But it does mean that the divine nature is not one of his parts, and that the human nature is not one of his parts. Divine and human natures will, on this view, be *properties* of his, and they will be so *simpliciter* (since they are not properties merely of a set of parts less than the whole Christ). The situation will thus be that Christ exemplifies certain properties in a qualified way – properties that are, perhaps, properties of his human parts. But there are no divine parts, and thus all intrinsic divine properties – and of course many human ones too – are exemplified by him *simpliciter*. These insights all presuppose the distinction between the ways in which something can be wholly F, as outlined above. No part of an incarnate divine person is divine, but the whole is divine; every part of an incarnate divine person is human, so the whole is human. This entails that, while Christ is both human and divine, there is (despite our common usage) no sense in which he is not-human, and no sense in which he is not-divine. Supposing, for example, that *being divine* and *being human* are compossible, there is thus no sense in which being divine entails being not-human, or in which being human entails being not-divine.[12]

---

12 I have mentioned above van Inwagen's claim to the contrary. Eleonore Stump has recently argued – in an illuminating paper on Aquinas's Christology – that 'in respect of' can be made to work in contexts where it is inappropriate to speak of parts: see the chapter on the Incarnation in her recent book, *Aquinas*, The Arguments of the Philosophers (London: Routledge, 2003, 411-415); I am very grateful to Prof. Stump for sending me both this chapter and one on parts that appear in the same work. Her example is a book whose contents can exhibit contradictory properties at one and the same time – e.g. a book can be both satirical (and thus not serious) and notable (and thus not satirical). But the contents of books are conveyed by parts of those books – chapters, paragraphs, sentences, and words – and in any case it is not clear to me that being satirical and being serious are contrary properties, and thus that they entail contradictory properties. (The problem here, then, is a failure to disambiguate the two predicates 'is satirical' and 'is serious'.) The other serious attempt to deal with the issue can be found in John Haldane, 'Incarnational Anthropology', in *Human Beings*, ed. David Cockburn, *Royal Institute of Philosophy Supplement*, 29 (Cambridge: Cambridge University Press, 1991), 191-211 (pp. 200-205). I offer a detailed argument against Haldane in ch. 8 of my *The Metaphysics of the Incarnation: Thomas Aquinas to Duns Scotus* (Oxford: Oxford University Press, 2002). The basic problem, as I show there, is Haldane's insistence on understanding the reduplicative sense of 'in respect of' truth-conditionally. There are other apparent counterinstances to my argument here. Consider, for example, the case of someone who is clever at philosophy but not at anything else. Surely in such a case we have a case of someone being qualifiedly clever in a context which is not explicitly mereological? I would argue in reply that the qualifiers here modify the *sense* of the predicate 'is clever', and show that it is, by itself, ambiguous. *Not being clever at chess* is not a contrary of *being clever at philosophy*. In the Christological context, contrariwise, *being impassible as God* is a clear contrary of *being passible as man*, since the qualifiers ('as God', 'as man') do not alter the senses of the predicate terms ('is impassible', 'is passible', respectively). Another interesting

This much could be contested, but only on the grounds that our common usage allows us to talk about Christ being both human and not-human (viz., in the case at hand, divine). Nothing substantive turns on this, so long as it is understood that the claim that Christ is not-human amounts to no more than that he is divine, though for the sake of consistency I would resist this sort of language.[13] To this extent, common usage may require us to make some sort of merely semantic distinction between the case of natural-kind words and words signifying other sorts of intrinsic properties. But these other cases are anyway clearly less controversial. Consider those intrinsic properties exemplified *simpliciter* in virtue of being divine, or in virtue of being human. The conjunction of these two sets of properties cannot simultaneously include any contradictory pairs.[14] For my argument implies that all intrinsic properties of the whole of a substance that are not themselves properties merely of a set of parts less than the whole of the substance are exemplified *simpliciter*.[15] (One property can be exemplified in virtue of another, but this does not allow us to import otherwise contradictory properties: refer to my remarks on reduplication at the beginning of this short chapter.) Suppose, for example, that being material is *simpliciter* a property of anything that is human. If this is correct, then there is no sense at all in which Christ is simultaneously immaterial (supposing that 'material' and 'immaterial' are genuine contradictories). He is not *simpliciter* immaterial, on pain of contradiction (since a substance's being *simpliciter* immaterial entails its not being the case that the substance is material). And he is not qualifiedly immaterial, because the divine nature is not a part, and as I have suggested the only way to secure the qualified

---

possible exception should be mentioned: the well-known physical analyses of simples such as electrons as both waves and particles. Of course, there are several possible responses here. A crude instrumentalist could reply that an electron is in fact *neither* of these things; it is merely the case that its behaviour can be equally well modelled as either wave or particle. A more sophisticated response could be that being a wave and being a particle are not in fact – despite appearances – genuinely contradictory properties. There are after all no mathematical inconsistencies involved in computing the behaviour of electrons.

13   Of course, claiming that there is no sense in which Christ is not-human does not entail that he is only human: just as the claim that there is no sense in which the red, solid surface is not-red does not entail that the surface is only red: it is, after all, red and solid. We could, I suppose, alternatively argue that apparently contradictory predicates such as 'is human' and 'is not-human' turn out not to be so in these specialized sorts of contexts. (This is not a controversial point: the claim is merely that the way in which we use words is often context-dependent, and in the case at hand we simply would not *mean* by 'not-human' the *contradictory* of 'human'.) But this disambiguation strategy would not work for all seemingly contradictory pairs in the case of the Incarnation, as I have noted.

14   Speaking about simultaneity in the case of a being whom many consider to be timeless does not present insuperable difficulty: we could substitute ET-simultaneity and generate the same difficulties. (On ET-simultaneity, see the well-known article by Eleonore Stump and Norman Kretzmann, 'Eternity', *Journal of Philosophy*, 78 (1981), 429-456 (p. 439)). It is clear enough, however, that the argument I am proposing here entails that God cannot be immutable, and thus cannot be timeless, though I will not draw out this entailment here.

15   Though, as noted above, I am not committed to the claim that there are no cases where a property that is *simpliciter* a property of a whole could not too be *simpliciter* a property of a part of that whole.

exemplification of an intrinsic property is if the property is exemplified by a whole in virtue of its unqualified exemplification by a part. Equally, if we suppose that Christ is qualifiedly material, and qualifiedly immaterial, this can only be because one of his human parts is material (e.g. his body), and another of them immaterial (e.g. his soul). Immateriality will not be the result of his being God at all.[16]

This does not entail monophysitism (the belief that there is only one nature in Christ, be it divine or a composite divine-human nature – the uniquely exemplified species of Christness). Being human – having a human nature – simply means having all the properties necessary for being human, and being divine – having divine nature – simply means (in this context) having all the properties necessary for being divine. An incarnate divine person satisfies these two conditions even in the case that the two sets of properties do not contain any contradictory pairs.

III

I have deferred consideration of the trope theory until now because, although it seems to me that fundamentally the same theological point can be made if we accept a trope theory, trope theories raise further mereological difficulties that need to be sorted out before we can make use of trope theories in this kind of theological context. This may come as something of a surprise, since trope theories are often understood mereologically: substances are bundles of compresent tropes, and tropes are the most basic parts of substances. Compresence, however, is a symmetrical but intransitive relation, and the intransitivity condition allows for compresent bundles to overlap. And overlapping means that mereological composition – if it is conceded that there be such, and that substances can include gross parts, as well as tropes – must involve some relation other than compresence. (As in the discussion in the previous section, I exclude merely homogeneous parts from consideration here. The literature does, however, include discussions of the difficult problem of homogeneity for trope theories.[17])

I will show in a moment that there is no plausible way for one bundle of compresent tropes to include contradictory pairs. If we suppose that this is the case, it is easy enough to see that mereological contexts actually require some relation other than compresence between two or more bundles of tropes – bundles the union of which includes tropes that fail to be compresent. After all, the different (non-homogeneous) parts of substances include contradictory pairs of properties, and as I shall show, such pairs cannot be included in any one bundle of compresent tropes. On this sort of view, the parts of substances are bundles of tropes too, and are instances of the items that D.C. Williams labels 'gross parts'.

---

16   There is a philosophical presupposition in all this, or perhaps a philosophical lesson that a theologian who denies a parts Christology needs to learn, and it is this: that the constitution of a substance from its parts is not sufficient to establish the identity of the substance. For in the case of the Incarnation, a person contains no parts other than human parts, and yet is not merely human, since he is also divine.

17   See e.g. Keith Campbell, *Abstract Particulars*, Philosophical Theory (Oxford and Cambridge, MA: Basil Blackwell, 1990), 136-138.

How might the tropes of a substance be related to those of any one of its gross parts? Presumably, one way is for the two sets of tropes to overlap. But it is no doubt possible for non-overlapping sets to be gross parts of one substance too. Furthermore, it is important to note that a mereologically complex substance is itself a further bundle of tropes, over and above its parts, some of whose tropes are not included in the bundles of tropes that are the gross parts of the substance. (Consider the property of being this human being, or of weighing 170lbs.)

The sorts of relation that obtain between the tropes of the whole and the tropes of the parts are in fact closely analogous to those suggested in section 2. For example, a cyclops's eye is a bundle of compresent tropes that includes various tropes that are not included in the bundle that is the cyclops himself: not only blueness (assuming that the skin of the cyclops is not blue), but also the relation of being a part of the cyclops. Still, there is clearly some sense in which the former of these, but not the latter, is a property of the cyclops, and, whatever the relation between the blueness of the cyclops's eye and the cyclops himself, I would suggest that it is sufficiently strong to warrant the qualified predication 'the cyclops is blue in respect of his eye', just as the relation between the cyclops and his skin is sufficiently strong to warrant the qualified predication 'the cyclops is brown in respect of his skin'.

In these mereological contexts there thus occurs what one writer has referred to as 'trope leakage': some or all of the tropes of one part can be tropes of another part, and some or all of them can be tropes of the whole mereologically complex substance too. But such leakage cannot be unrestricted, otherwise we will end up with a situation in which one substance unqualifiedly includes contradictory properties. Unlimited trope leakage would allow, for example, that 'Heraplem ... will be both beige and red, both slender all through and mostly round'.[18] The second of these is clearly problematic, for 'all through' prevents us giving a mereological account of Heraplem's being slender. But we may well want to claim that there is a sense in which Heraplem is slender: slender 'in a certain respect', because Heraplem's stick, Paraplete, is slender. ('All through' prevents us from using the qualifier 'in a certain respect'. Paraplete is both slender and slender all through. Slenderness is a property of Heraplem, such that Heraplem is slender in respect of Paraplete; but slenderness-all-through is not a property of Heraplem, because the claim that Heraplem is slender all through is inconsistent with the claim that Heraplem is round, or even mostly round.) I do not need to go into any detail in sketching a solution here. All I need is the concession that there are ways in which, given trope theory, we still have the mereological space for allowing that certain properties of complex substances are included in those substances merely 'in a certain respect': in respect of their being elements in a bundle (of compresent tropes) that is itself a (gross) part of the complex substance. Finally, those tropes of a part that are also compresent with the tropes of the whole will, on the argument thus far, belong to the whole *simpliciter*.

Is it true – as I have been supposing up to this point – that the only substances that can include contradictory tropes are complex substances? Why not, in other words, argue that bundles of compresent tropes can include contradictory tropes:

---

18   John Bacon, *Universals and Property Instances: The Alphabet of Being*, Aristotelian Society Series, 15 (Oxford and Cambridge, MA: Blackwell, 1995), 49.

say, F-ness in respect of being φ, and not-F-ness in respect of being ψ, where φ and ψ are compresent tropes? There is an answer to this, and it is closely analogous to the answer that I proposed in the case of the exemplification theory. The answer is that there is no obvious way in which compresence can allow for the presence of contradictory tropes. Take the simple surface that I have been talking about, and suppose that it is a bundle of two compresent tropes: its redness and its solidity. On trope theory it is usually considered true to claim, for example, that both the surface and its redness are red. The redness of the surface is red just because it is a *case* of red.[19] But it would be misleading to claim that the redness of the surface is not solid, for at least two independent reasons. First, suppose (very implausibly) that a trope corresponds to every significant predicate, such that there are as many tropes as there are predicates. On the supposition that the redness of the surface is not solid, the redness of the surface would – absurdly – include a trope of its own non-solidity, and indeed infinitely many others too, the complement of every property that the redness is not. Secondly, suppose (far more plausibly) that a sparse theory of tropes is true. In this case, it looks very plausible to claim that merely negative or privative predicates of tropes (e.g. the non-solidity of the surface's redness) are not tropes: and if such a predicate is not a trope, it is difficult to see why it can be truly predicated of the surface at all, given that one of the surface's tropes corresponds to the contradictory of the predicate. In short, if the surface's solidity is a trope, and the surface lacks any non-homogeneous parts, then it is simply not true of the surface that it is not-solid. And all this is just a way of affirming the eminently commonsensical claim that the ascription of contradictory properties to one and the same simple substance would render the principle of non-contradiction in effect useless.

The Christological application of all this is closely analogous to that suggested at the end of section II, so I will not spell out the details of such an application. In general, on this view, Christ will be a complex of various bundles of compresent tropes, and these bundles will include both the tropes that we would associate with divinity and the tropes that we would associate with humanity. Those tropes that are not included in his gross parts (i.e. the tropes included in the whole without thereby being included in any of the parts) are all compresent – as of course are those present at the intersection of the various gross parts, if there be one. And Christ possesses many of these tropes *simpliciter*. The ones that he does not possess *simpliciter* are those that he possesses qualifiedly, with respect to the parts of his human nature – just as any human person possesses some of his or her tropes qualifiedly in this way. These sets of tropes – the set included in the whole without being included in any of the parts, and the set that coincides with the intersection of the various gross parts, if there be one – cannot include any contradictory pairs. But the first of these two sets will include all the divine properties, and some of the human ones too. Among the human ones will certainly be properties such as passibility, which is clearly a property of a whole human person. And if the divine nature is not a part of Christ, it follows that impassibility, for example, cannot be included amongst the divine properties of Christ without that entailing that one bundle includes contradictory tropes. Analogous arguments can be constructed for most of the standard hard

---

19   See e.g. Campbell, *Abstract Particulars*, 42.

Christological cases. So accepting a trope theory is no help in dealing with putative Christological contradictions.

Again, this is not monophysitism. Christ's resembling the other divine persons is sufficient for him to be divine, and to have divine nature. His resembling other human persons is sufficient for him to be human, and to have human nature.

IV

The upshot of all this is that, if we deny a parts Christology, we cannot (except on one very unsatisfactory further strategy that I will outline below) allow Christ simultaneously to exemplify contradictory divine and human properties. Christ will indeed exhibit contradictory properties in different respects; but all of these will be *human* properties, properties possessed *simpliciter* by his different *human* parts. Whether or not the conclusion that we cannot allow Christ to exemplify contradictory divine and human properties creates insurmountable theological problems needs to be decided on a case by case basis, and is the work of other papers.[20] One lesson that the doctrine of the Incarnation teaches is that divine nature and (especially) human nature are not the way that we would otherwise think they are. (For example, being human does not entail being limited; neither does it entail being contingent. Being divine does not entail being impassible.) But this is not a bad lesson for a philosophical theologian to learn, provided that it does not entail abandoning conclusions about divine or human natures for which we have sound arguments. And I do not think that it does.

For now, however, I would like to suggest some reasons that we may have for believing that a parts Christology is false. The fundamental difficulty for a parts Christology is in showing how the two parts – most obviously, the two natures – can form just one person or substance. What sort of parts could they be? Clearly not material parts, since the divine nature is not a material part of anything. But not body and soul either. The divine nature could not be the soul of a human being, at any rate without that entailing that all three persons are incarnate. Equally, as I have outlined the distinction between parts and properties, parts are on one theory concrete objects that exemplify properties in their own right, and on another theory bundles of compresent tropes. It is easy enough to see how a human nature could be some such object. But it is very difficult to see how the divine nature could be anything like this. The divine nature, in standard Christian orthodoxy, is supposed to be shared somehow by the divine persons, and it is hard to see how any such shared object could be a concrete part, or a bundle of compresent tropes (tropes are not universals; any property shared by more than one substance is *ipso facto* a universal). So it seems to me that a Christology that posits divine and human natures as parts of an incarnate person is false.

So the soul-like part would need to be the divine person, and not the divine nature – or more precisely, some soul-like part of the incarnate person, such that this part

---

20 I attempt something of the sort for the properties of materiality and immateriality in my article, 'Incarnation, Omnipresence, and Action at a Distance', *Neue Zeitschrift für Systematische Theologie und Religionsphilosophie*, 45 (2003): 293-312.

fails to be identical with the divine nature, but is rather an object that, prior to the Incarnation, was identical with the divine person. This suggestion clearly raises some problems about identity: it is hard to see how two objects x and y could be identical at t and yet diverge at t_j. (If we denied that x and y were identical at t, we should most likely have to claim that they differed merely by modal or counterfactual properties: x does, and y does not, have the property of being possibly identical with the person of Christ. Discussion of the metaphysical issues raised here would take me well beyond the modest scope of my chapter here.)

There are less controversial objections to this sort of Christology too. Suppose materialism is true in non-Christological contexts, and that the divine person, or the soul-like constituent of this person, is related to his human nature in a way analogous to that in which a Cartesian soul is allegedly related to its body. This model is no help, since, with the exception of the interrelation of soul and body in sensation and emotion (i.e. such that the presence of the body is a necessary condition for certain mental states), the divine person is already related to every human substance in the relevant way.[21] So this model can specify the sufficient conditions for the embodiment of a divine person only if that person's embodiment is sufficiently described as his ability to experience the world – in sensation and emotion – by means of his body. And this looks to be an impoverished account of incarnation. In particular, it does not allow for a way for the mental life of the body (of the brain) to be the mental life of the divine person. After all, the human mental life of this person will be located in the brain, and (understandably) Cartesianism provides no way to allow for a soul to access the *intellectual* life of a brain.

If every human substance includes a created soul, then it is hard to see how the body-soul analogy can begin to work.[22] If the divine person is not just to have *access* to human experiences – which he has to every experience of every human being anyway – but also to have the experiences *as his*, then the human nature, including body and soul, must be a property of his, not just a part. Putting it more bluntly, how, on either of these scenarios, could the second person of the Trinity be said to possess, as his own, the mental acts and states of the human nature? Not merely by causing them, since merely causing a thought is not sufficient for the thought to belong to the agent. (An agent x could cause – directly and unmediatedly – something to have a belief that p even if x believes that not-p.) So it is not clear how this sort of union could guarantee the divine person's possession of human thoughts. But a minimal

---

21 For a useful if controversial summary of Descartes's position on the union of body and soul, including the claims about sensation and emotion, see Gordon Baker and Katherine J. Morris, *Descartes' Dualism* (London and New York: Routledge, 1996), 163-168.

22 Richard Swinburne, for example, accepts substance dualism and holds that the divine person is related to the living human body in such a way that there is no human soul other than that person. This looks very close to the condemned view of Apollinarius, despite Swinburne's express claim to the contrary: see his *The Christian God* (Oxford: Clarendon Press, 1994), 252. According to Apollinarius, Christ is a human being precisely because possessing a (living) human body is sufficient for being human. What a dualist on the mind-body question should assert is that Christ includes a created soul as well as a created body, even though the *whole* substance, whose only parts are created, is uncreated. I try to defend this position at length in 'Incarnation, Omnipresence, and Action at a Distance'.

requirement for the doctrine of the Incarnation is that the divine person possesses human mental states and acts.

Does all this mean that the doctrine of the Incarnation is fatal for classical theism, understood as including divine timelessness, immutability, and impassibility? I am inclined to think so. But it would be possible rationally to accept both classical theism and the doctrine of the Incarnation – despite the contradiction implicit in the two positions – provided that there were overwhelming and independent reasons for accepting both. The doctrine would then be a mystery, since it would involve the claim that two apparently contradictory positions in fact turn out not to be so. But it would be rational provided that the reasons in favour of both positions were strong enough. So if my conclusions in this paper are themselves reasonable, perhaps the question a Christologist should be asking is whether the arguments in favour of classical theism are sufficiently strong. I see no reason to think that they are, but on a question like this we would need to consider closely the arguments of classical theists, including notably the work of Paul Helm. Consideration of this question would take me far beyond the modest aims I have set for myself in this chapter.[23]

---

23   Paul Helm and Daniel von Wachter kindly read through a draft of this article. Thanks too to John Brooke, Peter King (Ohio) and David Mackie for conversations on some of these matters.

Chapter 11

Helm's God and the Authorship of Sin

Peter Byrne

Paul Helm's writings in the philosophy of religion are characteristically in the 'faith seeking understanding mode'. He does not offer a natural theology or endeavour to take his readers from unbelief to belief. In books such as *Eternal God*[1] and *The Providence of God*[2] orthodox doctrines about God as the creator and sustainer of all things are taken for granted. What is explored is the best means of articulating these beliefs in a philosophically sophisticated manner. Both books construe the doctrine of a sovereign, sustaining God in a way which shows another facet of Helm's character as a philosopher: his refusal to bow to fashion. Leading Anglo-American philosophers of religion are free will theists. They take it for granted that, if God is to be protected from the charge of being the author of human wickedness, the Christian scheme must suppose that human beings have libertarian free will, the liberty of indifference. Helm, in both of the above books, contends that God's sovereignty and libertarian free will cannot co-exist. The sovereign God is the one who determines all things, including human actions and their antecedents in human deliberation and motivation.

It is notable that this stance on the part of Helm puts him in the same company as recent critics of Christian theism. Thus it is part of J.L. Mackie's critique of theism via the problem of evil that, given that free will does not amount to the liberty of indifference, God could and should have made human beings such that they always freely chose the right.[3] That God did not do so, shows that he cannot be both omnipotent and omnibenevolent. Mackie thinks that without the free will defence, theism does not have even the beginnings of a credible theodicy. In the absence of a libertarian conception of freedom, theists cannot argue that it is conceptually impossible for human beings to have been made free by God and at the same time made such that they would never sin. With a compatibilist conception of freedom, as Helm acknowledges (*PG* 198), there is no significant distinction corresponding to the phrases 'moral evil' and 'natural evil'. All evil arises as a result of a deterministic causal process which is both initiated and continually sustained by God. All human goings-on are foreordained by Helm's God to the same degree as all natural goings-on.

Helm's theistic universe in *Eternal God* and *The Providence of God* is governed by necessity. In the latter book he outlines and defends a 'no risk' interpretation of

---

1   Oxford: Clarendon Press 1988. References to this work, abbreviated as *EG*, are given in the brackets in the text.

2   Leicester: Inter-Varsity Press 1993. References to this work, abbreviated as *PG*, are given in the brackets in the text.

3   'Evil and omnipotence' in B.G. Mitchell, ed. *The Philosophy of Religion*, Oxford: Oxford University Press, 1971, 100-101.

divine providence, according to which God infallibly determines what will happen in every particular case (*PG* 40). On Helm's account of the universe and creation (as on any version of determinism), nothing is really (as opposed to logically) possible but what actually happens in past, present and future. The way the past, present and future of the universe turn out is the only way they can turn out. Divine freedom, like human freedom, consists in the liberty of spontaneity – acting in accordance with his nature without external coercion or hindrance (*EG* 174). Says Helm: 'It is impossible for God now or at any time to choose or to have chosen differently' (*EG* 178). He allows that God's choices are logically contingent (alternative world histories are coherent). But only one world history is a real possibility and this is the actual one and it determines one, and only one, world future. The universe is the inevitable outcome of an inevitable choice (*EG* 181-182).

Helm's account of human agency and freedom fits in with this portrait of a deterministic universe in which every event is foreordained and decreed by God. Talk of human freedom and responsibility is appropriate in this universe because we can still make a distinction between those acts human beings do out of external compulsion and those that they do willingly. This is all to do with whether the line of causation determining an action goes through a person's desires and deliberations or is routed instead through some external, compelling agency.[4] Human responsibility for Helm is grounded on such things as: awareness by human agents of what they are doing; consent on the part of agents to what happens; identification by agents with the actions they perform (*PG* 186-188). Responsibility and freedom are grounded in agents' ability to act out of their beliefs and desires. Human agents, unlike purely natural ones, are moved by reasons. But acquiring beliefs and desires through reasons is but another example of a deterministic causal process at work (*PG* 222). Helm is explicit on the cardinal point in deterministic accounts of human agency: human beings have no power to do other than what they actually do. We can speak of a 'hypothetical power' human beings have to do otherwise than they choose to do. But that power is only hypothetical, because they only could act differently from the ways in which they do act if they willed differently. As determinists typically (though, in my view, absurdly) reason, Helm understands a person's motives and decisions as conferring power upon him or her (*PG* 189). This is because behind his account of responsibility and freedom is a denial of agent causality. He sees each and every human action as the product of a chain of causally related events, each one determined by the prior state of the universe. So if the state of the universe is viewed at any one moment, only one state is possible next. It is not just that, if Byrne had formed a different intention as to what to eat for breakfast this morning he *would* not have eaten muesli, but that in the absence of a different intention he *could* not have acted otherwise.

Defenders of libertarian free will consider that human agency is radically different from natural agency. If they are theists, they will accordingly regard the

---

4   The simple contrast between acts done willingly and those done through external compulsion will have to be refined to take account of those subjects who have lost the power to deliberate and form intentions through some pathological condition or other. Let us assume that the compatibilist can produce such a refinement.

relationship between divine providence and human doings as radically different from that between divine providence and natural events. The compatibilist cannot admit of such sharp contrasts. There is point to talk of human responsibility for this thinker, because behind human doings there is a background of character, motive and belief. There is reason then to treat human beings differently from non-moral beings. The theistic compatibilist can likewise embrace the existence of human responsibility for misdeeds. But human agency is not sufficiently different from natural agency to stop the all-powerful God determining human decisions and actions as much as he determines the behaviour of natural things. Critics of theistic determinism will thus conclude that its picture of human agency cannot provide a barrier which insulates God from being causally and morally responsible for human sin.

At one point Helm does state of evils 'all are finally attributed to the divine reason and will' (*PG* 198). Yet despite this admission, and the deterministic doctrines which lie behind it, Helm denies that God is the author of sin. One reason why he does so is that such an admission is contrary to the kind of Christianity he espouses. The Christian scriptures as interpreted by what Helm takes to be authoritative sources explicitly deny that God is the author of sin. Any version of orthodox Christianity must deny the divine authorship of sin. It has to make sense of the Biblical portrayal of a God who lays down a normative law which defines and forbids moral evil. The Christian God is portrayed as one who abhors and punishes sin. The entire scheme of things looks as if it will crumble if this righteous God is also the author of the sins for which he punishes human malefactors. Since Helm has admitted that human sins 'all are finally attributed to the divine reason and will', we ought to look closely at how he avoids conceding the divine authorship of sin. He has two main argumentative strategies. One consists in contending that theistic determinism is in no worse a position than secular determinism. If the latter can hold human beings fully responsible for morally evil acts which are not externally compelled (or pathologically caused), then so can the former. The second strategy consists in contending that theistic defenders of the liberty of indifference are in no better position than theistic determinists. Their God has as much responsibility for moral evil as Helm's. I shall argue that the first strategy fails. I shall concede something to the second strategy, while countering that the problem of evil *is*, *contra* Helm made much worse by the assumption of theistic determinism.

The first defensive strategy offers a robust challenge to the agnostic or atheistic critic of theism: rebut philosophical determinism before you make intellectual capital out of the fact that God determines human actions. The second strategy is powerful against those who are part of the faith seeking understanding enterprise, but it has no force in arguing with unbelievers. They will positively welcome the contention that the free will theism of Swinburne, Plantinga and Hasker has a God who is as deeply mired in human wrongdoing as the God of *The Bondage of the Will*. They will take many of the points in *The Providence of God* in favour of the dialectical equality of free will theologians and deterministic theologians as evidence of an insoluble intellectual problem at the heart of orthodox Christian, Jewish and Islamic theism: how can God's sovereignty obtain over the universe and yet human acts of torture, rape and murder not be laid at God's door?

Helm's first strategy is set out in pages 140-170 of *Eternal God* and pages 174-177 of *The Providence of God*. He notes that compatibilism has an account of the grounds of freedom and human responsibility. He contends against the likes of Flew and Kenny[5] that theistic compatibilism faces no additional difficulties in stating that human beings, despite being determined in all things that they think and do by the unchanging will of God, are nonetheless fully responsible for their evil deeds. If they are fully responsible, then God is not responsible. *Q.E.D.* Part of the defence of these claims is *ad hominem*, as noted above. Helm in particular takes Flew to task for talking about an all-determining God as a manipulator of human beings, someone who reduces human beings to mere puppets and then blames them for what he forces them to do. Such language is dismissed as anthropomorphic and castigated for missing the main point that the divine causation of human acts goes through the normal patterns of desire, belief and intention that are the source of non-compelled human agency. So God cannot be acting as a manipulator of human beings. Whatever he does by way of acting as all-determining cause does not subvert the normal processes which, according to compatibilism, make some human acts voluntary and others involuntary. The crux of his case comes when he considers Flew's contention that God could not rightly blame human beings for doing what is evil when he caused them to do those evil things. Says Helm, if on general determinism, it is right to blame human beings for evil deeds when those deeds are causally necessitated by prior events, then it is right to blame them on theistic determinism. They are blameworthy on general determinism and so blameworthy on theistic determinism. On general determinism it is fair to blame human beings for uncompelled evil acts. If it is fair to blame them, then it is fair for God to blame them (*EG* 153).

I think that Flew is nearer the mark in this dispute. As a compatibilist, Flew does not think that human agency introduces a radically new type of causality into nature. Nonetheless, we have the customs and institutions associated with human responsibility because human beings possess characters and all that pertains thereto – patterns of belief, desire and intention. Some things that happen reflect that peculiar purposive background and thus give rise to moral praise and censure. It would be very odd on this account to praise or blame the non-purposive, non-characterful causes that stretch behind any instance of human choice and action. But matters are different in the case of theistic determinism. Here there is a non-human cause of human choices which is purposive and which, however analogically, we can speak of as having motives, beliefs and intentions. The attitudes and modes of comment we fasten upon human agents *are* appropriate to this cause of our moral failings. It is appropriate to praise and blame this cause of Byrne's acts. By contrast, these attitudes are not appropriate to Byrne's genes or diet (or whatever determines his every thought and action on general determinism). Byrne's every thought and action is what it is because, and only because, Helm's God intends them. Helm's God purposes that Byrne does evil. In doing evil, Byrne does what this God has wanted and designed. Byrne's many evils reflect his character and dispositions, but they also reflect the character and dispositions of Helm's God, who infallibly and down

5   A.G.N. Flew *Crime or Disease?*, London: Macmillan, 1973, 102-106, A. Kenny, *The God of the Philosophers*, Oxford: Clarendon Press, 1979, 86-87.

to the smallest level of detail, decreed, planned and purposed that there should be someone who is Byrne and that this someone would have all the thoughts, values and intentions Byrne has. Helm's God is the purposer and originator of Byrne's evil deeds through Byrne's make-up. Helm's God plans that there be such a creature in being with his character. All of Byrne's acts and thoughts are foreordained and willed by God. On general determinism, we just cannot say these things of the non-purposive, beliefless, motiveless causal factors (presumably stretching back to the very first moments of the Big Bang) which determine Byrne's thought and conduct. Hence, given atheism responsibility stops with Byrne, but given theistic determinism it carries on to God.

Helm considers and endeavours to rebut an argument due to Kenny which tries to show that if God is the all-determining cause he is culpable of moral evil. Kenny, he contends, must be arguing that whenever a person X causes another person Y to do moral evil, X must do moral evil. But this cannot be right for, *ipso facto*, X cannot perform the moral evil that Y performs (*EG* 162). We may concede something to that. If the evil that Y performs is that of torturing someone in a death camp, then *ipso facto* Y is the torturer, not X – who caused Y to commit acts of torture. But if X infallibly and down to the smallest possible level of detail caused and necessitated Y's acts of torture, then Y is fulfilling X's purposes in committing torture. X wants Y to torture. X wants the suffering Y inflicts to take place and has acted so that it does take place. If, contrary to the hypothesis, Y had the power to forbear from torture and had exercised that power, then X's designs would have been frustrated. Y is X's agent in the commission of this horrid crime. The following looks like a plausible principle: whenever a person X causes a person Y to be his agent in the commission of evil, the evil that Y does is co-authored by X. Helm's God uses all of us as his agents and is the co-author of the evil we commit. ('Co-author' carries no very precise sense in this principle. It indicates merely that God has at least as much causal and moral responsibility for human evil deeds as their human authors.) Helm suggests that any principle Kenny could come up with to make God the author of evil would be equally troubling to a secular determinist like Flew (*EG* 163). Not so, for the reasons cited above. It makes no sense to say that I am the agent of my genes or my diet when I do moral evil or that they are the co-authors of my sin. Such descriptions make no sense when directed to entities which lack desires and beliefs. On secular determinism I am not fulfilling the plans of any other agents when I perform non-compelled acts. That is why it makes sense for secular compatibilists to praise and blame no one but me for those acts. It precisely does make sense to praise and blame God for human good and bad deeds on Helm's view of things, because those good and bad deeds do reflect God's purposes, plans and values as much as ours. Indeed, his purposes, plans and values are displayed in our deeds as least as much as ours, since we have ours only because he chose and wanted us to have them. Helm's God wants the torturer in the death camp to despise his victims and take pleasure in their degradation suffering and thus to be 'determined' by his character to inflict evil on them.

Helm has a further line of argument to rebut the charge that his 'no risk', deterministic view of providence makes God the author of sin. In *The Providence of God* he offers it after the important claim that God is the author of all goodness. This claim is made in connection with the endorsement of Anselm's statement that 'God causes both the essential being and the goodness of all good wills and good works' (Anselm, *On the Harmony* 168, quoted *PG* 190). Helm comments

> There are two linked reasons for insisting upon this. One is that God alone is good, and that creatures have whatever goodness they have from him in a derivative and dependent sense. For this reason, though human actions are good when their intention and end are good, those who perform them can claim no merit for them (*PG* 190).

So there is, according to Helm, an important asymmetry between human good and human evil deeds. The former, but not the latter, can be laid at God's door. God does not intend human evil acts as evil. He intends them so that good may come of them, that is he intends them under some description which takes in the good that God will bring from them. Under that description they are good acts and are intended as such (*PG* 190, cf. *EG* 162).

Helm's assertions here take us into his theodicy, which is based on the notion that though God is the ultimate and determining cause of all evil, he ordains evil in order to bring a greater good from it. I shall return to that later. I note now that the above argument for an asymmetry in God's authorship of good and of evil is based on a serious confusion. The confusion is that of running together two types of excuse for someone's commission of an evil act. An excuse might be one which deflects responsibility away from the accused. An excuse might be one which justifies the one accused, that is points to good reasons the accused had for doing that which appears to be evil. The first kind of excuse is the sort Helm proffers when faced with Flew's charges against the deterministic God. It is the excuse that, given compatibilism, human beings, not God, bear responsibility for evil acts. To say that God wills evil only as a necessary condition for bringing about a greater good justifies God in willing evil. But in order to do that it must accept God's responsibility for evil. If it were really the case that evil is not authored by God, Helm would have no need of the excuse that God does not will it as evil but only as part of an outweighing good. Furthermore, Helm cannot really have an asymmetry between the divine causation of, and responsibility for, good and evil acts. He cannot because on his account of divine sovereignty and human freedom *exactly the same kind of divine causal responsibility lies behind both good and evil acts*. For both kinds of acts it is the case that God foreordains, strictly determines and necessitates that they be done and that human beings have the plans, purposes and values that give issue to them. The only way to avoid this conclusion would be to claim that when human beings do good acts they never act in character; their characters are such that, left untouched by God, they would always do evil. Good action is always the result of intervening divine grace. This is a possible (and actual) theological position. But it has a consequence which rather strengthens the claim that Helm's God is directly responsible for sin, since will turn out on this view that God made human beings such that they would always and inevitably, albeit voluntarily, choose evil. God nonetheless intervenes in some way to give some human beings power to do good acts. Each instance of evil results from his failure to intervene.

I have contended that Helm's God is the co-author of human being's evil acts because:

i   those acts take place in accordance with God's purposes, plans and values;
ii those acts are therefore revelatory of his purposes, plans and values as much they are of human beings' character traits and intentions;
iii God sees to it that human beings necessarily and infallibly act in accordance with his purposes, plans and values.

We may say that God is the co-author of human evil. It follows from this that it is hard to accept that Helm can honour the distinction in the Christian tradition between two aspects of God's will: (1) God's decrees as to what ought to happen (or what happens when God's commands for creators are obeyed); (2) God's will embodied in what actually happens in creation. Everything, asserts Helm, is in accordance with the divine will (2) but only some things are in accordance with the divine will (1) (*PG* 131-133). On Helm's account, however, everything, but everything, is purposed down to the minutest detail by God. Nothing can happen that is contrary to the divine purpose. All happens as God wants it to happen. If God commands human beings not to murder, he is nonetheless set on infallibly and necessarily bringing acts of murder about. He is forbidding what he nonetheless wants to happen in history.

The means to get Helm's God off this particular hook may lie in his general theodicy. This is so far like traditional ones in claiming that the evil that exists in God's universe must do so for a reason. The reason is that it is the unavoidable consequence or precondition of a greater good, such that not even omnipotence could have brought that good about whilst not willing the evils our universe contains (*PG* 197). The good must be such, then, that it is conceptually impossible to bring it about and not purpose the evils we see. God wills and necessitates that human beings commit murder, rape and torture (not to speak of his willing the occurrence of natural evils), but these acts serve good purposes. Helm may claim that God is not evil when he purposes them, but his co-authors of evil acts, human beings, are, because they do not (or do not generally) purpose them for the sake of the good that will come of them. In a sense these evil acts are what God wants and in a sense they are not. They are individually distasteful but well worth planning, purposing and necessitating as part of an overall good. God then hates and forbids acts which he regards as distasteful in the short term but which are well worthwhile given the long term view he must take of events. It does not follow that human beings are doing what is justified when they perform these acts which God has planned, purposed and necessitated in accordance with his long-term interest. It may be that it is wrong for us to engage in the kind of planning for bringing good out of evil that God, *qua* creator, is forced to undertake. We shall return to this territory later.

This part of the discussion can close with one final point, which balances that made on behalf of Helm above. What happens when believers are persuaded of the merits of Helm's account of divine sovereignty and freedom? The ones who do evil deeds – the murderers, rapists and torturers – can be assured that when they do evil they are doing just what God planned, purposed and necessitated. They are doing just what is conceptually necessary for the attainment of God's long-term good for creation. All evil deeds, from the horrific crimes of the Nazi death camps down to every last little injustice, are purposed by God and inevitably reflect his plans. All are in accordance with what God wants overall. All are intended by God as well as being intended by their human co-authors. This looks to be highly comforting for the evil doers but less so for those who suffer evil.

There is an obvious question raised by the Helmian theodicy. How does it square with the Pauline injunction that one should not do evil that good may come of it? The place of that injunction in traditional moral theology is to set limits to how far we can pursue good by way of doing evil as its precondition. There are some acts that are so heinous that one may not do them for the sake of the bringing about a greater good or warding off a greater evil. One cannot murder that good may come of it. (The principle is thus part of the non-consequentialist ethical outlook which seems central to Christianity and assumed in most philosophical discussions of the problem of evil.) But Helm's God has precisely planned, purposed and necessitated acts of murder and instances of other kinds of horrendous wickedness so that good may come of them. Helm argues, following Marilyn McCord Adams, that the vision of God which will come to us (some of us? all of us? all of those who are victims of gross wickedness?) will swallow up and defeat all horrendous evils (*PG* 205). But why should we not say that such a vision would be sullied, dirtied by God having to purpose, and the innocent to endure, such evils? This is not the objection that the innocent have to suffer for the sake of others' benefit, but the complaint that even where they partake of the redeeming good, it is cheapened by the means employed to reach it (cf. *PG* 208).

Raising the question about using evil to achieve good means that at last we can turn to the second argumentative strategy Helm employs to ward off the charge that his God is the author of evil: those who combine theism with indeterministic freedom are in no better a position. I shall now argue that this contention is false. Theodicy is a dramatically easier proposition for theists who espouse the liberty of indifference than for Helmian theists, precisely because the God of Plantinga, Swinburne and Hasker does not purpose the morally evil acts of human beings but Helm's God does.

On standard libertarian theodicies, the free will defence is employed to this end: to show that God permits but does not purpose or bring about the moral evil committed by human beings. This God ordains that human beings have free will and with it the capacity to do evil and inflict harm on the innocent. He intends that they should enjoy the liberty to inflict this harm. Depending on the view of foreknowledge espoused, God either foresees the particular moral evils human beings commit or foresees in general that moral evil will be committed by human beings. God thinks, given his wider purposes, that it is overall good that he create the opportunity for human beings to perform morally evil acts and thinks that it is overall good that he permit the occurrence of the evil human beings commit. Free will is a great good in itself and its grant will lead to further greater goods (such as the development of significant moral and spiritual qualities). Thus it is worth occasioning and permitting moral evil for the sake of it. But the moral evil is not purposed by God. He does not bring about moral evil for the sake of the good he can get out of it. The harm inflicted by the human agents of moral evil is not inflicted by God in order to secure his purposes. That harm is incidental to his purposes. After all, libertarian theists such as Plantinga allow that God may have granted human beings free will and it *turned out* that they always freely chose the right. The divine grant of free will would not have thereby been negated.

We are now ready to grapple with one of Helm's key contentions against libertarian theists: their God is as much responsible for sin as Helm's own. Their God sets up the conditions for the occurrence of moral evil, knows it is taking place (at the very least, as it takes place), has the means of intervening to stop it but does nothing (see e.g. *EG* 159 and 164). There is an obvious truth to this claim but it masks the crucial asymmetry in the kinds of responsibility the all-determining and the libertarian Gods have for moral evil. We can bring out this asymmetry by recalling the import of the principle of double effect. Double effect is based on the fact that acts can have multiple consequences, some of them desirable, others not. Not all of the foreseen effects of an act are intended, even when the agent thinks it worthwhile to perform the act with those multitude effects. There is a difference between an effect that is foreseen and willingly brought about and an effect which is intended. An effect is intended when it is part of the act's objective (that is, its immediate purpose) or part of its end (that is, its larger purpose). The difference lies in this: an effect which is part of the agent's objective or end defines the act's success and failure. If objective and end are not realized, the act is to that extent abortive. An agent will not be endeavouring to bring about a merely foreseen effect. If it is not materializing, the agent will not take extra steps to bring it about. A merely foreseen effect, as opposed to an act's end and objective, are not relied on in further planning by the agent. By contrast, what is intended in the act will be fixed as a precondition of other acts which the agent plans.[6] We can illustrate the above theoretical account by two examples from Quinn.[7] 'Terror Bomber' acts to shorten a war by deliberately targeting bombs on civilians in order thereby to destroy morale. 'Strategic Bomber' acts to shorten a war by destroying an arms factory, foreseeing that civilians will be killed thereby. Each has the same end (shortening war) but the objective of the first is to attack civilians while the objective of the second is not to attack civilians. Attacking civilians is intended in the first case: if no civilians are in the area, the act is abortive; Terror Bomber is endeavouring to inflict harm on civilians; if Terror Bomber knows they are being moved, he will shift his target; he will plan further acts on the assumption that he intended by this one to inflict harm on civilians. Strategic Bomber inflicts casualties on civilians knowingly but he does not intend those casualties. His act is not abortive if it fails to harm civilians; he is not endeavouring to harm them; he will not re-target his bombs if he discovers that civilians have been moved away from the factory; he will not make further plans which are reliant on the aim of killing civilians having been accomplished.

It is evident that in both Quinn's cases the agents are responsible for the bad effects of their actions: harm to civilians. It is also evident that the type of responsibility is

---

6   For this account in greater detail see M. Bratman, *Intentions, Plans and Practical Reason*, Cambridge, Mass.: Harvard University Press, 1987, 141-142.

7   'Actions, intentions and consequences: the doctrine of double effect' *Philosophy and Public Affairs*, vol 18/4, 1989, 336 ff.

different. Terror Bomber intends harm to the innocent and has to defend that intended harm. Strategic Bomber does not intend harm to the innocent. He does not have to justify an intention to harm the innocent. He has to defend knowingly bringing about harm to the innocent in an act where the harm is tangential to its objective and end. It is equally evident that the type of responsibility for sin and moral evil borne by Helm's God is different from that borne by a libertarian theist's God. Helm's God intends morally evil acts to take place and he intends the harm that flows from them. The libertarian God does not intend morally evil acts to take place and he at best foresees the harm that flows from them. Evil and consequent harm are side effects of granting human beings free will. This difference is another way of supporting the point that Helm's God is the co-author of sin, while the libertarian God is not. That Helm's God intends moral evil to take place and intends the hurt and degradation its victims undergo should make the task of theodicy markedly more difficult for Helm than for a libertarian theist. The principle of double effect used in conjunction with the principle that one should not do evil that good may come of it raises the moral stakes for those who intend by their acts to harm and degrade the innocent.

Double effect states that an act may be licit if it is foreseen to bring about evil effects provided that:

i   the evil is not pursued as either the objective or the end of the act;
ii   the objective and end of the act are good;
iii the good intended in the act is sufficient to outweigh the evil in the foreseen effects.

More precisely, bad effects which are merely foreseen, as opposed to intended, do not fall under the ban of 'do not do evil that good may come of it'. Terror Bomber assaults and murders the innocent that good may come of it. Strategic Bomber does not. This is not to say that Strategic Bomber's act is necessarily licit. We may judge that the foreseen bad effects of his act are not at all outweighed by the good it accomplishes. The point is that Strategic Bomber's act does not partake of some of the harms crucial to non-consequentialist forms of moral reflection. Strategic Bomber has not intended the evil that befalls the innocent in order to further his goals. He has not wronged others in order to further his goals. He has not used their suffering as the means to gain his ends.[8] Terror Bomber has done these things. Helm's God is like Terror Bomber. He does intend that murder, rape and torture take place so that his ends may be fulfilled. He does intend the suffering and gross harm occasioned by such acts so that his plans can be accomplished. He does use death, suffering and degradation in others as a means to achieving his goals. Helm's God uses other persons and their suffering as part of his strategy for achieving his glorious ends. The victims of moral evil in the libertarian's universe are not so treated by God just in being victims of moral evil. The authors of moral evil may so treat them, but the libertarian God does not intend that they be so treated. He merely allows them to be treated so by others.

---

8   Quinn 342-344.

We might hang something else onto the asymmetries thus established between the Helmian and the libertarian God. The occurrence of moral evil reflects on the characters of these two Gods in different ways. We may judge the libertarian God to be reckless or heartless in allowing his human creatures to be the victims of sinful acts while this God stands by – not preventing sin and hoping that outweighing good will come of it. We may not share the evaluation implicit in standard theodicy that free will is so great a good that it is worth allowing the horrors of Auschwitz. Different, and more disturbing, reflections are mandatory when we consider Helm's God. His God actually planned, purposed and valued the occurrence of Auschwitz. He is a party to murder and torture in a way that the libertarian God is not. It is no use to say, as Helm so frequently does in *The Providence of God*, that his God did not plan moral evil as evil but under some description whereby it was part of a greater good (as on page 190). Here Helm ignores the wisdom in his own tradition's teaching that one should not do evil that good may come of it. This teaching tells us precisely that agents may not elide the evil objectives that they intend in favour of act descriptions which focus on good, overarching ends. Terror Bomber cannot answer the question 'what are you doing?' by merely saying 'I am trying to shorten the war'. He is doing that, let us grant, but he is doing so by means of the objective of attacking and harming the innocent. Helm's God is not merely planning, purposing and valuing the glory for himself and creation that will come with the Kingdom. He has from all Eternity been planning, purposing and valuing the performance of the most horrendous moral evils and the harms they occasion as objectives that are necessary for his ends to be achieved. Helm himself states that in ordaining the ends of creation God also ordains the means he employs to attain those ends (*PG* 219), means beset with the most awful moral evil, we might add. Only a deity flawed by the most terrible self-deception could tell himself that he did not plan, purpose and value the death camps as evil but only as part of an outweighing good. We would not let Terror Bomber elide his description and understanding of what he is about in this way and we cannot allow Helm's God the same luxury of morally blind self-deception.

The above does not prove that Helm's necessitarian theism cannot provide a successful theodicy. It does not show that the problem of evil defeats it. Helm has other elements to his theodicy apart from those considered. It does show that his theodicy does not get to grips with the fact that his God plans, purposes and values moral evil and is the co-author of sin as a consequence.[9]

---

9   I am grateful to Mark Wynn for comments on an earlier draft of this paper.

Chapter 12

Concept and Content

Keith Hossack

What is a concept? In this paper I suggest that a concept is a mental property. It is a quality or intrinsic property, and possessing the concept is just instantiating the property which the concept is. Since a concept is a quality, possessing a concept is a 'narrow' or intrinsic mental state. Referring to something by means of a concept is in contrast a 'broad' or relational mental state, for the referent of a concept is a function of the context and is therefore relational.

What is a content? I suggest that a content is also a mental property, and again it is a quality or intrinsic property. But whereas a concept is a property of a mind or mental substance, a content is a property of the mental event of the sort which Geach calls *mental acts* i.e. perceptions, judgements etc. Since a content is a quality, the content of a mental act is again a 'narrow' property of it. However, the state of affairs represented by a mental act with a given content is a function of the context of the act: like the referent, the state of affairs represented is a relational feature of the mental act.

What is the relation between concept and content? A Fregean answer is that they stand to each other as part to whole, for the concept is composed of the concepts it combines. According to Frege, content and concept are both of them abstract objects, outside of space and time: a content is a complex abstract object, composed of concepts, which in turn are simple abstract objects.[1] A part-whole theory is also implicit in Fodor's theory of the Language of Thought: according to Fodor, a concept is a word in the language of Thought, whereas a content is a sentence of the language.[2] Thus for Fodor as for Frege, concept is to content as part is to whole.

But on the account I shall offer, concept and content are not related as part to whole. Rather, a concept is a mental property which in cooperation with other such properties confers on its possessor a certain power: namely, the power to think thoughts with a certain range of contents. So whereas Frege and Fodor would say that a concept is part of the content itself, on the present account possession of the

---

1   Frege calls contents 'Thoughts'. Frege regards thoughts as eternal, timeless objects: he writes 'Thoughts are neither things in the external world not ideas. A third realm must be recognised' (Frege, 'Thoughts' in Frege (1984) p. 363). To explain compositionality, Frege posited a part-whole structure for thoughts. '...we look upon thoughts as composed of simple parts, and take these, in turn to correspond to the simple parts of sentences' (Frege, 'Compound Thoughts' in Frege (1984) p. 390).

2   '... concepts are the constituents of thoughts, and, in indefinitely many cases, of one another... For present purposes, it will do to think of thoughts as mental representations analogous to closed sentences, and concepts as mental representations analogous to the corresponding open ones.' Fodor (1998), p. 25.

concept is rather a part of the basis of the ability to *understand* the content, i.e. it is part of the ability to think a thought with the given content.

If a concept is the basis of a mental power, it would seem that the notion of a concept belongs to psychology, but here we must not be thinking of psychology on narrowly behaviourist or computationist lines. The mental power in question is the capacity for a certain range of thoughts. Now it seems evident that the proper function of thought is the getting of knowledge. For minds that can think, such as human minds, have an advantage over minds that cannot think, such as the minds of the simpler kinds of animals – there are many facts that human beings know, that simpler animals cannot know. Thinking yields extra knowledge, and that is the 'survival value' of thought. Thus if concepts give a power of thinking, and the function of thought is the getting of knowledge, then the notion of a concept belongs not just to psychology but to epistemology. We can put it like this: the notion of a concept belongs to the psychology of knowledge.

Thinking a thought can in the right circumstances cause knowledge. For example, if from what one already knows one infers that something beautiful shines, then thinking this thought in these circumstances causes one to know that something beautiful shines. The thought causes knowledge of the fact. Now if there is to be such a subject as epistemology, there needs to be a way of classifying thoughts in accordance with the facts they enable us to know. To classify a thing is to assign it to an explanatorily fruitful type: my suggestion is that to assign a content to a thought is to classify it in a way that is explanatorily fruitful in epistemology. Thus a content is an epistemological property of a thought, and a concept is an epistemological property of a thinker that confers the power of thinking thoughts with a given range of contents. The notions of concept and content alike belong to epistemology.

Background – The Metaphysics of Knowledge

Epistemology is the science of knowledge. There was a time when epistemologists thought their business was to define knowledge in terms of other concepts: as justified true belief, for example. But the enterprise of finding a definition of knowledge has not been a success: knowledge appears to resist definition in simpler terms. One reaction to this is to conclude that knowledge is too vague a notion to have a place in serious science: this is the conclusion reached by David Lewis, for example.[3] But a different conclusion is possible, for we might alternatively hold, as Tim Williamson does, that knowledge is a basic concept that is too fundamental to be defined.[4] The fact that knowledge is indefinable, if it is a fact, does not show there cannot be science of knowledge: any more than does the fact that spatial extension is indefinable shows that there cannot be a science of geometry. Extension is fundamental, though its properties can be studied in geometry; so there is nothing incoherent in supposing that knowledge is fundamental, though its properties can be studied in epistemology.

---

3   Lewis (1996).
4   Williamson (2000).

But what is knowledge? Here I assume that knowledge is a relation. Spatio-temporal distance is a fundamental relation, between material particles; knowledge is a fundamental relation, between minds and facts. A mind knows a fact: this means that the mind and the fact stand in the knowledge relation. If knowledge is a mental relation to a fact, then knowing the fact is a (relational) mental state.

What is the connection between one's mental *state* of knowledge, and the various *episodes* and *events* that make up one's mental life? Some of these mental acts, for example perceptions and judgements, are events of apprehending some fact: the mental act causes one to know the fact. Naturally the surrounding circumstances have to be favourable, for the very same episode of perception or judgement might fail to cause knowledge in a different context – in a sceptical scenario for example. But in suitable circumstances the event does cause one to know the fact. Thus to apprehend a fact is to be the subject of some or other mental act that causes one to know the fact concerned. After an act of apprehension, the faculty of memory may cause one to continue to know the fact, but remembering unlike apprehending is not a mental act. If knowledge is a relation, there can be no difference between knowing the fact that Hesperus shines and knowing the fact that Phosphorus shines. The fact that Hesperus shines is identical with the fact that Phosphorus shines, for facts are identical if they have the same constituents in the same order. The constituents of the fact that Hesperus shines are Hesperus and the property of shining; the constituents of the fact that Phosphorus shines are Phosphorus and the property of shining; since Hesperus is Phosphorus, the constituents are the same, and hence the facts are the same. Thus knowing the fact that Hesperus shines is the same thing as knowing the fact that Phosphorus shines.

However, it can be correct in English to say that someone knows that Hesperus shines, yet incorrect to say they know that Phosphorus shines. Therefore the English knowledge attribution 'knows that' is not simply a report of a relation between a thinker and a fact. Rather, the attribution gives not only the fact known, but also the content of the mental act whereby the fact was apprehended. Thus Pharaoh may apprehend the fact that Hesperus is shining by a judgement with the content *that Hesperus is shining*. It is correct to say that Pharaoh knows that Hesperus is shining. But Pharaoh does not know that Hesperus is Phosphorus, and so he does not judge that Phosphorus is shining. Therefore Pharaoh does not apprehend any fact by the judgement with the content *that Phosphorus is shining*, and therefore it would not be correct in English to say that Pharoah knows that Phosphorus is shining.

This raises the question of the logical form of reports of mental acts, e.g. the report '*S* judges that *C*'. I propose a Davidsonian analysis.[5] The report records a mental act, in this case a judgement, which is by *S* and classified as having the content *that-C*.

S judges that *C* =
$(\exists x)$(mental act (x) & judgement(x) & by(x, S) & *that-C*(x))

This treats 'that' in attitude reports as an operator which applied to a sentence yields a predicate which attributes the content expressed by the sentence. The analysis

---

5   Davidson, 'The Logical Form of Action Sentences' in Davidson (1980), pp. 105-148.

takes the content to be a property of a judgement. In contrast, the usual Fregean theory takes the judgement to be a relation between a mind and an abstract object. A disadvantage of the Fregean theory is that it forces the theory of thoughts to posit a special class of abstract objects, whereas the present theory requires no special entities proprietary to the theory of thought – a content is just a property.

The Epistemic Character of Content

What primitive notions will be needed in a philosophical account of thought and reasoning? We shall not be able to describe thought adequately without the standard psychological notions, such as *belief, desire, experience*, which presumably can all be defined functionally, i.e. causally and descriptively. But a complete account of thought will not be merely descriptive: there is a *right* way to reason, so we need to say what makes reasoning actually correct. The theory of thought therefore needs something that provides a standard of correctness. According to Frege, thought aims at truth, which is something absolutely primitive and indefinable. Logic is the study of the laws of truth, and we reason correctly only when we reason in accord with the laws of truth.[6]

Frege insisted on the norm of truth because he demanded that good reasoning be objectively correct. But he could have safeguarded objectivity just as well if he had made knowledge rather than truth the norm. For knowledge is factive, so the demand that thought aim at knowledge is also effective in safeguarding objectivity. Moreover, it was Frege himself who showed us that truth-preservingness alone is not sufficient to guarantee correctness, and that we need epistemic concepts in the theory of correct reasoning.

Consider the following argument, Argument (A):

Hesperus is beautiful
Hesperus shines
Therefore, something beautiful shines

By any standards, Argument (A) is a correct piece of reasoning. Now consider Argument (B):

Hesperus is beautiful
Phosphorus shines
Therefore, something beautiful shines

Argument (B) is not correct. We turn correct (A) into incorrect (B) by replacing 'Hesperus shines' with 'Phosphorus shines', so intersubstitution of the two sentences fails to conserve rationality of arguments. The sentences have failed a substitution

---

6   '... there will be laws of truth as well, and if there are, these must provide the norm for holding something to be true. And these will be the laws of logic proper.' Frege, 'Logic' in Frege (1979), p. 146.

test for synonymy: with respect to some notion of content, the sentences must differ in content.

So far as truth is concerned, arguments (A) and (B) are on a par: in both cases, it is impossible for the premisses to be true and the conclusion false. Therefore the notion of content with which we are concerned is not definable in terms of truth. But the arguments are not on a par epistemically. One can advance from knowledge of the premisses of (A) to knowledge of its conclusion. But if instead one was relying on (B), one would arrive only at a true belief; for knowledge the additional premiss that Hesperus is Phosphorus needs to be added. The difference in rational correctness between (A) and (B) is with respect to a norm not of truth but of knowledge. The difference in content between 'Hesperus shines' and 'Phosphorus shines' needs to be explained in terms of knowledge, for it is a difference in cognitive value.[7]

I have suggested that a content is a property of a mental act. A property is what its instances have in common, so we can ask what it is that mental acts with the same content have in common. We said that content is a concept of the theory of correct reasoning: the content of a mental act determines which inferences involving it are correct. It should follow that mental acts with the same content can be substituted for each other without affecting the correctness of the reasoning, provided the attitudes are the same.

This conception of content is due to Frege, who gives the following criterion for the sameness of content of two judgements:

> It may, or it may not, be the case that all inferences that can be drawn from the first judgement when combined with certain other ones can also be drawn form the second when combined with the same other judgements. Now I call the part of the content that is the same in both the *conceptual content. Only this* has significance for our symbolic language; we need therefore make no distinction between sentences that have the same conceptual content. In my formalised languages only that part of judgements which affects the *possible inferences* is taken into consideration. (*Begriffsschrifft* §3, original emphasis.) [8]

Frege's claim is that the content of two mental acts is the same if they have the same cognitive value, i.e. the same value for knowledge. We might also put it like this: two contents are the same if the one can be substituted for the other in any proof *salva demonstratione* – 'saving the proof'. Thus mental acts e_1 and e_2 of the same

---

7   It may be objected that Argument A fails to be correct for a reason that can be explained without appeal to knowledge. For on any reinterpretation of its non-logical terms on which its premisses are true, its conclusion is true also; whereas this is not the case for Argument B. But this is too strict a test, for there are plenty instances of correct reasoning that would fail it. For example,

Your nag kicked my steed
Therefore some horse kicked some horse

What this shows is that co-reference of the words is too weak a condition for correctness, but (syntactic) identity of words is too strong. Just as Frege taught us, sameness of reference is too little to require, sameness of tone is too much, and sense is that which is just right.

8   Frege (1952), p. 3.

attitude type have the same *content* if in any context either can replace the other in any course of reasoning without turning knowledge to ignorance.

Three remarks about this. First, it defines Content in general, not individual contents. What it tells us is that it is content properties that determine whether or not a thought-process is a proof. Let the *proof-value* of a thought process be the circumstance of whether or not it is a proof in a context. Then the definition tells us that content is what determines proof-value. Proof-value supervenes upon content: no difference in proof-value without a difference in content.

Secondly and conversely, let the *inferential role* of a content be the contribution it makes to the proof-value of the thought processes in which it occurs. Then the definition tells us that content supervenes upon inferential role – there can be no difference in the contents A and B unless there is some thought process whose proof-value would be altered by substituting the one for the other. Thus it is inferential role that determines the identity of a content.

Finally it is a consequence of the Fregean criterion that a thought that cannot appear in any proof has no content. Does this make the criterion verificationist – must we say that an undecidable statement is meaningless, since neither it nor its negation can be proved? No: the criterion requires only that a statement be capable of appearing *somewhere* in a proof – it need not figure as the last line. For Frege, though not perhaps for the verificationist, the Law of Excluded Middle is valid. Thus a statement and its negation could have an indispensable occurrence in a proof as an instance of Excluded Middle. This is sufficient to ensure a content for the undecidable statement, even though neither it nor its negation can occur as the *last* line of a proof. The verificationists were not mistaken in making occurrence in some proof the test of contentfulness; their only mistake was to suppose that the occurrence has to be in the *last* line.

If we take a content to be a mental property rather than an abstract object, we can take understanding the content to be a capacity for mental acts with that content. Understanding a content is in turn to be explained by concepts: grasping a concept is what underlies the mental subject's power or capacity for a mental act with a given content. Now in general what underlie powers are properties: so we can identify grasping the concept with having some categorical property that grounds the power. I propose that we simply identify the concept with the categorical property that grounds the power: then 'grasping' a concept is simply instantiating the property. Concepts are individuated by the contents they enable one to understand. Understanding supervenes upon concepts – no difference in understanding without a difference of concepts – so we can individuate concepts by the mental abilities to which they contribute.

Reference

A concept may have a referent. For example, the concept *Hesperus* refers at the actual world to Hesperus. What is the connection between a concept and its referent?

We noted above that facts are individuated by their constituents, so for each fact there is an ordered list of the things that are its constituents. In parallel fashion there is for each content an ordered list of the concepts activated in understanding it. For example, the judgement that Romeo loves Juliet activates in turn the concepts *love*, *Romeo* and *Juliet*; because one's possession of the concept *love* causes one's possession of the concept *Romeo* to cause one's possession of the concept *Juliet* to cause one's understanding of the content of the judgement. Similarly the judgement that Juliet loves Romeo activates the concepts *love*, *Juliet*, and *Romeo*, i.e. it activates the same three concepts in a different order.

Then to define reference we proceed as follows. For each concept C we find some knowledgeable judgement of the subject, such that C appears in the ordered list of concepts for the content of the judgement. Let p be the fact apprehended in this judgement. Then the referent of C is the object that occupies the corresponding position in the list of constituents of the fact p. Reference thus gets defined in terms of two other relations, *activation* and *combination*. Activation is a relation between a mental act and the concepts it activates: if mental act e activates concepts $c_1, ..., c_n$ in that order then we write:

activates $(e, c_1, ..., c_n)$

Similarly, combination is a relation between a fact and the particulars and universals of which it is the combination: if the fact p combines the particulars and universals $t_1, ..., t_n$ in that order then we write:

combines $(p, t_1, ..., t_n)$

To define reference now, we need to make an assumption about conceptual thought. The assumption in question is in the *Tractatus*, so I shall call it the Picturing Assumption.[9] The assumption is that whenever a mental act e is the apprehension of a fact p, then the concepts activated in the mental act correspond in order one for one to the particulars and universals combines in the fact. So if act e is the apprehension of fact p, and c_i is the ith concept activated by e and t_i is the ith constituent of p, then we say that t_i is a referent of c_i in the context in question. If we also assume that a concept never has more than one referent in the same context, we are able to define for every context, the referent of every concept which enters into the apprehension of some fact.

We have defined reference in terms of knowledge. If we wish to know the referent of concept C in a given context, we must find some knowledgeable judgement which the subject makes employing the concept; the logical forms of the judgement and the fact known then determine the referent. But in a context where the concept can figure in no knowledgeable judgement, its referent is undefined, and thoughts that rely on it are merely fictions. This is in accordance with Russell's Principle of Acquaintance:

Every proposition which we can understand must be composed wholly of constituents with which we are acquainted.[10]

---

9   Wittgenstein's extension of the *Tractatus* Picture Theory from language to thought is in his letter to Russell of 19.8.1919, in Wittgenstein (1961), pp. 129-130.

10   Russell (1980), p. 32.

Evans famously complained that 'the difficulty with Russell's Principle has always been to say what it means'.[11] Russell himself implausibly took acquaintance to be a matter of direct presentation to consciousness, whereas Evans suggested that we should think of acquaintance as discriminatory knowledge, i.e. 'the capacity to distinguish the object of judgement from all other things'. On either of these understandings of acquaintance, Russell's Principle seems straightforwardly false: one can think about things which are not immediately present to consciousness, and which one cannot discriminate from all other things. For example, one can think about the grain of salt one saw yesterday, though one is not seeing it today, and one would be hard-pressed to distinguish it from other grains of salt.

But suppose we define acquaintance with a thing simply as knowing something about it, i.e. knowing some fact of which the thing is a constituent. Then Russell's Principle does turn out to be a correct principle, at least for conceptual thought. For if subject S is capable of conceptual thought about a thing r, then S possesses some concept c whose referent is r; but if c can indeed be assigned the referent r it follows that there is some fact p which S knows and which has r as a constituent. Hence S is acquainted with r in the sense we have suggested, and Russell's Principle is verified.

The possibility of defining reference for concepts in the above way depends on the circumstance that the pattern of concept activation in human judgement mirrors the pattern of combination of the constituents of the fact represented. Our minds are well-designed, or well-adapted, and the human capacity for judgement is articulated in a way that corresponds to the logical articulation of facts. There is therefore an isomorphism between the mental properties that ground our powers of judgement, and the things which our judgements are about. In a given context we can index the properties to the things, and say if we like that (in that context) the concept is the power of thinking of a thing: but we must allow that in a different context we might have the concept without the thing, if in that context the concept should happen to be empty.

Truth

So far we have not needed the notion of truth. If we do need it, we can define it as the truth of a content. We can give a piecemeal definition in the spirit of Ramsey, with a separate clause for each atomic logical form, and recursive clauses for logically complex judgements.[12]

First we need to define a relation of *concatenation* between contents and concepts: we say the content C concatenates the concepts $c_1, \ldots, c_n$ in that order if for any mental act e, if e has the content C, then e activates $c_1, \ldots, c_n$. Then if in a given context w the referents of $c_1, \ldots, c_n$ are respectively $t_1, \ldots, t_n$, we say that $<t_1, \ldots, t_n>$ is *the referents-list* for C at w. We can then implicitly define truth by a Correspondence Schema:

$(\forall t_1) \ldots (\forall t_n)$(the list of referents for C at $w = <t_1, \ldots, t_n>$) $\rightarrow$ (true (C) $\leftrightarrow$ $\exists p(p$ is a fact & combines$(p, t_1, \ldots, t_n))$

---

11   Evans (1982), p. 89.
12   See 'Facts and Propositions' in Ramsey (1990).

We cannot turn this implicit definition into an explicit definition, for fear of the Liar paradox. The fact that truth is implicitly definable suggests that truth need not be taken as the theoretically central concept in the theory of thought, if we have knowledge available as an alternative primitive concept. The fact that truth is not explicitly definable means that we need not even take the predicate 'true' to name a genuine property: we arrive at a version of minimalism about truth.

Language

Our treatment of concepts so far has been entirely at the level of thought. Language has not been mentioned: there was no need to mention language, since there is no reason to think it is essential to concepts. But concepts are essential to language, for a language is only a map from words to concepts, i.e. a *lexicon*, together with a syntactic convention for representing logical forms, i.e. a *grammar*. The grammar allows us to pass from the list of words in a sentence to a corresponding list of concepts, and hence to the unique content associated with this list. Thus lexicon and grammar jointly determine a map from sentences to contents, and we may identify the language with this map. Then a language is the actual language of a population iff they use sentences of the language to express thoughts with the corresponding content. That is all that needs to be said here about the metaphysics of language – there is no need to bring a Fregean Third Realm into the account.

Interpretation

In interpreting the language of others, we wish to know which concepts they employ, and what these concepts refer to. According to Christopher Peacocke, the theory of concepts should individuate concepts by their possession conditions.[13] These allow us to determine what concepts a person has. If concept C is that concept such that a person who has the concept will in specified circumstances be willing to judge such and such, then the possession condition gives us a way of telling whether a person has concept C.

It seems doubtful to me whether Peacocke's method can work in practice. The reason is that his method is to give possession conditions in terms of inferential role. This may seem the right approach, for the inferential role does determine the concept, since if we have a different inferential role, we have a different concept. But the concept only supervenes upon inferential role: it does not follow that it is humanly definable in terms of inferential role. (Compare: the vague may supervene upon the precise, but it cannot be defined in terms of the precise.)

That we cannot define concepts in terms of their inferential role is suggested by the Quinean holism of confirmation. In Quine's slogan, anything can be evidence for anything. Therefore one cannot finitely define a concept by listing what would be conclusive evidence for a judgement involving it, because in the right circumstances anything could be evidence for it. Nor can one define the concept by listing some

---

13 Peacocke (1992).

favoured subset of the possible evidence, say the 'canonical' evidence. Anything can be evidence for the negation of anything, so in the right context anything can defeat even canonical evidence. Determining the concepts a person has by consulting possession conditions is unlikely to be a fruitful programme for the would-be interpreter.

Identifying Concepts by Their Definitions

It could be very difficult to learn the contents of a person's judgements simply by observing the circumstances in which they are prepared to make a judgement; meaning supervenes on use, but cannot be defined in terms of use. How then do we know which concepts people have? How can we be so successful in interpreting others?

It seems clear that part of the process of interpretation can begin by determining the words that express humanly universal concepts, which are innate and not learned: Quine suggests that interpretation begins in just this way, by determining which words stand for logical constants, for example. It seems that Quine is also right in saying that the interpreter seeks to build a holistic theory which makes overall good sense of the interpretee. But there is a resource available to interpreters who do not share Quine's reservations about the notion of analyticity. For we can use the notion of analyticity to explicate the notion of definition; definition is a process whereby new concepts are formed from concepts and contents we already possess; so we can identify some concepts from their definition, if we are willing to take analytic judgements more seriously than Quine does.

Definition is often regarded as a fairly trivial matter, but in fact it raises challenging issues. It is often said that in a definition, *definiens and definiendum* are synonyms, but this view is inconsistent with our Fregean criterion of concept identity. For Argument (C) below is a proof

x is unmarried & x is male
Therefore x is unmarried

But Argument (D) is not a proof

x is a bachelor
Therefore x is unmarried

To make (D) into a proof requires an extra premiss

(*) x is a bachelor $\leftrightarrow$ x is unmarried & x is male

This is true, by definition as we say, but its non-redundancy in the proof shows that by our substitution test 'bachelor' and 'unmarried male' are not synonyms. Indeed, we should not by now expect them to be, for 'bachelor' expresses a single concept, whereas 'unmarried male' expresses a combination of three concepts.

How is (*) itself known? This now seems to be a substantive epistemological question. To fix ideas let us take the case of the introduction of a singular term 'a' which is to be defined as referring to the denotation of some definite description 'the

F'. Suppose someone accordingly gives a definition of '*a*' by uttering the sentence
Def:

(Def)   *a* is the F

This utterance is not assertoric. The definer is not stating anything, but is stipulating
how the sentence is to be used in future, and a stipulation is a command. But if
everyone later utters the sentence in accordance with the definition, the later
utterances are not commands but assertions. Moreover, they are true assertions, and
indeed they are known to be true, for they express analytic truths. The philosophical
problem of definitions is then this: how can a mere command about the use of a *word*
produce subsequent knowledge of a *fact*, knowledge that is certainly not trivial, since
it indispensable in logic and mathematics?

To approach this, let us first ask: what is the logical form of the sentence Def?
The obvious suggestion is that it is:

(1)   *a* = the *F*

A difficulty with this is that what is 'true by definition' and analytic seems not to
be a merely contingent truth, whereas it may be contingent that *a* = the *F.*

Russell attempted to solve the problem of definitions by taking definitions to be
mere verbal abbreviations. Russell could not see how a definition could be knowable,
if it has the logical form (1), and instead took the true logical form to be '*a*' = 'the
F', i.e. the stipulation is that '*a*' is to be a mere abbreviation or verbal code for 'the
F'. On Russell's view, a definition is a mere verbal code: it can lead to nothing
beyond merely verbal knowledge. But Russell's code theory cannot do justice to the
non-trivial epistemology of analytic judgements. Without definitions, our current
knowledge of logic and mathematics would have been unattainable. As Wittgenstein
writes: 'If you have a proof-pattern that cannot be taken in, and by a change of
notation you turn it into one that can, then you are producing a proof, where there
was none before.'[14]

Definitions – changes of notation – allow us to prove results which we could
not prove previously, so they make accessible facts that were previously out of our
cognitive reach. Thus definitions have a substantive epistemology, and therefore
Russell's code theory must be rejected as inadequate.

We need a different account. I suggest that in definitions we rely on our capacity
for *demonstrative thought*. This is our ability, given a definite description 'the *F*'
which we understand, to apply to it the demonstrative concept *that*, so that we arrive
at the complex *that* (*the* F) whose referent, if it has one, is the denotation of the
description. Using this notation, we can distinguish the 'is' of definition from the 'is'
of identity. We can take the true logical form of Def to be not (1) but :

(2) *a* = that (the *F*)

14   Wittgenstein (1967), II §2, p. 65.

When this is uttered as a stipulation, it commands us to express by the word '*a*' a concept that is coreferential with the demonstrative complex *that* (*the F*).

But which concept coreferential with 'that (the *F*)' are we to express with the word '*a*'? To say that the referent is to be the denotation of the description 'the *F*' is not yet sufficient to determine the concept concerned uniquely: for example 'Hesperus' and 'Phosphorus' both refer to the denotation of 'the Evening star'. A purely referential condition is therefore not sufficient to characterize demonstrative thought. Thus if we remain at the level of reference, we cannot yet say, of all the concepts that refer to the *F*, which is the one *a* introduced by our definition. To identify the concept, we need to take cognitive value into account, i.e., we need to mention the inferential role of the concept in proofs.

Definitions are often appealed to in attempts to explain our knowledge of *a priori* truths, but I suggest it would be better to adopt exactly the opposite strategy. We are taking knowledge to be fundamental, and so we should try to explain definition in terms of *a priori* knowledge. Then we can say that the concept introduced by the definition is that concept *a* such that '*a* = that (the *F*)' is analytic: i.e. it is that concept *a* such that, if for some *x* it is known that *x* = the *F*, then it may be inferred *a priori* that *a* = the *F*. Then one's capacity to grasp new concepts by exploiting demonstrative thought is simply one's capacity, given a description 'the F', to form a concept '*a*' such that '*a* = the *F*' is analytic.

On this account, the new concept is defined whether or not it is known that the *F* exists. With or without a referent, there is a perfectly good concept. If the concept does refer, then of course it refers to the *F*, but it does so only in a context in which for some *x* it is known that *x* = the *F*. In that case one's evidence for the existence of the *F* acquaints one with the *F*, so that one's ability to refer to it is fully in accord with Russell's Principle. Note that it is not sufficient that the *F* exist – one must know it exists. Example adapted from David Lewis: Conan Doyle tells an audience the Sherlock Holmes stories as fiction, and the audience form the concept *Holmes* as 'that (the *G*)', where 'the *G*' is the description Doyle gave of Holmes. This concept refers to no one – it is all fiction. It still refers to no one even if, unknown to Doyle, there really is a person who satisfies the description 'the *G*'. This unexpected person is not the referent of *Holmes* for the audience, for they do not know of his existence so they are not acquainted with him. However, in a possible context where Doyle tells the story as testimony from his own knowledge, the very same *Holmes* concept does have a reference, and it refers to the person who in that context is the *G*.

By looking at how a person *S* acquired a concept, we may succeed in identifying the concept, and so interpret *S*. We need to know *S*'s history: then we identify the concept from its definition as 'that (the *F*)'. I would propose to extend this account to concepts arrived at by ostensive definition. In this case the content 'the *F*' may be partly non-conceptual, being made available to the thinker partly by current perceptual experience: in that case the function expressed by 'that' still returns a value that determines the referent of the ostensive definition. By following up concepts to the definitions by which they were acquired, including the ostensive definitions, we can succeed in interpreting others even if we do not have possession conditions for the concepts.

References

Davidson, D. (1980), *Actions and Events*, Oxford University Press, Oxford.

Evans, G. (1982), *The Varieties of Reference*, Oxford University Press, Oxford.

Fodor, J. (1998), *Concepts*, Clarendon Press, Oxford.

Frege, G. (1952), *Translations*, P. Geach and M. Black, eds, Basil Blackwell, Oxford.

Frege, G. (1984), *Collected Papers*, Basil Blackwell, Oxford.

Frege, G. (1979), *Posthumous Writings*, Basil Blackwell, Oxford.

Lewis, D. (1996), 'Elusive Knowledge', in his *Papers in Metaphysics and Epistemology*, Cambridge University Press, Cambridge, 1999.

Peacocke, C. (1992), *A Study of Concepts*, The MIT Press, Cambridge, Mass.

Ramsey, F. (1990), *Philosophical Papers*, Cambridge University Press, Cambridge.

Williamson, T. (2000), *Knowledge and its Limits*, Oxford University Press, Oxford.

Wittgenstein, L. (1961), *Notebooks 1914-16*, Basil Blackwell, Oxford.

Wittgenstein L. (1967), *Remarks on the Foundations of Mathematics*, Basil Blackwell, Oxford.

Chapter 13

Multiple Incarnations

Oliver D. Crisp

This paper is an attempt to make sense of the notion of multiple incarnations. It is an honour to be asked to contribute to a volume for my *doktorvater*, whose work has been one of the most important sources for my own thinking. Although Helm is not discussed in what follows, this, like much of my own labours, might be said to be 'Helmian' in that it is an attempt at what might be called 'analytic theology' – using the tools of analytical philosophy to make sense of certain traditional theological problems – inspired by the example of Helm's explorations in philosophical theology.

Traditionally, Christians have affirmed that the incarnation was the event in which the Second Person of the Trinity assumes a human nature in addition to his divine nature. But was that event unique and unrepeatable? Can one divine person assume two (or more) human natures? These apparently abstruse matters actually touch upon an important issue for any account of the incarnation. For if it turns out that God could have become incarnate more than once, then the incarnation, though a singularly important event for the salvation of human beings, may not be a singular event, all things considered.[1]

In what follows I argue that multiple incarnations are metaphysically possible, contrary to the objections raised in the recent literature by the Anglican theologian Brian Hebblethwaite. However, although such a divine act is metaphysically possible – there is no metaphysical obstacle to God becoming incarnate on more than one occasion – there is good reason to think that the incarnation is in fact a unique event in the divine life. Thus, the burden of this paper is that God could have become incarnate more than once, but he has not done so. The argument falls into five parts. In the first, I set out some important metaphysical distinctions that will be used in the main sections of the essay. Then, in a second part, Hebblethwaite's objection to the idea of multiple incarnations is explained, drawing, as Hebblethwaite does, upon the work of Thomas Morris. In the process of setting out Hebblethwaite's reasoning, I outline three assumptions that form the backbone of his objection. In the third section, I set out a metaphysical view that depends upon a particular account of

---

1   There are other, related problems having to do with the possibility of multiple incarnations. In the *Summa Theologiae IIIa. 3*, Thomas Aquinas maintains that more than one divine person could be incarnate in the same created nature and that more than one divine person could become incarnate, although there may be reasons why this is not entirely fitting. And in the recent literature there has been some discussion about whether a divine person would become incarnate in order to save some other race in a far-flung corner of the cosmos. See, for example Christopher L. Fisher and David Fergusson, 'Karl Rahner and the Extra-Terrestrial Question' in *Heythrop Journal* XLVII (2006): 275-290, and C.S. Lewis's novel, *Perelandra* in *The Cosmic Trilogy* (London: The Bodley Head, 1989 [1943]).

the metaphysics of human persons, which I shall call the Cartesian account. In this section, I show that two of the three assumptions that underpin Hebblethwaite's objection to multiple incarnations are questionable, and do not provide sufficient reason to doubt that multiple incarnations are metaphysically possible. In a fourth section I show how someone committed to the Cartesian account of human persons could accept all three of Hebblethwaite's assumptions and still hold to particular sort of multiple incarnations doctrine, where incarnation is taken to be equivalent to 'enfleshment'. Thus there are two independent, but related arguments against Hebblethwaite's analysis, and in favour of the possibility of a multiple incarnation doctrine. However, in a concluding section, I argue that the possibility of multiple incarnations should be distinguished from the actuality of multiple incarnations. There are important theological reasons for thinking that there is in fact only one incarnation, although God could have arranged matters otherwise.

Comments on the Metaphysics of the Incarnation

In what follows, I shall assume a certain sort of view about the human nature of Christ. It is important to state this view before progressing any further because much of what follows presumes this view about Christ's human nature. As I have made clear elsewhere, there are a number of different views that are current in the philosophical-theological literature about the metaphysics of the Incarnation.[2] The sort of view I presume requires that human natures, Christ's human nature included, are concrete particulars of a certain sort. A concrete particular is a discrete, real object, such as a table, a tortoise or a telephone. Some contemporary philosophical theologians maintain that natures, human natures included, are simply properties of things, like 'being red' or 'being west of London'. That is not the view I have in mind in what follows, and I think I have much of the Christian tradition in my favour in this particular regard. There are a number of different views about the sort of concrete particulars human natures actually are, if they are concrete particulars. Some think humans are essentially souls that just happen to be 'housed', so to speak, in the bodies they 'own'. Others think human nature is a compound of a human body and soul, or is the product of such a compound, where the soul organizes the matter of the body in some way. Yet another view might be that human natures are simply a certain kind of material object. But it is the first of these conceptions of human natures as concrete particulars that is assumed here, although I offer no argument for the superiority of this particular view or family of views over its rivals.

One final preliminary matter: in what follows, I shall assume that Christ's human nature is a concrete particular that is a human being, but is not a human person, strictly speaking. Christ is fully human, according to creedal orthodoxy. But he is not merely human. What is more, his human nature is, we might say, 'owned' by the divine person of the Word of God. In this important respect, Christ's human nature is unlike my human nature. I have a human nature and am a human person.

---

2 See Oliver D. Crisp, *Divinity and Humanity: The Incarnation Reconsidered* (Cambridge: Cambridge University Press, 2007), chapters 2-3.

I am fully human, but I am merely human. My human nature is not the human nature of a divine person; it is my human nature. And I am a person. In fact, I am a human person. By contrast, Christ is fully human, but not merely human. His human nature is the human nature of a divine person; it is never the human nature of a human person distinct from the divine person of God the Son. Hence, he is a human being with a human nature, like me. But he is not a human *person* in the strict and particular sense I shall be using here for the very good reason that if Christ were a human person as well as a divine person, then Nestorianism would be true.[3] But, of course, Nestorianism is a heresy; it cannot be true. This distinction is an important one for the argument of what follows.[4]

Hebblethwaite's Objection Outlined

With these distinctions in mind, we may turn to Brian Hebblethwaite. In a career which has involved a fair share of defending orthodox Christology, he has made the strong claim that it is not 'logically possible' for there to be multiple incarnations. In his most recent statement of this view, he says 'if God the Son is one divine subject, only one human subject can actually *be* the incarnate, human, form of that one divine life. Otherwise, we would be attributing a split personality to the divine Son'. He goes on to say, 'if Jesus was the same person as God the Son, so would other incarnations be. They would all have to be the same person. That makes no sense, least of all if they exist simultaneously in the eschaton'.[5] His reason for thinking this has much to do with what, following Thomas Morris, he calls the 'asymmetrical accessing relation' that obtains between the two natures of God Incarnate, as well as the 'unique metaphysical ownership' of the human nature of Christ by the Second Person of the Trinity.

These terms require some explanation. The idea seems to be this: The Second Person of the Trinity has immediate access to the conscious life of all created minds, including the mind of Jesus of Nazareth. But created minds do not have the same epistemic access to the divine mind. Nor, on this two-minds way of thinking about the hypostatic union, does the human mind of Jesus of Nazareth. According to the

---

3   Nestorianism is the heresy according to which Christ is composed of a human person and a divine person somehow co-existing in Christ.

4   Compare Anselm who says at one point, 'those who cannot understand anything to be a human being unless an individual will in no way understand a human being other than a human person. For [so they think] every individual human being is a person. Therefore, how will they understand that the human being assumed by the Word is not a person, that is, that another nature, not another person, has been assumed?' From *On The Incarnation of the Word* § 1 in *Anselm of Canterbury, The Major Works*, eds Brian Davies and Gillian Evans (Oxford: Oxford University Press, 1998), pp. 237-238.

5   Hebblethwaite, 'The Impossibility of Multiple Incarnations' *Theology* 104 (2001), pp. 324 and 327 respectively. Hebblethwaite traces the development of his own views in the first section of this essay. See also his earlier reflections upon the question of multiple incarnations in response to Thomas Morris's work in *The Incarnation, Collected Essays in Christology* (Cambridge: Cambridge University Press, 1987), pp. 166-168.

canonical Gospels, Christ appears unable to access certain information known only to the Father, including the time of his Second Coming. Hence, between the divine mind or consciousness the human mind or consciousness of Christ there is an intimate, but not symmetrical relation, whereby God can know what Christ *qua* human knows, yet the human mind of Christ does not know all that his divine mind, or range of consciousness does. In short, the divine mind contains, but is not contained by Christ's human mind.[6] This is Thomas Morris's 'asymmetrical accessing relation' that he concedes applies to all created minds, viz. the relation of such minds to the divine mind, Christ's human mind included. But this 'two-minds' Christology raises an immediate question, which is this: If this is the case, what distinguishes the epistemic access the Second Person of the Trinity has to the mind of Christ, as opposed to, say, the access he has to my mind? Morris allows that the Second Person of the Trinity enjoys a particular 'ownership' of Christ's human nature that does not obtain in the case of the divine relationship to my human nature. In short, Christ's human nature is the human nature of the Second Person of the Trinity.[7] Unlike Christ, my human nature is not hypostatically united to the divine nature and my human nature is not the human nature of God Incarnate. What is more, Morris sees no problem with maintaining that there is an asymmetrical accessing relation that obtains between the Word of God and Christ's human nature and that Christ's human nature is the human nature owned by the Word of God on the one hand, along with the idea that multiple incarnations are possible, on the other hand.

It is this Morrisian account of the possibility of multiple incarnations from which Hebblethwaite demurs. His objection to multiple incarnations depends upon three related assumptions. Although he does not declare them as such, the logic of his argument requires them in order for his objection to go through. They are:

1. Any human nature assumed by a divine person is numerically identical with that divine person.[8]
2. A divine incarnation has to be the same person, human as well as divine.[9]
3. A divine person can have at most one human nature.[10]

---

6   Thomas V. Morris, *The Logic of God Incarnate* (Ithaca: Cornell University Press, 1986), p. 103.

7   Ibid., pp. 161-162.

8   'For if God the Son is one divine subject, only one human subject can actually be the incarnate, human form of that one divine life. Otherwise, one would be attributing a split personality to the divine Son.' Hebblethwaite, 'The Impossibility of Multiple Incarnations', p. 324. This implies numerical identity between God the Son and his human nature. He makes similar comments elsewhere, e.g. his essay 'The Uniqueness of the Incarnation' in *Incarnation and Myth: The Debate Continued*, ed. Michael Goulder (Grand Rapids: Eerdmans, 1979), p. 189.

9   'Even he [Thomas Aquinas, whose account Hebblethwaite is criticizing] does not take seriously enough the fact that a series of divine incarnations would have to be the same person, human as well as divine.' Hebblethwaite, 'The Impossibility of Multiple Incarnations', p. 326.

10   'If Jesus was the same person as God the Son, so would other incarnations be. They would all have to be the same person. That makes no sense, least of all if they exist

The first assumption is a commonplace of catholic Christology: Jesus of Nazareth just *is* God Incarnate.[11] Hebblethwaite seems to think that the third assumption is implied by the second. But the second assumption is, it seems to me, false as it stands, and Hebblethwaite does not provide sufficient reason for endorsing the third assumption.

To see this, consider the following reasoning. First, as we have already noted, according to classical Christology Christ is a divine person with a human nature, that is, a theanthropic person. What is more, Christ *qua* human might not have existed had the Second Person of the Trinity not become incarnate. That is, Christ is truly but only contingently God Incarnate. For surely it is metaphysically possible for a given divine person to refrain from becoming incarnate, otherwise it would appear that God the Son is not free in his decision to become incarnate. Nor is it unorthodox to suggest that the Second Person of the Trinity might have taken a different human nature from the one he did take, although I grant that this is a more contentious Christological suggestion than the previous two. For instance, the Holy Spirit might have used a different ovum from which to form Christ's body in the womb of Mary *Theotokos* than in fact he did. In which case, the human body of God Incarnate would have been different from the one he did assume. This does not seem beyond the bounds of plausibility, and nothing in Hebblethwaite's argument is contrary to it.

But the crucial claim for present purposes has to do with whether, having decided to become incarnate as Jesus of Nazareth, the Second Person of the Trinity could have assumed another human nature *in addition to* the human nature of Jesus of Nazareth. Hebblethwaite says he cannot do so because any divine incarnation must be the same human and divine person on account of the fact that Christ is identical to the Second Person of the Trinity. In fact, he goes as far as saying 'the whole person of Jesus, his unique character and personality express God to us; for he is God the Son in person'.[12] But, according to catholic Christology no human *person* is generated or assumed by the Second Person of the Trinity at the incarnation. Strictly speaking, Christ has a human nature; he is not a human person. He is a divine person with a human nature. We might speak with the vulgar and say Christ is a human person, when if we were speaking with the learned we would be more careful to say Christ was a *theanthropic* (i.e. God-Man) person.[13] I suppose this is what Hebblethwaite has in mind when he speaks of the need for any divine

---

simultaneously in the eschaton.' Ibid., p. 327.

11   At least one commentator on Hebblethwaite's recent essay has overlooked this point. Peter Kevern remarks, 'if "Son of God" primarily designates a relationship rather than a separable self-conscious subject, Hebblethwaite's concern that the fullness of the Son's subjectivity be present in a particular incarnation becomes far less pressing.' But, of course, this can only be the case if the first of our three assumptions, affirmed by Hebblethwaite, is ignored. And in ignoring this, claiming instead that the incarnation might be a 'relationship' rather than a 'self-conscious subject' Kevern denies the catholic notion that Christ is identical with the Second Person of the Trinity. See Kevern, 'Limping Principles: A Reply to Brian Hebblethwaite on "The Impossibility of Multiple Incarnations"' in *Theology* September/October (2002), p. 346.

12   Hebblethwaite, *The Incarnation*, p. 167.

13   This is precisely what Thomas does at times.

incarnation to be 'the same *person*, human as well as divine'.[14] However, his strong language about the 'unique character and personality' of Christ suggests at times that Hebblethwaite has something more in mind, namely that Christ and Christ alone has the requisite capacities and properties *qua* human to be God Incarnate. In which case, applying a principle of charity to Hebblethwaite's second assumption regarding his comments about Christ being a person, whilst taking seriously his strong claims about the uniqueness of Christ, we could construe Hebblethwaite to mean that the particular human nature that is assumed in the incarnation is specially created for that purpose, to be the human nature of the divine person assuming it. Moreover, once a divine person 'owns' a particular human nature by assuming it in incarnation he cannot 'own' another human nature thereafter. It is 'part' of him from the first moment of assumption onwards. The relationship between the divine person and the human nature he assumes is a unique and unrepeatable one; a special sort of one-off metaphysical union between divine- and human natures.

Were this all Hebblethwaite said on the matter of the theanthropic personhood of Christ, we could proceed accordingly to analyse whether this charitable reading of his second assumption makes sense. Unfortunately, at times he goes beyond even the stronger language about the uniqueness of the human nature of Christ just mentioned, to say the following sort of thing:

> But multiple incarnations of the same Person of the Trinity – in actuality, of the divine Son – are ruled out by considerations of logic. Here the very idea makes no sense. One individual subject cannot, without contradiction, be thought capable of becoming a series of individuals, or, a fortiori, a coexistent community of persons.[15]

Thus, it appears that there are three distinct aspects to Hebblethwaite's second assumption. The first is simply that Christ is a person, which we can charitably take to mean Christ is a theanthropic person. This is conjoined with a second notion, that the theanthropic person of Christ somehow uniquely represents God to us, because his human nature has been specially created in order to be the human nature of God the Son. The third notion is that the very concept of multiple incarnations of the same person is somehow illogical: it simply makes no sense when analysed.

There is quite a leap from the second notion just described, to the third. The trouble with the third notion as it stands is that it is, as it were, tilting at windmills. For one thing, reference to one of the persons of the divine Trinity as one 'individual subject', which Hebblethwaite does, is problematic if one does not hold to a social model of the Trinity, where the divine persons of the Godhead are individuals bound together by a mysterious relation of mutual interpenetration or perichoresis.[16] But

---

14 Hebblethwaite, 'The Impossibility of Multiple Incarnations', p. 326. Emphasis added.

15 Hebblethwaite, 'The Impossibility of Multiple Incarnations', p. 333.

16 But perhaps all Hebblethwaite means to say on this point is that the human nature assumed is an instrument of the divine person assuming it. As Thomas points out, 'the human nature ... does not belong to the nature of the Word, and the Word is not its form; nevertheless the human nature belongs to his person' SCG IV. 41. 12. The human nature is not assumed into the divine nature or essence, although it belongs to the divine person assuming it. This is a common distinction in medieval and post-Reformation scholastic theology.

that aside, no creedally orthodox theologian would concede that the possibility of multiple incarnations implies that a divine person can become a series of individuals or a community of persons. In fact, Hebblethwaite seems to be confused about what the claims of classical Christology amount to. If an incarnation is simply the assumption of a human nature by a divine person, such that the divine person concerned comes to 'own' a particular human nature, no individual apart from the divine person exists, either before or after the first moment of incarnation. Nor can there be another individual on pain of unorthodoxy, as we have already had cause to note in the first section of this paper.[17] The point that Thomas Morris makes in relation to his own construal of a 'two-minds' Christology is that a divine person cannot be circumscribed by a human nature. Indeed, a divine person is capable of 'owning' more than one such human nature. Morris does not think of human nature as a concrete particular, but as a property. Yet even if human natures are concrete particulars, it does not seem *prima facie* 'logically impossible' for a divine person to 'own' more than one such concrete particular, given the sorts of metaphysical distinctions that Morris makes – aside from his particular construal of what a human nature is.[18]

We could put it like this. In the incarnation we are dealing with a divine person that has 'expanded', so to speak, to include a human nature. The 'expanded' divine person 'owns' his human nature, in a way similar to the manner in which I 'own' the limbs of my body. They are parts of me. In an extended or 'stretched' sense, the human nature of Christ is a 'part' of the Second Person of the Trinity.[19] But if this is the case, then there does not seem to be any reason why the Second Person of the Trinity cannot 'expand' in this way to assume more than one human nature. It would be like grafting more than one limb onto my body, where the limbs concerned have been specially prepared and grown for my body (rather than being removed from some donor before being attached to my body). Once grafted, the limbs become 'mine'. I 'own' them; they become 'part' of me.

Hebblethwaite's confusion is made clearest when he tackles Thomas Aquinas' well-known defence of the possibility of multiple incarnations.[20] In the *Summa Theologiae*, Thomas makes clear his advocacy of the view that Christ's human

---

17 Indeed, some medieval theologians were of the view that the human nature of Christ is necessarily such that it is sustained by a divine person. There is no possible world at which the human nature Christ actually assumes exists independent of God the Son, as a *suppositum*, or fundamental substance (a person). This, according to Alfred Freddoso, was Thomas Aquinas' position. See his fascinating essay, 'Human Nature, Potency and The Incarnation' in *Faith and Philosophy* 3 (1986): 27-53.

18 Thomas makes many of the same distinctions as Morris and holds that human natures a concrete particulars. See, for example, SCG IV. 41. 13 and IV. 42. 3.

19 Christ is a 'part' of God the Son in a 'stretched' sense because of the well-known objections to God having proper parts. For instance, defenders of divine simplicity deny God has any proper parts or properties. But aside from this, it might be problematic to think God has a human nature as a proper part. For then, God has a part that is physical. What is more, as many medieval theologians recognized, a being with parts is potentially fissile. But no perfect immaterial being can be fissile.

20 See *Summa Theologiae*, IIIa. 3. 7.

nature, like all human natures, is a concrete particular. In this connection, he has this to say concerning the metaphysical possibility of multiple incarnations of one and the same divine person:

> Now the power of a Divine Person is infinite, nor can it be limited by any created thing. Hence it may not be said that a Divine Person so assumed one human nature as to be unable to assume another. For it would seem to follow from this that the Personality of the Divine Nature was so comprehended by one human nature as to be unable to assume another to its Personality; and this is impossible, for the Uncreated cannot be comprehended by any creature.

No divine person can be circumscribed by a human nature he assumes, says Thomas, for the divine nature is infinite whereas human natures are finite. So it is not possible for a given human nature to somehow restrict the divine person that assumes it, in such a way as to prevent his assuming another human nature. Later in the same passage Thomas goes on to clarify how one divine person can assume more than one human nature thus:

> ... For a man who has on two garments is not said to be *two persons clothed*, but *one clothed with two garments*; and whoever has two qualities is designated in the singular as *such by reason of the two qualities*. Now the assumed nature is, as it were, a garment, although this similitude does not fit at all points.... And hence, if the Divine Person were to assume two human natures, He would be called, on account of the unity of suppositum [i.e. the unity of his fundamental substance], one man having two human natures.[21]

This is not quite right, if we are thinking with the learned, rather than speaking with the vulgar. For, I take it that if a divine person were to assume more than one human nature, where a human nature is a concrete particular, the consequence of this would be one divine person, or one God-Man having two human natures, not one *man* having two human natures as Thomas puts it in this passage. But, as the saying goes, even Homer nods. And if Homer may nod and make the odd mistake in his epic poetry, perhaps the Angelic Doctor can be forgiven the odd slip too. This brings us to Hebblethwaite's objection to Thomas's account of the possibility of multiple incarnations. In this regard, Hebblethwaite has the following to say:

> [O]ne cannot treat the human nature [of Christ] in a purely adjectival way, as a theoretically multipliable garment. Granted that there is only one ultimate metaphysical subject, namely God the Son, nevertheless, the human being God became is a human being, a personality, a subject, and a life that actually constitutes the human form of the divine life. One could even say that the human person is the divine person incarnate, though not, of course, an independent human person related to a divine person. Sadly, it is this generic, adjectival, talk of human nature being assumed that permits Thomas to envisage the possibility of multiple incarnations. Even he does not take seriously enough the fact that a series of divine incarnations would have to be the same person, human as well as divine.[22]

---

21 *ST* IIIa. 3. 7, trans. Fathers of the English Dominican Province (Notre Dame: Ave Maria Press, n.d. [1911]), pp. 2043 and 2044, respectively.

22 Ibid., p. 326.

Now, given the foregoing sketch of Thomas's views on this matter as a species of the notion that human natures are concrete particulars, coupled with an orthodox account of the assumption of human nature by the Son of God, the problems with Hebblethwaite's objection begin to become apparent. For one thing, how can God the Son be the one 'ultimate metaphysical subject' of the incarnation, where his human nature is also a 'personality' and a 'subject', without positing two subjects and two 'personalities' in the hypostatic union? The fact that Hebblethwaite repeatedly speaks of the human nature of Christ as a person, albeit in a qualified fashion, does not help matters.[23] Aquinas and Morris both understand that there is only one metaphysical subject in the incarnation, and that is God the Son. The language of two personalities or two subjects used by Hebblethwaite sounds rather unorthodox, and, in any case, hardly helps to shore up Hebblethwaite's case against multiple incarnations if, in one respect, there are already two subjects in the canonical incarnation without reference to other putative or possible incarnations! But more importantly, such inaccurate language muddies the theological waters. Once it has been made clear that a human nature is not a human person, and that the incarnation is akin to the expansion of God the Son so as to assume a human nature – all of which is consistent with the burden of what Thomas asserts – much of the force of Hebblethwaite's objection to the possibility of more than one such metaphysical arrangement dissipates. Nor is it true that Thomas' metaphysics of the Incarnation commits him to an 'adjectival' account of human nature, as Hebblethwaite supposes. As the citations from Thomas above make clear, in context Thomas is drawing an analogy between the assumption of human nature by a divine person and putting on a garment by a human person. He is clear that such an analogy is limited because 'this similitude does not fit on all points'. But such is the nature of an analogy. The point being made by Thomas is much like the illustration used in this paper of the expansion of a divine person, to wit, that a divine person can 'put on' or assume more than one human nature because no human nature can circumscribe or encompass the divine nature, nor a divine person.

Of course, analogies may be disputed, and perhaps it is the analogy Thomas uses here that Hebblethwaite means to object to. Similarly, my analogy with a body onto which extra limbs are grafted could be disputed. The incarnation is the assumption of a human nature that has a corporeal component by an essentially immaterial person. It is not the grafting of material components onto a material body. The two things are quite different, it might be thought. And this is true. In its place, let us construct a more adequate thought experiment that offers a model for thinking about multiple incarnations that rebuts Hebblethwaite's second assumption, and also has the advantage of suggesting an alternative way in which a doctrine of multiple incarnations could be set forth that avoids the problems Hebblethwaite sets out, which we shall pursue in the fourth section of the paper.

---

23 Thomas does speak of Christ as a human person, but only in the 'vulgar' sense, not in the strict-and-particular sense I am using here. Hebblethwaite's language concerning Christ's personhood is much less clearly articulated than that used by Thomas in this respect.

The Cartesian Account

Although now a hotly disputed issue, almost all orthodox classical theologians without exception held to some form of substance dualism with respect to human persons. According to substance dualists, humans are normally composed of a (human) body and soul. But there are a number of quite different philosophies of mind that go under the name 'substance dualism'. For present purposes we need only one: what I shall call the *Cartesian account*. For the sake of the argument it does not particularly matter whether Descartes actually held this view. It is sufficient that it is usually attributed to him in philosophical textbooks, and that it is usually thought of as the paradigm case of substance dualism in contemporary philosophy, even if it is not the only sort of substance dualism on offer.[24] The view in essence is this: a human is an essentially immaterial substance (i.e. a mind or soul) that is contingently related to a particular parcel of matter, which it 'owns' and by means of which it is able to act in the material world (i.e. a body). On this Cartesian account of substance dualism, the soul may be decoupled from the body at death. If the body perishes or is somehow annihilated, the human person continues to exist, since a human person is just a soul. Possession of a body is not a requirement for human personhood, on this view.[25] But it also appears that the Cartesian account is consistent with the idea that a human person (i.e. a human soul) on becoming decoupled from the body to which it was particularly related, might come into a new relationship of 'ownership' with respect to a different parcel of matter. That is, a particular human soul may be 'detached' from one human body and 'attached' to another body, whilst remaining the same person.[26] This is the case because, as we have already had cause to note, the Cartesian account presumes that embodiment is not a requirement of human personhood. If embodiment is a contingent matter, such that a human person may or may not have a body at a given time, then it would seem to be a small step to the

---

24 Trenton Merricks points out that the majority of substance dualists hold to the thesis that is central to what I am calling the Cartesian account, namely, that human persons are identical with souls and only contingently related to a certain physical body, which is not a part of that human person. So, according to Merricks at least, if one objects to this central claim of the Cartesian account, one is objecting to a central claim of the majority of substance dualists. Some substance dualists deny that human persons are identical with souls. Instead, they posit that human persons are soul-body composites. But, says Merricks, this raises a serious problem for this minority 'composite' version of dualism. For 'the dualist who denies that a person is identical with a soul must say that there are two objects with mental properties (a person and her soul) where normally we think there is one'. See Merricks, 'The Word Made Flesh: Dualism, Physicalism, and the Incarnation' in Peter van Inwagen and Dean Zimmerman, eds, *Persons, Human and Divine* (Oxford: Oxford University Press, 2007), p. 282, n. 2.

25 This is not to say that the body to which a particular soul is 'attached' has no influence over 'its' soul. For presumably, the soul comes to have true beliefs about the world through the body to which it is 'attached'.

26 In this context, 'detachment' from one body and 'attachment' to another is just shorthand for the soul relinquishing certain causal relations it has with one body, which enables it to act immediately in the material world via that particular body, and beginning to have similar causal relations with another body. No notion of *physical* attachment is implied.

conclusion that a particular human person (i.e. soul) may 'own' more than one body at different times, in succession.

On a certain construal of the general resurrection as reported by the Apostle Paul in passages like 1 Cor. 15, this is just what we should expect to happen when the disembodied souls of the dead are given 'spiritual bodies' in the eschaton. My body perishes and rots. The matter that made it up is scattered over a certain area and becomes the matter that makes up other living things in due course. But this does not yield an objection to the general resurrection because, given the Cartesian account, God may generate a new body for my soul which is not composed of the matter of my old body, even if it is a facsimile in every other respect. For, on the Cartesian account, possession of the same body pre- and post-resurrection is not a persistent condition required for the identity across time of human persons.

Now, apply this to Hebblethwaite's objection to multiple incarnations. The Second Person of the Trinity is essentially divine, but only contingently human. He might not have become incarnate, and he might not have become incarnate as the particular human he did.[27] Yet, the Second Person of the Trinity did become Jesus of Nazareth. He 'owns' the human nature of Christ. It is *his* human nature in an important sense. But from the fact that the Second Person of the Trinity owns Christ's human nature in a special, even unique way (meaning, he is uniquely Jesus of Nazareth), it does not follow that the Second Person of the Trinity cannot become incarnate in some other human nature in addition to the human nature he possesses. For who is to say that a divine person cannot possess more than one human nature, just as, in a similar fashion, a human soul can possess more than one human body?

But at this point, an obvious difficulty will be raised. This is that the analogy drawn between the Cartesian account of the mind-body relationship and the incarnation is tendentious. No classical theologian would agree that a human soul can 'own' more than one human body at any given time. Yet the argument just outlined presumes just this with respect to the incarnation. So the analogy is not to the point.

This objection is partially right. The Cartesian account outlined above is consistent with the idea that a human soul can only 'own' one human body at any one time (although this is not made explicit in the account offered thus far). And, at least one of the problems in view on the question of the possibility of multiple incarnations has to do with whether there could be simultaneous multiple divine incarnations – that is, more than one such divine incarnation obtaining at a given time, or where there is temporal overlap between two different incarnations. But this objection is not fatal to the case in favour of the possibility of multiple divine incarnations, for two reasons. The first is that, although human souls have traditionally not been thought capable of 'owning' more than one human nature at any given time, it does

---

27 As I have already pointed out, some of what Hebblethwaite says about the nature of the incarnation and the human nature assumed, militates against the notion that God the Son could have assumed a human nature other than the one he did assume. But if Hebblethwaite grants that the assumption of human nature is a contingent matter, and that the human nature assumed is only contingently related to the divine person assuming it, it is a small step to say that some other human nature could have been prepared for God the Son to assume than the one he did assume. Surely, in the councils of God, this is not metaphysically impossible.

not follow from this that the same conditions for 'ownership' of human natures (as opposed to human bodies) applies *mutatis mutandis*, to divine persons. For one thing, human souls are not omnipresent as the Second Person of the Trinity is.[28] And, as Thomas points out,

> whether we consider the Divine Person in regard to his power, which is the principle of the [hypostatic] union, or in regard to His Personality, which is the term of the [hypostatic] union, it has to be said that the Divine Person, over and beyond the human nature which He has assumed, can assume another distinct nature.[29]

For, to underline the point, the divine power of God the Son cannot be circumscribed by the human nature he assumes. Nor can the divine personhood of God the Son be limited by the human nature he assumes. The uncreated, as Thomas points out, cannot be comprehended by the created.[30] What is more, if the incarnation involves an asymmetrical accessing relation between the divine mind of Christ and his human mind, and such a relation obtains between all created human minds and the divine mind, there does not seem to be any obstacle to the possibility of multiple incarnations, even if they are simultaneous, or temporally overlapping, rather than consecutive. As Thomas Morris points out, echoing his medieval namesake, there 'could be only one person involved in all these incarnations – God the Son – but this one person could be incarnate in any number of created bodies and minds, such as the body and earthly mind of Jesus'.[31]

It might be thought that this still does not adequately account for the 'unique metaphysical ownership' of Christ's human nature by God the Son, and that this is what lies at the heart of Hebblethwaite's objection. If the Second Person of the Trinity 'owns' Christ's human nature in a unique way, then there can be only one such incarnation. The problem with this is that it simply does not follow from the fact that a divine person has metaphysical ownership of a particular human nature that this must be a *unique* metaphysical ownership of one human nature. It is this matter that is in dispute between Hebblethwaite on one side, and Thomas Aquinas and Thomas Morris on the other. In accordance with orthodoxy, both sides to the dispute are agreed that the metaphysics of the incarnation means any human nature owned by a divine person is in a particular personal union with that divine person. But from metaphysical ownership alone nothing follows about how many such metaphysical arrangements a particular divine person may have at any one time, or across time. Orthodoxy presumes only that the incarnation involves metaphysical ownership of a human nature by a divine person. But classical Christology is silent about whether such an arrangement is unique, and to presume this is the only viable position as Hebblethwaite does in speaking of it as a unique metaphysical arrangement, is to beg the question at issue. So the third assumption that underpins Hebblethwaite's

---

28 Even if one thinks souls are literally nowhere, having no spatial location, few will want to claim that created souls are omnipresent, even if this is not taken to imply some notion of physical location or co-location.

29 *ST* IIIa. 3. 7.

30 Ibid.

31 Morris, *The Logic of God Incarnate*, p. 183.

reasoning seems dubious. It is not clear given the tenets of classical Christology that divine person can have at most one human nature. Moreover, his second assumption also seems wide of the mark. The same *person*, human as well as divine is not involved in an incarnation according to classical Christology because any incarnation must involve the assumption of human nature by a divine person, not the assumption of a human person by a divine person or the generation of some hybrid divine-human person. Once the confusion at work in this aspect of Hebblethwaite's reasoning becomes clear, the second assumption collapses.

The Twist in the Tale

But more importantly, the Cartesian account provides a means of showing how, even if we concede to Hebblethwaite all three of the assumptions underlying his objection, the possibility of multiple incarnations is not precluded. For it could be that any human nature assumed by a divine person is numerically identical with that divine person; that a divine incarnation has to be the same 'person', human as well as divine; that a divine person can have at most one human nature; *and* that there are multiple consecutive incarnations.

To see this, let us return, once more, to the Cartesian account of the metaphysics of human persons. Recall that, on the Cartesian view, to be fully human the Second Person of the Trinity need only possess a human soul, even if, normally speaking, a human soul is 'attached' to a particular human body. Now, let us engage in a little theological make-believe. Suppose that at the incarnation, the Second Person of the Trinity assumes the human body and soul of Christ. But according to this hypothetical story about the death of Christ, instead of Christ's body dying on the cross, it is burnt, the ashes of his body being scattered to the four winds. Yet, on the third day after his immolation, Christ appears to his disciples in a body that appears to have all the same physical characteristics of the body that was burnt three days previously. Christ's resurrection body in this counterfactual version of his death and resurrection is numerically distinct from his pre-resurrection body, which has been scattered as ash to the four winds.[32] Yet, given the Cartesian view of the metaphysics of human persons, this counterfactual resurrected Christ has the same human nature he had prior to the destruction of his pre-resurrection body, because possession of a human body, let alone a particular human body, is not a requirement of human nature. Christ's human nature is essentially his soul that is only contingently related to the body his soul is 'attached' to at a given time. Furthermore, according to this story, Christ has two bodies, one prior to the resurrection and one afterwards, but only one human nature because the same human soul animates each body. One final caveat: As we have already noted, catholic Christology requires that Christ has a human nature, but is not a human person, strictly speaking. So the Cartesian account of human persons in view here will need to be modified in the case of Christ so that

---

32 Objection: God could reassemble the ash of Christ's body and use it to reform a body for Christ. Well then, assume that Christ's pre-resurrection body is somehow annihilated. Then there would be no metaphysical possibility of his pre-resurrection body forming the material basis from which any post-resurrection body could be fashioned.

it is clear that in this particular case we are dealing with a complete human nature but not a human person, strictly speaking. It is Christ's human nature that is in view here; were the Cartesian account applied to some other human being who is also a human person we would be able to speak of the human nature of that human person consisting essentially of a soul contingently related to a particular body. But, of course, this cannot obtain in the case of Christ, on pain of Nestorianism. So who is said to 'own' the human nature in question is an important matter, and Hebblethwaite is right to make this a central component of his own construal of the incarnation.

From this counterfactual story about the resurrection of Christ, consistent with the Cartesian account and Hebblethwaite's three assumptions, we can draw the following conclusion. This conception of the metaphysics of human personhood, which appears consistent with the requirements of catholic Christology, is also consistent with the Second Person of the Trinity having at most one human nature (i.e. human soul) as Hebblethwaite presumes. It is also consistent with the possibility of more than one incarnation, if by this is meant the assumption by God the Son of more than one human body (i.e. more than one 'enfleshment'). This is the case provided the multiple incarnations in question are consecutive, not simultaneous or temporally overlapping. And if this is the case (if we have in view only consecutive, not simultaneous or temporally overlapping incarnations), then on the Cartesian account, Christ could be enfleshed in more than one body. In fact, he could be enfleshed in a body located many miles and years away from the first century soil upon which he trod.[33]

The Possibility, but not Actuality, of Multiple Incarnations

We come to the final section of the paper. In his monograph of collected essays on the incarnation, Hebblethwaite observes that there is a distinction between the possibility and the actuality of multiple incarnations, and objects to both.[34] Thus far, I have provided two independent, though related, arguments for the metaphysical possibility of multiple incarnations. However, it seems to me that there are good theological grounds for thinking that in actuality there is only one incarnation. First of all, there is some evidence from the New Testament that Christ's incarnation has cosmic significance as a once-for-all event in which God is reconciling the whole of

---

33   In the foregoing I have assumed that human souls cannot have metaphysical ownership of more than one body at any given moment in time. But this assumption might be challenged. If human souls have no location because they are essentially immaterial beings, then it might be possible for one soul to have ownership of more than one body simultaneously, although, I admit that I have strong intuitions against this view, having to do with the first-person perspective I currently enjoy in my body. (How can I enjoy a first-person perspective in two bodies simultaneously?) But even if it turns out that, for some reason human souls cannot 'own' more than one body simultaneously, this can hardly apply univocally to God the Son, because he is omnipresent. In which case, it would seem that there might be reason to think the Second Person of the Trinity can be incarnate in more than one human body at-one-and-the-same-time, along the lines I have been pursuing in this section.

34   Hebblethwaite, *The Incarnation*, p. 167.

creation to himself, not merely human beings. Perhaps the most striking example of this can be found in Colossians 1: 19–20, where the author says 'For it pleased [the Father that] in Him all the fullness should dwell, and by Him to reconcile all things [*ta panta*] to Himself, by Him, whether things on earth or things in heaven, having made peace through the blood of His cross'.[35] Taken at face value, this suggests the cosmic uniqueness of Christ's work, which would seem to render any further incarnation otiose.

There are also grounds independent of scripture for thinking that the incarnation is a unique occurrence. Here I have in mind what we might call the fittingness of only one incarnation, given what God has ordained concerning the salvation of some number of humanity. This is hardly an overwhelming objection to the actuality of multiple incarnations. But it is, I think, an example of where considerations concerning what it is fitting for God to bring about, given his character and his commitments (such as creating the kind of world he did create), are important. Taken together, I think these considerations tell against the likelihood of multiple incarnations actually occurring.

Let us examine these claims more carefully. We begin with the biblical material. In his Bampton Lectures of the middle of the twentieth century, E.L. Mascall asserted that 'the arguments of both Ephesians and Hebrews rest upon the unquestioned, but also unformulated, assumption that there are no corporeal rational beings in the universe other than man'.[36] Such an objection could be expanded to include other New Testament passages relevant here (perhaps even Col. 1) since the main issue Mascall raises has to do with whether the New Testament authors he refers to thought that human beings were the *only* rational corporeal creatures in the cosmos to whom the work of Christ could be addressed. Perhaps this obtains in the case of all the New Testament writers, or at least all those writers whose work addresses this issue either directly or indirectly.

Let us expand Mascall's point to include all such New Testament authors. There are several things to be said by way of response to this. First, it might be thought that if scripture is revelation, the question is impertinent. The issue is whether God intends to convey to us that Christ's work is cosmically unique, as at least Col. 1 and Heb. 2 seem to indicate. What the human authors of these passages believed about the unique place of human beings in the cosmos is irrelevant. The question has to do with what the divine author of these passages intended to convey through them to his church. But that aside, it seems to me that all we may safely say about Eph. 1 and the Colossians and Hebrews passages with regard to the existence of

---

35 There are other passages in the New Testament that might be thought to point in a similar direction, although they do not seem to me to be conclusively in favour of the once-for-all cosmic significance of Christ's work. For example, Lk.1: 32-33 and Eph. 1. However, Heb. 2: 8b sounds much more like Col. 1. It says 'He [God the Father] put all in subjection under him, He left nothing that is not put under him. But now we do not yet see all things put under him'. Taken together with Col. 1 this seems to present a strong *prima facie* theological reason for holding that Christ's work is cosmically unique.

36 E.L. Mascall, *Christian Theology and Natural Science* (London: Longmans, Green and Co., 1956), p. 45, cited in Christopher L. Fisher and David Fergusson, 'Karl Rahner and the Extra-Terrestrial Intelligence Question', *Heythrop Journal* XLVII (2006): 280.

other corporeal intelligent creatures elsewhere in the cosmos is that as they stand these texts are commensurate with either the existence or non-existence of other such rational corporeal creatures. That is, these passages do not directly address this issue, nor do they imply a particular view of the existence of such creatures, because it does not seem to have been an issue these authors addressed, or even conceived of addressing. Mascall is guilty of over-reaching himself in stating otherwise.

But if the biblical material does not really address the question of whether or not there might be more than one incarnation, there may still be other reasons for thinking God only brings about one actual incarnation. It is here that considerations concerning the suitability of only one incarnation can be deployed. In order to make the case as simply and concisely as possible, I propose to set out one line of reasoning in favour of there being only one actual incarnation in terms of a theological 'just-so' story (with apologies to Rudyard Kipling). The story may not be the only way of making sense of the claim that God brings about only one actual incarnation. But it is one plausible way of thinking about this matter. Here it is:

> It is a theological commonplace in much, though not all, classical theology to claim that God is free to create or refrain from creating this world, or any world. On this way of thinking, nothing compels God to create; nothing compels him to create the actual world he does create; and God creates the world he does intentionally. It is an act of sheer grace.[37] It is also common to find classical theologians affirming that God has good reason to create this world, rather than some other world.[38] Suppose that is true. This is consistent with the possibility of multiple incarnations, because this is consistent with there being possible worlds at which God does become incarnate in more than one instance, though these worlds do not obtain. But this only underscores our initial question: why think there is only one incarnation? One reason has to do with the motivation for the incarnation. Following those in the Anselmian tradition, let us assume that God deigns to create this world knowing that human beings will fall and require a mediator in order to bring

---

37 There are, of course, exceptions to this rule. Jonathan Edwards is one such exception, Abelard another. Richard Muller does a good job of explaining the medieval debate in *Post-Reformation Reformed Dogmatics, The Rise and Development of Reformed Orthodoxy ca. 1520 ca. 1725, Vol. III* (Grand Rapids: Baker Academic, 2003), ch. 1, especially pp. 35 and 69. There have been several recent discussions of Edwards on this matter. See for example William Wainwright's essay 'Jonathan Edwards, William Rowe, and the Necessity of Creation' in *Faith, Freedom and Rationality, Philosophy of Religion Today*, eds Jeff Jordan and Daniel Howard Snyder (Maryland: Rowman and Littlefield, 1996), pp. 119-133 and William Rowe, *Can God be Free?* (Oxford: Oxford University Press, 2004), ch. 4. Interestingly, in the recent literature William Mann has defended something like Abelard's thesis. See Mann, 'Divine Sovereignty and Aseity' in *The Oxford Handbook of Philosophy of Religion*, ed. William Wainwright (Oxford: Oxford University Press, 2004), pp. 54-57.

38 Discussion of what is entailed by God having a good reason to create this world rather than another world would take us too far from our present concerns. However, it seems conceivable that God has a good reason for creating the world he does even if there is no best possible world. Thus, Muller, commenting on Aquinas' doctrine of divine freedom says, 'in the act of creation God necessarily wills his own absolute goodness as the end or goal of all his willing. Yet God freely chooses, without any necessity, the means by which he will communicate his goodness to creation'. Muller, *Post-Reformation Reformed Dogmatics III*, p. 60.

about their reconciliation with God. The incarnation is necessary, we might say, once God ordains to create this world, and to save some number of fallen humanity, in the knowledge that only a God-Man is able to bring about the reconciliation of human beings with God. According to this story, God cannot simply pass over or forgive sin without adequate satisfaction. Or, at least, if he could pass over or forgive sin without adequate satisfaction, he has good reason not to do this, and for ordaining the incarnation and work of Christ instead.[39] This is a kind of consequential necessity, because it depends upon God ordaining the creation of this world and the reconciliation of some number of fallen humanity through the saving offices of the God-Man. For many medieval and post-Reformation theologians, this sort of distinction would be a familiar aspect to the distinction between the so-called absolute power of God, that is, what God has power to do in abstraction from any particular action he has ordained, and his ordained power, according to which God must act only in accordance with what he has ordained once he has ordained what he decrees.

Here endeth the narrative. This brief sketch of what we might call a consequentially necessary account of the incarnation gives one reason for thinking that the primary motivation for the incarnation is the reconciliation of some number of humanity. If no human being had fallen, there would be no motivation for the incarnation, on this view. Such an account of the motivation for incarnation can be found in the work of a number of Protestant as well as Catholic theologians, such as John Calvin, although Calvin is not entirely consistent in his application of this doctrine. Calvin maintains that 'the only reason given in Scripture that the Son of God willed to take our flesh, and accepted this commandment from the Father, is that he would be a sacrifice to appease the Father on our behalf'.[40] Let us assume, for the sake of argument and with theologians like Calvin, that this is what motivates the incarnation. We can apply this to the question of the fittingness or suitability of there being only one incarnation in actuality (i.e. in the actual world that obtains) in the following manner, using the tenets of our just-so story as our theological frame of reference.

1. The creation of this world, or of any world, is an act of divine grace.
2. The incarnation is consequentially necessary given that God ordains to create this world and reconcile some number of fallen human beings to himself (and God has good reason to bring this state of affairs about even if he could have simply forgiven sin without satisfaction).

---

39 Richard Swinburne has recently advocated a version of the satisfaction theory of atonement that presumes God could have foregone atonement, but that there are good reasons why God ordains atonement rather than foregoing it. See Swinburne, *Responsibility and Atonement* (Oxford: Oxford University Press, 1989).

40 Calvin, *Institutes of the Christian Religion*, trans. Ford Lewis Battles, ed. John T. McNeill (Philadelphia: Westminster Press, 1960), II. xii. 4, p. 468. Compare Gal. 4: 4, which Calvin cites in the course of his argument in *Institutes* II. xii. 7, p. 474. However, in *Institutes* II. xii. 1, p.465, Calvin says 'Even if man had remained free from all stain, his condition would have been too lowly for him to reach God without a Mediator'. This runs contrary to everything Calvin goes on to argue against Osiander in the remainder of this chapter of the *Institutes*. It is difficult to know what to make of this, but it would appear to be a slip of the pen on Calvin's part.

3. The motivation for the incarnation is the reconciliation of some number of fallen humanity, such that, without a fall there would have been no need for an incarnation.

To this we may add the idea that

4. The satisfaction offered by the God-Man has a value sufficient to the divine purpose of reconciling fallen human beings.

Now, it would seem that this provides a motivation for the incarnation. But it also provides a reason for thinking that more than one incarnation would be superfluous because the reason for the incarnation – the reconciliation of some number of fallen human beings – is achieved through the incarnation of Christ. If the incarnation is motivated (at least in part) by a desire to bring about such reconciliation, and the incarnation of Christ successfully achieves this end, another incarnation is redundant. So it would seem most fitting for God to become man in only one instance, although multiple incarnations are metaphysically possible, given the Cartesian account of human nature outlined earlier.

Much of the dialectical force of the just-so story of a consequentially necessary incarnation depends on assumptions about the divine nature and the work of Christ that are now hotly disputed by contemporary theologians. Yet this story, or something very like it, has been espoused by a number of western theologians in what we might call the Anselmian tradition, broadly construed. Swallowing this story without more by way of explanation of some of its key assumptions or assertions might be a tall order for some. And more would need to be said by way of dogmatic exposition in order for this story to withstand such criticism. Nevertheless, it seems to me that this offers one way of thinking about why a single incarnation might be most fitting, although multiple incarnations are metaphysically possible. And that is all we set out to provide. But this does leave one final query in addition to the foregoing, having to do with the existence of other life forms in the universe that might also require reconciliation to God. The existence of such life forms is, of course, entirely speculative and there may be reasons to think that the likelihood of the emergence of corporeal intelligent life elsewhere in the cosmos is slim.[41] Be that as it may, some theologians have argued that if there exist other cosmic life forms that also need salvation, it would be strange to think God has not provided some means of salvation for them too. And for all we know, this involves some sort of incarnation in addition to the incarnation of Christ. If this is right, then there seem to be several possibilities with respect to the question of the salvation of some putative extra-terrestrial corporeal life forms. The first is that God does not save such beings and the work of Christ does not apply to them. The second is that no additional incarnation is required because the scope of Christ's work includes them as things stand. So God does save these beings, but through the work of Christ. The third option is that the work of Christ might apply to them (it is cosmic in its scope) but God has not deigned to save any of these creatures. And the fourth option is that the

---

41 See, for example, the evidence adduced by Fisher and Fergusson in 'Karl Rahner and the Extra-Terrestrial Intelligence Question'.

work of Christ does not apply to them, yet God has deigned to provide some means of salvation for these creatures. It is this fourth option that opens the door to the possibility of the applications of a multiple incarnation doctrine to the salvation of putative corporeal extra-terrestrial intelligent life.[42]

Theological issues of such a speculative nature are difficult to adjudicate. Still, it would be strange to think God would not provide some means of salvation to such a benighted race of extra-terrestrials, and that God would not ordain the salvation of at least some of them. For the Christian God is gracious and merciful, a matter attested to by scripture. Such theological considerations would mean discounting the first and third options stated above. Of the remaining two, it seems to me that God could provide another incarnation. But granted considerations of fittingness as set forth in our just-so story, and the biblical evidence of the cosmic significance – even uniqueness – attributable to the incarnation (that actually obtains), my tentative conclusion is that the second, rather than the fourth, option, is the more likely, all things considered.

Conclusion

In their recent essay on Rahner's understanding of extra-terrestrial intelligence and its implications for the incarnation, Christopher Fisher and David Fergusson claim that 'in a world of multiple incarnations, salvation must take place in ways other than through a single action of cosmic healing significance'. They go on to say that this 'raises the question of whether even one incarnation would be necessary, as opposed to multiple indwellings of conscious persons by the divine Spirit. A multiplicity of occurrence must inevitably compromise the singularity of the incarnation'.[43] Multiple incarnations necessarily compromise the *singularity* of the incarnation – that is analytically true. But multiple incarnations might not compromise the saving significance of the work of Christ, if that work is restricted in its salvific scope to *homo sapiens* and there are other extra-terrestrial life forms God wishes to reconcile to himself. And it is surely this matter that is behind the sort of unease expressed by theologians like Fisher and Fergusson. Whether there are extra-terrestrial corporeal life forms in need of salvation, and whether God provides for this through an additional incarnation of some kind, is a matter of theological speculation. But this does emphasize the important modal distinction between the possibility and the actuality (i.e. obtaining) of multiple incarnations. In this paper I have argued that there are two arguments in favour of the possibility of multiple incarnations, *pace*

---

42 This fourth option is not restricted to a doctrine of multiple incarnations, however. It is consistent with some other means of salvation, as C.S. Lewis imagines in his novel, *Perelandra*. In this regard, God may simply forgive the sin of the fallen extra-terrestrial creatures without the need for an incarnation or atonement. But I shall leave this possibility to one side, since if this is true, then the doctrine of multiple incarnations is straightforwardly irrelevant to the question of the salvation of other fallen corporeal creatures that might exist elsewhere in the cosmos.

43 Fisher and Fergusson, 'Karl Rahner and the Extra-Terrestrial Intelligence Question', p. 282.

Brian Hebblethwaite. Yet, there is reason to think that as a matter of fact, God has created this world with only one incarnation in mind. The cosmic significance of Christ's person and work, spoken of in various places in the New Testament points in this direction. And there are other considerations, having to do with the fittingness of such an arrangement that may also be pressed into service here. Thus, on balance, I think that although Hebblethwaite is mistaken in thinking there is a logical, or even metaphysical impediment to the possibility of multiple incarnations there are good biblical and theological reasons for thinking that in actuality there is only one incarnation of the Son of God.

Index